THE CAMBRIDGE COMPANION TO
THOMAS MORE

This *Companion* offers a comprehensive introduction to the life and work of a major figure of the modern world. Combining breadth of coverage with depth, the book opens with essays on More's family, early life and education, his literary humanism, virtuoso rhetoric, illustrious public career and ferocious opposition to emergent Protestantism, and his fall from power, incarceration, trial and execution. These six chapters are followed by in-depth studies of five of More's major works – *Utopia*, *The History of King Richard the Third*, *A Dialogue Concerning Heresies*, *A Dialogue of Comfort against Tribulation* and *De Tristitia Christi* – and a final essay on the varied responses to the man and his writings in his own and subsequent centuries. The volume provides an accessible overview of this fascinating figure to students and other interested readers, whilst also presenting, and in many areas extending, the most important modern scholarship on him.

George M. Logan is the James Cappon Professor of English (Emeritus) at Queen's University, Canada, and a Senior Fellow of Massey College in the University of Toronto. A leading More scholar, he is the author of an influential book on *Utopia*, principal editor of the Cambridge edition of that work and editor of More's *History of King Richard the Third*, as well as senior editor of the sixteenth-century section of the distinguished *Norton Anthology of English Literature*.

CAMBRIDGE COMPANIONS TO RELIGION
A series of companions to major topics and key figures in theology and religious
studies. Each volume contains specially commissioned chapters by
international scholars which provide an accessible and stimulating
introduction to the subject for new readers and non-specialists.

Other titles in the series

THE CAMBRIDGE COMPANION TO CHRISTIAN DOCTRINE
edited by Colin Gunton (1997)
ISBN 0 521 47118 4 hardback   ISBN 0 521 47695 × paperback

THE CAMBRIDGE COMPANION TO BIBLICAL INTERPRETATION
edited by John Barton (1998)
ISBN 0 521 48144 9 hardback   ISBN 0 521 48593 2 paperback

THE CAMBRIDGE COMPANION TO DIETRICH BONHOEFFER
edited by John de Gruchy (1999)
ISBN 0 521 58258 × hardback   ISBN 0 521 58781 6 paperback

THE CAMBRIDGE COMPANION TO KARL BARTH
edited by John Webster (2000)
ISBN 0 521 58476 0 hardback   ISBN 0 521 58560 0 paperback

THE CAMBRIDGE COMPANION TO CHRISTIAN ETHICS
edited by Robin Gill (2001)
ISBN 0 521 77070 × hardback   ISBN 0 521 77918 9 paperback

THE CAMBRIDGE COMPANION TO JESUS
edited by Markus Bockmuehl (2001)
ISBN 0 521 79261 4 hardback   ISBN 0 521 79678 4 paperback

THE CAMBRIDGE COMPANION TO FEMINIST THEOLOGY
edited by Susan Frank Parsons (2002)
ISBN 0 521 66327 × hardback   ISBN 0 521 66380 6 paperback

THE CAMBRIDGE COMPANION TO MARTIN LUTHER
edited by Donald K. McKim (2003)
ISBN 0 521 81648 3 hardback   ISBN 0 521 01673 8 paperback

THE CAMBRIDGE COMPANION TO ST PAUL
edited by James D. G. Dunn (2003)
ISBN 0 521 78155 8 hardback   ISBN 0 521 78694 0 paperback

THE CAMBRIDGE COMPANION TO POSTMODERN THEOLOGY
edited by Kevin J. Vanhoozer (2003)
ISBN 0 521 79062 × hardback   ISBN 0 521 79395 5 paperback

THE CAMBRIDGE COMPANION TO JOHN CALVIN
edited by Donald K. McKim (2004)
ISBN 0 521 81647 5 hardback   ISBN 0 521 01672 × paperback

THE CAMBRIDGE COMPANION TO HANS URS VON BALTHASAR
edited by Edward T. Oakes, SJ and David Moss (2004)
ISBN 0 521 81467 7 hardback   ISBN 0 521 89147 7 paperback

Continued at the back of the book

THOMAS MORE

Edited by George M. Logan

CAMBRIDGE
UNIVERSITY PRESS

CAMBRIDGE UNIVERSITY PRESS
Cambridge, New York, Melbourne, Madrid, Cape Town, Singapore,
São Paulo, Delhi, Dubai, Tokyo, Mexico City

Cambridge University Press
The Edinburgh Building, Cambridge CB2 8RU, UK

Published in the United States of America by Cambridge University Press, New York

www.cambridge.org
Information on this title: www.cambridge.org/9780521888622

First published 2011

Printed in the United Kingdom at the University Press, Cambridge

A catalogue record for this publication is available from the British Library

Library of Congress Cataloging-in-Publication Data

The Cambridge companion to Thomas More / edited by George M. Logan.
    p. cm. – (Cambridge companions to religion)
  Includes bibliographical references and index.
   ISBN 978-0-521-88862-2 Hardback – ISBN 978-0-521-71687-1 (Pbk.)
1. More, Thomas, Sir, Saint, 1478–1535.   2. Great Britain–History–Henry VIII,
1509–1547–Biography.   3. Henry VIII, King of England, 1491–1547–Relations with
humanists.   4. Great Britain–Politics and government–1509–1547.   5. England–
Intellectual life–16th century.   6. Christian martyrs–England–Biography.
7. Statesmen–Great Britain–Biography.   8. Humanists–England–Biography.
  I. Logan, George M., 1941–   II. Title.   III. Series.
  DA334.M8C19 2011
  942.05′2092–dc22

2010029549

ISBN 978-0-521-88862-2 Hardback
ISBN 978-0-521-71687-1 Paperback

For Clarence H. Miller

Contents

Notes on contributors

Dominic Baker-Smith, OBE, is Professor of English (Emeritus) at the University of Amsterdam. He taught formerly at the University of Cambridge and at University College, Cardiff. He has also served as chairman of the Society for Renaissance Studies. In addition to numerous other publications on Renaissance literature, he is the author of *More's 'Utopia'* (1991, 2000) and editor of the three volumes of Erasmus's *Expositions of the Psalms* (1997–2010) in the Toronto *Collected Works of Erasmus*.

Caroline M. Barron is a Professorial Research Fellow at Royal Holloway, University of London, whose work has focused on the history of medieval London: on its government and relations with the Crown, and on the lives of the men and women who lived in the city. Her most recent book, *London in the Later Middle Ages: Government and People 1200–1500*, was published in 2004. She is a corresponding Fellow of the Medieval Academy of America.

Cathy Curtis is currently an Honorary Associate of the Department of History at the University of Sydney. Her recent publications include the entry in the *Oxford Dictionary of National Biography* on More's friend and fellow royal secretary Richard Pace (2004); 'From Sir Thomas More to Robert Burton: the laughing philosopher in the early modern period', in *The Philosopher in Early Modern Europe* (2006); '"The best state of the commonwealth": Thomas More and Quentin Skinner', in *Rethinking the Foundations of Modern Political Thought* (2006); 'The social and political thought of Juan Luis Vives: concord and counsel in the Christian republic', in *A Companion to Juan Luis Vives* (2008); and 'The active and contemplative lives in Shakespeare's plays', in *Shakespeare and Political Thought* (2009).

Eamon Duffy is Professor of the History of Christianity at the University of Cambridge and a Fellow of Magdalene College. His principal works include *The Stripping of the Altars: Traditional Religion in England c.1400–c.1580* (1992, 2nd edn 2005; Longman–*History Today* Book of the Year Award for 1993), *The Voices of Morebath: Reformation and Rebellion in an English Village* (2001; Hawthornden Prize for Literature), and *Marking the Hours: English People and Their Prayers, 1240–1570* (2006).

George M. Logan is the James Cappon Professor of English (Emeritus) and former head of the Department of English at Queen's University, Canada, and a Senior Fellow of Massey College in the University of Toronto. He is the author of *The Meaning of More's 'Utopia'* (1983), principal editor of the Cambridge edition of *Utopia* (Latin–English 1995; English, 2nd edn 2002) and editor of *The History of King Richard the Third* (2005). He is also senior editor of the sixteenth-century section of *The Norton Anthology of English Literature.*

James K. McConica, CSB, is a past president of the University of St Michael's College and the Pontifical Institute of Mediaeval Studies at the University of Toronto. He is vice-president of the *Conseil Internationale* responsible for the critical edition of the *Opera omnia* of Erasmus and chair of the editorial board of the Toronto *Collected Works of Erasmus.* His books include *English Humanists and Reformation Politics* (1965), *Thomas More* (1977), *Erasmus* (1991) and, as editor and part-author, *The Collegiate University,* Volume 3 of *The History of the University of Oxford* (1986). He is a Fellow of the Royal Historical Society and of the Royal Society of Canada, a Foreign Member of the Belgian Royal Academy of Sciences, Letters and Fine Arts, a Corresponding Member of the British Academy and an Officer of the Order of Canada.

Elizabeth McCutcheon is Professor of English (Emerita) at the University of Hawaii. A former Guggenheim Fellow, she is the author of *My Dear Peter: The 'Ars Poetica' and Hermeneutics for More's 'Utopia'* (1983) and of many articles on More, Erasmus, Margaret More Roper, Renaissance humanism, rhetoric and other subjects; among these works is what is probably the single most frequently cited article on *Utopia,* 'Denying the contrary: More's use of litotes in the *Utopia*' (1971).

Peter Marshall, FRHS, is Professor of History at the University of Warwick. He is the author of *The Catholic Priesthood and the English Reformation* (1994), *Beliefs and the Dead in Reformation England* (2002), *Reformation England 1480–1642* (2003), *Religious Identities in Henry VIII's England* (2006), *Mother Leakey and the Bishop: A Ghost Story* (2007), *The Reformation: A Very Short Introduction* (2009), and, among his many other publications, is editor of *The Impact of the English Reformation 1500–1640* (1997) and co-editor of four other books, including *The Beginnings of English Protestantism* (2002) and, most recently, *Catholic Gentry in English Society: The Throckmortons of Coughton from Reformation to Emancipation* (2009).

Anne Lake Prescott is the Helen Goodhart Altschul Professor of English (Emerita) and former chair of the Department of English at Barnard College in Columbia University. She is the author of *French Poets and the English Renaissance* (1978) and *Imagining Rabelais in the English Renaissance* (1998), and co-editor of the Norton Critical Edition of *Edmund Spenser's Poetry* (3rd edn, 1993), *Approaches to Teaching Shorter Elizabethan Poetry* (2000) and *Female and Male Voices in Early Modern England* (2000). Her study of More's reception in the century following his death forms the introduction to Jackson Campbell Boswell's *Sir Thomas More in the English Renaissance: An Annotated Catalogue* (1994). Her work has won prizes from the Sidney Society and the Donne Society, and has earned her the Spenser Society's Lifetime Achievement Award.

Richard Rex is Reader in Reformation History at the Faculty of Divinity in the University of Cambridge and Director of Studies in History at Queens' College Cambridge. He is a leading scholar of the English Reformation, whose publications include *The Theology of John Fisher* (1991), *Henry VIII and the English Reformation* (1993, 2nd edn 2006), *The Lollards* (2002), and *The Tudors* (2002, rev. edn 2003).

Katherine Gardiner Rodgers is Professor of English at American River College in Sacramento, California, and the editor of *The Last Things* in the Yale edition of More's *Complete Works*. Her recent publications include 'Early modern aging: Erasmus's epigram "On the Troubles of Old Age"', in *Erasmus of Rotterdam Society Yearbook* 27 (2007), and 'Thomas More as witness in the prison letters', in *Moreana* 46, no. 176 (2009).

Andrew W. Taylor is Fellow and Director of Studies in English, Churchill College Cambridge. In addition to articles on the poet Henry Howard, earl of Surrey, he is the author of several book chapters on Tudor religion, including 'Versions of the English Bible' and 'The translation of biblical commentary' in *The Oxford History of Literary Translation in English*, Volume 2: 1550–1660 (2010), and '*Ad omne virtutum genus?* Mary between piety, pedagogy, and praise in early Tudor humanism', in *Mary Tudor: Old and New Perspectives* (2010). He is co-editor of *Neo-Latin and the Pastoral* (2006), is co-editing *Ovid in English, 1480–1625* for MHRA Tudor and Stuart Translations, and is completing a monograph on biblical humanism and poetry in the early English Reformation.

Preface

Selecting and apportioning the subject matter for a Thomas More *Companion* is not an easy job. More's life and public career span a large and broad range of significant subjects; and he was also a voluminous and influential writer whose collected works run to fifteen volumes (really twenty-one, since four of the volumes are in multiple parts) in the Yale edition – and these must be supplemented by his correspondence. And while Companions are intended to give a comprehensive overview of their subject, I did not want the book to accord equal but therefore uniformly thin coverage to everything. I thus decided to divide it into three parts, as follows.

Part I comprises six essays on what I have called More's 'Life, times and work'. The section opens with Caroline Barron's essay on More's family and education and his early adult life – a decade divided between law, literary studies and his exploration and final rejection of the possibility of taking religious orders. It then continues with James McConica's treatment of a topic of fundamental importance not only for More's writings but for his public career, 'Thomas More as humanist'; the essay opens by tracing the development of Renaissance humanism and its advent in England and continues with an examination of its impact on More and an overview of his specifically humanist writings. Next comes Elizabeth McCutcheon's study of 'More's rhetoric', discussing the centrality of revived classical rhetoric to humanism and to More's writings in many different genres. The following essay is Cathy Curtis's heroic survey of the huge topic of More's public career, taking him from his early days as a young London lawyer to his resignation, three decades later, of the lord chancellorship of England. Richard Rex then treats the single most controversial aspect of both More's public career and his writings: his dealings – as an officer of Henry VIII's government, as the king's adviser in the anti-Lutheran treatise that earned him from Pope Leo X the (retrospectively ironic) title of 'Defender of the Faith', and finally in his own polemical writings –

with those whom we know as early Protestants but whom More could know only as heretics. The essay includes overviews both of More's polemical writings and, in its opening pages, of the history of religious dissent in England *before* Luther. The final essay in the section is Peter Marshall's study of More's last years, which begins with the afternoon in 1532 when More surrendered the Great Seal of England to the king and includes, in addition to an account of the stages of the deterioration of More's relationship with Henry that led finally to his execution, an overview of the Tower Works, the devotional writings that occupied most of More's time in his final years.

Part II of the book then offers detailed accounts of five of More's major writings. (I regard it as a strength of the volume that these works have also been treated, although briefly, by other hands, in the overviews of the broad categories of More's writings included in Part I.) The section opens with Dominic Baker-Smith's exemplarily non-reductive reading of More's endlessly enigmatic and rewarding humanist dialogue *Utopia*, a seminal work of modern Western political thought and writing. Next comes my own treatment of More's other greatest and most influential humanist (and political) work, the coruscatingly brilliant and shrewd *History of King Richard the Third*. Eamon Duffy then treats the most admired of More's polemical writings, *A Dialogue Concerning Heresies*, which C. S. Lewis declared to be a 'great Platonic dialogue: perhaps the best specimen of that form ever produced in English'. The section closes with essays on More's two most highly regarded devotional works, both written while he was imprisoned in the Tower of London. Andrew W. Taylor offers a nuanced reading of More's third major work in dialogue form, *A Dialogue of Comfort against Tribulation*, in which, in the aftermath of the catastrophic 1526 defeat of the Hungarian army by the westward-advancing Ottoman Turks under their emperor Suleiman the Magnificent, two fictional Hungarians discuss the proper response to the religious persecution, even unto death, that they believe threatens Hungarian Christians: the subject has an obvious analogue in More's concern for English Catholics like himself who decline to side with Henry VIII in his contest with Rome over his desire to put aside his queen in order to marry Anne Boleyn. Katherine Gardiner Rodgers then treats More's last – unfinished – large-scale work, *De Tristitia Christi*, on 'the sadness, the weariness, the fear, and the prayer of Christ' in Gethsemane: another topic with obvious parallels to More's own situation when he wrote, awaiting trial and execution, but, like all the other works he published or intended to publish, written not for himself but for what he liked to call 'the whole corps of Christendom', where (as of course in the whole corps of humankind) *all* have sorrows and weariness, and all face death.

Part III of the book comprises a single essay: Anne Lake Prescott's treatment, in 'Afterlives', of the enormous topic of the later impact of More's life, death and writings, and especially the two most influential of these writings, *Utopia* and *The History of King Richard the Third*.

Each of the essays has a 'Further reading' appendix, and the book also includes a general bibliographical appendix of 'Foundational resources for More studies'. In addition, I have provided a network of cross references between essays, and a detailed index, which has as one of its main purposes the provision of help in locating the book's scattered treatments of topics – such as More's letters and poems – that are not accorded chapters of their own but are treated, sometimes in considerable detail, in one or more of the essays. Taken all in all, the book amounts to something close to what literary scholars call a critical biography.

I have been fortunate to have a subject such as More, whose enormous stature and endless fascination made it possible for me to recruit so many first-rank scholars – several of whom, although eminent in fields that obviously have great bearing on More studies, have previously written on More (if at all) only in passing. Their superb scholarship, now brought to bear directly on him, sheds new light on a number of topics. I am proud to have been responsible for this enriching of the More community.

Four of the earlier recruited contributors were extremely helpful in discussing with me the shape of the book and other possible recruits to it: my old friend Elizabeth McCutcheon and my new friends (though long admired from afar) Dominic Baker-Smith, Richard Rex and Peter Marshall. The book is dedicated to another old friend, Clarence H. Miller, whose work – astonishing for both quality and quantity – as executive editor of the Yale *Complete Works of St. Thomas More* is only the most signal accomplishment of a lifetime of fruitful labour that has earned him an enduring place in the pantheon of the greatest humanistic scholars. Clarence's generosity to me over the past two decades has made a tremendous difference to my own work. He gave me invaluable advice on many aspects of the *Companion*. So, too, did the unsurpassed Tudor historian and biographer John Guy. I am deeply grateful to both of these magnificent students of Thomas More.

I have greatly enjoyed working on the book with a series of highly capable, pleasant and patient individuals at Cambridge University Press: first Kate Brett, who in 2006 approached me about editing a

Thomas More *Companion* and for nearly three years thereafter impeccably guided me through manifold intricacies of the task; latterly Laura Morris, who took over from Kate, and others who have been in charge of various phases of editing and production: Joanna Garbutt, Rosina Di Marzo and, finally, the copy-editor, Philippa Youngman. I want to offer my sincere thanks to all of these fine professionals and also to take this opportunity to say how proud and pleased I am to have been associated with the Press, in a series of projects, for a quarter of a century.

Abbreviations

Works in the following list, including the early biographies of More by Roper, Harpsfield, Stapleton and Cresacre More (Thomas More's great-grandson), are cited throughout only by abbreviation plus page number (and volume number, if any), e.g., Roper 208; *CW* 12:319. Modern biographies are cited only by author's surname, shortened title and page number, e.g., Ackroyd, *Life of More*, 201. For publication details of early and modern biographies and a list of the individual volumes of *CW*, together with other important modern editions of individual works by More, see pages 288–91.

1557	*The workes of Sir Thomas More Knyght ... wrytten by him in the Englysh tonge*, London, 1557
CMore	Cresacre More, *The Life of Sir Thomas More*, ed. Joseph Hunter, London, 1828
Corr.	*The Correspondence of Sir Thomas More*, ed. Elizabeth Frances Rogers, Princeton University Press, 1947
CSPSp	*Calendar of Letters, Despatches, and State Papers Relating to the Negotiations between England and Spain (1485–1558)*, 13 vols., London, 1862–1954
CSPV	*Calendar of State Papers and Manuscripts, Relating to English Affairs, Existing in the Archives and Collections of Venice, and in Other Libraries of Northern Italy (1202–1675)*, 38 vols., London, 1864–1947
CU	*Utopia: Latin Text and English Translation*, ed. George M. Logan, Robert M. Adams and Clarence H. Miller, Cambridge University Press, 1995
CW	*The Complete Works of St. Thomas More*, 15 vols., New Haven and London: Yale University Press, 1963–97
CWE	*The Collected Works of Erasmus*, 86 vols., University of Toronto Press, 1974–

EA	R. S. Sylvester and G. P. Marc'hadour, eds., *Essential Articles for the Study of Thomas More*, Hamden, Conn.: Archon Books, 1977
EE	*Opus Epistolarum Des. Erasmi Roterodami*, ed. P. S. Allen, H. M. Allen and H. W. Garrod, 12 vols., Oxford: Clarendon Press, 1906–58
EETS	Early English Text Society
EW	*The English Works of Sir Thomas More*, ed. W. E. Campbell *et al.*, 2 vols. (edition not completed), London: Eyre & Spottiswoode, 1931
Harpsfield	Nicholas Harpsfield, *The life and death of Sir Thomas Moore, knight, sometimes Lord high Chancellor of England* (1558–59), ed. Elsie Vaughan Hitchcock, EETS, 1932
LP	*Letters and Papers, Foreign and Domestic, of the Reign of Henry VIII*, 21 vols., London, 1862–1932
LCL	Loeb Classical Library
ODNB	*Oxford Dictionary of National Biography*, 60 vols., Oxford University Press, 2004
OED	*The Oxford English Dictionary*, 2nd edn, 20 vols., Oxford: Clarendon Press, 1989
PRO	Public Record Office (London)
R3	Thomas More, *The History of King Richard the Third*, ed. George M. Logan, Bloomington and Indianapolis: Indiana University Press, 2005
Roper	William Roper, *The Life of Sir Thomas More* (c. 1557), in *Two Early Tudor Lives*, ed. Richard S. Sylvester and Davis P. Harding, New Haven, Conn.: Yale University Press, 1962
SL	*St. Thomas More: Selected Letters*, ed. Elizabeth Frances Rogers, New Haven, Conn.: Yale University Press, 1961
SP	*State Papers ... Henry the Eighth*, London, 1830–52
Stapleton	Thomas Stapleton, *The Life and Illustrious Martyrdom of Sir Thomas More* (pub. 1588), trans. Philip E. Hallett, ed. E. E. Reynolds, London: Burns & Oates, 1966
STC	*A Short-Title Catalogue of Books Printed in England, Scotland and Ireland, and of English Books Printed Abroad, 1475–1640*, ed. A. W. Pollard *et al.*, 2nd edn, 3 vols., London: Bibliographical Society, 1976–91

Chronology

1478 (1477?), 6 or 7 February	More born, in London.
c. 1482–90	Attends St Anthony's School.
1483	Death of King Edward IV; disappearance of his son and successor, Edward V; accession of Richard III.
1485	Defeat and death of Richard III at battle of Bosworth Field; accession of Henry VII.
c. 1490–2	More serves as page in the household of John Cardinal Morton (d. 1500), Henry VII's lord chancellor.
c. 1492–4	At Oxford.
c. 1494	Enters the Inns of Court to study law.
1499	Meets Erasmus.
c. 1501	Delivers lectures on St Augustine's *City of God*.
1503	Writes 'A rueful lamentation' on the death of Henry VII's queen, Elizabeth. (Most of More's few other surviving English poems probably also date from his early adulthood.)
1504	In parliament?
Late 1504 or January 1505	Marries Joanna Colt.
1506	More and Erasmus publish a volume of translations (from Greek to Latin) of the 2nd-century AD ironist Lucian.
1509	Death of Henry VII; accession of Henry VIII. Erasmus writes *The Praise of Folly* (published 1511).
1510	More in parliament; appointed an undersheriff of London.

c. 1510	Publishes *The Life of John Picus* (Pico della Mirandola).
1511	Death of Joanna Colt; More marries a widow, Alice Middleton.
1513	Machiavelli writes *The Prince* (published 1532).
c. 1513–20	More writes *The History of King Richard the Third*.
1515, May–October	On trade embassy to Flanders; meets Pieter Gillis; begins *Utopia*.
1515–19	Writes four letter-essays in defence of Erasmian humanism.
1516	*Utopia* published in Louvain.
1517	Second edition of *Utopia* published in Paris. Martin Luther's ninety-five theses on indulgences signal the beginning of the Reformation.
1518	More joins Henry VIII's council. March and November: third and fourth editions of *Utopia* published in Basel, together with Latin poems (written over the preceding two decades).
1520, May–June	In Henry VIII's entourage at the Field of Cloth of Gold (meeting between Henry and the French king, Francis I). July–August: takes part in trade negotiations with representatives of the Hanseatic League, at Bruges.
1521	Becomes under-treasurer of the exchequer; knighted; appointed to assist Henry VIII with his anti-Lutheran treatise, *Defence of the Seven Sacraments*.
c. 1522	Writes *The Last Things*.
1523	Made speaker of the House of Commons; writes *Responsio ad Lutherum* (a defence of Henry VIII against Luther).
1525	Appointed chancellor of the duchy of Lancaster.
1527, October	First consulted by Henry VIII about the possibility of divorcing his queen, Catherine of Aragon.
1529, June	Publishes *A Dialogue Concerning Heresies*, against William Tyndale and Luther. 25 October: succeeds Wolsey as lord chancellor. 3 November: opens the 'Reformation Parliament' (which sat until 1536).

1532, January	Publishes the first part of *The Confutation of Tyndale's Answer*, his longest anti-Protestant polemic (second part published 1533, along with several other polemics in that year and the next). 16 May: resigns the chancellorship over the 'Submission of the Clergy', ceding veto power over ecclesiastical legislation to the king.
1533, 25 January	Henry VIII marries Anne Boleyn (pregnant with Elizabeth I). 1 June: More refuses to attend Anne's coronation as queen. 11 July: Henry excommunicated by Pope Clement VII.
1534, 13 April	More refuses to swear support for the Act of Succession acknowledging Henry's children by Anne Boleyn as heirs to the throne. 17 April: More imprisoned in the Tower of London, where, over the course of the next fourteen months, he writes *A Dialogue of Comfort against Tribulation*, *De Tristitia Christi* and other devotional works.
1535, 1 July	More tried and convicted of treason. 6 July: beheaded.
1551	*Utopia* first translated into English, by Ralph Robinson.
1557	Collected edition of More's English works.
1563 and 1565	Collected editions of More's Latin works.
1935, 19 May	More canonized.

The family tree of Thomas More

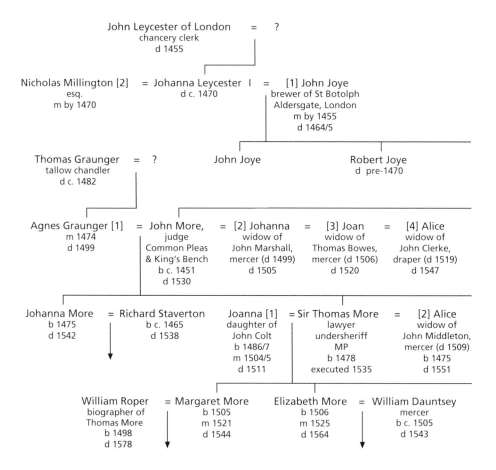

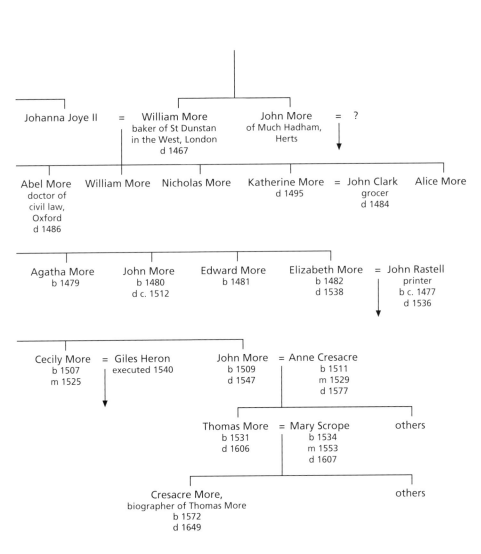

Johanna Joye II = William More
baker of St Dunstan
in the West, London
d 1467

John More = ?
of Much Hadham,
Herts

Abel More
doctor of
civil law,
Oxford
d 1486

William More

Nicholas More

Katherine More = John Clark
d 1495   grocer
d 1484

Alice More

Agatha More
b 1479

John More
b 1480
d c. 1512

Edward More
b 1481

Elizabeth More = John Rastell
b 1482   printer
d 1538   b c. 1477
                d 1536

Cecily More = Giles Heron
b 1507   executed 1540
m 1525

John More = Anne Cresacre
b 1509   b 1511
d 1547   m 1529
            d 1577

Thomas More = Mary Scrope
b 1531   b 1534
d 1606   m 1553
              d 1607

others

Cresacre More,
biographer of Thomas More
b 1572
d 1649

others

Part I
Life, times and work

1 The making of a London citizen

CAROLINE M. BARRON

Thomas More, like everyone else, had thirty immediate ancestors stretching back to the generation of his great-great-grandparents: we know the names of only eight of these thirty men and women, but, even so, that is probably more than is known about the forebears of most middle-ranking Londoners in the late fifteenth century. We might think, perhaps, of these thirty ancestors forming a chorus line on a stage, each lit by a spotlight and all equally important. But twenty-two of the spotlights have broken and so only eight of the chorus are visible. In the epitaph which he composed for himself, More wrote that he was born 'urbe Londinensi, familia non celebri sed honesta' (*EE* 10:260).[1] And, indeed, those members of his family whom we can trace bear out this modest claim. Both his parents were Londoners, and so were his known grandparents, great-grandparents and great-great-grandparents. Such a long London pedigree is very unusual in the fifteenth century. The population of the City in this period – numbering about 50,000 – was replenished, indeed maintained, by a flow of immigrants from the surrounding countryside; so the thick London blood that coursed through Thomas's veins was distinctive.

Thomas's father, John More, was the son of a citizen and baker, William More, who died in 1467, a decade before the birth of his famous grandson.[2] John More's mother, William's wife, was Johanna, the daughter of a London brewer, John Joye, and his wife Johanna Leycester, the 'graunt mother' whom John More remembered specifically in his will.[3] And he had good reason to remember his grandmother, because it was from her that he received a considerable inheritance, including the manor of Gobions in North Mimms in Hertfordshire and also substantial tenements in London itself.[4] Johanna Leycester/Joye was the daughter of John Leycester, a chancery clerk who had come from Leicester in the 1430s and settled in London in the extramural parish of St Botolph Aldersgate.[5] He, together with his son-in-law John Joye, the brewer, played a prominent role in the parish fraternity dedicated to the Holy Trinity in St Botolph's Church. John Joye served several times as a warden and master of the fraternity in the years between 1438 and 1463.[6] He was often involved in property transactions on behalf of the fraternity and was frequently an auditor of the wardens' accounts.[7] John Joye also served as a common councilman for the ward of Aldersgate in 1454.[8] John Leycester, the chancery clerk and Joye's father-in-law, had probably come to live in the parish after John Joye had established his brewery there.[9] Although he never held office within the Holy Trinity fraternity, Leycester acted as an arbiter in disputes and sometimes audited their accounts.[10] In 1449 he lent the fraternity the considerable sum of £20, and some of this money was still owing to him when he died in 1455.[11] His executors, his son-in-law John Joye and Joye's son-in-law William More, arranged that the debt would be repaid by allowing Joye and his wife, Johanna Leycester, to live rent-free for fourteen years in their house, called the Falcon on the Hoop, which belonged to the fraternity.[12] The Falcon was a substantial brewhouse, fronting onto Aldersgate Street and lying just north of the church, and it later became the meeting hall of the fraternity.[13] So these London ancestors of Thomas More were moderately prosperous men and women living purposeful and successful lives in this bustling London parish, and playing significant roles in its affairs. John Leycester the chancery clerk was clearly a man of some wealth (since he had the resources to lend money to the fraternity), and his daughter Johanna was his heir. Although she and her husband had several children, only *their* daughter Johanna appears to have survived, and it was she who married the baker William More and brought much of the accumulated Leycester and Joye inheritance to her eldest son John.[14] Perhaps also young John More inherited from this line stretching back through a baker to a brewer and then to a chancery clerk, a commitment to the parish church, to the corporate activity of its fraternity of lay people and to industry and hard work.

More unusually, perhaps, we also know something about Thomas More's mother, because her husband carefully recorded that John More, gentleman, was married to Agnes, the daughter of Thomas Graunger, on 24 April 1474 in the parish of St Giles without Cripplegate.[15] This Thomas Graunger was a London citizen and tallow chandler who had been one of the wardens of his craft in 1467 and can be found acting as a trustee, receiving gifts of goods and chattels and witnessing documents in the years between 1459 and 1474; and on most of these occasions, the property involved lay in St Giles Cripplegate parish.[16] Conclusive evidence that Thomas Graunger the tallow chandler was the father of

Agnes More would seem to be provided by the gift of goods and chattels which he made in January 1479 to three men: Richard Morley, a fellow tallow chandler; John Swerder, a goldsmith; and John More, gentle-man.[17] There were numerous reasons for making such gifts, which might provide security for debts or a means of avoiding legal liabilities. In this case, it is likely that Thomas Graunger may have been intending (with the help of his wily legal son-in-law) to forestall a forfeiture, avoid liability for a debt or prevent his executors having to pay death duties in the ecclesiastical courts.[18] Thomas Graunger's will has not survived, so it is hard to trace the ancestry of his daughter Agnes More any further back, and there are no surviving medieval records for the parish of St Giles Cripplegate, which might have revealed the activities of the Graunger family. But it appears that members of the family were enrolled in the fraternity of parish clerks dedicated to St Nicholas. Membership of this fraternity (for which a small annual fee was pay-able) seems to have been composed of 'middle-ranking Londoners' who wished to secure the continual prayers of the fraternity priest after their deaths and also the attendance of professional singing lay clerks at their funerals.[19] The death in 1481–2 of Thomas Graunger is recorded in the Bede Roll of the fraternity, and there are several other Graungers, possibly members of the same family, also recorded as members in the years between 1453 and 1506.[20] It is possible that the Agnes More inscribed as a member between April 1478 and May 1479 was Agnes Graunger, the wife of John More who, perhaps, chose to be enrolled following the birth of her son Thomas in February 1478.[21]

Brewers, bakers and tallow chandlers were not numbered among the great merchants of medieval London such as the mercers, drapers and goldsmiths, who supplied the city with a stream of wealthy alder-men and mayors. But these middle-ranking London citizens were, as Thomas More later claimed, respectable if not famous. And it is clear that those of More's ancestors whom we can trace were men of some substance, if not great wealth. His great-grandfather, John Joye, the brewer, ran a large brewhouse – sufficiently large to become, later, the meeting hall of the parish fraternity. His paternal grandfather, the baker William More, at his death was owed £87 – a very considerable sum – for bread he had supplied to the household of the earl of North-umberland. And Thomas More's maternal grandfather, Thomas Graun-ger the tallow chandler, had been involved in 1460 in the safe-keeping of property deeds and other documents for Sir Edmund Montfort, a Lancastrian supporter who fought at the battle of Towton and was attainted in July 1461.[22] But, substantial as these men were, William

More's marriage to Johanna Joye, the heiress of the Joye/Leycester wealth, moved the family up an economic and social peg.

William and Johanna appear to have had six children, and we know something about three of them.[23] Katherine married, first, a London fishmonger, William Howes, and then a grocer, John Clark, and her will drawn up in 1495 reveals a wealthy and substantial widow well established among the mercantile elite of the city, who appointed her brother, John More, gentleman, to act as one of her executors.[24] But the significant social shift is that of the two eldest sons, John More and his brother Abel. They did not follow their father into the world of the London trades but, instead, turned to the law, and to do this they must have had some significant financial backing, since training in the law, then as now, took many years and only slowly yielded financial rewards. Abel More appears to have gone to Oxford University, and by 1482 he had secured his doctorate of civil law and was earning fees for giving legal opinions and acting as an arbitrator. He was employed by Lincoln and Merton Colleges, and in 1486 he was retained by the priory of St Frideswide at the substantial annual salary of £10 13s 4d.[25] But this promising career was nipped in the bud when Abel died, in 1486; he was buried in the London parish church of St Michael Bassishaw, close to his brother John's London home.[26]

John More, the eldest son of William and Johanna More, chose to pursue a career in the common law and was admitted to membership of Lincoln's Inn in 1474, the same year that he married Agnes Graunger.[27] He rose steadily through the hierarchy of offices of the Inn: butler in 1482–3, reader in 1489–9 and again in 1494–5, governor in 1490–1 and again in 1494–6, and in 1503 he was created one of the serjeants at law, a group of distinguished lawyers chosen for their legal skill to act particularly for the crown and the court.[28] It is difficult to know exactly how he made enough money to support his burgeoning family: by 1482 Agnes had borne him six children. Doubtless he picked up odd fees here and there for providing legal advice and serving writs for city companies and individuals, and in 1501–2, for example, he received an annual fee of 13s 4d for providing legal advice to the wardens of London Bridge.[29] An inspection of the various deeds enrolled in the Husting Court of London between 1481 and 1503 reveals John More, gentleman, acting as an attorney and, most frequently, as a feoffee, or trustee, holding tenements for groups of individuals before passing them on to other owners. Although he was never a salaried official of the City (unlike his son Thomas who became an undersheriff in 1510), he was frequently to be found acting together with men who were closely associated with City government such as Miles Adys, the City chamberlain,[30] William Dunthorne and Nicholas Packenham, the common clerks,[31] John Haugh, John Greene and Thomas Marowe, who all held the office of common serjeant at law,[32] and Richard Higham and John Shelley, both undersheriffs.[33] John More in these years also acted frequently in association with leading London aldermen, many of whom went on to be lord mayor. In particular he seems to have worked with the draper Sir William Capell, the alderman of Walbrook ward and mayor of London in 1503–4, and the very wealthy merchant Sir Stephen Jenyns, who was an alderman from 1499 and mayor in 1508–9.[34]

Although it is possible to gain some idea of John More's career as a jobbing lawyer working his way around the courts of the City (and doubtless also at Westminster), it is harder to gain an understanding of the genial *pater familias* depicted by Holbein in 1527. All Thomas More's sixteenth-century biographers draw attention to the role played by John More in his son's upbringing and education and emphasize the respect which Thomas showed to his father, notwithstanding that he had surpassed him in rank (Roper 221, Harpsfield 54, Stapleton 3–4). His perceived influence on his son may, in part, be due to the fact that he lived to be nearly eighty years old (marrying for the fourth and last time when he must have been seventy) and so was a well-known figure in the households of his children and grandchildren. And he was a man for whom family, in its widest sense, was important. After the birth of his second child and first son, Thomas, on 6 February 1478, John More decided to begin to record the births of his children.[35] The book he used for this purpose was his fourteenth-century copy of Walter of Bibbesworth's treatise on French vocabulary, doubtless a useful tool for a young lawyer at a time when legal proceedings (including those in parliament) were still recorded in French. But it was not a grand, or expensive or, indeed, a religious book – which suggests that, at this date, John More did not own many books.[36] He recorded the date and details of his marriage, the birth of his daughter Johanna in 1475, then Thomas in 1478, followed by Agatha in 1479, John in 1480, Edward in 1481 and Elizabeth in 1482. Agatha, John and Edward appear to have died young, but John More remained on close terms with his surviving children: Johanna, who married Richard Staverton (a lawyer who was admitted to Lincoln's Inn on the same day as his brother-in-law, Thomas More, in 1496[37]); Elizabeth, who married the printer John Rastell; and, of course, with his son Thomas. In addition to recording the details of his marriage and the births of his children, John More also copied out a recipe for curing 'le agu' and a brief inventory of plate: two basins weighing 111 ounces, two ewers weighing 47 ounces, and one gold chain of 96 links weighing 11¾ ounces and worth £23 5s.[38]

John More was making a reasonable success of the law, and he was determined that his able son should be given every opportunity to succeed and to shine. He sent him to the lively new grammar school at the Hospital of St Anthony in Threadneedle Street, where he was 'brought up in the Latin tongue' and where he soon 'farre surmounted his coequalls' (Roper 197; Harpsfield 10). The master of the school at the time was 'a famous and learned man, called Nicholas Holt' (CMore 15–16). There is no surviving record of Nicholas Holt at Oxford or Cambridge, but a Master Nicholas received wages of £10 p.a. as 'Master of the Grammar school' at St Anthony's in 1494–5, so this may be the same man who taught the young Thomas More some ten years earlier.[39]

The grammar school at St Anthony's Hospital had been established in 1441 by the enterprising provost of Oriel College Oxford, Dr John Carpenter, who took over the nearby church of St Benet Fink to provide the revenue to pay the salary of a master who was to teach all boys who wished to learn, free of charge.[40] In the next decade the Hospital acquired a clerk who was to teach boys plainsong and singing (presumably polyphonic) with the organ, and the first song master was the notable musician John Benet.[41] Whereas the singing children received their board and lodging in the Hospital (together with the Hospital bedesmen), the grammar school boys lived in their own homes and attended the school on a daily basis. We can know something about the school curriculum because a school book from St Anthony's has survived.[42] Its contents suggest the style of teaching at St Anthony's: how to conjugate irregular Latin verbs; rules of syntax; the construction of Latin sentences and the use of cases; instruction in orthography; and lists of towns and countries with their names in English and Latin. But the book also contains some lines of music, notes on the moves in chess and references to the making of garlands on the feast of St Anthony, which was a day of celebration in the Hospital, when the glum daily diet of cheese and mutton stew was enlivened with chicken, custards and strawberries. The antiquary John Stow recorded that in his youth (in the 1520s) the boys of the different grammar schools in the City would dispute publicly in St Bartholomew's churchyard and compete to win prizes which, Stow sagely remarked, 'made both good schoolmasters and good scholars'. But when walking around the City the scholars, 'their satchels full of books', would get into fights when the boys of St Paul's and St Anthony's taunted each other as 'Anthony's pigs' or 'Paul's pigeons'.[43] It is likely that Thomas More was well instructed in the reading and writing of Latin, and he may also have taken part in some of the music-making that took place in the Hospital. In later life, although not a singer, More played the viol, and he emphasized the religious and recreational importance of music in his *Utopia* (*CW* 4:407, note to 128/15; *CU* 127, 143, 239).

But Thomas was not allowed to remain long at St Anthony's school. His father, 'being carefull for his farther good and vertuous education' (Harpsfield 10), found him a place, in about 1490, as a page in the household of John Morton, the archbishop of Canterbury (and, from 1493, a cardinal), at Lambeth Palace. It is not clear how John More was able to achieve this coup for his son. It is possible that his legal services to Edward Stafford, third duke of Buckingham, who was a powerful member of Henry VII's council and an ally of Morton, may have enabled John More to secure a favour from his client.[44] Another possibility is that Master Nicholas Holt who taught young Thomas at St Anthony's may have spoken of him to his (supposed) relative Master John Holt, at that time an usher at Magdalen school in Oxford but by 1496 the schoolmaster of the boys in Morton's household. Thomas certainly knew John Holt, for he wrote Latin verses for his grammar book, *Lac puerorum* ('Milk for children'), and one of his first surviving letters is to him (*SL* 1–3).

The years spent in Morton's household had a lasting effect on Thomas. In the first place he greatly admired Morton, a wily Lancastrian at heart who reconciled himself to Edward IV but not to Richard III, joined the failed rebellion of Henry Stafford, duke of Buckingham, in 1483 and then fled to join Henry Tudor. More wrote of him that he had been 'whirled about by violent changes of fortune' with the result that he had 'learned practical wisdom, which is not soon lost when so pur-chased' (*CU* 55). Clearly he was an imposing man and More observed that in conversation 'he was not forbidding, though serious and grave'. He had a prodigious memory, a great knowledge of the law and spoke carefully and with polish. It is interesting that although Morton was an archbishop More does not comment on his spiritual or pastoral qualities. It is the statesman and lawyer whom More admires and who must have gone some way towards shaping his own career path and ambitions. And it seems likely that it was Morton (among others) who influenced More's hostile portrait of Richard III. The events of Richard's usurpation and death, and the accession of Henry VII, were less than a decade away when More was in Morton's household. It is inconceivable that such momentous events were not frequent topics of conversation among Morton's servants (see further below, 174). But there was another aspect of life in the archbishop's household which must have influenced young Thomas, and that was the entertainments put on for the household at Christmas and on other festive occasions. At the time that More was at Lambeth, the playwright Henry Medwall was a member of the household and wrote dramatic interludes, of which two – *Fulgens and Lucrece* and *Nature* – have survived.[45] It appears that Thomas on occasion would join impromptu with the players and win applause from the onlookers (although what the players thought of this is not recorded). It would seem that Thomas's natural talents in speaking and dramatic acting were fostered in Morton's household, and he clearly made an impression on the archbishop, who is recorded to have said, 'This child here waiting at the table, whosoever shall live to see it, will prove a marvellous man' (Roper 198).

But Morton must have perceived that this talented young scholar and actor needed to take his studies to a higher level, and so, when Thomas was about fourteen, he moved away from London and his family to study at Oxford. More's great-grandson Cresacre More records that young Thomas was 'placed ... in Canterbury College ... now called Christ Church' (CMore 18; cf. below, 26), and although this cannot be verified it seems very likely, since Archbishop John Morton took a particular interest in this college, which had been established in 1361 for the university education of Benedictine monks, particularly those from Christ Church, Canterbury. But there were also five scholarships for poor boys 'of free and legitimate birth', three of whom could be chosen by the archbishop of Canterbury. These *pueri collegii* received their board and lodging, but no allowance for clothes or books. In return for their scholarships, they had to assist in the chapel and wait on the wardens and fellows in hall, doubtless tasks similar to those More had already been performing at Lambeth.[46] Morton's concern for the education of young men at Oxford and Cambridge is evident in his will (1500), in which he left £128 6s 8d to provide exhibitions for poor scholars, two-thirds at Oxford and a third at Cambridge.[47] More remained at Oxford for barely two years, but, nonetheless, 'he wonderfully profited in the knowledge of the latin and greeke tonges' (Harpsfield 12; cf. Roper 198).

Although More's time at Oxford was brief, it was to have a profound effect on him. Doubtless Morton hoped that Thomas would find, in

Oxford, a vocation to the priesthood, and More's father may have hoped that he would study civil law, although it seems clear that he really wanted his son to return to London to enter a legal inn and become a common lawyer. But what Thomas encountered at Oxford was men who were passionate about the study of classical authors and, in particular, the study of Greek. William Selling, the learned prior of Christ Church, Canterbury, had studied at Canterbury College before travelling to Italy, where he learned Greek at Bologna. Following his return to England, he was elected prior of Christ Church, in 1472. His influence over Canterbury College was strong, although the study of the classics and humanism did not form part of the official curriculum there of theology and canon law.[48] But there were others who had been at Oxford before Thomas arrived and had begun to infect the university with the 'new learning' (cf. below, 25–6). Thomas Linacre was a fellow of All Souls and had travelled to Italy with Selling, acquiring Greek books while he was abroad. William Lily had been at Magdalen in the 1480s and travelled to the eastern Mediterranean and Rhodes, where he studied Latin and Greek before returning to London and marriage in the 1490s. John Colet had originally studied at Cambridge, but he too travelled to Rome before returning to lecture at Oxford in 1496.[49] But the most direct intellectual influence on Thomas More while he was at Oxford is likely to have been William Grocyn, who had studied at New College and been appointed as a divinity reader at Magdalen before leaving England in 1488 for Italy, where he studied in Florence and met up with Thomas Linacre and William Latimer, another young English scholar who was travelling in Italy in the 1490s (*BRUO* 2:1106). When Grocyn returned to Oxford in 1491 he rented a room in Exeter College and gave the first public lectures on Greek in the university.[50] It may be fanciful to suggest that Thomas More heard these lectures, but there is no doubt that when he was brought back to London by his father *c.* 1494 he knew some Greek and was anxious to learn more. And there is a possible indication of a link at this early stage between Grocyn and More. When the vicarage of St Lawrence Jewry, the parish in which John More and his family lived, became vacant in 1496, William Grocyn was appointed to the living, where he remained until his death. It would seem that Grocyn lived in the vicarage at St Lawrence – where he would doubtless have kept his remarkable library of Latin and Greek books (*BRUO* 2:828–30) – and it seems likely that the friendship between the two men (Grocyn was thirty years older than More) may have flourished in this parish context. Indeed, the presence of Grocyn may have reconciled More to being called back to London in order to embark on the practical study of law.

Thomas More began his study of law at one of the Inns of Chancery – New Inn, lying just north of the Strand in Aldwych Lane, near the church of St Clement Danes.[51] Here he was enrolled, so William Roper tells us, and 'for his time he very well prospered' (Roper 198). At this period the ten Inns of Chancery acted as preparatory schools for the four greater Inns of Court: Lincoln's Inn, Grey's Inn, Inner Temple and Middle Temple. At the Inns of Chancery young men learned the elements of law before graduating to one of the Inns of Court, and while they lived in these lesser inns they could attend the courts at Westminster and drop into one of the many drinking houses in the western suburbs for refreshment on their way back.[52] Sir John Fortescue in his book in praise of the laws of England (written in the 1460s) described, perhaps a trifle fancifully, the quiet academy or university comprising the legal inns in London's western suburbs, where young men, mostly of the noble class, learned not only about the law but also 'to sing and exercise themselves in every kind of harmonies'. They learned how to dance and to play the games to be found in the royal household, and on holy days they studied scripture and after divine service devoted themselves 'to the reading of chronicles'. In Fortescue's opinion, at the legal inns young men were trained not only in the 'science of laws' but also 'to acquire virtue and discourage vice'. They were, in effect, finishing schools for men.[53]

Thomas More clearly made short work of the lessons to be learned at New Inn, and only two years later, on 12 February 1496, he was admitted to Lincoln's Inn, where his father was currently serving as a governor, together with Richard Staverton, who married his elder sister, Johanna. Both young men were pardoned four vacations – that is, let off four terms' residence – at the instance of John More.[54] The careers of father and son then moved forward in tandem at the Inn. Thomas seems to have avoided the burdensome offices associated with the Christmas festivities, and having twice declined to serve as the Christmas marshall, in 1510 paid a fine of £5 and was permanently exonerated. But he did serve as an auditor, pensioner and butler, and as the autumn reader in 1510–11, Lent reader in 1515 and as a governor in 1511 and again in 1514.[55] Only six years after being admitted to Lincoln's Inn, Thomas More was 'made Reader of Furnivall's Inn, so remaining by the space of three years and more' (Roper 198). Furnivall's Inn, another of the Inns of Chancery, was attached to Lincoln's Inn, and it was the task of the reader to hear the moots, or disputations, in the

Chancery Inn and to provide a link between the two inns, conveying messages and making effective the academic control which Lincoln's Inn claimed to exercise.[56] During the time that Thomas More was the reader, there was a dispute about the election of the principal at Furnivall's Inn, and William Warham, the lord chancellor (who had oversight of all the legal inns), chose More as one of the two men to examine the case.[57]

After Thomas More returned to London from Oxford he certainly began to climb the legal ladder. But he had other concerns. He was still exploring his call to the religious life, and he was pursuing his interest in the new humanist learning that he had encountered at Oxford. The years between his return to London in about 1494 and his marriage to Joanna Colt in late 1504 or January 1505 – that is, between the ages of sixteen and twenty-six – must have been a time of intellectual and emotional turmoil and excitement for Thomas. For four of those years, we are told by More's early biographers, he chose to live in association with the London Charterhouse. His later martyrdom, two months after that of the prior of that monastery, John Houghton, together with two other Carthusian priors, makes this early association with the Charterhouse of particular significance to these biographers. Roper records that More lived for about four years 'in the Charterhouse', where he gave himself to 'devotion and prayer' but 'without vow' (Roper 198). Harpsfield suggests that his purpose was to see 'whether he could frame himselfe to that kind of life or, at least for a time to sequester himselfe from all temporall and worldly exercises' (Harpsfield 17). Cresacre More believed that at that time More thought of becoming a Franciscan friar 'that he might serve God in a state of perfection' (CMore 25).[58]

So what did living with the Carthusians 'without vow' mean? Although the Carthusians aspired to cut themselves off from the world (and to some extent from each other), the founding of a house in the suburbs of a large city like London made complete exclusion impossible. In practice the London house had many contacts with Londoners who were their most important benefactors, established chantries within the conventual church, chose burial in the Carthusian graveyard and, of course, supplied the house with much of its provisions.[59] Successive priors, prompted by directives from the General Chapter of the order at the Grand Chartreuse, attempted to keep lay people (especially women) at bay and confined them to the perimeters of the precinct in the outer courtyards and the cemetery.[60] But More would not have been unique in seeking to associate, as a lay person, with the spiritual and ascetic life of a Carthusian house. In 1490 Bishop John

Russell, like John Morton a civil servant bishop, who had been Richard III's lord chancellor, received permission from the General Chapter to build a residence in the grounds of the London Charterhouse.[61] He died in 1494, before More would have been living there. In spite of Russell's association with Richard III, More thought him 'a wise man and a good and of much experience, and one of the best-learned men, undoubtedly, that England had in his time' (*R3* 30). Secular visitors, or prospective monks like Thomas More, might be allocated special accommodation recently built for visitors in the south-west corner of the monastic precinct, adjoining the main convent buildings but separated from them by a small cloister.[62]

Thomas More may well have participated in the daily services in the chapel, and he must, surely, have been attracted by the richness of the library.[63] Although More would not have been encouraged to communicate with the monks when they attended services, he might have joined them for the meal which they took together in the *frater* (communal dining hall) on Sundays, or when they went out on their weekly walks. In 1500 an Irishman of great holiness, William Tyn-bygh, became prior, of whom Dom David Knowles wrote that 'To him, more than to any other, must be attributed the high standard of discipline and observance that distinguished the House of the Salutation among even its sister houses in the reign of Henry VIII'.[64] At this distance we cannot know what influence this pious man may have exerted on Thomas More, but the books in the Carthusian library provided a strong traditional and spiritual input which countered (or enriched) the diet of classical texts which More was studying with his humanist friends.

It may well be that, as his biographers wrote, More wanted to test his own vocation to the religious life; but he might also, like many other young men, have wanted to get away from home. It seems likely that More moved out of the family home following the death of his mother, Agnes, and his father's remarriage, in 1499. Thomas More's biographers pay no attention to the role of Agnes in the upbringing of her son, but it may have been her influence which led to his being named Thomas after her father, and it may have been she who directed her brilliant son (albeit unsuccessfully) towards the life of a religious. Thomas's feelings for his mother should not be judged by the misogynist jokes men recount to each other but rather, perhaps, by the care which he lavished on the upbringing of his daughters.[65] It is worth remembering that Margaret Roper and her husband William, who wrote the early and highly influential biography of Thomas More, were both grown up when they knew John More as an old man, whereas Agnes More had died before Margaret was born and when William Roper himself was barely two years old. It is not surprising, therefore, that John More's influence on his son is more frequently noted by his biographers. But there is another aspect to Agnes More that gives one pause. When she died in 1499 she appears to have been buried in the same tomb as her Oxford brother-in-law, Dr Abel More, who had died thirteen years earlier, and her son Thomas composed a twelve-line Latin epitaph for their joint tomb in St Michael Bassishaw church.[66] For a wife to be buried with her brother-in-law rather than with her husband was certainly unusual, if not unique.[67] And why was Agnes More not buried in the church of St Lawrence Jewry where John More's family were parishioners? It may have been simply a matter of economy that led John More to bury his wife in his brother's tomb: we shall probably never know what lay behind this unusual course of action. But when John More remarried, to his neighbour, the widow Johanna Marshall, before the end of the year, Thomas himself may well have moved out, near to the Charterhouse at Clerkenwell.[68]

And although More might well have joined in the spiritual exercises and prayers of the Charterhouse monks, he certainly continued with a number of temporal and worldly exercises. More was studying law at Lincoln's Inn, he was the reader at Furnivall's Inn (both, in Holborn, easily accessible from the Charterhouse), and he was also writing Latin and English poetry (below, 29, 48, 52). Of great significance for More was his first meeting with Erasmus, who visited London in 1499.[69] And it was also in these years (1494–1504) that More was developing his friendship with William Grocyn, now the rector of the church of St Lawrence Jewry. More gave a series of lectures on St Augustine's *City of God* in St Lawrence Jewry about 1501, the year that Grocyn lectured on the Dionysian *Celestial Hierarchy* at St Paul's Cathedral.[70] More also pursued his study of Greek, with Grocyn and with Thomas Linacre, returned from Italy and lecturing on Aristotle's *Meteorologica* as well as acting as tutor to Prince Arthur and physician to Henry VII. Moreover, William Lily had returned from Rhodes and was now teaching in London. Cresacre More describes Lily as More's 'faithful companion' with whom he debated the question of ordination to the priesthood. But God, so Cresacre More tells us, 'had allotted him for another state' (CMore 26). More also developed his friendships with John Colet, from 1504 the dean of St Paul's and refounder, along humanist lines, of St Paul's School, and with John Holt the schoolmaster of the boys in Morton's household and, since

1502, schoolmaster to the young Prince Henry. So, although Thomas More may have been testing his vocation by associating with the Carthusians 'without vow', he was certainly also out and about in the lively legal, courtly and intellectual world of early-sixteenth-century London. And around the beginning of 1505 he took the decisive step away from the religious life when he married Joanna Colt and set up house in the substantial property known as The Barge in Bucklersbury, in the London parish of St Stephen Walbrook. He was now launched on a meteoric civic career which was to take him, within a decade, to membership of the prestigious Mercers' Company, to parliament as a member for London, to the well-paid office of undersheriff of the City and on diplomatic missions to Paris and Louvain. Cardinal Morton had been right: the child who had waited at his table was, indeed, proving to be a marvellous man.

FURTHER READING

For a map of the City of London at the time when Thomas More was walking its streets, see Mary D. Lobel, ed., *The City of London from Prehistoric Times to c.1520*, Vol. 3 of *The British Atlas of Historic Towns* (Oxford University Press, 1989). The 1520 map has been reprinted in a revised edition as *The City of London Five Hundred Years Ago* (Moretonhampstead, Devon: Old House Books, 2008). Although he first published his great work *A Survey of London* in 1598, some fifty years after More's death, John Stow's account remains the crucial starting point for the topography and buildings of the medieval city. The best edition is still that of C. L. Kingsford (Oxford: Clarendon Press, 1908). The government of the city and the realities of life in London in the medieval period are described in Caroline M. Barron, *London in the Later Middle Ages: Government and People 1200–1500* (Oxford University Press, 2004).

Barbara Hanawalt examines the experiences of children in *Growing Up in Medieval London* (New York and Oxford: Oxford University Press, 1993), and Caroline Barron discusses the educational opportunities available to London children in 'The expansion of education in fifteenth-century London', in John Blair and Brian Golding, eds., *The Cloister and the World: Essays on Medieval History in Honour of Barbara Harvey* (Oxford: Clarendon Press, 1996), 219–45. The legal training available in the Inns of Chancery and the Inns of Court is discussed by J. H. Baker in 'The English legal profession, 1450–1550', in Wilfrid Prest, ed., *Lawyers in Early Modern Europe and America* (London: Croom Helm, 1981), 16–41, and by Caroline Barron in chapter 3 of *The Parish of St Andrew Holborn* (London: Diamond Trading Co., 1979). Penny Tucker, in her book *Law Courts and Lawyers in the City of London 1300–1550* (Cambridge University Press, 2007), has a very useful discussion of the operation of the city's courts and the duties of the various legal officers, including the undersheriff.

The history of the London Charterhouse has been excellently surveyed by Bruno Barber and Christopher Thomas in *The London Charterhouse* (London: Museum of London Archaeology Service, 2002), and Andrew Wines offers a cool appraisal of the finances of the house when Thomas More was living nearby in 'The University of Life and the London Charterhouse: practical experience versus scholarly attainment within the Carthusian leadership', in Caroline M. Barron and Jenny Stratford, eds., *The Church and Learning in Later Medieval Society* (Donington: Shaun Tyas, 2002), 100–9.

The expectations and attainments of women in London during More's lifetime can be explored in Caroline M. Barron and Anne Sutton, eds., *Medieval London Widows* (London: Hambledon, 1994), and in Barbara A. Hanawalt, *The Wealth of Wives: Women, Law, and Economy in Late Medieval London* (Oxford University Press, 2007).

Notes

1. '[I]n London of respectable, though not distinguished, ancestry' (*SL* 181).
2. Margaret Hastings, 'The ancestry of Sir Thomas More', *Guildhall Miscellany* 2 (1961), 47–62. Hastings discovered and published a number of key documents, mostly in the City archives, which she used to settle several important issues concerning More's family. See the family tree, above, xxiv–xxv.
3. Hastings, 'Ancestry of Sir Thomas More', 55.
4. *Calendar of Close Rolls* [*CCR*] *1454–61* (London: Public Record Office, 1939), 68; Hastings, 'Ancestry of Thomas More', 57–8, 60–1.
5. Ibid., 68.
6. Patricia Basing, ed., *Parish Fraternity Register: Fraternity of the Holy Trinity and SS Fabian and Sebastian in the Parish of St Botolph without Aldersgate* (London Record Society, 1982), nos. 128, 129, 130, 51, 95, 94, 55, 56, 103.
7. Ibid.: property, nos. 63, 110, 122, 112, 95, 94; auditor, nos. 50, 52, 53, 54, 55, 56, 58, 59.
8. Corporation of London Record Office [CLRO], Journal 5, fo. 155.
9. John Joye appears to have been active in the City as early as 1426 (CLRO Husting Roll 155/13) and began to play a role in the Holy Trinity fraternity in 1434: Basing, *Parish Fraternity Register*, no. 63.

10. Ibid., nos. 40, 78, 53, 54, 55, 56, 58.

11. Ibid., nos. 46, 49, 52, 57, 60.

12. Ibid., no. 123; for Leycester's will and the appointment of his executors see Hastings, 'Ancestry of Thomas More', 50–1.

13. Basing, *Parish Fraternity Register*, xvii–xix; Mary D. Lobel, ed., *The City of London from Prehistoric Times to c.1520* (Oxford University Press, 1989), 96.

14. In his will, drawn up in 1455, John Leycester mentions John Jr and Robert, the sons of his daughter Johanna and her husband John Joye. In 1470 the Leycester inheritance appears to have been divided between John Jr and his sister Johanna and thence to her son John More: Hastings, 'Ancestry of Thomas More', 56–8, 61–2; *CCR 1468–76*, 113.

15. Trinity College Cambridge, MS 0.2.21 fo. 139v; and see below, nn. 35 and 36.

16. M. F. Monier-Williams, ed., *Records of the Worshipful Company of Tallow Chandlers London* (London, 1897), 55–64; CLRO, HR 187/45, 195/10, 195/3 and 11; *CCR 1468–76*, nos. 787 and 1270. It used to be thought that Agnes Graunger's father was the Thomas Graunger, skinner, who became an alderman and sheriff of London in 1503 and died in 1510. But, as George Ramsay pointed out in 1982, this Thomas Graunger only emerged from his apprenticeship in the early 1470s, at the time when his supposed daughter was marrying John More: see 'A saint in the City: Thomas More at Mercers' Hall', *English Historical Review* 97 (1982), 269–88, esp. 273–4. There is nothing in the will of Thomas Graunger, skinner, to suggest any connection with the More family.

17. Philip Jones, ed., C*alendar of Plea and Memoranda Rolls ... of the City of London, 1458–1482* (Cambridge University Press, 1961), 176.

18. On the uses of gifts of goods and chattels, see Philip Jones, ed., *Calendar of Plea and Memoranda Rolls ... of the City of London, 1437–1457* (Cambridge University Press, 1954), xxii–xxviii.

19. N. W. and V. A. James, eds., *The Bede Roll of the Fraternity of St Nicholas*, 2 vols. (London Record Society, 2004), 1:xxviii.

20. Ibid., 1:128 no. 229, 2:378.

21. Ibid., 1:115 no. 201. For the date of Thomas More's birth, see below, n. 35.

22. *CCR 1468–76*, 367, no. 1326.

23. On 12 March 1470 Johanna Leycester/Joye/Millington granted several London tenements to her grandson, John More son of William More, and his heirs, but, failing heirs, the properties were to go to his brothers and sisters, named as Abel, William, Nicholas, Katherine and Alice: Hastings, 'Ancestry of Thomas More', 57–8.

24. The National Archives, PROB 11/10; will drawn up 18 September 1495 and proved 9 October. I am grateful to Justin Colson for help in interpreting this will. John More in his own will, drawn up in 1530, over thirty years after his sister's death, named her and her husband, John Clark, grocer, among those to be remembered in the prayers of the two scholars at Oxford and Cambridge whom he was funding: Hastings, 'Ancestry of Thomas More', 55.

25. Most of the information about Abel More can be found in A. B. Emden, *A Biographical Register of the University of Oxford to A.D. 1500* [*BRUO*], 3 vols. (Oxford: Clarendon Press, 1957), 2:1302. But see also John Fletcher and Christopher Upton, eds., *The Domestic Accounts of Merton College, Oxford 1482–1494* (Oxford Historical Society, 1996), 4, 8, 157. I am grateful to David Lepine, Nicholas Orme and Julian Reid for help in elucidating the Oxford career of Abel More.

26. The year of Abel More's death is confirmed by the reference in the Merton accounts to offerings made on the 'day of the obit for Doctor Abel Moore', Fletcher and Upton, *Domestic Accounts*, 157; his death and burial in St Michael Bassishaw was commemorated in a Latin verse epitaph recorded (not very accurately; e.g., '*Exoniensum*' instead of '*Oxoniensum*') in John Weever, *Ancient Funerall Monuments* ... (London, 1631), 398. See Germain Marc'hadour, 'The death-year of Thomas More's mother', *Moreana* 16, no. 63 (1979), 13–16. For further discussion of this epitaph, see below, 15.

27. W. P. Baildon, ed., *The Records of the Honorable Society of Lincoln's Inn: Admissions 1420–1893*, 2 vols. (London: Lincoln's Inn, 1896), 1:19.

28. E. W. Ives, *The Common Lawyers of Pre-Reformation England* (Cambridge University Press, 1983), 469–70; Ives, 'John More', *ODNB* 39:51–3, at 52; J. H. Baker, *The Order of Serjeants at Law* (London: Selden Society, 1984), 166.

29. In 1497 the Pinners' Company paid him 3s 4d for a writ of *scire facias*. See B. Megson, ed., *The Pinners' and Wiresellers' Book 1462–1511* (London Record Society, 2009), 30; V. Harding and L. Wright, eds., *London Bridge: Selected Accounts and Rentals 1381–1538* (London Record Society, 1995), 161.

30. CLRO 1486, Husting Roll 215/14, 15, 16; 1490, HR 220/2.

31. 1486, HR 215/14, 15, 16; 1490, HR 219/23.

32. 1477, HR 207/11; 1486, HR 215/15, 25; 1484, HR 214/4; 1497, HR 225/49; 1501, HR 228/4.

33. 1486, HR 215/29; 1487, HR 217/8; 1490, HR 220/2; 1496, HR 223/18.

34. Capell: 1486, HR 215/29; 1487, HR 217/8; 1497, HR 225/37; 1505, HR 231/32; 1517, HR 238/8. Jenyns: 1490, HR 220/2; 1496, HR 223/18.

35. Trinity College Cambridge, MS 0.2.21 fo. 139v. John More's original entry recorded that Thomas was born on the Friday after the Feast of the Purification in the seventeenth year of Edward IV's reign, i.e. 6 February 1478. He later inserted a note above the line to record that the date was 7 February, which would suggest that Thomas More was born in 1477, when 7 February fell on a Friday. It seems probable that John More's first recording of the date, which occurred nearer to the actual birth, is the correct one and that his later addition of 7 February was a mistake for the 6th.

36. The Trinity College MS 0.2.21 is, in fact, two volumes bound together at a later date: a thirteenth-century copy of Geoffrey of Monmouth's *History of Britain* and the fourteenth-century text of Walter of Bibbesworth which begins on folio 120.

37. W. P. Baildon, ed., *The Records of the Honorable Society of Lincoln's Inn: The Black Books*, 4 vols. (London: Lincoln's Inn, 1897–1902), 1:105.

38. Trinity College MS 0.2.21, fos. 139, 140v. The recipe for the ague comprised a selection of herbs, boiled up with conduit water, sweetened with sugar and then drunk with white wine.

39. St George's Chapel, Windsor, Records of St Anthony's Hospital, XV.37.21, fos. 15 and 31.

40. *Calendar of Patent Rolls [CPR] 1436–41*, 238.

41. *CPR 1446–52*, 279–80; Brian Trowell, 'John Benet d. 1458' *ODNB* 5:70.

42. British Library MS Additional 37075; see David Thomson, *A Descriptive Catalogue of Middle English Grammatical Texts* (London: Garland, 1979), 219–32.

43. John Stow, *A Survey of London*, ed. C. L. Kingsford, 2 vols. (Oxford: Clarendon Press, 1908), 1:74–5. The Hospital was dedicated to St Anthony of Egypt, one of whose attributes was a pig, and so, in regard to this, pigs belonging to the hospital (distinguished by wearing bells around their necks) were allowed, unlike other pigs, to roam freely in the City. For the history of St Anthony's Hospital and School see Rose Graham, 'The order of St Antoine of Viennois and its English commandery, St Anthony's, Threadneedle Street', *Archaeological Journal* 84 (1927), 341–406, and Caroline M. Barron and Matthew Davies, eds., *The Religious Houses of London and Middlesex* (London: Institute of Historical Research, 2007), 228–31.

44. Guy, *A Daughter's Love: Thomas & Margaret More*, 18, 79, 283, 292–3.

45. Alan Nelson, 'Henry Medwall', *ODNB* 37:698.

46. W. A. Pantin, *Canterbury College Oxford*, 4 vols. (Oxford Historical Society, 1985), 4:85–9. Pantin considers whether More might have been a sojourner at the college but thinks that his placement there by Morton as a *puer collegii* was more likely (4:99–100).

47. *BRUO* 2:1320. For Morton's will see C. Eveleigh Woodruff, ed., *Sede Vacante Wills … Proved before the Commissary … Christ Church, Canterbury* (Canterbury: Kent Archaeological Society, 1914), 85–93, esp. 89. For the possibility that More spent some of his Oxford time at Magdalen College School – a centre of humanist learning at the university – see below, 25–6.

48. Pantin, *Canterbury College*, 4:83.

49. Jonathan Arnold, *Dean John Colet of St Paul's: Humanism and Reform in Early Tudor England* (London: Tauris, 2007), 20–4.

50. *BRUO* 2:827; J. B. Trapp, 'William Grocyn', *ODNB* 24:56–8.

51. C. L. Kingsford, 'Historical notes on medieval London houses', *London Topographical Record* 11 (1917), 28–81, esp. 51–4.

52. For the Inns of Chancery and Inns of Court see Caroline M. Barron with Penelope Hunting and Jane Roscoe, *The Parish of St Andrew Holborn* (London: Diamond Trading Co., 1979), ch. 3.

53. Sir John Fortescue, *On the Laws and Governance of England*, ed. Shelley Lockwood (Cambridge University Press, 1997), 68–9.

54. *Black Books of Lincoln's Inn*, 1:105.

55. *Black Books*, 1:132, 145, 146, 162, 163, 165, 175.
56. Barron *et al.*, *St Andrew Holborn*, 26.
57. D. S. Bland, *Early Records of Furnival's Inn: Edited from a Middle Temple Manuscript* (Newcastle upon Tyne: King's College, 1957), 39 and 25. The record simply says 'Moore de Lincoln's Inn', so it could refer to John More, who was made a serjeant in 1503, rather than to his son Thomas, then the reader.
58. He goes on to say that More did not take this course of action because he found that religious men in England had degenerated from their earlier strictures.
59. For lay burials within the London Charterhouse, see Andrew Wines, 'The London Charterhouse in the later Middle Ages: an institutional history', D.Phil. thesis, Cambridge, 1998, 235–6.
60. Bruno Barber and Christopher Thomas, *The London Charterhouse* (London: Museum of London Archaeology Service, 2002), 70–2.
61. Wines, 'London Charterhouse', 255.
62. Ibid., 33–4, 39, 54.
63. E. Margaret Thompson, *The Carthusian Order in England* (London: S.P.C.K., 1930), 313–30; Vincent Gillespie and A. I. Doyle, eds., *Syon Abbey and the Libraries of the Carthusians* (London: British Library, 2001), 614–29.
64. Barron and Davies, *Religious Houses*, 255.
65. Guy, *A Daughter's Love*, 46; Ackroyd, *Life of Thomas More*, 9–10.
66. Weever, *Ancient Funerall Monuments*, 398, discussed by Germain Marc'hadour in 'The death-year of Thomas More's mother'. Guy believes that Agnes More was buried with her brother (*A Daughter's Love*, 77), but it is clear that her companion was her brother-in-law. Abel is a very unusual name at this period, so what are we to make of John More's bequest in his will drawn up in 1530 of 5 marks to 'Abell the sonne of Emme'? It is possible that Emme was a servant of Abel More who bore him a son: see Hastings, 'Ancestry of Thomas More', 56.
67. Christian Steer, who is studying the medieval burials in London parish churches, confirms that he has not found a single instance of a wife being buried with her brother-in-law.
68. The will of John Marshall, mercer of London, was proved 9 February 1499. He was a wealthy parishioner in St Lawrence Jewry, and William Grocyn was one of his executors (National Archives PROB 11/11). His widow had married John More by October 1499 (Marc'hadour, 'Death-year', 16). For indications that Johanna Marshall had a difficult personality, and a hint that Thomas More may not have been fond of her, see Guy, *A Daughter's Love*, 19, 23 and 78–9.
69. For more on this meeting and the other instances of More's humanist connections and activities mentioned in this paragraph, see below, 26–7.
70. Trapp, *ODNB* 24:57. In 1504 More wrote that, in the absence of Colet, Grocyn was 'the sole guide' of his life (*SL* 6).

2 Thomas More as humanist

JAMES McCONICA

In 1439 the first books from the bequest of Humfrey, duke of Gloucester, arrived at Oxford, seeding the outlook of Italian humanism in the scholastic bower of the English medieval university.[1] It is a date that will serve as well as any to announce the arrival in England of the new priorities associated with the subtle cultural stimulus that we now call 'northern humanism'. In the subsequent unfolding of that influence its most celebrated exponent and disciple, in his own day and after, was Thomas More. Indeed, although his celebrity extends far beyond that of the humanist enterprise of the early Tudors, his achievement in that literary milieu of itself would have ensured his lasting reputation. His early intellectual formation also defines the period and manner in which northern humanism took root in England. By the time More arrived at Oxford around 1492, being some fourteen years of age, his privileged education had begun to prepare him to participate fully in the cultural sea-change foreshadowed by the reception of this new outlook on learning and civil life. We must therefore begin with a brief discussion of what is implied in the term 'humanism' as well as what is not.

The humanism of the European Renaissance was subtle precisely because it was not an ideology or philosophy. Its adherents could indeed be passionate in pursuit of aims that could be widely varied, but in their origins, the central texts of their enterprise were the same as those of the medieval university: the magisterial legacy of Greece and Rome, of antique grammar and rhetoric, of Aristotle and, especially in the north, of the foundational texts of Christian antiquity, notably those of scripture and the Church Fathers. This was the bedrock of European culture, revisited from time to time in a 'classical revival' marked by a fresh resort to antiquity and a new period of intellectual achievement.[2] The classical revival – the renaissance – associated with the name of Thomas More was widespread, enduring and profound. It is usually associated with 'civic humanism' and the advent of 'modernity'.

This renaissance developed from the twelfth century onwards, not in the feudal domains of northern Europe but in the city republics south of the Alps. There the educational formation of the antique Roman governing class, derived in its turn from ancient Greece, found a congenial new home. Education in the service of the city-state – the *polis* – was intended to prepare (free, male) citizens to govern. The object was to produce the 'suitably learned' speaker – the *doctus orator* – who was a citizen trained in the art of persuasive speech (hence grammar and rhetoric) and guided by appropriate knowledge. That knowledge came from the repositories of practical political experience, in history, politics, the arts of war, drama and 'poetry' (literature in general), all enshrined in the speeches and achievements of the great citizens of the past. As an educational programme it carried an inherent moral purpose in the furtherance of the common good, so that another component was moral philosophy, especially directed to the obligations of the ruler and the citizen.[3]

This Ciceronian ideal found its great proponent in the fourteenth century in the works of Petrarch, who more than any other individual impressed on his age the consciousness of historical change.[4] That awareness was at the core of a new, critical attitude to received opinion and established certainties. The texts inherited from the past had now to be re-examined in the context of their time. The cry of *ad fontes!* – 'Return to the sources!' – became the clarion call of the humanist community, determined to recover the elegance of classical Latinity along with the integrity of the antique texts purified of their accumulation of medieval commentaries and scribal misunderstandings. They hoped, indeed, to recover the very outlook of the original authors. Scholastic culture was rejected in its entirety: the arts of disputation and dialectic, and the textual glosses of medieval annotators, were seen alike as corrupt and uncritical, and entirely irrelevant to the needs of the day. What Petrarchan humanism retained from the medieval curriculum was essentially the *trivium* – grammar, rhetoric and dialectic – but the studies of the *quadrivium* – arithmetic, geometry, astronomy and music – were supplanted by history and moral philosophy. In modern terms, it was a 'liberal arts' curriculum.

That the higher studies of the medieval university were seen as irrelevant identifies the most radical break with the medieval past. The culture of humanism, with its emphasis on the issues of the present, was entirely hostile to philosophical system-building and abstract speculation. Instead, the emphasis fell on education that served the needs of the day in seeking the best course of action to nourish civil life, promote marriage and the family, encourage the pursuit and regulation

of wealth, and refine the arts of politics. Thus moral philosophy, drawing on the experience of the past, and rhetoric, as the art of persuasion
in the public forum, were the studies at the heart of the humanistic
curriculum. To serve such practical needs the humanists turned not to
metaphysics or abstract principles but instead to the civic culture of
antiquity, where they resolved to recognize themselves. It became
necessary therefore to revisit the texts, to study them according to the
methods of their own time as advocated by such classical rhetoricians
as Quintilian, to discover their literary context in a sweeping search for
new authors, and, most important, to master the original languages in
which those texts were conceived. Without any intended repudiation of
their religious heritage, the emphasis in this reassessment was on the
potential of the human spirit, and the prospects and travails of life in
this world rather than the next.

Thus the culture that emerged in fourteenth- and, especially,
fifteenth-century Italy was civic, lay and literary in orientation, and
recovered many new texts, literary and philosophical, most notably
those associated with Greek letters and the Platonic tradition.
A command of classical Latin and Greek came to be deemed essential
for proficiency in both secular and sacred letters, so that the study of
Greek became a new and distinguishing imperative; and, for the study
of scripture, Hebrew was added to Greek. The unforeseen result was a
profound reappraisal of the cultural and religious heritage of the Christian West.[5] Early evidence of how disturbing all this might be to
received opinion in the religious sphere was given by the Roman
humanist Lorenzo Valla (1407–57), who, among other feats of philological criticism, exposed the inauthenticity of the 'Donation of Constantine', an eighth-century forgery purporting to embody the cession
to the papacy, by the fourth-century Roman emperor, of political
authority over all of western Europe.

By contrast, the culture of the medieval universities in the north,
firmly in place by the twelfth century, reflected the interests of feudal
monarchy and the Church and was designed to serve the needs of the
landed classes and the monarchy. It was clerical and speculative, and
confined to comparatively few texts and authors, studied entirely in
Latin. The study of grammar and rhetoric was propaedeutic to the
higher studies – among them theology – in which dialectic was dominant. Nonetheless, the medieval curriculum achieved a remarkable
degree of sophistication in fields that were the preserve of a restricted
intellectual elite, such as theology itself, grammatical logic,[6] and
Modist or 'speculative' grammar. Oxford's distinction in those fields

had made it an international European destination for the great religious orders and for the training of clergy, amongst whom the English crown sought out its religious leaders, diplomats and civil servants.

Duke Humfrey's benefaction, with its preponderance of theological books, reflected the evolving situation in fifteenth-century England, where the widespread popularity of endowed schools and the expanding mercantile and urban populace foreshadowed a receptive home in the next century for the developments in Italy.[7] As a cultivated nobleman, he exemplified the class whose interests were allied with governance, whose contacts were international, and whose wealth facilitated innovation. He presented the university with a generous supply of texts in traditional subjects such as medicine, civil and canon law, philosophy and scholastic theology. At the same time, his gifts embraced a wide range of subjects not familiar to the scholastic curriculum and included some intimately associated with humanistic priorities, such as patristic authors, including new translations from the Greek Fathers, classical texts, Leonardo Bruni's Latin translation of Plutarch's *Lives*, Plato's *Republic* in the Latin version of Piercandido Decembrio and new works by such French and Italian humanists as Tito Livio Frulovisi and Antonio Beccaria – both of whom served as secretaries to Duke Humfrey – as well as by Bruni, Coluccio Salutati, Poggio Bracciolini and Andrea Viocchi.[8]

Thomas More emerged from precisely the milieu for which this blend of traditional study and new influences was appropriate. A Londoner who was the eldest son of a successful advocate and whose origins were rooted in the life of the City (the More family lived in Cripplegate ward),[9] he had excellent schooling at St Anthony's in Threadneedle Street. For his further education he was then placed as a page in the household of England's most influential churchman, John Morton, archbishop of Canterbury and chancellor of England. This arrangement typified provision for the advanced education of the young nobleman or other individual of high status who was intended for the world of affairs. As Morton was also chancellor of Oxford University, it is not surprising to find Thomas More at Oxford about 1492.

It was most likely at Oxford that he was introduced to the study of Greek and humanistic Latin (Roper 198). Coincidentally, our first information about the public teaching of Greek in the university comes from precisely this time, when William Grocyn was lecturing on Greek literature. While it is likely that occasional teaching in Greek was available in Oxford from the 1460s, and certainly by the 1490s, Grocyn's are the first public lectures of which we know.[10] More may have spent some of his time at Magdalen College School, then outstanding for the reform of grammar teaching in England, where the Italian humanist and Grecian, Cornelio Vitelli, was recently a guest. The link would have been John Holt, schoolmaster to the boys in Morton's household at Lambeth Palace in 1495, and a sometime master at Magdalen College School as well. The Greek scribe John Serbopoulos was producing Greek manuscripts in Oxford between 1484 and 1500, some of which were acquired by Grocyn, and might well have tutored Thomas More in the language.[11] The earliest attributed testimony about More's Oxford affiliation appears to be that of the antiquary Miles Windsor about 1555, recorded a century later by Anthony Wood. Windsor was in Oxford in the reign of Queen Mary, at a time when recollection of More would have been both fresh and of recent interest, and he places his chamber at St Mary's Hall. Another tradition that places him at Canterbury College can be explained by Morton's practice of maintaining his Oxford scholars, scattered throughout the university and often located at St Mary's Hall, through that Canterbury foundation.[12] Wherever More was located, with his prestigious connections he could have found introductory instruction from a competent teacher, possibly Grocyn himself.

In 1494 More was recalled to London and to the legal studies that were plainly to be his destiny. Erasmus records Sir John More's hostility to his son's liberal studies, to the point of depriving him of all support,[13] but it was soon evident that More's humanist ambitions were nonetheless persistent. Ironically, he was now in the proper milieu for the pursuit of such studies, as the early influences from Italy took root in court circles and in the professional legal world of the Inns of Court rather than in the universities. When around 1497 John Holt wrote a Latin grammar, the first in English, called *Lac puerorum* ('Milk for children'), More supplied epigrams for the introduction and conclusion of the book. In a letter to Holt in 1501 he also writes of having made additions to a comedy about Solomon and, in describing his studies, says that he has set Latin aside and has taken up the study of Greek (*SL* 2). We learn, too, that his Greek instructor is none other than William Grocyn, lately of Oxford.

At this time Grocyn was the best-trained Grecian in the kingdom, having studied for two years in Florence under Demetrius Chalcondyles and Angelo Ambrogini, the eminent humanist also known as Poliziano. By 1501 Grocyn held the living of St Lawrence Jewry and was lecturing at St Paul's on the *Celestial Hierarchies* of Dionysius the Areopagite. This neo-Platonist work, thought until the sixteenth century to have apostolic authority, comments on the mediation of the nine orders of angels between God and Man.[14] Our source of information is More's account of the matter in the same letter, where he describes a varied audience in light-hearted and familiar terms. Shortly afterwards, and clearly at the invitation of Grocyn, More delivered a course of lectures in the church of St Lawrence Jewry on St Augustine's *City of God*. Introduced by now to John Colet and to Thomas Linacre and William Lily as well, evidently through his association with Grocyn, he had found a place at the very heart of an eminently distinguished humanist circle.[15]

Those connections were responsible for an introduction exceptionally important for the future. In the spring of 1499, the Dutch humanist Erasmus 'of Rotterdam' arrived in London with his aristocratic pupil William Blount, Lord Mountjoy, who was a friend of More's family. More took him to call on the royal children at Eltham Palace,[16] a politic indication of his personal status. More was twenty-one years old, Erasmus about thirty-two. Erasmus spent most of this first British visit in Oxford, where he was at work on the *Antibarbari* ('The anti-barbarians'), his manifesto arguing for the appropriation of pagan learning and wisdom precisely to enrich and purify the Christian faith; he was probably also assembling the collection of Greek and Latin proverbs that would be called the *Collectanea*, the first form of the *Adagia*. Although Erasmus left England for a time in January 1500, the friendship between the two men was firmly established.

In the years to follow, More pursued his legal studies whilst lodging with the Carthusian monks at the London Charterhouse.[17] He was called to the Bar in 1501, then employed as reader at Furnival's Inn for three years, a time during which he undoubtedly debated the exact form of his future calling, whether to a life of lay service to the commonweal, or one of monastic and/or priestly vocation. He continued as well with the study of Greek under Grocyn and then with Thomas Linacre. The latter had recently returned (1499) from some twelve years' study of Greek and medicine in Italy, bringing with him Greek manuscripts of Galen (the great medical authority of ancient Greece, whose views remained highly influential), from which Linacre would make the translations into Latin that won him international acclaim. In Venice he had assisted Aldus Manutius in the preparation of the first printed edition of Aristotle.[18] Now the most learned Greek scholar in the realm, he was appointed tutor to Henry VII's first son, Prince Arthur, who, however, died in 1502. More's perseverance with these studies while weighing the prospect of a vocation in the Church is sufficient evidence of his commitment to the learned Christian humanism of which Erasmus was to be the pre-eminent exponent.

His lectures on St Augustine's *De civitate Dei*, already mentioned, are exemplary of such a formation and in themselves were a bold and unusual venture. According to Roper, More's auditory included his teacher, 'Doctor Grocyn, an excellent cunning man, and all the chief learned of the City of London' (Roper 198).[19] From Roper's account and later sources it is easy to conclude that More was well known to learned contemporaries in the City, and that lectures on such a subject by a young layman would have had its appeal, if only as a novelty. Of the nature of his lectures, however, we can say little. The topic itself was clearly in keeping with humanistic interest in the early sources of the Christian faith, and More's biographer Thomas Stapleton, writing in 1588, said that More discussed the *City of God* 'not from a theological point of view, but from the standpoint of history and philosophy' (Stapleton 7–8), thus reflecting both his lay status and humanist priorities. His Greek studies continued also with William Lily, the man later chosen by John Colet as first headmaster of the school he refounded at St Paul's. A godson and pupil of Grocyn, Lily had left Oxford in about 1490 and travelled to Jerusalem, Rhodes and Italy, pursuing his studies in Greek and Latin. He was a companion of More in the Charterhouse and the two competed in preparing Latin translations from the *Greek Anthology*, some of which found their way into More's *Epigrammata*, which appeared in 1518 from the press of Froben in Basel, together with *Utopia* and epigrams of Erasmus.[20]

A parallel undertaking – More's translation of the life of Pico della Mirandola composed by his nephew Giovanni Francesco Pico – bears more importantly on his interior debate about future vocation. His text was derived from the Latin edition of Pico's *Complete Works* and was finished in about 1504 according to Stapleton, who associated it with More's decision to marry (Stapleton 9). More's brother-in-law John Rastell printed it about 1510 as the *Life of John Picus*.[21]

The earl of Mirandola had been a devout layman as well as a remarkable humanist scholar and syncretic philosopher, and More dedicated the translation to a friend and fellow-parishioner of St Stephen Walbrook, Joyce Lee, who had decided to become a nun of the Franciscan Order of the Poor Clare Sisters. A member of a family close to that of Sir John More, More's 'good syster' was also the sister of the future archbishop of York, Edward Lee, with whom More was to have further dealings. The translation was accompanied by extracts from the devout and erudite Pico's writings on spiritual matters and, whether it was written at the start or near the end of the decade, it must be associated with More's decision to remain in the lay state and pursue a civic vocation.[22]

More's humanistic productions up to this point, including his lectures, his translations from the *Greek Anthology*, his Latin poems and the *Life of John Picus* may be seen in part as the finger exercises of an ambitious tyro in the new culture of humanism.[23] Nonetheless, they demonstrated his growing expertise in the humanistic literary arts. The *Epigrams* in particular were singularly advanced from the uninspired productions of contemporary humanists, including Erasmus. As their editor has said, 'If More had written nothing but his Latin poems, he would have been assured of a modest but important place in neo-Latin and vernacular literature. The same cannot be said of Erasmus.'[24] More took as his themes not conventional pieties and ingratiating tributes to notable persons, but rather the practical affairs of the day. He touches frequently on the difference between a good king and a tyrant, and although perhaps not too much should be made of this – since reflection on the nature of the tyrant and on the virtues of a republic were commonplaces in the culture of humanism[25] – More's long poem on the coronation of Henry VIII includes a daring attack on the late policies of Henry VII, a sharp critique that lends credence to his views on the advantages of senatorial government over that by a king.[26]

These productions should be placed as well in the context of More's marriage to Joanna Colt, his taking a house, 'The Barge [often 'The Old Barge'] in Bucklersbury', in the parish of St Stephen Walbrook, and his likely election to parliament as a burgess[27] – all in the years 1504–5 – a bold if tacit confirmation of his commitment to a family and public service.

In late 1505 Erasmus joined More and his family at The Barge for a six-month stay, during which the two friends set themselves to Latin translations from Lucian of Samosata, the second-century Greek satirist and master of the dialogue, who was a tireless commentator on the manners of his age.[28] With this undertaking More was moving to a new level in the humanist agenda. His collaborator was his senior by a decade, but Erasmus had come to the study of Greek later than More, at about the time More was in Oxford, so that their relationship was more companionable than that of master and pupil. Lucian was a serious commitment for both of them in more ways than one. Unknown to the medieval West, his satirical dialogues, recently rediscovered,[29] were coruscating and highly ironic in their moral stance, as well as irreverent towards and dismissive of popular religion, including the early Christianity known to him. His contempt for common credulity and for superstitious fraud under the cloak of devotion was particularly congenial to Erasmus's aim of replacing a religion of observances with pure devotion focused on the scriptural portrait of Christ. At the same time Lucian's Greek was considered pure and exemplary and, like the humanists of More's day in relation to classical antiquity, Lucian belonged to a later generation of Greek intellectuals – the 'Second Sophistic' – who, half a millennium away from the Attic civilization they admired, were self-consciously promoting its rehabilitation. His allure needs no further explanation.[30]

The translations by More and Erasmus from Lucian formed an advanced stage in their mastery of classical Greek. More translated three of the dialogues,[31] Erasmus four; and both did translations of Lucian's declamation *Tyrannicida*. More's dialogues touch on Lucian's typical concerns: the moral virtues of a simple life free from cupidity, the futility of philosophical speculation as opposed to the usefulness of practical wisdom in the search for the good life, and, in *Philopseudes*, the ageless human weakness of credulity for which the only corrective is a resolute scepticism. A dedicatory letter written by Erasmus in May 1506 suggests that it was More's idea that in addition to their translations, both of them write a Latin reply to the *Tyrannicida*,[32] which is thus the work among the four he translated in which More showed most explicit interest. It posed a complex problem in legal morality, touching on the place of the tyrant in the community. Their immersion in the irony and satiric postures of Lucian left an indelible impression on the writing of both men, and in More probably appealed to a penchant for taking on roles, for adopting various voices, that was deeply embedded in his nature.[33] As a literary device it was to be fully realized in his most enduring work, *Utopia*.

More dedicated his translations to Thomas Ruthall, bishop of Durham since 1503 and sometime chancellor of Cambridge University, who was an experienced diplomatist and servant of the crown. The dedicatory letter seems to forestall some possible concern on Ruthall's part when More remarks that the *Cynicus* had been quoted in a sermon of St John Chrysostom, that the *Necromantia* rebukes the fruitless contentions of the philosophers on trivial questions, and that the *Philopseudes* is aimed at habitual lying, even if it also shows a pagan disregard for some of the cherished doctrines of the Christian faith. Indeed, says More, in a strikingly Erasmian turn of phrase, Christians who propagate pious falsehoods do greater harm, as if truth needed the support of lies (*CW* 3, Part 1:6–7).

Within a short span of time, More had occasion to intervene with more robust and explicit defences of the humanist position. In August 1509, by which time Joanna Colt had borne More three daughters and, most recently, a son, Erasmus returned to England from Italy, bringing with him for completion his most celebrated satire, the mock encomium *The Praise of Folly*, the Latin title of which – *Moriae encomium* – enshrined their friendship in a pun on More's surname. *The Praise of Folly* appeared in print in Paris in 1511, and the following year in its authorized edition by Josse Bade. By Erasmus's intimates and such supporters as Thomas More and Pope Leo X, it was received with delight; others received it with consternation and dismay. An early critic of uneasy and inconsistent stance was Maarten van Dorp (1485–1525), a humanistic Latinist who turned eventually to scholastic theology at the University of Louvain.[34] Having met Erasmus in 1514 and seen some of his *Opuscula* through the press, Dorp wrote to him 'reporting' objections to the *Folly* by Louvain theologians for its lack of reverence, and criticizing Erasmus's audacity in proposing to emend the New Testament in the light of the Greek text, exposing all the discrepancies between it and the Vulgate. At stake in the eyes of the common people, he protested, was the authority of the theologians and the 'received' text. An expanded version of this letter, taking into account a conciliatory reply[35] by Erasmus, was dated 27 August 1515.

At this time More was involved in an embassy to the Netherlands, having been drawn into part-time royal service. He arrived in Bruges on 17 May 1515 to renegotiate an alliance of friendship and commerce with Flanders, in company with Cuthbert Tunstall (the chancellor to the archbishop of Canterbury) and three others. In the course of these extended discussions More found opportunities to explore Erasmus's homeland and met Pieter Gillis, a scholarly friend of Erasmus who was town clerk of Antwerp. Gillis showed More Erasmus's recently published defence of *The Praise of Folly* and Dorp's response, in which he continued to deny the need for Greek and maintained the superiority of the Latin Vulgate over the Greek text of the New Testament on the grounds that the Greeks had become heretics.

More's reply to Dorp's letter of 27 August is his first extended defence of the humanist agenda in a series that followed publication of the *Folly*. It was composed towards the end of his embassy and dated from Bruges on 21 October. In a friendly but firm tone he replies to Dorp's positions and admonishes him for adopting condescending attitudes, and for misrepresenting Erasmus's views. Characteristically, More's letter adopts the rhetoric of dialogue, reporting conversations and maintaining the stance of a friendly onlooker who is persuaded of the good will of both participants, Dorp and Erasmus.[36] At the same time, More's familiar irony is incisive, even lethal, thus: Dorp's criticism of the *Folly*, his dislike of the grammarians and of Erasmus's insistence on annotating the Vulgate, his dismissal of Greek literature – these are after all legitimate opinions, and what is more, Dorp has stated his views in such a way that More does not doubt that arguments for Erasmus's position will occur to everyone reading the letter (*CW* 15:9–11). More also defends the grammarian's approach to theology, one formed through close study of the text rather than through the anachronistic and distorting framework of Aristotelian dialectic. Such an approach is made, as in antiquity, with a helpful knowledge of every branch of literature, every relevant discipline. And from this point More turns to defence of Erasmus's intended emendation of the Vulgate in the light of the early texts (*CW* 15:81 ff.), concluding with a strong personal appeal that Dorp should render himself truly competent and take up the serious study of Greek.

Defence of such study in More's own university was his next work of humanist advocacy. Although we know nothing about the exact circumstances that provoked his letter of 29 March 1518 addressed from Abingdon 'to the reverend Fathers, the Vice-Chancellor, the Proctors, and the other members of the Masters' Guild of the University of Oxford' (*CW* 15:130–49), we know from Erasmus that More himself reported the conservative attack on Greek studies to the king.[37] His argument includes an essential article of the humanist creed, that an informed knowledge of the legacy of pagan letters will help, not hinder, the quest for a life of virtue. Moreover, such literacy is essential if the preacher is to reach the ordinary man and not just the academic initiate – another favourite theme. Thus classical learning is a vital foundation for mastery of the sources of Christianity and for their propagation to the public, especially in preaching. More even invokes a humanist *topos* when he commends approaching theology by way of philosophy and the liberal arts, thus adorning the queen of the sciences 'with the spoils of the Egyptians' (*CW* 15:138–41). In one passage he encapsulates perfectly the humanists' dissatisfaction with the established medieval curriculum, directed as it was to the cultivation of abstract, speculative disciplines that might bring satisfaction and even international reputation to an individual scholar, but brought no return at all to the ordinary citizen:

> Furthermore, not everyone who comes to Oxford comes just to learn theology; some must also learn law. They must also learn prudence in human affairs, something which is so far from being useless to a theologian that without it he may be able to sing

well enough for his own pleasure, but his singing will certainly
be ill suited for the people. And I doubt that any study contributes
as richly to this practical skill as the study of poets, orators, and
histories.

(*CW* 15:139)

More's support of Erasmus also extended to a distinctly awkward
intervention in a dispute between his friend and Edward Lee, mentioned above in connection with More's dedication of the *Life of John
Picus* to his sister Joyce. Lee was an Oxford graduate and churchman
who would accede in 1531 to the see of York. As it happened, the
relationship between the More family and that of Lee was of long
standing. In 1516 Lee matriculated at Louvain, where he hoped to
further his knowledge of Hebrew and Greek. For a time he contributed
suggestions to Erasmus for revisions to his edition of the Greek New
Testament (which had been published in 1516 and would be issued in a
revised edition in 1519), but he came to believe that Erasmus paid
insufficient attention to his contributions. Lee felt slighted and accused
Erasmus of plagiarism, of being too proud to accept his advice and of
being a slanderer of scripture.[38] Erasmus, highly sensitive both about
attacks on his scholarship and about charges of heterodoxy, turned
furiously on Lee – writing against him and enlisting his supporters to
do so as well – when, after the publication of the revised New Testament,
Lee finally published his criticisms. Despite attempts by many to mediate, the quarrel between the two lasted for years.

Like other English friends of Erasmus, More was anxious to quell the
embarrassing dispute, and on 1 May 1519 he wrote a long letter to Lee,
urging him not to publish (*CW* 15:152–95). The letter is of interest here
for its rhetorical form as much as its content. In the light of Lee's belief
that he has been highly offended, More begins with a strong assertion of
personal goodwill, and invokes the remembered friendship of their
parents. He insists that his friendship remains firm, but confesses also
to his fondness for Erasmus, for the reason that the Dutch scholar is
admired by all of Christendom due to his unceasing exertions to advance
sound learning in both secular and sacred studies. Accordingly More is
the more alarmed at Lee's determination to pursue a course of action
that can only damage his own reputation and that of his country.
Although saying that he declines to take sides in the dispute, More
nonetheless makes it clear that he thinks Lee's case is weak, and he
informs Lee of the impression his actions are making on others, including the appearance of insincerity and duplicity in his proposing that

Bishop John Fisher mediate. He goes on to specify other instances of what appear to be dissembling, and urges caution and restraint, especially given Erasmus's reputation: the first edition of the New Testament had, after all, the approval of the pope, Leo X. Lee should realize that Erasmus could bring against him a battery of learning and invective. Above all, More fears that Lee will bring discredit upon himself for defending his honour where More cannot see that Erasmus has impugned it. Finally, he urges Lee to abandon his accusations, resume friendly relations with Erasmus (who will not refuse), abandon a quarrel that will continue to haunt him (a prescient observation) and return to constructive scholarship and a peaceable life by recalling his Christian charity. There is an interesting note of patriotism in closing: if compelled to do so by Lee's continued obduracy, More will make it clear that the learned community understands that Lee acts alone as a Briton, not for Britain. Humanist themes inform the entire letter: the cause of true learning, the need for concord, the discredit such quarrels can bring upon the reform of good letters, and the assurance of continuing friendship.

More set forth a final, general epistolary defence of the Erasmian reform programme in a letter written at about the same time as his letter to Lee. This letter is described simply as 'to a monk' (*CW* 15:198–311). In it he responded to an epistolary attack on Erasmus, widely circulated in manuscript in 1519 and addressed, as it seemed, to More as Erasmus's associate. The anonymous author was a member of the London Charterhouse where More had lived a few years earlier, a young monk known to him personally who was an active conservative polemicist.[39] More's response became the centrepiece of a volume published in 1520, in which a group of English and German supporters of Erasmus directed a joint counterattack against Lee and Lee's attack on Erasmus's New Testament.[40]

More's letter begins with that same issue, but moves on to the wider issues of the Erasmian reform programme. With typical irony he thanks the monk for the loyal concern he shows for his welfare by warning him against dangerous familiarity with Erasmus, but responds by protesting his own concern over the grave dangers in the monk's position. As he has done before, More points to the eminent supporters of Erasmus's New Testament, including the pope, and with respect to Erasmus's orthodoxy, to the formidable reputation of his close associates, including John Fisher, John Colet, Tunstall, Richard Pace and Grocyn (*CW* 15:208–9). To the objection that Erasmus accuses some of the great figures of Christian learning of having been in error – men such as Jerome, Augustine, Ambrose and Hilary – he points out that they are known to have disagreed among themselves: in such instances, could both have been right? To speak as the monk has spoken is to reveal that he has never read these Fathers, or certainly never understood them. Simply laughable is the monk's contention that Erasmus lacks eloquence. More points out further that the version of the scriptures by Jerome scarcely survives in the received text – the Vulgate – and, indeed, that the received text has never (contrary to the monk's belief) been sanctioned by the Church. On the sensitive issue of Erasmus's translation of the Greek *logos* by *sermo* rather than the received *verbum* in the first chapter of the Gospel of John, More replies that in this Erasmus had the support of Jerome himself, who indicated (among other things) that the words *verbum* and *sermo* are used interchangeably in scripture whenever the Greek term *logos* occurs (*CW* 15:238–9). Dealing trenchantly with other objections of the monk to Erasmus's New Testament, and repeating some arguments he has used before with Lee, More turns then to other of Erasmus's works similarly disparaged by his opponent, starting with the *Folly*.

Declining to defend the *Folly* himself, More again appeals to the consensus of distinguished judges who approve of it, and quickly refers to Erasmus's own comprehensive defence of the work in his response to Dorp. Of greater interest is the next issue, that of the dialogue *Julius exclusus e coelis* ('Julius barred from heaven') – a virulent and anonymous attack on Pope Julius II, whose warlike pontificate epitomized all that the reform party found wrong with the contemporary papacy. The monk argues (as did many at the time) for Erasmus's authorship. In truth, it seems entirely likely that Erasmus wrote it[41] – at least in large part, while in Cambridge – but he refused to acknowledge the authorship of something that was such a gift to his enemies and now to the Lutheran party. It is very likely that Thomas More, too, knew the truth,[42] and in his efforts here to distance Erasmus from the notorious satire he evaded the kind of forceful denial one might have expected from him had he been convinced of Erasmus's innocence of the work. Instead, he adopts the stance of a disinterested witness in a less than persuasive rebuttal. The monk, like many others then and since, claims that the style is unmistakably 'Erasmian'. More's response to this is amusingly convoluted, before he moves on to the 'what if he did' argument, attempting to place the blame for untimely publication on the publishers, then reproving the monk for exposing an error by a fellow religious.[43] It is not More's finest moment as an apologist.

With rising emphasis he berates the monk's failure to observe his vows of seclusion by reading heretical (Lutheran) and controversial works, a constant theme in the voluble humanist critique of monks and friars who neglect their vows and proper duties to take up worldly concerns and self-indulgent habits. More makes it clear that he is undeceived by the pretence of the other to give him timely advice, and recognizes the letter as an extended, bitter and unjustified attack on Erasmus in which the monk exhibits the same abusive traits he repudiates. More regrets that the monk has fallen away from the amiable character he enjoyed as a young man, and hopes that his present conduct is an aberration. He must after all take into account the eminent character of those of his English contemporaries who are avowedly grateful to Erasmus for what they owe to him: Bishop John Fisher of Rochester, John Colet, the dean of St Paul's, and the dean of Salisbury, John Longland, here with explicit reference to Longland's admiration for Erasmus's New Testament. Using another humanistic theme, he reproves the monk for attempting to break up a friendship, and then concludes the letter with a lengthy and animated defence of Erasmus as a critic not of the religious life as such, nor of conventional pieties, but as one who is concerned only with abuses of the consecrated life, and with superstitious legalism displacing informed, true piety.

The letters of advocacy for the humanist agenda that we have considered were all composed within a few years of the two principal works that secured More's fame in the English and international world of letters, his *History of King Richard the Third* and *Utopia*.[44] *Utopia* was written, in Latin, in 1515 and 1516, beginning in the Netherlands when More was also composing his long letter to Maarten van Dorp in defence of *The Praise of Folly*. What is now Book II of the work (with the opening of Book I) was written first, containing a detailed description of the fictional island of Utopia and the life of its inhabitants. Book I, an open-ended dialogue on civic duty, along with the conclusion of the work and the prefatory letter to Erasmus's and More's humanist friend Pieter Gillis, was composed in 1516, when More, back in England, was engaged in the business of the court and contemplating entry into full-time royal service.[45]

The History of King Richard the Third was composed in its two versions, Latin and English, starting in about 1513, when he was involved in the world of business in London, and More had probably discontinued them, unfinished, by the end of the decade.[46] The Catholic exile community brought out the Latin text from Louvain in the *Opera omnia* of 1565. The English *History* was published authoritatively in More's English Works in 1557, but the text must have circulated in manuscript well before that date, since a corrupt version of it was incorporated into some chronicle histories from 1543 on.[47] More's English version informed and shaped Shakespeare's portrait in his *Richard III*, and his account passed thence to popular understanding.

Both of these works take up the humanist debate about the duty of the man of 'good letters' in the world at large, and in particular about the respective merits of a life of scholarly leisure and informed seclusion against that of active engagement with the practical affairs of the day (cf. below, n. 22). This tension will have been at the heart of More's personal debate during the years when he lived in the Charterhouse whilst studying the law, as his father wished him to do. It is a theme that surfaces again and again in his epigrams and other writings; it is a core issue in the *Life of Pico*.

It is reasonable to ask why More took time in a very busy schedule to write the *History* – and in two languages. It is unlikely that he ever considered publication, if only for reasons of prudence: too many of the actors were still alive, too many of them in a position to hinder his career, to say the least (see *R3* xl–xliii). The work may have been intended in part for circulation among a very close group of friends who would appreciate its artistry as an exercise in rhetorical form and who shared an understandable interest in its theme, and the doubling of his composition suggests that strongly. It was, after all, informal circulation of the text that ultimately ensured its becoming known, via the chronicle histories. At heart, however, More's *History* is rooted in his preoccupation with the uses of power in promotion of the welfare of the commonweal, especially in the England of his day, and the writing of it will have served to deepen his long reflections on that theme.

Throughout classical antiquity the study of history was part and parcel of the vocation of the man of letters concerned with the needs of the commonweal. Like poetry, drama, philosophy and 'good letters' in general, historical writing was a branch of rhetoric, intended to be both instructive and entertaining, and was seen to convey the accumulated experience and wisdom of the past.[48] More's informed venture into the events surrounding the death of the usurper Richard and the accession of the Tudor dynasty can be appreciated in that light. It was a complete departure from the annalistic traditions of earlier English historiography, and the only antecedent local history with humanistic credentials was the *Anglica historia* of Henry VII's court historian, Polydore Vergil, who was a close friend (see below, 175).

No doubt the existence of Vergil's work was an incentive to More, whose *History* became an unforeseen supplement to it. He presented the king as a tyrant in the classic mould, and his enduring portrait, one

version of it powerfully written in his native tongue, was a pinnacle
achievement of the English Renaissance. The classical historians on
whom his work was modelled were chiefly the Romans Tacitus and
Sallust.[49] For Sallust, history writing was a restorative after he was
constrained to withdraw from public life, his personal career thus
sounding a chord in More's interior world. Sallust wrote two biographies of public villains, Catiline and Jugurtha, and the frequent echoes of
the latter in particular reveal More's familiarity with his works, which
he had first read in school. With Tacitus, More shared a sense of the
high dignity and moral purpose of history. The Roman historian's
portrait of Tiberius as a devious tyrant following the peaceful reign of
Augustus provided him also with a template for his account of Richard's
rule, a narrative that far transcends mere imitation, and in which there is
a counterpoint of ironies and circumstance that illuminates brilliantly
the aims of the humanist historian.

With *Utopia*, published first in 1516 in Louvain, we arrive at a
singular work that is one of the enduring creations of the northern
Renaissance, and surely among the most provocative. The full title,
*On the Best State of a Commonwealth and on the New Island of
Utopia*, is alluring. The way in which More's coinage 'Utopia' has
entered the language would nevertheless be a matter of wry amusement
to its author, whose complex purposes are entirely obscured in the
common understanding of 'a utopia' as 'an imaginary place with a
perfect social and political system'.[50] The book has caused More to be
seen variously as the designer quite simply of the 'best state', as a
forerunner of the Reformation, as a nostalgic conservative looking back
to medieval ideals, as a utopian socialist, a prophet of the communist
revolution, and a humanist critic of European society in his day. The
Greek roots of the name – *ou* + *topos*: noplace – indicate that it has no
real existence, while simultaneously evoking the opposite, '*eutopia*' or
good place.[51] Thus there is paradox at the threshold to beguile the
unwary. More's most famous creation may be regarded with more
assurance as the culmination of those long reflections on the nature
and purpose of the commonweal – of the *polis* of his day – that began in
earnest in the Charterhouse, and as it takes the form of an extended
dialogue, its lineage from Lucian cannot be overlooked, any more than
its pervasive irony.

Its relationship to Plato's *Republic* is evident, but not obvious. An
influential commentator states that, 'While Utopia is unquestionably
the greatest contribution to the political theory of the northern Renaissance, it also embodies by far the most radical critique of humanism

written by a humanist.'[52] As such, it evokes Machiavelli's undertaking in *The Prince* (written 1513, published 1532), while its kinship to Erasmus's *Praise of Folly*, completed and dedicated to More under his own roof, must also be considered in reading something written by More while exploring Erasmus's domestic world – the Low Countries – for the first time. Yet Erasmus, who was entrusted with seeing the work through to publication, was remarkably slow to comment, and in his famous portrait of More, written in 1519 to Ulrich von Hutten (*CWE* 7:15–25; on *Utopia*, 23–4), he gives the work perfunctory attention, commenting only that it shows the reasons 'for the shortcomings of a commonwealth', the English commonwealth in particular. A modern reader approaching *Utopia* for the first time may wish to know that Erasmus's reaction signalled some general hesitation within the humanist community, where withholding comment was far from customary.[53] Why such reticence? It was not that *Utopia* was stillborn. The early editions (five in More's lifetime) were buttressed in the humanistic fashion of the day with commendatory epistles and poems from prominent members of the world of letters (see below, 142, 148–9). It was clearly intended primarily for a select humanist readership, as the thematic interplay with Greek itself suggested.

The reader of *Utopia* should be aware that the ideal society presented in Book II by a famously Christian author is in some respects strikingly at odds with Christian ideals, as it is also just as clearly intended to reflect upon the society of the day. More appears as an actor in the book, but in a fictional persona better described by his Latin name, *Morus*. His interlocutor and notional informant about the world of Utopia is 'Hythloday' (*Hythlodaeus*), whose name means 'expert in nonsense'. We are reminded of the *Moriae encomium*, the 'Praise of Folly' – in which Folly's praises are sung by Dame Folly herself. Paradox pervades the work as it does the *Folly*, and haunts its interpreters. A secure starting point is the knowledge that *Utopia* was written for a highly sophisticated humanist audience, that it deals with the issues of politics and statecraft, and that it does so with constant reference to the familiar traditions of the Stoic political philosophy found in works like Cicero's *De legibus*, *De officiis* and *De republica*. For all its irony and paradox, parts of it – notably those concerned with such social problems as enclosures – are written with direct and unmistakable passion. Moreover, modern interpreters have recognized how many of the ideas in *Utopia* – social, religious and political – were those of More himself.[54] With all of its complexity, *Utopia* can be read as a highly personal and deeply considered conclusion to More's long reflection on

the place of the citizen in a European state, a work above all of political
philosophy if not exactly of 'political science'.

Recently, following on from (but in part contesting) the work of
Quentin Skinner,[55] the view that More's critique is directed not at the
prevailing social order as such but rather at the humanist community
itself has stimulated a reassessment that carries implications for his
entire outlook on the world of letters. This approach is rooted in More's
attachment to Greek and the culture of Greece, and postulates a division between the agenda of the classic Latin humanist adoption of
Stoic, Ciceronian principles adapted to the circumstances of the Italian
city-states, and the far more radical outlook of those drawing their
ideals from Plato and the Platonic tradition found in writers like Pico
della Mirandola and another fifteenth-century Florentine philosopher,
Marsilio Ficino. From this perspective the attempt to see the Utopian
constitution as a variant of the civic ideals of what Skinner has called
'neo-Roman' republicanism is mistaken. The critical and defining
issue, among others, is the abolition of private property and the attendant radical egalitarianism in the Utopian commonwealth, contrasted to
the norms of the traditional humanist programme, where social inequal-
ity and private property were unquestioned as fundamentals. This was
the framework still of Machiavelli, despite his inversion of 'virtue', as it
was of Erasmus; for More the object of a perfect society is spiritual; it is
beatitude.[56] Yet another interpretation holds that the dialogue within
Utopia is unfinished, and intentionally so: that the radical reform of
society envisaged in *Utopia* (as in Plato's *Republic*) is only to be attained
by a continuing conversation between proponents of the kind of moral
absolutes proposed by Plato and the pragmatism of the civic humanist.[57]

However *Utopia* is understood, it was the apogee of More's humanistic career. In the troubled decade that followed, its author moved from
the rhetoric of familiar dialogue and exploratory, ambivalent ironies
to far more direct and unambiguously polemical prose. What is abun-
dantly clear is that the conversation about *Utopia* itself shows no
sign of abating, that in every age the work evokes reflection on the
nature of civil society, on its shortcomings and its potencies, and that
Utopia's challenge to its readers has not abated in the five centuries
since its birth.

FURTHER READING

In addition to works cited in the endnotes, Jozef IJsewijn's 'The
coming of humanism to the Low Countries' is an informative, close

study of the transmission of humanism from Italy to the north, and is found in *Itinerarium Italicum*, a Festschrift for Paul Oskar Kristeller edited by Heiko A. Oberman with Thomas A. Brady, Jr (Leiden: Brill, 1975), 193–301. For a foundational study of the historiography, see Wallace K. Ferguson, *The Renaissance in Historical Thought* (Cambridge, Mass.: Houghton Mifflin, 1948). L. D. Reynolds and N. G. Wilson's *Scribes and Scholars: A Guide to the Transmission of Greek and Latin Literature*, 3rd edn (Oxford: Clarendon Press, 1991), deals not only with antiquity and the early Byzantine period, the Carolingian revival and the twelfth-century renaissance, but also with printing, the discoveries of texts, paleography and the origins of textual criticism. Charles Nauert's article 'Humanism as method: roots of conflict with the scholastics' is a fine summary of recent scholarship on that critical issue: *Sixteenth Century Journal* 29 (1998), 427–38.

On England in particular, the Kristeller Festschrift cited above also contains Denys Hay's 'England and the humanities in the fifteenth century', which usefully compares the Italian and the English scene in social and political terms as well as cultural, and includes information on vernacular as well as Latin literature. On the early Oxford Grecians see, in addition to Roberto Weiss's *Humanism in England During the Fifteenth Century* (below, n. 8), the essay by Cecil H. Clough, 'Thomas Linacre, Cornelio Vitelli, and humanistic studies at Oxford', in Francis Maddison *et al.*, eds., *Essays on the Life and Work of Thomas Linacre c.1460–1524* (below, n. 18), 1–23. On Cambridge, see Damian Riehl Leader's *The University to 1546*, Vol. 1 of Christopher Brooke, ed., *A History of the University of Cambridge* (Cambridge University Press, 1988).

On More, the revisionistic biography by Richard Marius, *Thomas More* (1984), includes much interesting and often provocative material. Alistair Fox's highly useful overview of More's writings, *Thomas More: History and Providence* (Oxford: Blackwell, 1982), has at its core a psychological portrait of More similar to Marius's. John Guy's compact biography *Thomas More* (2000) is judicious and authoritative; his latest work on More is a rich double biography, based largely on newly discovered documentary sources, of More and his favourite child: *A Daughter's Love: Thomas & Margaret More* (2008). On the intellectual background specifically to More's personal development as a humanist, see Eric Nelson's *The Greek Tradition in Republican Thought* (below, n. 56). Ann Moss, *Renaissance Truth and the Latin Language Turn* (Oxford University Press, 2003), argues that the change from medieval Latin to the humanists' revived classical

Latin was both a manifestation and a cause of a set of fundamentally important changes, in the early modern period, in Western modes of thought.

Notes

1. M. B. Parkes, 'The provision of books', in J. I. Catto and T. A. R. Evans, eds., *Late Medieval Oxford: The History of the University of Oxford*, Vol. 2 (Oxford: Clarendon Press, 1992), 473–4; A. C. de la Mare, 'Manuscripts given to the University of Oxford by Humfrey, duke of Gloucester', *Bodleian Library Record* 13.1 (1988), 30–51, and 13.2 (1989), 112–21.
2. Charles G. Nauert, Jr, *Humanism and the Culture of Renaissance Europe* (Cambridge University Press, 1995), 2–3.
3. Nicholas Mann, 'The origins of humanism', in Jill Kraye, ed., *The Cambridge Companion to Renaissance Humanism* (Cambridge University Press, 1996), 1–19; Dominic Baker-Smith, *More's 'Utopia'* (London: HarperCollins, 1991; repr. University of Toronto Press for the Renaissance Society of America, 2000), 3–6.
4. Nauert, *Humanism*, 19 ff.
5. On the broadly subversive influence of Greek, see Simon Goldhill, *Who Needs Greek? Contests in the Cultural History of Hellenism* (Cambridge University Press, 2002).
6. Terrence Heath, 'Logical grammar, grammatical logic and humanism in three German universities', *Studies in the Renaissance* 18 (1971), 9–64; *CW* 15:lviii.
7. Nicholas Orme, *English Schools in the Middle Ages* (London: Methuen, 1973), ch. 7.
8. On the works acquired by Duke Humfrey see R[oberto] Weiss, *Humanism in England During the Fifteenth Century*, 2nd edn (Oxford: Blackwell, 1957), 62–7.
9. James McConica, 'The patrimony of Thomas More', in Hugh Lloyd-Jones, Valerie Pearl and Blair Worden, eds., *History and Imagination, Essays in Honour of H. R. Trevor-Roper* (London: Duckworth, 1981), 56–71. On More's early life and education, see above, 8–11.
10. Grocyn's lectures appear to have been a private initiative during his stay in rented rooms in Exeter College from Hilary Term 1491 to Trinity 1493. The first teaching of Greek initiated by the university was in 1512: see James Kelsey McConica, *English Humanists and Reformation Politics* (Oxford: Clarendon Press, 1965), 83. On the Greek teachers Emanuel of Constantinople and John Serbopoulos, see Catto and Evans, *Late Medieval Oxford*, 780–1; Weiss, *Humanism in England*, 142–8, 173–4.
11. Catto and Evans, *Late Medieval Oxford*, 781; Weiss, *Humanism in England*, 173–4; McConica, *English Humanists*, 50; Robert S. Stanier, *Magdalen School, A History of Magdalen College School Oxford*, 2nd edn (Oxford: Basil Blackwell, 1958), 58–61.

12. Anthony à Wood, *Athenae Oxonienses*, Vol. 1, col. 36 in the edn of 1721; Vol. 1, col. 79 in the edn of 1813–20 (repr. Hildesheim: Georg Olms, 1969); W. A. Pantin, *Canterbury College Oxford*, 4 vols. (Oxford: Clarendon Press, 1985), 3:227–45.

13. *CWE* 7:19; note Erasmus's view that 'the law as a profession has little in common with literature truly so called'.

14. Erasmus stated in 1532 that thirty years before, Grocyn, like Valla, had concluded that the author was not St Paul's convert of Acts 17:34. However, for reasons to doubt that Grocyn held this view at the time of his lectures, see J. B. Trapp, 'William Grocyn', *ODNB* 24:57.

15. See further above, 15–16. For Erasmus's admiring account of Grocyn's learning and the accomplishment of the circle of Grocyn, Colet, Linacre and More, see *CWE* 1:235–6. Allowance must be made for rhetorical hyperbole.

16. For Erasmus's account of this visit – which caught him off-guard and without the expected literary tribute – see his Epistle 1341A (*CWE* 9:299–300).

17. According to the biography by his son-in-law William Roper, More lived at the Charterhouse for 'about four years' (Roper 198). The much later biography by his great-grandson Cresacre More says that he dwelt 'near' the Charterhouse (CMore 25. Cf. above, 13–14).

18. Francis Maddison, Margaret Pelling and Charles Webster, eds., *Essays on the Life and Work of Thomas Linacre, c.1460–1524* (Oxford: Clarendon Press, 1977), xix.

19. On wider implications of the event see Baker-Smith, 'Who went to Thomas More's lectures on St Augustine's *De Civitate Dei*?', *Church History and Religious Culture* 87 (2007), 145–60.

20. Leicester Bradner and Charles Arthur Lynch, eds., *The Latin Epigrams of Thomas More* (University of Chicago Press, 1953), xii.

21. When the *Life* was issued among More's *English Works* in 1557, Rastell's son William stated from within the family circle that it had been written shortly before its original publication. On the date, see the editor A. S. G. Edwards in *CW* 1:xxxvii–xxxix, who concludes that the *Life* was indeed written shortly before its publication, i.e. in 1509; see also *CW* 1:xl.

22. See Guy, *Thomas More*, ch. 2, on More's interior debate between a life of 'action' or 'contemplation', especially the relevance of Pico, 37–9.

23. The chronology is difficult, and some of the poems and epigrams were certainly produced towards the end of the decade. On More's progress in Greek and his sources see the introduction to Bradner and Lynch, *Latin Epigrams*, xii, xix–xxi.

24. Clarence H. Miller in *CW* 3, Part 2:55. See his 'The epigrams of More and Erasmus', ibid., 38 ff., Bradner and Lynch, *Latin Epigrams*, xxvii–xxviii, and below, 48.

25. Nauert, *Humanism*, 30–3.

26. Note especially *CW* 3, Part 2:145 ('Death unassisted kills tyrants'), 165 ('That the tyrant while he sleeps is no different from the commoner'), 229–31 ('What is the best form of government').

27. Guy, *Thomas More*, 43–4 and notes. See further below, 89 n. 10.
28. On Lucian see Goldhill, *Who Needs Greek?* ch. 2.
29. The *editio princeps* was published in Florence in 1496. See Erika Rummel, *Erasmus as a Translator of the Classics* (University of Toronto Press, 1985), ch. 3.
30. 'A certain adroitness of appeal to the less reflective side of human nature has preserved his work in spite of contemporary disregard', a judgement on Lucian in the *Oxford Classical Dictionary*, is one that his critics might apply with enthusiasm to Erasmus, although the final phrase would be wildly inappropriate.
31. *Cynicus*, *Menippus* and *Philopseudes*.
32. *CWE* 2:112. For a comparison of the two men as translators see Rummel, *Erasmus as Translator*, 64–9.
33. Roper 198 on his ability to improvise roles in the Christmas plays in Morton's household; the early letter, mentioned above, to the schoolmaster John Holt recording his additions to a play, *Solomon* (the work is otherwise unknown); and Erasmus's report to Ulrich von Hutten that More wrote brief comedies and acted in them, *CWE* 7:19.
34. On Dorp and More's letter to him in defence of *The Praise of Folly* see the introduction by Daniel Kinney in *CW* 15:xix–xxviii.
35. *CWE* 3:111–39 (Ep. 337) is an extended version of the original, which is lost. The existing version was included with Erasmus's *Apologiae* and from 1516 on it appeared with *The Praise of Folly* in the early editions of that work.
36. 'The qualified familiarity of More's style in the *Letter to Dorp* permits formal discussion with no loss of informal candor; in this letter, as in *Utopia*, conversation is once again elevated into a speculative work of art': Kinney, *CW* 15:cxvii.
37. *CWE* 6:317. The court was frequently at nearby Abingdon. See McConica, *English Humanists*, 92–4, and 'The rise of the undergraduate college', in *The Collegiate University*, ed. James McConcia, *The History of the University of Oxford*, Vol. 3 (Oxford: Clarendon Press, 1986), 67.
38. See the account by Kinney, *CW* 15:xxxiii–xxxvii.
39. See the discussion by Kinney, *CW* 15:xli–xliii.
40. *Epistolae aliquot eruditorum*; see Kinney, *CW* 15:xliii. In the same year, More published a fifth open letter, *Epistola ad Germanum Brixium* (*CW* 3, Part 2:594–659, with an introduction by Kinney, 551–92), a ferocious attack on the French humanist Germain de Brie that formed part of More's protracted and generally unappealing controversy with him. On Erasmus's advice, More quickly suppressed the letter, buying up all the unsold copies.
41. See Michael J. Heath's introduction to the work, *CWE* 27:156–60.
42. See Kinney, *CW* 15:585, note on 260/21.
43. Erasmus was an Augustinian canon.
44. What follows is a brief overview of these works in the perspective of humanism. For full treatments, see the essays devoted to each, below.
45. On the complex history of the text see George M. Logan, *The Meaning of More's 'Utopia'* (Princeton University Press, 1983), 3–18.

46. On the dating, see *R3* xxi–xxiii. On the complex textual history, see Richard S. Sylvester's introduction in *CW* 2:xvii–lix and (a necessary supplement to Sylvester) Daniel Kinney in *CW* 15:cxxxiii–cliii.
47. First as a continuation of Hardyng's *Chronicle*; see *R3* xliii–xliv, where the publication history is described.
48. For more on classical historiography, see below, 175–8.
49. See *CW* 2:lxxxvi–xcviii; *R3* xxxv–xl; and below, 179–82.
50. *The Concise Oxford Dictionary.*
51. More's earliest references to the book (*SL* 73, 76, 80) give it a *Latin* name: *Nusquama* (Nowhere).
52. Quentin Skinner, *The Foundations of Modern Political Thought*, 2 vols. (Cambridge University Press, 1978), 1:256. On the relevance of Plato see Baker-Smith, *More's 'Utopia'*, ch. 3 and *passim*.
53. Cf. the observation of Guy: 'The main responsibility for the critical vacuum which accompanied the first publication of *Utopia* lies at the door of Erasmus. He was uncharacteristically slow to publish his own commendation' (*Thomas More*, 91).
54. See Logan, *Meaning*, 10–11.
55. *Foundations* 1:255–62; 'Sir Thomas More's *Utopia* and the language of Renaissance humanism', in Anthony Pagden, ed., *The Languages of Political Theory in Early-Modern Europe* (Cambridge University Press, 1988), 123–57. Cf. Logan, *Meaning*, 268–70.
56. For a powerful exposition of this view, see 'Greek nonsense in More's *Utopia*', ch. 1 of Eric Nelson's *The Greek Tradition in Republican Thought* (Cambridge University Press, 2004).
57. Brendan Bradshaw, 'More on Utopia', *Historical Journal* 24 (1981), 1–27; and cf. below, 162–3.

3 More's rhetoric

ELIZABETH McCUTCHEON

Thomas More, 'the man for all seasons', could also be characterized as 'rhetorical man'. As Peter Ackroyd observes, rhetoric was 'the basis of all his work. His wit, his ingenuity as a writer, his skill as an actor, and his public roles, were all part of the same dispensation'.[1] A single essay cannot cover all these aspects of the man or his writing. More wrote voluminously, and even the Yale edition of his *Complete Works* – in fifteen volumes, two languages and multiple kinds – needs to be supplemented with editions of his personal letters and with his professional writings as lawyer, judge, king's secretary, orator, diplomat and lord chancellor, in so far as they are extant.[2] Furthermore, for More and his fellow humanists rhetoric was essential and indispensable to writing, regardless of type. Obviously formative in what we call literature (which they thought of more broadly as *bonae litterae* – 'good writing'), it was equally important in polemics; and devotional writing, too, had its rhetoric, even if it was little interested in aesthetics.[3]

More excelled in each of the rhetorical kinds he used. Among readers in general, *Utopia* and his *History of King Richard the Third* have proven pre-eminent; but many have found solace and strength in his *Dialogue of Comfort against Tribulation*, his *De Tristitia Christi* and his prayers; and his polemical works, especially the *Dialogue Concerning Heresies*, have strong defenders. Many of More's 'literary' works belong to his humanist period, which lasted through the second decade of the sixteenth century or a few years later. These include almost all his English poems, most of his Latin epigrams, *Utopia*, several long Latin letter-essays and the Latin and English versions of the *History*. Additionally there are his personal or familiar letters, which span his entire life, although, unfortunately, many are no longer extant.[4] These are the writings that this essay will mostly be concerned with, although it will not ignore his life, his polemics and his devotional writings. Even so, what follows will be selective.

RHETORIC, HUMANISM AND MORE

More grew up at a distinctive and in some respects particularly propitious moment for a writer and an intellectual, when rhetoric had once again risen to primacy in western European culture.[5] Defined as the art of verbal persuasion, rhetoric flourished in classical Greece and Rome.[6] There it evolved from oral discourse – legal and political speech-making – and, in consequence, always centred in three major oratorical genres: judicial, deliberative, and demonstrative or epideictic. The first refers to rhetoric as practised in the law courts, and is concerned with past actions; deliberative rhetoric looks ahead, debating a choice to be made (especially on a matter of political policy); and demonstrative is the rhetoric of praise or blame. The many textbooks of rhetoric – among which those by Aristotle, Cicero and Quintilian were pre-eminent – had as their fundamental organizing principle the five 'faculties' or skills that a successful orator must master. These are invention (the finding out of pertinent material, for which the numerous 'topics' (from Greek *topoi* – literally, 'places'), lists of tried-and-true headings for thinking about particular kinds of subjects, are central); arrangement (the optimal disposition of the materials collected in the process of invention); style (encompassing such matters as the different levels of language appropriate to different subjects and circumstances, and ornament – especially the many rhetorical 'figures'); and, finally, memory and delivery: these last two faculties apply, of course, only to *oral* discourse, whereas the other faculties apply to written works as well as speeches. The manuals also lay down rules for secondary genres, including the philosophical dialogue, history and the letter. Although Socrates and Plato, among other members of the rival educational tradition of philosophy, argued that rhetoric could (and often did) make the worse the better case, that it flattered and deceived its audience, it had important legal and political functions in the democratic city-states of Greece and in the Roman republic. But as the institutions and culture of western Europe changed over the following centuries, rhetoric shrank in relation to grammar and logic, the other two parts of the fundamental *trivium* of medieval liberal education. It also became fragmented and specialized, emphasizing the arts of letter-writing, preaching and poetry, and often being reduced to little more than the decorative application of the 'figures'.[7]

Beginning in the fourteenth century, however, rhetoric in its classical form enjoyed a renaissance in Europe, and came to shape much of its discourse, educational practices and culture for several centuries. This was due in large part to the humanist movement, which recovered aspects of classical learning that had long been lost or diverted to non-classical purposes (see above, 22–5).[8] More's formal education, first at St Anthony's School and the school provided for the pages at Cardinal Morton's palace, and later at Oxford and the Inns of Court, was substantially shaped by the humanist revival of classical rhetoric, which gradually transformed the curriculum and instruction in the language arts, first in the grammar schools and subsequently the universities; and by the early 1500s, while still a young man whose career lay ahead of him, he already knew well the major figures of early Tudor humanism, including John Colet, William Grocyn and Thomas Linacre, and had made the acquaintance of the foremost humanist of the era, Erasmus.[9]

The young More was simultaneously student and teacher, continuing his study of Greek and promoting humanist learning while pursuing his legal studies. His earliest verses, translations and other compositions show both how quickly and how well he mastered humanist ideas about language, rhetoric and classical letters, and how actively he promoted them. Before 1500 he had already composed two Latin poems (*CW* 3, Part 2:65, 294–9) in praise of a Latin grammar that John Holt (above, 9, 26) wrote for English schoolboys who were beginning their studies. The 'Progymnasmata', or 'Preparatory Exercises', is a later, more ambitious effort, consisting of eighteen epigrams, all based on Greek texts, which More and another fellow humanist, William Lily – the headmaster of St Paul's, the cathedral school refounded on humanist principles by John Colet – translated into Latin in friendly rivalry. This little collection, which demonstrates various ways to develop an idea, proved popular at a time when *copia* (rhetorical fluency and fullness) was highly prized. Revilo P. Oliver, one of the editors of More's epigrams, calls it 'a stroke of pedagogical genius', pointing out that the two men 'may be credited with the invention of the variorum translation of selected Greek epigrams that was to have a brilliant history in the schools and beyond' (*CW* 3, Part 2:13).

In fact, More was always something of a humanist teacher: witness the education he designed for his own children and others in what came to be called his 'school'. Challenging the then common belief that learning would corrupt a woman, More promoted a liberal education for the girls as well as the boys in his household, so that his daughters, in particular Margaret More Roper, became exemplars of learning and virtue and proof of women's intellectual and ethical potential.[10] Employing some of the best young scholars in England as tutors, More fashioned and oversaw a well-rounded curriculum that emphasized rhetoric, was based on a mastery of Latin and Greek, stressed *bonae litterae* and embraced the liberal and humane arts – grammar, rhetoric, poetry, logic, mathematics, philosophy and astronomy, as well as theology and medicine.[11]

Two other of More's early works – his translations of Lucian and of a life of Pico della Mirandola (above, 29–30, 28) – provide further evidence of his mastery of rhetoric and commitment to humanist literary and intellectual developments. Lucian and Pico can seem worlds apart. Lucian was thought of as a cynic, atheist and mocker of sacred things, in sharp contrast to Pico, whose devotion More emphasized, so that his translation of Pico's biography has been treated as a secular version of a saint's life (*CW* 1:liii–lv). But More's defence of his translations from Lucian says much about his view of literature and rhetoric in general. He argued that Lucian 'fulfilled the Horatian maxim and combined delight with instruction', adding that 'he everywhere reprehends and censures, with very honest and at the same time very entertaining wit, our human frailties' (*CW* 3, Part 1:3). This appreciation of wit and a double emphasis on entertainment and education are equally characteristic of More's later works, including *Utopia*, and reflect his love of irony, satire, drama and a seriocomic wit that amuses, tests and exercises its readers.

Another tendency is evident in these early works. More is already going beyond imitation or a literal translation; as he translates, he improvises, adds writing of his own and combines rhetorical forms, leading his editor Anthony S. G. Edwards to speak of the *Life of Pico* as an anthology (*CW* 1:xxxvii, xliii, lv) and foreshadowing later works such as *The History of King Richard the Third* and *Utopia*, which contain multiple forms and resist easy classification as to genre. It is also striking that as early as about 1510 (the approximate date of publication of the *Life*) More had already written and published in both Latin and English, and was writing both prose and poetry.[12] In addition, he had explored virtually all the kinds of writing he later employed, with the seeming exception of polemics. Even here, though, his early explorations in declamations – the set speeches that were a standard rhetorical exercise, involving arguments for or against a particular position – gave him the rhetorical tools he later used in his defences of humanism and the Catholic Church.[13]

LANGUAGES AND AUDIENCES

The popularity of More's *Utopia*, so often translated and retranslated, the publication of the Yale edition of his *Complete Works*, and the multiple translations of some of his devotional writings and personal letters can obscure just how much More originally wrote in Latin. It is essential to note the language he chose, however, because it reflected his awareness of audience and shaped his whole rhetorical process, manifested in his adherence to the key rhetorical precept of decorum, which mandates that all features of a piece of writing be appropriate to the subject, speaker, audience and occasion. More wrote in Latin for a well-educated elite, persons (mostly male) who shared his educational and cultural background; in many cases, too, this meant an international readership and, frequently, a coterie of fellow humanists or, alternatively, scholarly opponents. Think, then, of correspondents such as Erasmus, John Colet, Peter Giles and Antonio Bonvisi, an Italian merchant and good friend; of other well-placed lawyers, doctors, clerics and administrators, including William Warham and Guillaume Budé; or, in his middle and later years, of opponents such as Martin Luther and Johann Bugenhagen. By contrast, he wrote in the vernacular for fellow English men and women, anxious to reach a broader and more popular audience of both readers and auditors, since reading aloud in a group was a popular activity[14] – as with his many defences of the Catholic Church, for which he was authorized by Bishop Cuthbert Tunstall in 1528. He also wrote many of his most personal and intimate communications in English – to his daughter Margaret More Roper; other members of his family; and English colleagues. There was some overlap, but, in general, Latin was the language he preferred for elite intellectual discourse, while English, paradoxically, could be both more intimate and more common. So it is important to realize, for example, that More wrote *Utopia* in Latin and subsequently opposed its translation. Once published, however, he could not control its dissemination, to his discomfort in later years, when Tyndale and other Protestant reformers attacked both it and him.[15]

The two languages that More wrote in share a common Indo-European origin but otherwise not only are different but were in different stages of development. Latin is a heavily inflected language and much less dependent on word order; the conclusion of the main clause of a sentence – and thus the meaning of the sentence as a whole – was often suspended until its very end. English, however, characteristically depends on succession and relies heavily on subject, verb, object or subject-predicate constructions. Latin also tends to be polysyllabic, whereas many English words, especially those from Anglo-Saxon, are short. On the other hand, Latin is a more economical language; an English translation will almost inevitably be longer. And the rhythms are different as well; classical Latin prose had complicated rules for chimed endings, and its verse was quantitative (based on patterns of long and short syllables), not accentual. Humanist Latin can be particularly complex; the humanists looked down on medieval Latin prose and rhymed verse, and called for a return to the highly polished and elaborate Latin compositions of the classical period. A major issue, for those aspiring to write 'good' Latin, was just how closely to imitate classical writers; above all, the great exemplar of Roman rhetoric, Cicero. In his dialogue *Ciceronianus*, Erasmus argued against those who insisted upon a scrupulous, even slavish, imitation, preferring a more flexible Latin style that would be truer to the spirit of the classics, to contemporary concerns, and to the nature of the individual writer. By contrast, Tudor English was an evolving vernacular, much influenced by its oral forms.[16] It was also in flux. A number of words More used are now obsolete. On the other hand, the *Oxford English Dictionary* credits him with the first use of many words that have since become familiar. Unlike those who thought that Tudor English was 'crude' or 'unpolished' in comparison with a classical tongue, More defended it. In his *Dialogue Concerning Heresies* he specifically rejected the claim that the Bible could not be translated into English: 'For as for that oure tonge is called barbarouse / is but a fantasye. For so is as euery lerned man knoweth / euery straunge langage to other. And yf they wolde call it barayne of wordys / there is no doute but it is plentuouse ynoughe to expresse oure myndys in any thynge whereof one man hathe vsed to speke with another' (*CW* 6:337).[17] His writing in the vernacular can be diffuse, even redundant, but later English writers such as Ben Jonson looked back to More as a founding father of eloquence in England, and in the twentieth century R. W. Chambers insisted that 'More was the first Englishman to evolve an effective prose, sufficient for all the purposes of his time: eloquent, dramatic, varied'.[18]

Thanks to his interest in language generally, and to his translations, both from Greek to Latin and from Latin to English, More acquired a heightened consciousness of the uniqueness of each language – its technical aspects, so to speak, its range of references and allusions, and its cultural implications. No one English word conveys quite the same meaning as its Latin equivalent or vice versa – so much so that More, who liked doublets anyway, often used doublets or even triplets to suggest the range of meaning when translating a Latin original (see further below, 173). Moreover, as he moved from one language to another, he moved from one world to another, importing (and reshaping) ideas and values and expanding his own cultural mentalité and that of his various readerships. He also developed a more consciously historical point of view, becoming aware of how language and thought evolved over the centuries, and of the potential of Tudor English. At the same time, More, who respected the languages of the Church Fathers and saw Latin (rather than English) as authoritative with respect to Church doctrine, developed a vernacular that took on some of the attributes of Latinity, notably elements of suspension, in his English defences of the Roman Catholic Church.[19]

For More, the language he chose was a fundamental rhetorical tool, and his early 'Pageant Verses' show just how sensitive to language he was. He wrote these nine stanzas, eight in English and one in Latin, to accompany a cycle of pictures on painted cloth in his father's house in London. In the first seven stanzas, one figure after another, from Child-hood, to Manhood, Venus and Cupid, Age, Death, Fame, and Time, ironically declares his, her, or their 'triumph', only to be defeated by the one that follows, as More weaves together two motifs, one derived from the traditional notion of the ages of man, the other from Petrarch's *Triomphi*. Stanza 8 is transitional: Eternity speaks – still in English – as the poem begins its shift from a circular movement from womb to tomb to an otherworldly perspective. But More makes a complete break in stanza 9. Now an authority figure, the Poet, speaks in Latin, the language associated with prayer, the Church, and the salvation of the soul, reminding viewers that 'Gaudia laus & honor, celeri pede omnia cedunt, / Qui manet excepto semper amore dei' (*CW* 1:6, lines 115–16): 'Pleasures, praise, homage, all things quickly disappear – except the love of God, which endures forever.'[20]

The Latin and English versions of his history of Richard III show how extensively the mature More interrelated audience, language and rhetoric. Although left unfinished, they are brilliant instances of humanist 'rhetorical historiography' (see below, 175–8) and demonstra-tive rhetoric that have much in common. Both respond to the same classical historical models and highlight many of the same incidents. The historical actors are the same, and in each case there is a shrewd, often ironic, narrative voice. As examples of *vituperatio* (a rhetoric of blame), they incorporate many of the same rhetorical forms, including deliberative oration, panegyric, sermon and debate;[21] and here, as so often, More is a master of dialogue. They draw on similar rhetorical strategies, including *enargia* (vivid description), innuendo and equivo-cal explanations, to show Richard III's evil nature and behaviour.[22] Tonally, the two versions are also similar, being ironic, tragi-comic and dramatic – so much so that some critics have treated the English history, in particular, as a drama (see below, 185); and, indeed, Shakespeare's *Richard III* owes much to More's.

But neither version is a translation of the other, and striking differences in their rhetoric and decorum reflect major differences in audience and language: in the one case, an international and sophisticated readership, for whom humanist Latin is the language of choice; in the other, a home-grown readership. For his international audience, More needs to explain English customs, institutions and places, and the Latin version includes information of this kind not found in the English (below, 170–1). The Latin version is also full of verbal echoes of numerous classical works, so that its readers experience a densely layered text, albeit one that seems somewhat removed from the English scene. These echoes and allusions inevitably are much less apparent in the English version.[23] On the other hand, the English version is more colourful and vigorous than the Latin, its metaphors bolder. Consider the famous comparison between the so-called election of Richard as king and the action of a stage play. The Latin is abstract: 'Iam qui imperatorem ludat in tragaedia / populusne ignorat forsitan esse cerdonem?' (*CW* 15:482; in the facing editorial translation, 'And when someone plays an emperor in a tragedy, are the people unaware he might be a mere craftsman?'). By contrast, the English reads: 'And in a stage play all the people know right well that he that playeth the sowdaine is percase a sowter' (*R3* 94). More's English prose is more colloquial, direct and emphatic; his nouns are crisper, more vivid and more ominous, since the narrator mentions the *sultan*, not just *any* emperor, at a time when the Ottoman empire gravely threatened Europe. Similarly, alliteration and assonance bind sultan and shoemaker together with a play of 'p' and 's' sounds, so that sound reinforces sense. As well, each version has its own rhetorical structure or design. Although the Latin version is presumably unfinished (as the English version unambiguously is), its action is so concentrated that its formal design seems virtually complete: the *Historia Richardi Tertii* covers less than three months (not counting flashbacks and prequels), from the death of Edward IV on 9 April 1483 to the accession of Richard III on 26 June, with a brief appended account of his coronation on 6 July. The English *History* is looser and somewhat closer in form to the unhurried, digressive English chronicle histories, and continues through the summer and early autumn of 1483, breaking off in the midst of an exchange between the duke of Buckingham and Bishop (later Cardinal) Morton that anticipates plots and rebellions to come.

EPIDEICTIC, DELIBERATIVE AND UTOPIAN RHETORIC

As *vituperatio*, More's *History/Historia* is a brilliant example of the branch of epideictic or demonstrative rhetoric that indicts and blames. Obliquely insisting that kings should serve the people, it offers no example of a good king, instead dramatically representing examples of more or less bad ones who usurp the throne and misuse rhetoric for perverse ends. This made More's history intrinsically dangerous, indeed subversive; using rhetoric to boldly and ironically deconstruct the mystery of kingship and other authority, clerical as well as secular, he uncovered the modus operandi of power and showed political theatre for the tragi-comic game or performance it is, one which could end on the scaffold.

More never completed his history, which was, accordingly, not published in his lifetime. He was, however, eager to publish *Utopia* (1516), a companion piece to the history which he probably worked on at about the same time (below, 171–2). But where the history indicts kingship and paints a wholly negative and very dark picture of fifteenth-century England, *Utopia* couches its own caustic account of English social conditions and European politics in an open-ended, ironic and sometimes comic investigation of 'the best state of the commonwealth' that adroitly links historical fact with speculative fiction.[24] It is also more rhetorically and formally complex, giving its name to a new genre.[25]

Utopia as a whole is a fictionalized example of deliberative rhetoric, at once literary, philosophical, political and social, that subsumes the deliberative rhetoric of Book I[26] and the epideictic of Book II (*CU* xxvi–xxix), where 'Morus', a fictionalized version of the author, reports the altogether imaginary Raphael Hythloday's encomiastic account of Utopia. In effect, we can construe the first part of the original title, *De Optimo Reipublicae Statu*, as a question: what *is* the best state of the commonwealth? Or, more radically still, *is* there a best state of the commonwealth, or at least a better (or less bad) one than those in western Europe? While Book II offers possible answers, each book and the work as a whole invite more questions. The deliberative rhetoric in Book I, which spells out the problem, is negative or dystopian – Europe, and, more particularly, England, is a place where money is the measure of value and injustice is rampant. By contrast, the epideictic rhetoric of praise in Book II is focused on Utopia, which Hythloday represents as a eutopia (etymologically, 'happy' or 'fortunate place'), where all things are held in common and the citizens, who are well housed, well fed and well educated, have work that is tempered with leisure, enjoy good medical care and follow a natural religion that includes belief in an afterlife with rewards for good deeds and punishments for vices (*CU* 161). His account is extraordinarily vivid: here, as in the *History*, More exhibits his remarkable skill in rhetorical *enargia*, the creation of powerful visual imagery.[27] Occasionally Raphael claims (ironically) that he is only *reporting* what he saw, not praising it. But Utopia's putative European discoverer also insists that there, and only there, can justice be found. Hythloday's auditors have grave reservations, however (*CU* 105, 247–9), so that in this and other ways both books are finally two parts of a larger rhetorical and fictional structure that More invented and that we can call a meta-utopia.

This larger structure is a dialogue, one that draws on all three leading classical species of this genre – the Platonic, the Ciceronian and the Lucianic[28] – and also on another ancient genre, the traveller's tale (then as now notoriously unreliable). Moreover, the dialogue not only incorporates entire deliberative and demonstrative orations but in itself can be regarded as including most of the components that rhetorical theory prescribed for an oration. The result of this elaborate conglomerative process is an inherently unstable, intentionally provocative and complexly ironic text.

The traditional oratorical form – developed especially for the judicial oration but applied with modifications to the theory and practice of deliberative and demonstrative – consists of an exordium (introduction), narration (a statement of the facts), proposition (statement of issue or thesis), division (outline of the argument that is to follow), proof, refutation (of opposing arguments) and peroration (conclusion); allowance is also made for an optional digression.[29] The opening of Book I of *Utopia*, which introduces the circumstances – the setting and speakers – functions as an exordium, portraying an urbane humanist discourse among men of good will in a pleasant garden. In particular, the biographical credentials of Hythloday are given, thus beginning the fundamentally important rhetorical task of establishing *ethos*, the speaker's attractiveness and his authority for speaking on the topic at hand; we also learn a good deal about Morus – the other major interlocutor – in these pages.[30] In a few quick strokes More also indicates what will become the subject matter of Book II, 'the customs and institutions of the Utopians' (*CU* 49), here contrasted with the monsters and other strange beings that strew the usual traveller's tale. At this point, though, More postponed Hythloday's monologue in Book II (which he had already written) and inserted the 'Dialogue of Counsel' which makes up so much of Book I (see below, 148). Rhetorically, this is a digression – and is in fact introduced as one: 'Now I intend to relate only what . . . [Hythloday] told us about the customs and institutions of the Utopians, but first recounting the conversation that drew him into speaking of that commonwealth' (*CU* 49–51). But in a larger perspective it is an integral part of the exploration *de optimo reipublicae statu*, for it explores important ancillary questions: can change for the better be brought about, and if so, by whom and how, given the political structures in place and the nature of human beings? And what are the obligations of the informed and conscientious humanist? It also shows England and western Europe at a critical moment of disequilibrium, where crime is rampant, basic human necessities are unequally distributed, and the poor and helpless are exploited by a powerful and wealthy elite.

Only after this dialogue do we have Raphael's picture of Utopia, which constitutes the 'proof' or confirmation of his proposition or thesis: that

> wherever you have private property, and money is the measure of all things, it is hardly ever possible for a commonwealth to be just or prosperous – unless you think justice can exist where all the best things are held by the worst citizens, or suppose happiness can be found where the good things of life are divided among very few, where even those few are always uneasy, and where the rest are utterly wretched.
>
> (*CU* 101)

Raphael returns to this point in his peroration (*CU* 241–7), where, in an emotionally charged speech that ends by indicting that master vice, pride, which has infected most of humankind, he insists that Utopia is the only commonwealth worthy of the name. This is in its rightful place, at the end of his speech. But More displaces, reassigns and otherwise rethinks the refutation, which, in the standard oratorical structure, follows the confirmation. Instead, he places major arguments against the proposition *before* the confirmation, which is offered explicitly as a refutation of arguments that Morus and Giles, rather than Hythloday, raise at the end of Book I (*CU* 105). So the actual refutation is woven into the confirmation. But interestingly (and enigmatically), Morus raises some of the same objections, as well as *others*, at the very end of Book II (*CU* 247–9), although these are directed at the reader, and Hythloday knows nothing about them. To Hythloday, he offers only 'praise for ... [the Utopians'] way of life and his account of it' – but this just after confiding to the reader that he finds key Utopian laws and customs 'absurd': these include their ways of waging war, their religious practices, and their 'communal living and their moneyless economy', which 'alone utterly subverts all the nobility, magnificence, splendour and majesty which (in the popular view) are the true ornaments and glory of any commonwealth'. More's intentions in having Morus make this claim have been much disputed.[31] But whether we interpret it as sincere, as ironic, or both, it is not the final word either. Instead, Morus reopens the issue, hoping for further discussion with Hythloday and remarking that 'I freely confess that in the Utopian commonwealth there are very many features that in our own societies I would wish rather than expect to see.'

Finally, the rhetoric of *Utopia* is further complicated – and enriched – by the materials that More and others (with his approval) added as supplements to its two books. The last thing that More wrote before entrusting his manuscript to Erasmus – and encouraging him to solicit commendatory letters to be published with it (*SL* 73, 76, 80–1) – was his own prefatory letter to Peter Giles. Although not always treated as an integral part of *Utopia* (some editions relegate it to the back of the book or simply omit it), the letter is essential to the work, framing it and establishing the spirit in which readers are invited to approach a jocoserious and ambiguous text that depends on an aesthetic of honest deception.[32] The four earliest editions also include a collection of other materials, which vary from one edition to another but include a map of Utopia, poems praising it, marginalia and the commendatory letters that Erasmus collected; for the second, 1517 edition, More himself wrote a second letter to Giles (*CU* 266–9), which offers – with characteristic indirection and irony – some guides to reading the book. These materials, collectively called the parerga, offer a variety of views of *Utopia* and constitute another indication that the work is a metautopia, to be approached as an open-ended and polysemous dialogue that explores what are in fact many-faceted and still unresolved political and philosophical questions: what *is* the best state of a commonwealth, and *why*? is the realization of the best state – or even modest improvement of existing ones – possible, and if so, how? Thus *Utopia*, ever mindful of its audience and exploring the probable or contingent, exemplifies what rhetoric is at its best – not, as Jennifer Richards has said, merely 'an art of plausible speaking', but 'a "critical" method, which prompts us always to think again'.[33]

DIALOGUES AND LETTERS

More's fondness for the dialogue is evident not only in *Utopia* but in three English examples of the form, the *Dialogue Concerning Heresies* (1529), the dialogue that is embedded in the long letter that More and/or Margaret Roper wrote to Alice Alington (1534) answering one from her, and the *Dialogue of Comfort against Tribulation* (1534).[34] Each has its own setting and shape; their framing narratives are, for example, successively more complicated. But they share an overriding concern with the salvation of the soul, and they all depend, for conviction, on faith as well as reason. Where *Utopia* is open-ended, these dialogues mime a movement towards enlightenment and understanding under the guidance of a wise and paternalistic authority figure, and critics have called the first two, which are defences or apologies – in the first, of Catholic Christendom, in the second, of More's refusal to sign an oath in support of the Act of Succession – Platonic dialogues.[35]

Accordingly, the interlocutors are not (in contrast to the situation in *Utopia*) evenly matched. In the *Dialogue Concerning Heresies*, More, here 'Mayster chauncellour' – an obvious authority figure – is urged to meet a young scholar who is 'of nature nothynge tonge tayed' (*CW* 6:25) and has some sympathy with Lutheran ideas. Meeting in More's study, they debate the major issues challenging the English Church in a peaceful, sometimes humorous, and friendly way that models a recursive educative process. As the older man defends traditional Christian doctrines and practices, the younger one gradually comes to understand and accept them, rejecting the ideas of Luther, Tyndale and other reformers. In the letter to Alice Alington, More, now imprisoned in the Tower of London, speaks on his own behalf and defends his refusal to sign the oath, in a dramatic dialogue between himself and his favourite daughter, who is reluctant to accept her beloved father's refusal and the execution that will almost certainly follow. Cast, half-teasingly, as Mother Eve, Margaret Roper urges her father to sign the oath, as so many others have done. But More rejects the idea that his refusal is a mere scruple or that he should follow the example of those who have signed, and insists that he must instead follow his conscience, which he has well informed, on peril of his soul.[36]

The third dialogue, also written in 1534, takes place in another enclosed but otherwise unspecified space, between Antony, an old man who feels his age and knows that death is imminent, and Vincent, his young nephew, who seeks consolation against the many terrors at hand, embodied in a threatened invasion by the Turks that shadows More's situation vis-à-vis Henry VIII. Vincent is a solicitous and attentive listener who also asks questions and voices fears that take three books for Antony to overcome or, more precisely, transcend. The conversations move easily – Louis Martz characterizes More's strategy here (as in the dialogue letter) as an 'art of improvisation' (*CW* 12:lvii). But there is an underlying structure; despite Antony's garrulity and the many comic stories and digressions, the dialogue slowly but surely moves to the most painful tribulation of all: persecution for the faith. Finally, faith transforms suffering into an act of love, and the dialogue ends with a meditation on the last things and the passion and death of Christ.

Throughout his life More was engaged with another rhetorical form with an ancient tradition, the letter.[37] Like other humanists, More favoured both its open or public form, where it lent itself to discussion and debate on intellectual and polemical issues, approximating an essay, and its more personal form as the familiar epistle. A personal and private (or quasi-private) form, associated with the study, the letter was thought of as maintaining a conversation carried on in absence between good friends and as a gift carrying the good wishes of the sender. Rhetorical theory stipulated that it be written in a 'plain' – informal, unadorned – style, and it was to be flexible and improvisatory, although hardly unmediated: like all other genres, the letter had its own decorum, necessitating a consideration of circumstances, the addressee or addressees, the writer's stance and the subject matter. More's letters lent themselves to any number of topics; they could facilitate an exchange of ideas, share current news and gossip, promote a sense of community, serve as a form of self-promotion, advance particular interests among a coterie, introduce or dedicate a piece of writing, and create or advance friendship between persons separated in space. And letters often had several audiences in addition to the original correspondent, since they frequently circulated in manuscript and sometimes were printed.

Four of More's open or public letters, all written in Latin, constitute a 'defense of humanism', where More worked out 'a truly progressive prescription for the continual renewal and refinement of the "living gospel of faith"' (*CW* 15:lxxvii). These are treated elsewhere in this volume (above, 31–6). More's personal and quasi-personal letters, some in English, some in Latin, are quite diverse, and they are indispensable for an understanding of his life, friendships, ideas, values and beliefs. His letters to Erasmus and to his eldest daughter are among his best known, and are typically wide-ranging. Thanks to the letter to Erasmus which begins 'I am sending you my "*Nowhere*", which is nowhere well written' (*SL* 73), we know that More finished the book that was later renamed *Utopia* by or before 3 September 1516; a much later letter (*c.* June 1533), which More urges his friend to print, explains his resignation from the chancellorship and includes a transcript of the long epitaph – a review of his public career – that he had written for himself and already had incised on his tombstone (see below, 69). More's letters to Margaret – his closest confidante – are among his most significant. He carried on an extensive correspondence with her while imprisoned in the Tower of London in 1534–5, and she was able to preserve some of his letters, which were subsequently published.[38] They were certainly personal; at the same time, under cover of writing to his daughter More was able to establish an invaluable written record of his three final interrogations. Written shortly after each interview, while the events were fresh in More's mind, these letters are dramatic, detailed, and carry evidentiary weight. His letter about the interrogation on 3 June 1535 (*SL* 249–53) even raises questions about the official record, which claims to cite More verbatim but misrepresents an all-important conditional 'if' as More reported it.[39] By contrast, some of More's other letters to Margaret are intensely private, including several written in 1534 (*SL* 234–42) and his last letter, of 5 July 1535, bidding her and the rest of his family farewell (*SL* 257–8).

ORNAMENT AND ESSENCE

Up to this point I have not said much about More's practice of rhetorical ornamentation, especially his use of the many 'figures' that the rhetorical manuals expatiated on at length. In mediocre writers, ornament *was* merely ornamental: self-conscious virtuoso decoration of their texts. But with a good and serious writer, ornamentation is subject (like everything else) to the governance of decorum, and the figures become integral parts of the work, not just gilding its surface but enriching its meaning and sometimes even manifesting its themes and deep structure. This is profoundly true of More, and it will be appropriate to end this essay with observations on his use of two key figures.

Rhetorical theory associates certain figures with particular topoi of invention.[40] As a consummate rhetorician, More selected topoi and figures appropriate to each individual piece of writing, so that one always needs to examine the context in order to understand what he is doing in this regard. But, at the risk of over-generalizing, many of More's favourite topoi are based on opposition or negation, or otherwise involve a play of perspectives; and, accordingly, his favourite figures are those that are especially associated with such topoi: tropes such as antithesis, paradox, hyperbole, metaphor, irony and understatement, which exercise the mind and make for lively, energetic and provocative texts that challenge readers and encourage thought.

I want to comment specifically on More's use, in *Utopia*, of one particular figure of understatement, litotes, in which something is affirmed by stating the negative of its opposite. Seemingly a small matter, litotes recurs with great frequency in More's book and mirrors the ambiguity and muscular tension of the work as a whole.[41] Litotes was a common figure in the Renaissance; often used for understatement, politeness or modesty, it was also thought of as a form of praise or dispraise, hence useful in demonstrative rhetoric. But More's litotes go far beyond that, as a form of negation that requires negotiation on the part of the reader, who is presented with an assertion that often remains ambiguous and calls attention to itself while seemingly not doing so. 'I don't doubt' (*non dubito*), for example, is not the same as 'to be sure', or 'certainly', because it implies that the speaker has weighed the possibilities and reached a decision – hence its persuasiveness. At the same time, though, a certain ambiguity often remains; if something is 'not the worst' (*non pessime*), does that mean it is 'the best', 'not bad', or ... ? Likewise, 'not a few' (*haud pauci*) may mean 'some', 'many', or even 'almost all'. Hence litotes contributes quietly, but effectively, to the open-mindedness and pervasive irony of *Utopia*. A litotic note is even struck on the title page, where More's work is described as 'A Truly Golden Handbook, No Less Beneficial than Entertaining' (*CU* 3). Thus the value of the little book (as it originally appeared) is emphasized by a weighing process of qualities that might otherwise seem antithetical.

Three of More's favourite metaphors also involve a play of perspectives. One explores variations on the subject of the world or life as a stage; another, the world or life as a prison; the third, the idea that life is a pilgrimage.[42] The first metaphor appears prominently in both *Utopia* and *The History of King Richard the Third*. Morus rejects the 'school philosophy which supposes every topic suitable for every occasion' (*CU* 95), recommending 'another philosophy, better suited for the role of a citizen, that takes its cue, adapts itself to the drama in hand and acts its part neatly and appropriately' (*CU* 97). Better to be silent, he adds, than to appear in philosophical garb and recite Seneca's speech to Nero in the midst of a comedy of Plautus. The immediate point is rhetorical: follow decorum of speech and behaviour and adapt to the play at hand. But for Hythloday (here sounding Platonic) this amounts to lying: and his objection, with its sense that this world is less than real, lingers. When More employs the same metaphor in the *History*, it is less tragi-comic than tragic: the people who have watched the staged election of Richard know that 'these matters be kings' games, as it were stage plays, and for the more part played upon scaffolds ... And they that wise be, will meddle no farther' (*R3* 95). The metaphor is grimmer still in the unfinished treatise on the Four Last Things (*c.* 1522). Asking if we would not laugh at a 'lorel' (rogue) who is vain about wearing 'a gay golden gown' when he 'playth the lord in a stage playe', but who, once it ends, 'shal go walke a knaue in his old cote' (*CW* 1:156), More goes on to point out that we are *all* that lorel: 'Now thou thinkest thy selfe wyse ynough whyle thou art proude in thy players garment, & forgettest that whan thy play is done, thou shalt go forth as pore as he. Nor thou remembrest not that thy pageant may happen to be done as sone as hys.'[43] And then he leaves this metaphor, 'which be to mery for this matter', and turns to expatiate on the world as a prison, in which all are under immutable sentence of death.

The metaphor of the world as prison is in fact pervasive in More's writings.[44] It accommodated some of his most deeply held thoughts, feelings and beliefs about the human condition and could be onto-logical, satiric and epistemological. More liked to use it as an image of the corrupt and sinful condition of humankind – transformed later in his life into a sense that suffering in this world can be purgative. He often used it satirically to point out the world's manifest injustice. It let him make distinctions between the blind or short-sighted, who take what they see as real, and those who remember that their true home is elsewhere. It also does much to explain More's pervasive sense of irony. It appears early, in Epigram 119 (*CW* 3, Part 2:166–9), is much expanded in his treatise on the Four Last Things, and is fully developed in the *Dialogue of Comfort against Tribulation*, where Antony insists at least four times that it is not metaphoric but literal – as it was for More, writing from the Tower (see further below, 230–1).

The third metaphor is related to the first two, but the emphasis is reversed; each person is a traveller, whose true home is not in this world and whose life is preparation for another.[45] Tellingly, More sub-sumes elements of all three metaphors in a joco-serious moment in Book II of *Utopia*, when the Anemolian ambassadors parade down the street in Amaurot. They are resplendent in cloth of gold, with heavy

gold chains round their necks and jewels on their caps, all intended to
impress the Utopians. But, ironically, their finery is inferior to the gold
chains that Utopia's slaves wear and the jewels that children there play
with. So a parent tries to explain to her bemused child that they must
be looking at 'one of the ambassadors' fools' (*morionibus*), as More
plays on his own name (*CU* 153). Significantly, this tale comes in the
section headed '*De peregrinatione Utopiensium*' (*CU* 144), which says
only a little about their travel but a great deal about their value system,
which is so mindful of a life to come. Although the life of the Utopians,
with its many constraints, can also seem prison-like, they are represented as true travellers, for whom death is the way to life.[46] By spelling
this out, though, I understate More's subtle wit, which leavens his
ideas and is an intrinsic part of a man who never lost his sense of
humour, even when he was about to step onto the scaffold.

FURTHER READING

Rhetoric, a complex field with a long tradition, is currently experiencing a renaissance. Jennifer Richards, *Rhetoric* (London and New
York: Routledge, 2008), concisely discusses its theory and practice
and the recent emergence of 'rhetoricality'. George A. Kennedy, *Clas-
sical Rhetoric and Its Christian and Secular Tradition from Ancient to
Modern Times*, 2nd edn (Chapel Hill: University of North Carolina
Press, 1999), and Thomas M. Conley, *Rhetoric in the European Tradition* (University of Chicago Press, 1994), include full treatments of
Renaissance rhetoric. Paul Oskar Kristeller, *Renaissance Thought:
The Classic, Scholastic, and Humanist Strains* (New York: Harper
Torchbooks, 1961), 3–23, is an authoritative introduction to the relationship between humanism and rhetoric, and Quentin Skinner, 'Clas-
sical eloquence in Renaissance England', Part 1 of his *Reason and
Rhetoric in the Philosophy of Hobbes* (Cambridge University Press,
1996), 19–211, is an invaluable treatment of rhetoric and its role in
civic life, politics and political thought in Renaissance culture. For
useful definitions, see Richard A. Lanham's *Handlist of Rhetorical
Terms*, 2nd edn (Berkeley: University of California Press, 1991).

More found in rhetoric an inexhaustible art that he used in countless ways. The introductions and commentaries in *CW*, *CU* and *R3* are
indispensable on this subject. Two especially valuable introductions to
editions of More's devotional works must be singled out: Louis
L. Martz's introduction to the *Dialogue of Comfort against Tribulation*
(*CW* 12), also available in his *Thomas More: The Search for the Inner*

Man (New Haven and London: Yale University Press, 1990), and Clarence H. Miller's introduction to *De Tristitia Christi* (*CW* 14), which includes an invaluable discussion of More's habits of composition and his later Latin style. Two important general studies of *Utopia* that touch on rhetoric are George M. Logan, *The Meaning of More's 'Utopia'* (Princeton University Press, 1983), and Dominic Baker-Smith, *More's 'Utopia'* (London: HarperCollins, 1991; repr. University of Toronto Press, 2000). Other especially useful studies include Logan, '*Utopia* and deliberative rhetoric', *Moreana* 31, no. 118–19 (1994), 103–20; Elizabeth Story Donno, 'Thomas More and *Richard III'*, *Renaissance Quarterly* 35 (1982), 401–47, on More's rhetorical approach to history; Elizabeth McCutcheon, 'Denying the contrary: More's use of litotes in the *Utopia'*, *EA* 263–74; and McCutcheon, *My Dear Peter: The 'Ars Poetica' and Hermeneutics for More's 'Utopia'* (Angers: Moreana, 1983). K. J. Wilson, *Incomplete Fictions: The Formation of English Renaissance Dialogue* (Washington: Catholic University of America Press, 1985), is incisive on More's later dialogues.

Notes

1. Ackroyd, *Life of More*, 46.
2. For examples of the professional writing and oratory, see William Nelson, 'Thomas More: grammarian and orator', *EA* 150–60, at 157–9, and below, 72–8, 84, 86.
3. It of course *remains* the case that all writing that aims to persuade is rhetorical. For a compact overview of the field, see Richards, *Rhetoric* (in 'Further reading'); also Brian Vickers, *In Defence of Rhetoric* (Oxford: Clarendon Press, 1988), on rhetoric's relationship to other arts and modern literary forms.
4. They continue to be discovered. See *Morus ad Craneveldium Litterae Balduinianae Novae: More to Cranevelt: New Baudouin Letters*, ed. Hubertus Schulte Herbrüggen (Leuven University Press, 1997).
5. John Monfasani, 'Humanism and rhetoric', in Albert Rabil, Jr, ed., *Renaissance Humanism: Foundations, Forms, and Legacy*, 3 vols. (Philadelphia: University of Pennsylvania Press, 1988), 3:172–235, surveys the early development of Renaissance rhetoric, especially in fifteenth-century Italy. See also Quentin Skinner's superb account of 'Classical eloquence in Renaissance England', Part 1 of his *Reason and Rhetoric in the Philosophy of Hobbes* (in 'Further reading'), 19–211.
6. Especially valuable are George A. Kennedy, *Classical Rhetoric and Its Christian and Secular Tradition from Ancient to Modern Time*s, and Thomas M. Conley, *Rhetoric in the European Tradition* (in 'Further reading').
7. Kennedy, *Classical Rhetoric*, 196–225.

8. See also Monfasani, 'Humanism and rhetoric', and Paul Oskar Kristeller, *Renaissance Thought: The Classic, Scholastic, and Humanist Strains* (in 'Further reading'), 3–23.

9. On More's education and humanist associates, see above, 8–12, 15–16, 25–8.

10. I am drawing here on my study 'Margaret More Roper: the learned woman in Tudor England', in Katharina M. Wilson, ed., *Women Writers of the Renaissance and Reformation* (Athens, Georgia: University of Georgia Press, 1987), 449–80.

11. Because the teaching of Latin was the equivalent of a puberty rite for males only, this was a radical departure: see Walter J. Ong, SJ, 'Latin language study as a Renaissance puberty rite', *Studies in Philology* 56 (1959), 103–24.

12. Erasmus, who particularly liked 'rhetorical poems' and 'poetical rhetoric, such that one can sense poetry in the prose and the style of a good orator in the poetry' (*CWE* 2:271), said in his *Ciceronianus* (1528) that he saw such cross-fertilization in More: 'As he spent a considerable time in his younger days on writing poetry, you can spot the poet even in his prose writing' (*CWE* 28:423; see further *CW* 3, Part 2:41).

13. On declamations, see *CW* 3, Part 1:xxxii–xxxiv. Erasmus remarked More's fondness for this form (*CWE* 7:23). His surviving declamation is his answer to Lucian's *Tyrannicida* (see above, 30).

14. Aural reading occurred in a variety of contexts throughout the Middle Ages and early modern Europe. See Keith Thomas, 'The meaning of literacy in early modern England', in Gerd Baumann, ed., *The Written Word: Literacy in Transition* (Oxford: Clarendon Press, 1986), 97–131. Compare the resisting hearers in More's *History of King Richard the Third* (*R3* 62–3 and 76–80) and the Utopians' enjoyment of some 'reading on a moral topic' at the beginning of lunch and supper (*CU* 143).

15. David Weil Baker discusses this at length in the chapter on 'Heresy and Utopia' in his *Divulging Utopia: Radical Humanism in Sixteenth-Century England* (Amherst: University of Massachusetts Press, 1999), 48–75.

16. Walter J. Ong, 'Oral residue in Tudor prose style', in *An Ong Reader: Challenges for Further Inquiry*, ed. Thomas J. Farrell and Paul A. Soukup (Cresskill, N.J.: Hampton, 2002), 313–29.

17. More did not oppose a translation of the Bible into English so long as it was done 'well and faythfully' (*CW* 6:337), but objected to Tyndale's translation of the New Testament, questioning his choice of words and the Reformers' doctrine of *sola scriptura* (below, 195, 206–8).

18. Jonson's *Timber: or, Discoveries*, in his *Works*, ed. C. H. Herford and Percy and Evelyn Simpson, 11 vols. (Oxford: Clarendon Press, 1925–52), 8:591; Chambers, 'The continuity of English prose from Alfred to More and his school,' in Harpsfield liii. See too Clarence H. Miller's astute comments in *CW* 14:742–3.

19. Janel M. Mueller, *The Native Tongue and the Word: Developments in English Prose Style 1380–1580* (University of Chicago Press, 1984),

201–25. Cf. *CW* 6:508–10 on More's practice in his *Dialogue Concerning Heresies*.

20. Translation from the Yale edition of More's Latin poems (*CW* 3, Part 2:293).
21. On More's histories as examples of *vituperatio*, see Elizabeth Story Donno, 'Thomas More and *Richard III*' (in 'Further reading'), 401–47.
22. Ibid., 418–41, and, on *enargia* itself, Richard A. Lanham, *A Handlist of Rhetorical Terms* (in 'Further reading'), 64. Especially in the English version, More's practice of *enargia* is extremely striking. Consider the famous description of Richard after the murder of the little princes, where his internal state is conveyed primarily through astonishingly vivid visual images: 'Where he went abroad, his eyes whirled about, his body privily fenced [i.e. shielded], his hand ever on his dagger, his countenance and manner like one alway ready to strike again. He took ill rest a-nights, lay long waking and musing, ... suddenly sometimes start up, leap out of his bed, and run about the chamber' (*R3* 102). Richard's apologist biographer Paul Murray Kendall speaks ruefully of the tremendous damage inflicted on his subject's reputation by 'the stunning vitality of More's literary talent': *Richard the Third* (London: Allen & Unwin, 1955), 423; quoted *R3* xvi.
23. See *R3* xxxiii–xl, and the detailed documentation by Daniel Kinney in his edition of the Latin history in *CW* 15.
24. Major studies include George M. Logan, *The Meaning of More's 'Utopia'*, and Dominic Baker-Smith, *More's 'Utopia'* (in 'Further reading').
25. Gary Saul Morson, *The Boundaries of Genre: Dostoevsky's 'Diary of a Writer' and the Traditions of Literary Utopia* (Austin: University of Texas Press, 1981), discusses More's work as both a utopia and a meta-utopia. See, too, William J. Kennedy, *Rhetorical Norms in Renaissance Literature* (New Haven: Yale University Press, 1978), 94–105, on the rhetoric and style of ironic discourse in *Utopia*.
26. There is an excellent analysis of Book I in these terms by Logan, '*Utopia* and deliberative rhetoric' (in 'Further reading').
27. One critic of utopian fiction, Bertrand de Jouvenel, has argued that this '"causing to see" by means of a feigned description ... is ... the essential feature of the utopian genre': 'Utopia for practical purposes', in Frank E. Manuel, ed., *Utopias and Utopian Thought* (Boston: Beacon Press, 1967), 220.
28. *Utopia* most resembles the Ciceronian type, because of its historic grounding, its development of character and its open-ended nature. K. J. Wilson discusses all three kinds, and More's transformations of them, in *Incomplete Fictions: The Formation of English Renaissance Dialogue* (in 'Further reading'). David Marsh, *The Quattrocento Dialogue, Classical Tradition and Humanist Innovation* (Cambridge, Mass.: Harvard University Press, 1980), 1–23, treats Cicero's and later humanist dialogues, pointing out that humanist dialogue 'intentionally seeks to create ambiguities' (14).

29. For more on this structure, and the way that Sir Philip Sidney used it in his *Defence of Poetry*, a fictional judicial oration, see Kenneth Myrick, *Sir Philip Sidney as a Literary Craftsman*, 2nd edn (Lincoln: University of Nebraska Press, 1965), 46–83. On the structure of More's Latin poem for the coronation of Henry VIII, which follows a standard classical pattern for an encomiastic speech, see *CW* 3, Part 2:43–4.

30. For both, some of this work has already been accomplished in the prefatory letter to Peter Giles (*CU* 30–9). The way that More handles *ethos* for his interlocutors, sometimes undercutting their authority, is especially complex and helps to explain the widely varying opinions of Hythloday and Morus held by readers.

31. *CU* 247–9 n. 142 usefully summarizes the major issue; and see below, 161–2.

32. I have explored the letter in detail in *My Dear Peter: The Ars Poetica and Hermeneutics for More's 'Utopia'* (in 'Further reading').

33. Richards, *Rhetoric*, 62–3.

34. The first and third of these works (*CW* 6 and 12) are treated in detail elsewhere in this volume. The texts of the More–Alington dialogue are in *Corr.* 511–32.

35. C. S. Lewis, *English Literature in the Sixteenth Century Excluding Drama* (Oxford: Clarendon Press, 1954), 172; Chambers, 'Continuity of English prose', clxii.

36. Louis L. Martz discusses this letter in *CW* 12:lx–lxv. See also Guy, *A Daughter's Love*, 238–42; and Alison V. Scott, 'More's letters and "the comfort of the truth"', in A. D. Cousins and Damian Grace, eds., *A Companion to Thomas More* (Madison, N.J.: Fairleigh Dickinson University Press, 2009), 53–76.

37. I know of no comprehensive study of More's letters. But see my article 'The humanism of Thomas More: continuities and transformations in his Latin letters', in J. F. Alcina *et al.*, eds., *Acta Conventus Neo-Latini Bariensis: Proceedings of the Ninth International Congress of Neo-Latin Studies* (Tempe, Ariz.: Medieval & Renaissance Studies, 1988), 25–40.

38. Guy, *Thomas More, passim*, and *A Daughter's Love*, 229, 235–6, 247–50, 263–4, 266, discusses these letters.

39. Cf. *SL* 251 with the corresponding passage of 'Sir Thomas More's indictment', Appendix 3 in Harpsfield 274; and see below, 128–31.

40. See Sister Miriam Joseph, *Rhetoric in Shakespeare's Time: Literary Theory of Renaissance Europe* (New York: Harcourt, Brace & World, 1962), 308–53.

41. I am drawing on my study 'Denying the contrary: More's use of litotes in the *Utopia*', *EA* 263–74.

42. These are examples of what George Lakoff and Mark Turner call 'conceptual' metaphors, that is, metaphors that 'affect the way we think and talk every day': *More than Cool Reason: A Field Guide to Poetic Metaphor* (University of Chicago Press, 1989), 8–9, 127.

43. *CW* 1:264 n. 156/16–22 calls attention to More's reminiscence, here and in the *History*, of Lucian's *Menippus*, which he had translated into Latin. (An English translation of Lucian's passage is in *R3* 126–7.)

44. See Elizabeth McCutcheon, '"This prison of the yerth": the topos of immurement in the writings of St. Thomas More', *Cithara* 35 (1985), 35–46.
45. See my essay '*Homo viator*: aspects of the works and life of Thomas More', *Moreana* 42, no. 164 (2005), 17–42.
46. In this respect the Utopians are like Hythloday, whose two frequently repeated quotations (*CU* 45) intimate this same idea. And cf. More's remark to his wife, Alice, when she visited him in prison: 'Is not this house ... as nigh heaven as my own?' (Roper 243).

4 More's public life

CATHY CURTIS

In an act of characteristic prescience and with lawyerly clarity, More composed his own epitaph, which he had cut in stone and which survives to this day in Chelsea Old Church.[1] It was the month following his resignation as lord chancellor of England, some eight months before King Henry VIII sought his arrest and two years before his execution. He sent a copy with a letter of explanation (in Latin, like the epitaph) to his great Dutch friend Erasmus for publication and dissemination on the Continent, describing the epitaph as 'a public declaration of the actual facts', which anyone could refute if they were able (SL 178–83, at 179). In the epitaph More presents himself as a Londoner, alludes briefly to his literary interests and underscores his several years spent as a pleader in the law courts. He then lists his various public offices, duties and particular achievements in an admirably compressed form which conveys much about the period 1518–32, which primarily concerns this chapter:

> [A]fter having held the office of judge as an Under-Sheriff in his
> native city, he was admitted to the Court by the Unconquerable
> Henry the Eighth, who is the only King ever to have received the
> unique distinction of meriting the title 'Defender of the Faith', a
> title earned by deeds of sword and pen; he was received at
> Court, chosen member of the King's Council, knighted, appointed
> Under-Treasurer and then Chancellor of Lancaster, and finally,
> Chancellor of England by the special favor of his Sovereign.
> Meanwhile he was elected Speaker of the House of Commons;
> furthermore, he served as the King's ambassador at various times
> and in various places, last of all at Cambrai.
>
> (SL 181)

More goes on to note that he alienated neither the nobility nor commons, but that 'he was a source of trouble to thieves, murderers, and heretics'. In an earlier letter to Erasmus he had justified his decision to resign, citing health problems (probably cardiac insufficiency), which he argued prevented him from continuing to discharge properly the highest office in the land (*SL* 173).

That More thought such a pre-emptive defence of his integrity necessary after such faithful and diverse service as the king himself acknowledged 'frequently in private, and twice in public' (*SL* 180) after his resignation suggests the extreme difficulties confronting those who accepted high office in the complex and fluid politico-religious national and international contexts of the early sixteenth century. At the beginning of his public life, More could not have predicted the appearance of Luther and the religious reformers, the Ottoman advances as far as Vienna and Henry VIII's desire for both an annulment of his marriage to Catherine of Aragon and an imperial realm independent of Rome. As early as 1516, however, *Utopia* had revealed apprehensions concerning the corruption and dissension within European states, and the internecine wars between them, which generated injustice and the impoverishment of the common people. That kings and princes tend to tyranny without wise counsel and that courtiers resort to flattery because they lack virtue are major themes. Yet More was engaged in his first diplomatic mission for the crown when he began *Utopia*, and a little over two years after its publication he became a full-time royal servant and was launched on the brilliant court career that he summarized in the epitaph. Knowing what he did about the corruption, frustrations and perils of royal service, why did he take this path? And what talents, skills and attributes of character enabled him to advance so steadily along it, bringing him eventually to the very apex of service to Henry? What made him so useful to his legal clients, to the courts he presided over as a judge, to his diplomatic missions and royal offices and, until the final rupture, directly to his king?

LAWYER AND HUMANIST SCHOLAR

After attending St Anthony's grammar school, where he first studied Latin, More was, around 1490, sent by his father as a page into the household of Cardinal John Morton, archbishop of Canterbury and Henry VII's lord chancellor.[2] It was common in this period for boys to be placed as servants in the houses of powerful men; that John More secured such a position for Thomas with Morton indicates that he intended to direct his son towards a career in public life. Morton was pragmatic and politically adept, having (as More says of him in *The History of King Richard the Third*) 'gotten by great experience (the very mother and mistress of wisdom) a deep insight in politic worldly drifts' (*R3* 106; *CW* 2:91). The chancellor recognized More's precocity, and was so impressed by the boy's extempore performances at Christmas revels that, according to the biography of More by his son-in-law William Roper, he predicted that 'This child here waiting at the table, whosoever shall live to see it, will prove a marvellous man' (Roper 198). In 1492, Morton sent More to study at Oxford, where he would have continued the liberal studies he had begun at St Anthony's (see above, 10–11, 25–6). More's father, however, was intent on his first son's following him into the profession of law, and he brought Thomas back to London to enter legal studies at the Inns of Court at about sixteen years of age. Thomas first attended New Inn before proceeding, in 1596, to Lincoln's Inn.

Students (mainly from the gentry) attending the Inns of Court lived a communal life. Instruction was intensely aural and practical, based on increasingly challenging disputation exercises rather similar in form at least to the scholastic exercises More would have encountered at Oxford.[3] 'Case-putting' involved difficult legal questions, formulated by a bencher (a senior barrister in the inns permitted to sit on the benches at moots), which were debated by small groups that could include all members of an inn, from student through to bencher, and argued every day during term. 'Moots' were based on more complex case arguments, and had the form of a trial, with utter ('outer' – another title deriving from seating arrangements) barristers or benchers acting as mock judges, and students or barristers acting as opposing counsel. The 'readings' were lectures delivered twice yearly by the most skilled lawyers, on a statute or a branch of law, and might continue for days or weeks. More's abilities and application enabled him to advance rapidly through the ranks, becoming an utter barrister about 1501. In addition to a constant diet of the theory and practice of law, life in the inns was leavened by a yearly calendar of 'revels', which were festivities held in hall and included dramatic productions.[4] All in all, legal education in the period was rigorous and detailed, and fostered exceptional skills in memory, forensic analysis and argumentation that would serve More well throughout his legal and political life. And doubtless his years in the inns informed his conception of political life as pageants played upon scaffolds (as stages were rather ominously called), most vividly embodied in a passage in his *History of King Richard The Third* (*R3* 94–5; *CW* 2:80–1; see further below, 179).

More's early inclination, though, was evidently stronger for the contemplative life, both literary and spiritual, than the active public life.[5] Around 1500 he became connected to, and perhaps resident in, the London Charterhouse (that is, the Carthusian monastery, a connection he may have retained until close to the time of his marriage, around the beginning of 1505). About 1501, he gave a series of public lectures on Augustine's *City of God* (Roper 198; Harpsfield 17, 13). Erasmus tells us that More's father was hostile to his son's application during these years to the extra-legal studies of Greek literature and philosophy, theology and history that Thomas pursued under the Italian-educated humanist scholars Thomas Linacre, William Grocyn and William Lily (*CWE* 7:19–21).[6] One would think, however, that John More must have realized that some, at least, of these studies might prove useful to his son's career, given the interpenetration of the legal, political and administrative life of the realm. Law was, then as now, the most obvious road to advancement in public life: the speaker of the House of Commons, for example, was invariably a common lawyer. But the crown also needed skills in writing, speaking, argument and translation which could be applied in government business such as the negotiation and drafting of international peace and trade treaties, in conducting commissions abroad and in serving the king's various law courts. Both legal training and a humanist education in the liberal arts – especially in rhetoric – were extremely useful to a public career in the period.[7] More himself maintains, in the defence of humanistic learning in his *Letter to Oxford*, that 'the study of poets, orators, and histories' is of unrivalled value in the acquisition of the 'practical skill' of 'prudence in human affairs' (*CW* 15:139, trans. Daniel Kinney).

EARLY EMBASSIES AND LEGAL PRACTICE FOR THE CITY OF LONDON

More's abilities as a commercial diplomat, orator, arbitrator and lawyer were highly regarded in the City of London and by the crown, and his workload grew quickly.[8] He held a series of offices in the legal inns (see above, 12–13), and was granted honorary membership in the rich and powerful Mercers' Company in 1509, speaking on their behalf on the occasion of Henry VIII's coronation.[9] Also in 1509, he was appointed justice of the peace for Middlesex, and was elected to represent Westminster in Henry's first parliament.[10] He was appointed as one of two undersheriffs for the City of London in 1510, an office which continued until his resignation after joining

Henry's council in 1518. The undersheriff functioned as a permanent legal adviser to the sheriffs, and served as a judge in the Sheriff's Court, which sat on Thursday mornings.[11] According to Erasmus, More settled many cases with great integrity, frequently remitting fees due from litigants (*CWE* 7:22).

In 1512 More was in parliament attending debates regarding Pope Julius II's call to arms in the Holy League against France.[12] May 1515 marked the first of his many royal commissions. On this occasion More and Cuthbert Tunstall negotiated commercial treaties regarding the Anglo-Flemish wool and textile trade, and *Utopia* is set in Antwerp during a hiatus in these lengthy and difficult discussions.[13] More complained to Erasmus that the office of diplomat had never attracted him; apart from missing his family, the expenses of supporting both his domestic and ambassadorial households were heavy (*CWE* 3:234–5). Henry VIII did offer him a pension on his return, which, as he told Erasmus, he felt compelled to refuse, as he thought it would compromise his position in the City of London. According to Roper (who is, however, not necessarily accurate on all points), More's income as a private lawyer was £400 a year (Roper 200), which his later royal service increased only marginally, as by 1525 he was earning between £400 and £500.[14]

More was chosen by Wolsey and the king's council to ascertain the cause of the Evil May Day rioting of 1517, when the grievances of apprentices against aliens in London threatened serious civil unrest (*CSPV* 2, nos. 879, 881, 887). He would later reflect on the dangers presented to the commonwealth by loose talk and rebellion (*CW* 9:156). A number of the rioters were hanged for treason, although many others were pardoned by Henry. In August that year More was a junior envoy to the seasoned ambassadors Richard Wingfield and William Knight, again negotiating to resolve a dispute between English and French merchants in Calais. He also successfully assisted the papal counsel to Leo X in a complex and sensitive matter concerning a ship carrying alum (used to fix cloth dyes and in other commercial applications) which had been seized by the duke of Suffolk. According to Roper, More argued so learnedly in the Court of Star Chamber for the pope's side that not only was the ship restored to the pope but Henry VIII concluded that he could no longer be without More's full-time service (Roper 201). John Guy more accurately identifies More as having been simultaneously a translator and adviser for the pope's agent and a go-between for the commercial interests of the City of London.[15] An out-of-court settlement was reached, thus satisfying the diplomatic requirements of Henry and Wolsey that the pope be maintained as an ally.

KING'S ORATOR, SECRETARY AND DIPLOMAT

More expressed great reservations about the inconveniences and threats to reputation entailed in public service (*SL* 69–70, 88–9), and initially resisted the urgings of Henry VIII and Wolsey that he join the royal council. To Bishop John Fisher he wrote that '[m]uch against my will did I come to court, as everyone knows ... So far I keep my place there as precariously as an unaccustomed rider in the saddle', and it was only because Henry VIII was possessed of all the qualities necessary in a good monarch that life was tolerable at court (*SL* 94). The biographical sketch of More that Erasmus wrote in 1519 also claims that More was dragged reluctantly to court (*CWE* 7:22). Yet it must be recognized that his entire humanist education and accumulated experience made that destination highly predictable. More was guided by his Christian humanist understanding of the civic duty of a virtuous man: citizenship was aligned with the life of Ciceronian *negotium*, active political service, in preference to that of Platonic *otium*, or contemplative withdrawal.[16] Morus and Hythlodaeus debate just this opposition in *Utopia*, the former arguing for dedication to the needs of the commonwealth, especially in times of political difficulty. More's earlier musings concerning tyranny and the abuse of counsel in his *Epigrammata* and *The History of King Richard The Third* had revealed dark suspicions (however elliptically and ambiguously expressed) about Henry VIII's propensity to pass from mild rule in his early years to full-blown arbitrary rule and More's preference for republican and consultative government over that of a single ruler.[17] More's comment to Fisher regarding his monarch expressed more hope than fact, and no doubt he felt impelled to do what he could to yet guide the youthful Henry in the ways of virtuous kingship.

The precise date of, and motives behind, More's entry into full-time royal service have been contested. G. R. Elton maintained that More was already sworn as a king's councillor when he was a commercial envoy at Calais in the autumn of 1517, and questioned More's professed lack of enthusiasm for public life. This view, which Elton first propounded in a lecture of 1970,[18] and which gained wide acceptance, was finally laid to rest in 2000 in Guy's *Thomas More* (49–58). Elton's argument was based mainly on the fact that More's annuity as a councillor, although granted on 21 June 1518, had its first instalment backdated to the previous September; therefore More must have been a councillor by that time. But Guy pointed out that this backdating of annuities was a bureaucratic technique employed in various circumstances, so that, in More's case, it cannot be taken as determinative evidence of a 1517 appointment. Meanwhile, three contemporary witnesses – Roper, Erasmus and the Venetian ambassador – unanimously date More's entry into full-time royal service to spring or early summer 1518. Following a study by David Starkey of the relationship between the court and the council, Guy noted that when More's friend Richard Pace, who had been the much-favoured king's secretary for two years, returned from his embassy to the Swiss in early 1518, Wolsey placed him in court as Henry's attendant councillor. More was then recruited to help Pace by 26 March 1518. Pace and More were used interchangeably as royal secretaries until 1521. My own researches suggest an alternative explanation for More's entry into service at this time, having to do with the aftermath of Pope Leo X's proposal in a bull of 6 March 1518 for a truce among European powers, which would enable a crusade against the Turks in response to recent Ottoman successes in Egypt and Syria.[19] There are grounds for thinking that More consented to enter royal service at this point because of the obvious potential importance of this collective security initiative to early modern European peace-making. While it is true that Henry and Wolsey opportunistically appropriated and modified the papal proposal to enhance England's power with respect to France and Spain, it must also be recognized that the Universal Peace Treaty – proclaimed in London in October 1518 – evolved into a sophisticated and important attempt to address European international relations. And additional skilled public servants were required to bring it to fruition. More gave a brief Latin oration (not extant) in London on the arrival of the papal legate Cardinal Campeggio for the treaty negotiations, praising the pope's desire for peace; he was also one of the treaty's signatories.

More had many other duties beyond the diplomacy surrounding the Universal Peace. As acting royal secretary, he exchanged letters with Wolsey on the king's business (of these only some twenty, of perhaps hundreds, survive); he read to Henry letters from Wolsey and other members of the council, as well as diplomatic dispatches, wrote letters to the king's dictation, and acted as an access point to him in epistolary matters.[20] More was also responsible for checking various grants and appointments, and required to sign warrants and witness royal documents. When Henry visited Oxford or Cambridge in his progresses,

More was called on to answer extempore to the Latin orations of the universities, and he attended and participated in the official readings and disputations (Roper 209).

Humanist hopes for peace continued between 1518 and the sumptuous Field of Cloth of Gold of June 1520, at which Henry and Francis I were to meet face to face at Calais and affirm the Universal Peace. More accompanied the king, along with a large proportion of the English nobility. He left no reference to the extravagant event, but the sentiments expressed in *Utopia* on conspicuous consumption and display (in an ironic inversion the Utopians use gold for chamber pots and the chains of slaves) suggest that he would have viewed such princely posturing as deeply corrupt. At this meeting Henry VIII and Pace both made orations praising the benefits of perpetual peace between the two kings (*LP* 3, Part 1, no. 869).[21] But Gustiniani, the Venetian ambassador to France, mused that these sovereigns were not at peace in fact, but rather accommodated themselves to circumstances and hated each other most cordially (*CSPV* 3, no. 119) – indeed, France would soon breach the Universal Peace Treaty of 1518, by engaging in hostilities with Charles V in 1521.

From Calais More went to Bruges, where he helped to negotiate a commercial treaty between England and the Hanseatic League over July and August, and again in autumn the following year. The detailed records by the Hanse commissioners reveal that all the fruits of More's Latin education, legal training and experience in representing the Mercers' guild were brought to bear.[22] On the first occasion, More was third of four commissioners, and on the next, second of six – but on both occasions More spoke more than anyone else and was clearly acting as spokesperson. The negotiations were difficult and protracted, with More determined not to cede too much on the king's behalf. While the Hanse commissioners thought More's mild speech and calm demeanour to be customary among the English, he was also considered to be a tough, dissimulating and subtle negotiator.

More was knighted and appointed under-treasurer of the exchequer in May 1521, and given lands and perquisites which enabled him to buy his estate at Chelsea. He acted as a supervisor of officers responsible for collecting and disbursing money and keeping accounts, and also had custody of the treasury of the receipt, which was the government's archive for treaties and diplomatic documents.[23] In July 1521, Henry instructed Pace to write to Wolsey that as 'old men doith nowe decaye gretly within thys Hys realme', he was minded to acquaint other young men with his great affairs, and therefore More should be privy to all matters that Wolsey would soon treat at Calais (*LP* 3, Part 2, no. 1437). Those matters involved the secret machinations surrounding France's breach of the Universal Peace Treaty; as the aggressor, she should be subject to punishment at the hands of the other signatories, especially England, the arbiter of the treaty. Wolsey in fact sought to negotiate a secret treaty with Charles V to mount a joint invasion of France. More accompanied Wolsey on the embassy, which departed in August.[24] On his return, More was again attending the king, acting as an intermediary between Henry, who travelled incessantly, and Wolsey, who stayed at Hampton Court transacting the executive business of government.[25] Wolsey applied the strategy of gathering most councillors around himself, while allowing a smaller group to attend the king. In this way the lord chancellor kept a tight rein on policy and communication. More was clearly trusted not to threaten Wolsey's position of favour with the king. His attendance on the king was constant, as evidenced by surviving letters between More and Wolsey in 1523.[26]

As sole secretary in 1521, More became involved with the anti-Lutheran campaign which had already begun on the Continent.[27] With the assistance of More and the theologically astute John Fisher, Henry VIII had composed an anti-Lutheran tract that year which earned him the title 'Defender of the Faith' from Leo X. When Luther replied with venom, More retaliated on behalf of the king (who could not reply in kind) with his *Responsio ad Lutherum* of 1523. His forensic method of refuting Luther point by point was combined with an *ad hominem* attack, which came readily to one equipped as lawyer and rhetorician (Intro. *CW* 5:715–31). More's voluminous controversial writings in defence of the traditions and authority of the Roman Catholic Church would absorb enormous energy for the remainder of his public career and even after his withdrawal from public office in 1532, and would later attract opprobrium from scholars who felt uneasy with the vituperative tone and at times scurrilous matter (below, 101–5).

In April 1523 More was chosen as speaker of the House of Commons. His oration on the occasion of his presentation to Henry VIII is not extant, but he recounted the striking story, taken from Cicero, of vainglorious Phormio, who invited Hannibal to his lecture room and then presumed to instruct the great general on the art of war: More feared to speak before his king concerning the ordering of the commonwealth.[28] The comparison was apt, given that the speaker would have to represent the commons on the topic of war (and the attendant taxation) in this very parliament. More also made a second speech, which Roper reports verbatim (Roper 202–5). It is legendary as the first recorded example of a petition for the exercise of freedom of speech in parliament, although clearly the liberty had existed to some extent earlier.[29] More insisted that every man must be free to discharge his conscience and boldly declare his advice, and asked that Henry 'take all in good part, interpreting every man's words, how uncunningly [i.e. unskilfully] soever they be couched, to proceed yet of good zeal towards the profit of your realm and honor of your royal person'. Effective governance, then, depended on parliamentarians' freedom of speech without fear of reprisal, and the king's receptivity to honest, if at times unadorned, counsel.

During this busy parliament, Wolsey appeared with all pomp and retinue in order to intimidate the commons, demanding £800,000 for war with France on behalf of the king, which he contended the realm was wealthy enough to sustain.[30] Wolsey then tried to subvert parliamentary privilege by asking individual members to answer, and when met with silence asked More as the mouth of parliament to speak for them. The wily More knelt before Wolsey and offered 'many probable arguments proving that for them to make answer was it neither expedient nor agreeable with the ancient liberty of the house' (Roper 207). The opinion of the house was that a lesser sum should be accepted because of the economic hardship the larger one would impose on the commonwealth. Wolsey raged that he would rather have his tongue plucked out of his head with a pair of pincers than communicate this to his king, and he was furious with More, unsuccessfully attempting to have him sent to Spain on an embassy and ruing the day he had been made speaker.

Many in the English ruling elite, including More, Tunstall and Pace, held that an alliance with the Holy Roman Emperor best served English interests, especially with respect to trade. Furthermore, the emperor could serve as a protector and even reformer of the Church, should the papacy fail in its duties.[31] Wolsey was pragmatic and expedient in his approach; the highest good was evidently to serve Henry's best interests. With Charles V's lack of interest in a projected Anglo-imperial invasion of France after Francis I's defeat and capture at Pavia in February 1525, and the failure of the widely resisted and resented extra-parliamentary 'Amicable Grant' demanded by Wolsey for the cost of the invasion, Henry and Wolsey moved to negotiate a truce with France. Thomas More and Nicolas West were appointed in August to negotiate the five agreements with envoys of the French regent, Francis's mother, Louise of Savoy. These agreements made up the Treaty of the More (named after the royal house where it was concluded), under which Francis had to pay Henry two million crowns in yearly instalments, with peace proclaimed between England and France on 6 September. During this period, English opinion as to the desirability of war was divided. Sections of the nobility and soldiers preferred peace; extra taxation associated with war was certainly highly unpopular with the people more generally.[32] More had warned years earlier in *Utopia* that the excessive taxation of the commons by a king could provoke rebellion in his subjects (*CU* 93).

In July 1525, More was made chancellor of the duchy of Lancaster. The chancellorship proved to be a burdensome but highly useful experience. His chief role was as an equity judge (equity involved tempering the letter of the law by reference to the particular circumstances of a case).[33] At this period, the king appreciated More's 'merry' company, and Roper recounts that Henry would so frequently send for More to discourse with him on astronomy, geometry, theology and worldly affairs that he was forced to 'dissemble his nature' – that is, deliberately make himself into less pleasant company – so as to have some time to spend with his family (Roper 202). Nor was More deluded as to Henry's ultimate scale of values. When Roper enthused about the obvious fondness the king had displayed for More during an impromptu visit to his home at Chelsea, More replied that he had no cause to be proud: 'for if my head could win him a castle in France (for then was there war between us) it should not fail to go' (Roper 208).[34] Charles V would later unwittingly invert this comment, declaring that he would have given up a city to have such a counsellor.[35]

Roper's admittedly partisan account of More's intense but precarious relationship with Henry nevertheless conveys an element of psychological truth about their contrasting personalities and discharge of office.[36] More is presented as patient, moderate, affable and as a master of his passions through the exercise of reason, years of study and religious reflection. His settled domestic life and marriage, and his devotion to service and the needs of the poor, evince his concern for the proper ordering of a just society (Roper 210–12, 219–22, 223–4, 237–8). By contrast, Roper's Henry VIII has an inconstant and mutable disposition, easily led and prone to anger (Roper 208, 238). More perceived that Henry could move from personal intimacy to mortal threat if policy or passion required, indicating his king's lack of capacity for constant friendship. Henry's later infidelity to his marriage vows to Catherine (not to mention subsequent wives), and his failure to honour international peace treaties, also revealed a pattern of deep subversion of the sanctity of relationships. Despite all attempts to educate the king in the ways of the virtuous Renaissance philosopher-prince, he remained stubbornly lacking in the virtues that More had doubtless hoped to encourage when he first entered service.

For three years beginning in 1526, More (now replaced as secretary by William Knight) was largely away from court, travelling on the king's business. In 1527 large embassies crossed the Channel in both directions, securing the Peace of Amiens between England and France. More was again intimately involved with negotiations which again promised an eternal peace and culminated, this time, in the solemn swearing of the treaty in the cathedral of Amiens.[37] Along with Tunstall, More accompanied Wolsey to France in the summer; the Cardinal-Peacemaker (as he was now styled) travelled in such royal state that it brought much negative comment. A few months earlier, imperial troops, many of them thought to be Lutherans, perpetrated the notorious Sack of Rome, the horrors of which More described in *A Dialogue Concerning Heresies* (CW 6:370–2) and which may have further hardened his attitude to heresy as constituting the gravest threat to the very survival of civil society.[38]

From 1526 until 1528 a combination of domestic events threatened England's prosperity and had international repercussions: bad weather, a poor harvest and an outbreak of plague led to scarcity of grain and inflated prices, followed by unemployment and civil unrest.[39] The pursuit by Henry VIII of an unpopular divorce, which led to an anti-imperial stance with implications for the importation of vital food and the exportation of cloth to the Netherlands, further stoked dissent from the king's policies. Two of More's closest friends – Pace and the Spanish humanist Juan Luis Vives – were supporters of the queen's case and pro-imperial in outlook, and both were briefly imprisoned by Wolsey and interrogated.[40]

The king's desire for an annulment on the grounds of a legal defect in the original dispensation from Pope Julius II (which had allowed him to marry his deceased elder brother's wife) was on the agenda before More had left for France in spring 1527. After returning from Amiens in late September, he reported to the king at Hampton Court, who 'brake with me of his great matter', to the effect that his marriage to Catherine was against scriptural, canon and natural law and so grievously compromised that 'it could in no wise by the Church be dispensable' (SL 207). Asked for his opinion, More demurred that he would need to consult the authorities, and after reading Edward Foxe's manuscript of the writings on the divorce, he remained unconvinced. Henry did not approach More again until after he was lord chancellor, when the king implored him to 'look and consider his great matter' again. He told More, however, that he 'never was willing to put any man in ruffle or trouble of his conscience' (*SL* 209, 210).

In December 1527 Wolsey wrote to Pope Clement VII intimating that the unity of Christendom depended on the succession to the English crown, and in 1528 suggested more directly that England would break with Rome if the pope did not commission Wolsey to try the divorce in England. Wolsey's strategy seems to have been to link the matter of the marriage to the succession of the crown and thence to the potential for English civil war. It has been argued that at this time Wolsey was less concerned with punishing heretics per se than in proving to the pope that active measures were being taken to maintain Catholic orthodoxy.[41] More became involved with Wolsey's diplomatic cum theological policy, although his motivation was more simply to protect the Catholic Church. In March 1528 Tunstall, as bishop of London, authorized More to possess and read Lutheran books so that he could write books against heresy in English (*Corr.* 186–8; see further below, 99). More's *Dialogue Concerning Heresies* duly issued in 1529; other polemical works followed.

At about this date, More told Roper that 'upon condition that three things were well established in Christendom', he would be content to be 'put in a sack and here presently cast into the Thames' (Roper 210). He desired a universal peace, perfect uniformity of religion instead of the present errors and heresies, and that the matter of Henry's marriage be brought to a good conclusion; otherwise he considered that there would be much disturbance in Christendom. With the Peasants' War of 1525–6 in Germanic Europe, and the Turkish sultan Suleiman's defeat of the Hungarians at the Battle of Mohács in 1526 followed by his siege of Vienna in 1529, More shared the apocalyptic fear of many across Europe that the Christian world might face destruction, and argued that the blame for this situation could be laid squarely at the feet of Christian rulers who had indulged in the blinding passions of ambition and envy (see below, 216–17). As he wrote in the *Dialogue Concerning Heresies*, while each prince has aspired to the expansion of his own dominion, they have cared little for 'what came of the comen corps of crystendome', and so God has punished their 'inordynate appetytes' by withdrawing his help and allowing them to eat one another up, while the Turk prospers and threatens to soon 'swalowe them all' (*CW* 6:413–14). Princes are urged to protect and defend their territory; such action is commendable, especially given that the perdition of souls, as well as the loss of property and bodily harm, will follow from the invasion of the Turks.

The Franco-imperial Treaty of Cambrai of August 1529 brought a temporary peace to Europe, which allowed the emperor Charles V to provide leadership against the Turks the following year and call a council of the 'universal church' to address the threat the Roman Church thought was posed by reformed religion. More was among the English ambassadors who met those of the emperor, pope and king of France to negotiate this treaty, which was signed in the cathedral by Francis I, Margaret of Savoy on behalf of Charles V, and by More, Tunstall and John Hacket on the part of Henry. The jointly written and partly mutilated dispatches of the three English ambassadors (More was ranked second after Tunstall) reveal the complexity of the gruelling negotiations over the release of the French king's sons by Charles V (who had exchanged Francis I for his sons, who were then held as hostages), payments due to England under the Treaty of Windsor of 1522, and cases of offensive war (*LP* 4, Part 3, nos. 5679, 5822, 5824, 5829, 5830). The treaty itself paid scant attention to English interests, with the French originally suing for peace with Charles V after being routed at the battle of Landriano in June, without so much as consulting England.

Whatever the treaty's shortcomings for England's interests, in its aftermath Tunstall was promoted to bishop of Durham and More became lord chancellor. In his epitaph, More referred to Cambrai as his culminating achievement in public office – the renewal of a peace treaty between the princes of Christendom and 'the restoration of a long-desired peace to the world' (*SL* 181), which in 1532 he fervently prayed would last. It would not, of course, but at least England would not engage in another foreign military adventure for thirteen years after the ratification of this treaty.

LORD CHANCELLOR

Henry had become increasingly impatient with Wolsey's inability to secure a papal dispensation for the annulment of his marriage, making it inevitable that the cardinal would sooner or later fall from power. The Treaty of Cambrai made the position much worse, since it left Charles V – the nephew of Henry's queen – with commanding power over the pope, Clement VII. The end came on 17 October 1529, when Wolsey pleaded guilty to a charge of *praemunire* – of obeying a foreign authority over the statutes of England by assuming a papal legateship (which Henry had in fact bestowed on him).[42] More signed the articles of attainder against Wolsey formulated by the 'Reformation Parliament' (which, convened in November 1529, sat for six and a half momentous years).[43] More was appointed to the office of lord chancellor on 25 October 1529, receiving the main emblem and instrument of office, the Great Seal, from his king and taking an oath to 'do right to all manner of people, poor and rich, after the laws and usages of this realm'.[44] Erasmus wrote to Tunstall, Pace and Lord Mountjoy that he could not congratulate More nor the cause of good letters on his new office, but he did congratulate England (*EE* 8, Eps. 2263, 2287, 2295). Writing to Erasmus, More emphasized his loyalty to Henry VIII and stressed that the post involved the interests of Christendom (*SL* 172).

Why was More chosen by Henry and the ascendant factions at court, now dominated by men such as the dukes of Norfolk and Suffolk, Stephen Gardiner and Sir Thomas Boleyn – men who sought to please their king and apply pressure on Clement VII to refer the divorce suit to England for consideration, and who supported reform of the privileges of the English Church and its clergy?[45] This was a period of intense anti-clericalism, designed to bring both pope and the local clergy to heel.[46] And why did More *accept* the chancellorship, given that he knew Henry so well, and how things lay with his desire for an annulment? More was the first common lawyer in a hundred and fifty years to become chancellor, the office usually being filled by an ecclesiastic. Wolsey himself, however, thought More the best person for the office and, indeed, More continued his predecessor's work in extending equity through the Court of Star Chamber and in prosecuting heresy.[47] It has been suggested that More provided propaganda value for Henry as a true philosopher-king, served by learned, moderate and conscientious men.[48] More commented that, given that so great a prelate as Wolsey had taken a fall, he himself had 'no cause to rejoice' (Roper 219). But one did not simply refuse the request from one's monarch for service in the highest office of the land, and this was especially true in More's case, since he perceived multiple and interrelated dangers, not just to England but to Christendom itself, from internecine discord and religious dissension and the aggressive movement of the Turks into Europe. As 'Morus' had argued in *Utopia*, one ought not to desert the ship of the commonwealth in a storm just because one cannot control the winds, but should rather attempt to make the situation at least a little less dire (*CU* 97). Henry VIII also promised More his freedom of conscience (although only after he had accepted the chancellorship) and

had instructed him as far back as March 1518 – on his first entry into
royal service – that he should 'look unto God and after God unto him'
(*SL* 209). More's later advice to Thomas Cromwell is revealing of his
own struggle to reconcile God's injunctions with the king's desires: 'in
your counsel-giving unto his grace, ever tell him what he ought to do
but never what he is able to do … For if a lion knew his own strength,
hard were it for any man to rule him' (Roper 228).

Having been installed as chancellor, More gave a long and eloquent
oration at the ceremonial opening of parliament on 3 November. The
first part (not extant) concerned the cancellation of Henry's debts,
indicating that the expense incurred by securing the universal peace
at Cambrai had guaranteed unity in Christendom, eliminated the risk
of foreign invasion and restored England's trade. The second part (also
not extant) called for reformation of 'divers new enormities sprung
amongst the people' (presumably, religious enormities), and the final
part addressed the reasons for the fall of Wolsey.[49] This surviving
section of the speech does not employ the usual flourishes of classical
rhetoric but is accommodated to the audience of burgesses and knights:
it is blunt, stern and, insomuch as it departs from the literal, uses
uncomplicated and vivid metaphorical language suited to the parliament of a wool-based economy. Building on the conventional comparison of a king to a shepherd, More argues that it is the multitude of his
people rather than his wealth and honour which makes the king a
governor of might and puissance. This is followed by a devastating *ad
hominem* attack on Wolsey, supporting Henry VIII's action against
him, as well as by an oblique criticism of the king's compromised
sovereignty:

> [A]s you se that emongest a great flocke of shepe some be rotten and
> fauty, which the good sheperd sendeth from the good shepe, so the
> great wether which is of late fallen … so craftley, so scabedly, yea
> and so untruly juggled wyth the kynge, that all men must nedes gesse
> and thinke that he thought in him self, that he had no wit to perceive
> his craftie doing … but he was deceived, for his graces sight was so
> quicke and penetrable, that he saw him, ye and saw through hym,
> both with in and without, so that all thing to him was open.[50]

Considering the seriousness of his crimes, More continues, Wolsey was
punished lightly; but whoever tries the same will not escape so easily.
Wolsey, with whom More had worked closely for so many years, was
now the diseased 'great wether', a danger of contagion in the body
politic. This was none too subtle counsel to Henry himself (who was

seated beside More in parliament), as well as to any other servant who might be tempted to exceed the limits of office. Why was it that the king had allowed Wolsey to usurp his power, as had been long rumoured throughout Europe?

Wolsey indeed left More a mixed legacy, for alongside the ambition, pride and greed with which More (like others) taxed him was a desire to see justice done equally to all who sought it, and his extraordinary administrative talent and energy.[51] As chancellor, More continued Wolsey's reforms, simplifying legal procedures in common law and increasing access to equity courts, rather than achieving any fundamental reform of the common law itself.[52] In general terms, More regarded law as applying equally to all, and its proper operation as fundamental to a healthy secular and ecclesiastical society; and the administration of the laws required the greatest prudence, courage and moderation.[53] Like Wolsey, he emphasized the importance of the concept of equity. The treatment of law in *Utopia* reveals the same concern: More identifies the social origins of the crime of theft and endorses the application of equity to moderate the severity of punishment for it (*CU* 55–71).

More presided over the two equity courts of Star Chamber and Chancery. When the notoriously slow common-law courts provided inadequate access to justice, the equity courts could make good their shortcomings. Like Wolsey, More was criticized for his use of injunctions which halted legal proceedings by common-law judges and passed them to the Court of Chancery for review. Roper says that in a meeting with the common-law judges over dinner, More discussed in detail his recently issued injunctions, and after debate the judges were forced to 'confess that they in like case could have done no otherwise themselves' (Roper 221). More then instructed the judges that they should use their own legal discretion to ameliorate defects in the law. As a judge himself, More was considered to be incorruptible, impartial and efficient – his biographers provide anecdotes to this effect, such as More's refusal to show special favour to his son-in-law Giles Heron in a suit in Chancery, but rather binding him over to appear in Star Chamber or face prison (Roper 20; Harpsfield 53).

Sources for More's activities in 1530 are patchy. With the rise of the talented Thomas Cromwell, who supported the divorce and became Henry's close adviser, More was sidelined in much government business because it increasingly involved matters relating to the divorce and included the development of Henry's imperial vision of a united English commonwealth with its church under the control of the secular crown.[54] This most experienced of diplomats was now entirely removed from the diplomatic efforts to obtain a papal dissolution of the marriage. Wolsey's name and policy appear everywhere during *his* tenure as chancellor, whereas More is mentioned far less, and foreign diplomats seek out other of Henry's councillors.

The imperial ambassador Eustace Chapuys recorded that Charles V wrote a letter thanking More for his support for the queen, news of which came to More just before he was required by Henry VIII to address both houses of parliament regarding the king's great matter. Chapuys reported to the emperor that More 'begged me for the honour of God to forbear, for although he had given already sufficient proof of his loyalty that he ought to incur no suspicion', yet any visitor might yet provoke it. If any mistrust should arise in this way, More would not have 'the liberty which he had always used in speaking boldly in those matters which concerned your Majesty and the Queen' (*LP* 5, no. 171). He explained to Chapuys that the peace and welfare of Henry VIII and the realm was his objective. This is evidence that More was still pursuing a pro-imperial foreign policy behind the scenes.

In the House of Lords More had to speak against those claiming that Henry sought his divorce out of love for a woman rather than from a sincere scruple of conscience, showing that the king's case was supportable by adducing the seals of various European universities that had ruled in Henry's favour according to scripture and canon law.[55] A clerk read the opinions, which were not presented for debate but rather to inform the House. Asked his own opinion by one of the members, More replied that he had given his opinion many times to Henry, and would not to anyone else (*LP* 5, no. 171; *CSPV* 4, no. 664). Then More, along with Norfolk, Suffolk and the bishops of London and Lincoln, went down to the House of Commons to deliver the king's message there. Once more, members were advised that the matter was not open to debate, nor were the opinions of the universities to be questioned. Hall recorded More's speech to the Commons: 'if thys mariage be good or no, manye clerkes do doubt. Wherfore the kinge lyke a vertuous prince willinge to be satisfied in his conscience, and also for the suretie of hys realme hath with great deliberacion consulted with great clerkes [scholars], and hath sent my lord of London here present to the chiefe Universities of all Christendome to know their opinion and judgement in that behalfe'.[56] More no doubt found this episode excruciating, knowing full well that his own reputation for justice and probity was being exploited, even though he carefully resisted stating his own position (unlike the bishops of London and Lincoln). But his silence was eloquent. He well understood Henry VIII's strategy of appearing to take broad and learned counsel, to consult and deliberate with parliament, and pay heed to his conscience. All the humanists' efforts to educate Henry in the principles of kingly taking of counsel and consultation were in one sense well learned by Henry: he knew how to talk the talk while in fact remaining utterly resistant to any opinion which contradicted his desired outcome.[57]

As uncongenial as serving such a ruler must have been to More, he would resign only a year later, on 16 May 1532, apparently believing up to about that time that it might still be possible to pull Henry back from his present policy, or at least to do some good on matters other than the divorce. But early in 1532, after bullying by Henry, parliament passed the Act in Conditional Restraint of Annates (payments to Rome made by clergy). After opposition, the Submission of the Clergy to the Crown was passed on 15 May, making the English Church subordinate to the crown. Chapuys reported that More and the bishops in the Lords opposed Henry, who was 'very angry, especially with the Chancellor and the bishop of Winchester, and is determined to carry the matter' (*LP* 5, no. 1013). The day after the passage of the act, More went to Henry in his privy garden at Whitehall and returned the Great Seal, asking of his king that he might withdraw from public life to concentrate on spiritual matters. Henry, apparently, graciously accepted (see below, 116).

The emphasis in this study of More's public life has rested on the discharge of his various offices in the highly charged and fluid domestic and international context of his times. More's career as a humanist, lawyer, diplomat, negotiator and orator was defined by his understanding of the opportunities and limitations entailed in the particular offices he swore oaths to serve, and was profoundly dependent on the nature and temperament of both Henry VIII and Wolsey. He accommodated as he judged best to Henry's increasingly tyrannical behaviour, Wolsey's usurpation of the king's proper exercise of power and pursuit of war, an ever-changing diplomatic environment and the spread of the European religious reform movement. My view is that More achieved much in public office, but frequently through indirect and private counsel, and unobtrusive but diligent diplomacy. Although he always presented a dutiful and discreet public persona in office, and in his surviving letters to Henry and Wolsey reveals little of his own opinions and judgements, he was quite capable of influencing opinion behind the scenes or actively orchestrating opposition in parliament, while being acutely aware that, as Norfolk warned him, 'the wrath of the king is death' (Roper 237).

Much, of course, remains unknown and unrecoverable, but the frustrations and defeats More suffered were clearly immense.

Three months before More became chancellor, his friend and fellow humanist Vives issued, in his *De concordia et discordia in humano genere* ('On concord and discord in humankind'), a warning to monarchs who fall short of the Platonic ideal of the philosopher-king. In a clear allusion to Henry VIII, Vives argued that just as a monarch averts his countenance from a courtier with whom he has fallen out, as if the courtier no longer existed, God may well reject that monarch in the same manner when he meets his maker.[58] And Vives argued that the 'Defender of the Faith' should be exposed if in promoting war he is not behaving as a Christian, since Plato and Seneca had not hesitated to instruct *their* rulers. Christians should dare to offend, even at the price of martyrdom, just as Socrates and Christ had done. Although More – the 'Christian Socrates', as his biographer Harpsfield called him (199) – chose indirection and even silence to avoid open rebellion against Henry VIII in the hope of continuing to influence policy, his public career was yet lived according to these principles.

FURTHER READING

Among modern biographies of More, three of the most accessible which deal with his public career are T. E. Bridgett's *Life and Writings of Blessed Thomas More*, 3rd edn (London: Burns, Oates & Washbourne, 1924), Richard Marius's revisionist *Thomas More* and Peter Ackroyd's *Life of Thomas More*. Readers must navigate the difficult waters of confessional bias that swirl around the treatment of More's public career not only in the earliest lives, by William Roper, Nicholas Harpsfield, Thomas Stapleton and More's great-grandson Cresacre More, but also in two popular and influential modern ones, R. W. Chambers's *Thomas More* and E. E. Reynolds's *The Field Is Won*. John Guy's brief, excellent *Thomas More* not only covers More's career but lays out the scholarly debates regarding More's political motivations, activities, relationships and reputation as 'hard man' or 'soft man'. Also essential are Guy's *The Public Career of Sir Thomas More* and his double biography *A Daughter's Love: Thomas & Margaret More*. William Nelson's 'Thomas More, grammarian and orator', in *EA* 150–60, originally published in 1943, is a pioneering study of the importance to More's career of his humanist education.

Robert P. Adams, *The Better Part of Valor: More, Erasmus, Colet, and Vives on Humanism, War, and Peace, 1496–1535* (Seattle:

University of Washington Press, 1962), provides the humanist context for More's ideas on war and peace. Guy's 'The rhetoric of counsel in early modern England', in Dale Hoak, ed., *Tudor Political Culture* (Cambridge University Press, 1995), 292–310, and his 'Tudor monarchy and its critiques', in John Guy, ed., *The Tudor Monarchy* (London: Arnold, 1997), 78–109, are important discussions of Tudor conceptions of counsel and monarchy. For the relationship of humanism to early modern political service, see Quentin Skinner, 'Political philosophy', in Charles B. Schmitt *et al.*, eds., *The Cambridge History of Renaissance Philosophy* (Cambridge University Press, 1988), 389–452. For more information regarding the European and English political context, see Glenn Richardson, *Renaissance Monarchy: The Reigns of Henry VIII, Francis I and Charles V* (London: Arnold, 2002).

Notes

1. By 1795 the original stone had been replaced and the epitaph modified, with More no longer identified as a troubler of heretics. See Guy, *A Daughter's Love*, 313, and cf. below, 105.
2. For More's schooling and early years, see above, 8–12 and 25–6.
3. On training in the inns, see J. H. Baker, *The Third University of England: The Inns of Court and the Common-Law Tradition* (London: Selden Society, 1990), 12–22; Eric Ives, *The Common Lawyers of Pre-Reformation England: Thomas Kebell: A Case Study* (Cambridge University Press, 1983), *passim*; Ackroyd, *Life of More*, 50–61.
4. Richard J. Schoeck, 'Thomas More and Lincoln's Inn revels', *Philological Quarterly* 29 (1950), 426–30.
5. Guy, *Thomas More*, 27–41.
6. On this phase of More's life see Guy, *Thomas More*, 23–9; see also above, 15–16, 26–9.
7. See Quentin Skinner, *Reason and Rhetoric in the Philosophy of Hobbes* (Cambridge University Press, 1996), 66–110. The present chapter expands William Nelson's short but useful discussion of More's humanist training as crucial to a career at court: 'Thomas More, grammarian and orator', *EA* 150–60.
8. The development of More's legal and political career is traced in Guy, *The Public Career of Sir Thomas More*.
9. G. D. Ramsay, 'A saint in the City: Thomas More at Mercers' Hall, London', *English Historical Review* 97 (1982), 269–88; Guy, *A Daughter's Love*, 27–9; Ackroyd, *Life of More*, 122–4.
10. According to Roper (199), More had previously been a member of the parliament of 1504, and Roper tells a colourful story of his provoking the wrath of Henry VII by frustrating the avaricious king's demand for an exorbitant tax. None of this is independently corroborated, but in support of Roper see Guy, *Thomas More*, 43–4.

11. Ibid., 45.
12. For background to Henry's early military adventures and failures, see J. J. Scarisbrick, *Henry VIII* (London: Eyre & Spottiswoode, 1968), 21–31.
13. On Tunstall, whom More greatly admired, see D. G. Newcombe's account, *ODNB* 55:551–5.
14. Guy, *Public Career*, 26.
15. Guy, *A Daughter's Love*, 49–51, 286–7.
16. Quentin Skinner, 'Thomas More's *Utopia* and the virtue of true nobility', in *Visions of Politics*, 3 vols. (Cambridge University Press, 2002), 2:213–44. For a radically different interpretation of More's attitude on this matter – at least as embodied in *Utopia* – see Eric Nelson, 'Greek nonsense in More's *Utopia*', ch. 1 of Nelson's *The Greek Tradition in Republican Thought* (Cambridge University Press, 2004), 19–48.
17. Cathy Curtis, '"The best state of the commonwealth": Thomas More and Quentin Skinner', in Annabel Brett *et al.*, eds., *Rethinking the Foundations of Modern Political Thought* (Cambridge University Press, 2006), 93–112, at 102–6.
18. Published as 'Thomas More, councillor', in R. S. Sylvester, ed., *St. Thomas More: Action and Contemplation* (New Haven: Yale University Press, 1972), 87–122; see 87–91.
19. I intend to publish a detailed study of this matter. On the treaty, see Garrett Mattingly, 'An early non-aggression pact', *Journal of Modern History* 10 (1938), 1–30, and Nicholas Craft, 'The 1518 Treaty of London and early modern approaches to international relations', MA thesis, University of Melbourne, 2006; and on the development of a peace discourse by More, Pace and Tunstall in this context, see Catherine Curtis, 'The social and political thought of Juan Luis Vives: concord and counsel in the Christian republic', in Charles Fantazzi, ed., *A Companion to Juan Luis Vives* (Leiden: Brill, 2008), 113–76, esp. 116–23.
20. For these and other duties mentioned in this paragraph, see Ackroyd, *Life of More*, 199–203.
21. Joycelyne G. Russell, *The Field of Cloth of Gold: Men and Manners in 1520* (London: Routledge & Kegan Paul, 1969), 175–6.
22. See John Headley's Introduction to *CW* 5, 799–800 and n. 6.
23. Marius, *Thomas More*, 202; G. R. Elton, *Studies in Tudor and Stuart Politics and Government*, 4 vols. (Cambridge: Cambridge University Press, 1974–92), 1:134.
24. Ackroyd, *Life of More*, 215–16.
25. Marius, *Thomas More*, 204.
26. Chambers, *Thomas More*, 206–8.
27. For a detailed account of More's anti-Lutheran activities, see below, 95–112.
28. Edward Hall, *Henry VIII*, introduction by Charles Whibley, 2 vols. (London: T. C. & E. C. Jack, 1904), 1:279. (Whibley reprints the section on Henry VIII from Hall's chronicle history, *The Union of the Two Noble and Illustre Families of Lancaster and York*, originally published in 1548.)

29. For the speech's significance, see John Neale, 'The Commons' privilege of free speech in parliament', repr. E. B. Fryde and E. Miller, eds., *Historical Studies of the English Parliament*, 2 vols. (Cambridge University Press, 1970), 2:147–76; J. S. Roskell, *The Commons and their Speakers in English Parliaments 1376–1523* (Manchester University Press, 1965), 324–32.

30. John Guy, 'Wolsey and the parliament of 1523', in Claire Cross *et al.*, eds., *Law and Government under the Tudors: Essays Presented to Sir Geoffrey Elton* (Cambridge University Press, 2002), 1–18.

31. Peter Gywn, *The King's Cardinal: The Rise and Fall of Thomas Wolsey* (London: Barrie & Jenkins, 1990), 552–5.

32. Ben Lowe, *Imagining Peace: A History of Early English Pacifist Ideas, 1340–1560* (University Park: Pennsylvania State University Press, 1997), 179.

33. On More's duties as chancellor see Guy, *Public Career*, 27–9.

34. The reference to war dates this famous remark to the period between autumn 1524 (when More moved to his new Chelsea estate) and August 1525 (England's truce with France).

35. Chambers, *Thomas More*, 287–90.

36. For contemporary corroboration of Roper's view of More's personality by Erasmus and the Venetian and Spanish ambassadors to England, see, respectively, *CWE* 7:16–25, *CSPV* 2, no. 1010, and *LP* 5, no. 120. On Henry's personality and way of conducting himself, see Eric Ives, 'Henry VIII: the political perspective', in Diarmaid MacCulloch, ed., *The Reign of Henry VIII: Politics, Policy and Piety* (London: Macmillan, 1995), 13–34, esp. 31–4, and J. Christopher Warner, *Henry VIII's Divorce: Literature and the Politics of the Printing Press* (Woodbridge, Suffolk: Boydell, 1998), 13–16.

37. Glenn Richardson, 'Eternal peace, occasional war: Anglo-French relations under Henry VIII', in Susan Doran and Glenn Richardson, eds., *Tudor England and Its Neighbours* (Basingstoke: Palgrave Macmillan, 2005), 44–73, at 48–52.

38. On More's heavy involvement during this period in the campaign against Lutheranism, which encompassed not only polemical writing but personal engagement in the detection and prosecution of heretics, see below, 98–106.

39. John Guy, 'Wolsey and the Tudor polity', in S. J. Gunn and P. G. Lindley, eds., *Cardinal Wolsey: Church, State and Art* (Cambridge University Press, 1991), 54–75. See also Gunn, 'Wolsey's foreign policy and the domestic crisis of 1527–8', in the same volume, 149–77.

40. Curtis, 'The social and political thought of Juan Luis Vives', 130–2.

41. William Rockett, 'Wolsey, More, and the unity of Christendom', *Sixteenth Century Journal* 35 (2004), 133–51.

42. Gwyn, *The King's Cardinal*, 583–98; G. W. Bernard, 'The fall of Wolsey reconsidered', *Journal of British Studies* 35 (1996), 277–310.

43. Eric Ives, 'The fall of Wolsey', in Gunn and Lindley, *Cardinal Wolsey*, 286–315.

44. Guy, *Thomas More*, 140, citing PRO C 54/398 (no. 18).
45. See Guy, *Public Career*, 141–51, for more detail on the various court groupings.
46. See Richard Rex, *Henry VIII and the English Reformation*, 2nd edn (Basingstoke: Palgrave Macmillan, 2006), 30–1, 35–6, 38–42; Guy, *A Daughter's Love*, 189–90, 206–14.
47. Chambers, *Thomas More*, 236–40; Guy, 'Thomas More as successor to Wolsey', *Thought: Fordham University Quarterly* 52 (1977), 275–92.
48. Warner, *Henry VIII's Divorce*, 1–25.
49. Various partial accounts survive: see Hall, *Henry VIII*, 2:163–4; *CSPSp* 4, Part 1, no. 211; Guy, *Public Career*, 111–15.
50. Hall, *Henry VIII*, 2:164.
51. S. J. Gunn and P. G. Lindley, 'Introduction', in *Cardinal Wolsey*, 1–53, esp. 4–11, 18–21.
52. See Guy, *Thomas More*, 126–45; *Public Career*, 50–79; and *The Cardinal's Court: The Impact of Thomas Wolsey in Star Chamber* (Hassocks: Harvester, 1977), 40–5, 109. See also Ackroyd, *Life of More*, 285–90.
53. See Gerard B. Wegemer, *Thomas More on Statesmanship* (Washington: Catholic University of America Press, 1996), 67–74.
54. Guy, *Public Career*, 127–40; Marius, *Thomas More*, 372, 376, 381–5.
55. Marius, *Thomas More*, 383–5.
56. Hall, *Henry VIII*, 2:185.
57. Warner, *Henry VIII's Divorce*, 15–16.
58. Joannis Ludovici Vivis Valentini, *Opera omnia*, ed. Gregorio Mayans y Siscar, 8 vols. (Valencia: Montfort, 1782–90; repr. London: Gregg, 1964), 5:400.

5 Thomas More and the heretics: statesman or fanatic?

RICHARD REX

Thomas More's dealings with heresy and heretics have been the most bitterly contested aspects of his career. Even within his lifetime they aroused controversy, as his own *Apology* demonstrates. John Foxe's famous 'Book of Martyrs' cast More, along with the Tudor bishops, among the deepest-dyed villains, and the stories it told, true and false alike, have been handed down and continue to be supplemented and embellished to this day. Thus Brian Moynahan has bizarrely proposed that More, from his confinement in the Tower of London, masterminded the taking of William Tyndale in Antwerp; while the numbers of heretics executed during More's chancellorship were recently inflated from half a dozen to 'a few hundred' by one of England's leading journalists; and in 2009 a novelist won the Man Booker Prize for Fiction (appropriately enough) with a story in which she has More admit in conversation the allegations of torture he denied in print.[1] Which all goes to show that, while there have always been admirers for whom Thomas More was a 'man for all seasons', there have always been critics for whom he was a fanatical persecutor.

More's Tudor critics mostly censured him not for persecution as such but for persecuting the wrong people, namely Protestants. Today's critics censure him rather for the fact of the persecution, and for his emotional intensity in going about it, than for his particular choice of victims. The contrast that mattered for John Foxe was between papist and Protestant; the contrast that matters more today is between the apostle of tolerance some detect in the author of *Utopia* and the inquisitorial magistrate who became Henry VIII's lord chancellor. The benefits of religious toleration and the fruitlessness of protracted religious polemics are now so self-evident that even sympathetic historians are troubled by More's pursuit of heresy. One of the greatest living authorities on More once went so far, in assessing the tension between the author of *Utopia* and the antagonist of heresy, as to talk of a 'schizophrenia' too great to permit of 'final reconciliation' given the 'available historical evidence'.[2]

The aim of this essay is to see whether it is possible to find a properly historical reconciliation of that tension. After outlining the religious situation in which More found himself, it will proceed in three stages. First, we need to consider More's attitude to heresy as developed in his extensive polemical writings. By this I mean not merely his views on the particular heresies he faced, namely the doctrines of Protestantism as they developed in the 1520s (which we might summarize as the undermining of traditional notions of Church and sacraments through the application of a new understanding of scripture and faith), but also his views on the formal nature and implications of heresy.

Second, we need to consider his actual dealings with heretics. The point here is not to split hairs over precisely how many heretics were condemned to be burned in England during his chancellorship – the total is generally agreed to be six, More himself being actively engaged in the proceedings (as opposed to merely issuing the writs) in the cases of three. Rather, the point is to show that More was far more active in the repression of heresy than we might suspect from a historiography obsessed with the balance sheet of victimhood. This was not merely an incidental part of his life and work.

Finally, we need to set More's attitudes and actions in the context not of twenty-first-century Western politics but of the English and European politics of the 1520s and 1530s, in order to ascertain whether they show us, to borrow Jasper Ridley's contrast, a statesman or a fanatic.[3] My contention will be that the data do indeed show us a statesman, not a fanatic: a statesman of conscience, and a statesman of extraordinary insight and foresight.

PROLOGUE: HERESY IN ENGLAND

An undercurrent of heretical dissent from the dominant orthodoxies of the Catholic Church had run through English history since the late fourteenth century, when a loose-knit movement inspired by the teachings of John Wycliffe had spread out from Oxford. These teachings anticipated elements of Protestantism by challenging ecclesiastical, and especially papal, authority; by promoting vernacular scripture; and by discrediting many aspects of priestly mediation and popular piety. Royal and ecclesiastical authorities had combined to repress 'Lollardy', as it became known, but they did not succeed in eliminating it, even though it survived only among a small minority in a few scattered areas. The reaction against Lollardy bequeathed three important legacies: the death penalty for heresy, introduced by the statute *de heretico comburendo* ('for burning heretics') in 1401; a profound suspicion of the English Bible, because followers of Wycliffe had produced a translation to help spread their teachings; and an assumed association between heresy and sedition, arising from the outbreak of the Peasants' Revolt (1381) at just the time when Wycliffe's teachings were attracting both official disapproval and a degree of popular support.

The reign of Henry VII had seen renewed persecution of Lollardy, which some historians have seen as reflecting a revival of the heresy, but which others, more plausibly, interpret as reflecting the first Tudor's aspirations to control and legitimation. This persecution intensified still further in the reign of Henry VIII, largely because the English bench of bishops was increasingly preoccupied with ecclesiastical reform, but perhaps also because the young king modelled himself on Henry V, who had put the resources of the crown firmly behind the fight against Lollardy. In any case, there were both more burnings and more recantations under the first two Tudors than under their fifteenth-century predecessors. Thomas More would certainly have been aware of the public executions of or recantations by Lollards that took place in London in the late fifteenth and early sixteenth centuries. And a throwaway remark in the *Apology* (*CW* 9:126) might indicate that he had once talked with Richard Hunne, the subject of the most notorious heresy process in England in the 1510s, although, notwithstanding his own extensive discussion of that case, he had certainly taken no part in it at the time. Elsewhere in the *Apology*, he recalls a mass recantation by a dozen or more heretics in Lincoln diocese that was much discussed at court (*CW* 9:115, alluding to John Longland's purge against heretics in the Chilterns in 1521).

It was in 1521 that More first became actively involved in proceedings against heresy. The target, however, was not Lollardy but the new teachings of Martin Luther, which became the centre of attention thanks to Henry VIII's decision to refute Luther's *Babylonian Captivity of the Church*. More was called in to help with Henry's *Assertion of the Seven Sacraments*, and it may be no mere coincidence that his first major preferment in royal service – knighthood and appointment as undertreasurer of the exchequer – came in the selfsame month (May 1521) that Luther's books were burned in London and Henry's refutation was announced to the public.[4] At this early stage there were some signs in the universities of sympathy with Luther's ideas, but it was not until the mid-1520s that these ideas threatened a wider impact in England, at a moment when, for the English regime, their seditious potential was made manifest in the Peasants' War, the great uprising that ravaged southern and central Germany in the first half of 1525. What most worried the English authorities was first the rumour and then the arrival of a freelance English translation of the New Testament. This translation, the work of William Tyndale, was heavily influenced by Luther's German version. Printed abroad, Tyndale's New Testament was smuggled into the country from 1526 and enjoyed instant success, despite the efforts of the bishops to suppress it. In the furore over its arrival, the authorities uncovered a network that distributed forbidden books (the works of Luther, Zwingli, Bugenhagen, Lambert and others) in London, Oxford and Cambridge. By the end of the decade investigations in England were turning up not only old Lollards but new Lutherans.

Thomas More was closely involved in the campaign against Lutheranism from the start, and regarded it as an integral part of the service he owed as an officeholder under the crown. However, the story of the early 'Protestant Reformation' in England rapidly became entangled with a very different story – the 'King's Great Matter', Henry VIII's six-year search (1527–33) for a divorce from his first wife, Catherine of Aragon, to enable him to marry the great love of his middle age, Anne Boleyn. Most of Luther's keenest English opponents were opposed to Henry's divorce, while England's evangelicals, such as Robert Barnes and Hugh Latimer, soon showed themselves enthusiastic in support (ignoring the lead of Luther and Tyndale, who both declared against Henry), not least because Anne herself was showing sympathy for their cause as early as 1528. In the kaleidoscopic politics of England in the early 1530s, arguments about theology became mixed up with arguments about the divorce and arguments about the status and behaviour of the clergy, as Henry's regime fomented anticlerical agitation in an effort to intimidate or discredit both the clergy and the papacy, which was increasingly overt in its refusal to grant Henry's petition for annulment of his marriage. Failing the death of one of the key figures in the affair, the eventual resolution was almost inevitable. Henry formally separated the realm and church of England from papal jurisdiction in order to enable his matrimonial difficulties to be sorted out at home. In the aftermath of the divorce, he was declared Supreme Head of the Church of England, and started to steer his church in a direction that would lead ultimately, although not in his lifetime, to a Protestant settlement. Thomas More, refusing to accept this dénouement, became in summer 1535 the most illustrious victim of Henry's Reformation.[5]

I

Not, of course, that he knew that. This essay was originally commissioned under the title 'Thomas More and the Reformation', but that title was abandoned on the realization that Thomas More never encountered 'the Reformation': history had not yet bestowed that appellation on the crisis in which he lived.[6] What More encountered, as he saw things, were heretics, and if we are to understand More rather than merely pass judgement on him, we must ascertain how he saw things. What were heretics? More himself provides a definition: 'all they that obstinately holde any selfe mynded opynyon, contrary to the doctryne that the comen knowen catholyke chyrche, techeth & holdeth for necessary to saluacyon' (*CW* 10:30). More's own cautiously trodden path to the scaffold illustrates one particular element he identified in the heretics of his day: egotism. Nothing could be more absurd, in his view, than to go willingly to death on account of a personal opinion.[7] It was precisely this, for him, that characterized the Protestants he condemned. Heresy was the preference of personal opinion over the consensus of the Church, a consensus providentially guaranteed by the Holy Spirit. He was well aware, of course, that Protestants claimed to ground themselves not on personal opinion but on the literal sense of scripture and on that alone. However, he argued, this was self-contradictory (in that scripture does not identify itself, but is identified by the Church), contrary to scripture (which itself affirms the authority of the Church), and contradicted by experience (in that those who appealed to scripture alone soon came to differ over almost every major theological topic).

Thomas More saw heresy as damaging in both the temporal and the spiritual order. Religion was in his view fundamental to social order: hence the attention given to religion in *Utopia*. Historically, he saw heresy as tending to foment civil disorder, and he appealed to the examples of Wycliffe in England, Huss in Bohemia and Luther in Germany to substantiate this claim (*CW* 8:29). Religious division, he felt, was intrinsically divisive of society, while Lutheranism was a particularly potent solvent of obedience and order. But it was not the case, as was argued by R. W. Chambers, the biographer and apologist who defined More's reputation for the mid-twentieth century, that

More's justification for the repression of heresy rested solely on its temporal effects.[8] The spiritual dimension of heresy was still more awful. As Brad Gregory has shown in his magnificent study of early modern martyrdom, *Salvation at Stake*, for serious Christians in the sixteenth century heresy was not just a matter of life and death; it was a matter of eternal life and unending death.[9] Heretics therefore took pride of place in the triad of criminals against which More set his face in his epitaph: 'thieves, murderers, heretics'.[10] Thieves robbed people of their goods; murderers robbed them of life; but heretics robbed them of their immortal soul. Finally, heresy constituted treason against God (*CW* 9:136). Thus, for More, 'Heresye of al crimes is the wurste' (*CW* 9:45). This was his theoretical basis for the repression of heresy by measures up to and including, in cases of obstinacy or relapse, the death penalty. Heresy was a legitimate subject for the intervention of Christian temporal jurisdictions. Like so many of his contemporaries, More saw Christian kings as sacral figures, 'speciall consecrate personys' (*CW* 9:50), with a divine calling to promote not only the temporal but also the spiritual welfare of their subjects. Henry VIII was, in the 1520s, the very model of such a king.

As we have seen, it was at Henry VIII's instigation that More first took an active interest in countering heresy. After helping with the *Assertion of the Seven Sacraments*, he was called on to defend his king against Luther's intemperate reply, the *Contra Henricum Regem Angliae* (Wittenberg, 1522). He probably had a hand in Henry's letter to the dukes of Saxony, appealing to them to deal appropriately with the troublesome friar, and his own *Responsio ad Lutherum* appeared over the *nom de plume* of Guilielmus Rosseus towards the end of 1523. When the great German Catholic polemicist Johannes Eck came to England in 1525, More met him at court, and gave him a copy, letting him in on the secret of its authorship (about which More did not boast, but which he did not take great pains to conceal – it was something of an open secret).[11] Martin Luther's unaccountable *démarche* of 1525, when he wrote an apologetic letter to the king because he had heard a rumour that Henry was becoming more receptive to 'the Gospel', provoked Henry to a stern reply in which, again, we can probably detect More's hand.[12] It was at much the same time that More drafted a response to an open letter from one of Luther's lieutenants, Johannes Bugenhagen, which had offered comfort to England's nascent evangelical community (*CW* 7:1–105). This response was not published at the time, perhaps because official attention in England turned towards a more pressing issue, the arrival and circulation of Tyndale's New Testament.

Growing concern with the impact of Tyndale's translation and the emergence of vernacular polemics led to the remarkable decision of the bishop of London, Cuthbert Tunstall, to license and thus in effect to commission More to own and read forbidden books for the purpose of refuting them in English (*Corr.* 386–8). The first fruits of this were seen in the *Dialogue Concerning Heresies* (1529), which is the subject of specific consideration elsewhere in this volume. The three main thrusts of this work, which appeared shortly before More's promotion to the chancellorship, were to defend practices relating to the cult of the saints that had been impugned by Thomas Bilney, to criticize Tyndale's New Testament as heretically tendentious, and to justify the English government's repression of heretics by any lawful means up to and including the death penalty. After this More turned to the popular sensation that had been made early in 1529 by Simon Fish's *Supplication of Beggars*, a pithy polemic against Catholic provision for the souls of the departed. More's *Supplication of Souls* lodged a lengthy counter-plea in defence of prayers for the dead on behalf of the souls in Purgatory. A powerful case has been made for the idea that More, whether as ghostwriter or prompter, was responsible for the *Dyaloge ... of these Lutheran faccyons* that appeared in 1531 over the name of William Barlow, who had at that point recanted the evangelical beliefs to which he would soon return.[13] Tyndale's *Answer unto Sir Thomas More's Dialogue* (1531) in its turn provoked the massive *Confutation of Tyndale's Answer*, which came out in two parts, the first early in 1532. The second part, which appeared late in 1533, also turned its attention to Robert Barnes, who in 1531 had addressed a *Supplicatyon* to Henry VIII.

In the meantime More put out a briefer and more accessible pamphlet, his *Apology* (1533), which took up a variety of charges that were being made against him in evangelical circles regarding his public actions against heretics in his capacity as chancellor. The elegance of this work was somewhat compromised by his decision to use it also to mount a defence of the English clergy against an attack from another quarter, the *Treatise concernynge the Diuision betwene the Spiritualtie and Temporaltie* (1532), an anonymous pamphlet (in fact by the common lawyer Christopher St German) that under a pretence of even-handedness lambasted the clergy of England for a range of moral and procedural failings, most especially an excessive readiness to detect heresy in harmless criticism and an undue rush to judgement in heresy cases. This in turn embroiled More in further controversy, although by now he had resigned the chancellorship and thus had time on his hands. St German reiterated and amplified his charges in dialogue form as *Salem and Bizance* (1533), against which More felt obliged to launch his *Debellacyon of Salem and Bizance* (1533). His last polemical salvos were fired against a target he found even more threatening: 'sacramentarian' heresy, denying the real presence of Jesus Christ in the consecrated elements of the Mass. His largely conventional but relatively learned arguments, centring on the scriptural narratives of the Last Supper and on the sixth chapter of the Gospel of John, read through the lenses of patristic interpretation and ecclesiastical definition, were developed in *A Letter ... Impugning the Erronyouse Wrytyng of John Fryth* and *The Answere to the Fyrst Parte of the Poysened Booke*. Although written and printed nearly a year apart, these books were released together late in 1533, More's last publications before confinement in the Tower of London turned his attention to his own fight for survival against Henry's regime and to the safeguarding of his immortal soul.

The lines of argument developed by More in his polemics are consistent to the point of repetitiveness. While the shorter texts concentrate on one or two topics, the longer works (*Responsio ad Lutherum*, *A Dialogue Concerning Heresies* and *The Confutation of Tyndale's Answer*) range across the field of Protestant theology but give exhaustive attention to its two foundations: justification by 'faith alone' and the appeal to 'scripture alone'. More's arguments were already becoming commonplaces, although he often sets them out with distinctive rhetorical skill and dialectical acuteness. Against faith alone he invokes the strong emphasis on charity in Paul's Epistles, the role ascribed to good works in the Epistle of James, and the many biblical texts that accord eternal rewards to good works, along with the almost complete undetectability of any such doctrine in the long patristic and medieval tradition. His response to the appeal to scripture alone focuses on the fundamental difficulty that the scriptures themselves did not specify which books should or should not be regarded as scriptures, as well as on the need for authoritative interpretation. For More, such interpretation can be delivered only by the Church, the 'knowen catholyke chyrche' as he later terms it (*CW* 8:275). The Church, indeed, bears ever more weight in his polemics, and the massive *Confutation* is to a large extent a series of reflections on the nature and authority of the visible Church as the divinely constituted and guaranteed vehicle of saving truth. From first to last, its argument is a *reductio ad absurdum*: namely, that Christ promised to send the Holy Spirit to guide the Church in all truth, and that if the teachings of the evangelicals were true, then Christ's promise, the guidance of the Spirit, and the Church must all have turned out to be false.

It has been suggested that More was ambivalent and evasive on the subject of the role of the papacy in the Church, but this is at best a half-truth.[14] In his polemics in the 1530s he steers clear of arguments about the papacy, explicitly because his argument with his evangelical opponents does not depend on the papacy but on the consensus of the Church, and no doubt also, but implicitly, because the political tensions then obtaining between Henry VIII and Clement VII made it wiser to do so. But his own position is made perfectly clear in the *Responsio ad Lutherum*, which affirms papal headship of the Church by divine right, referring his readers not only to John Fisher's extensive discussion of the subject in his *Assertionis lutheranae confutatio* but also to the conciliar declaration of papal headship that Fisher cited there.[15] It was to this same conciliar definition of papal headship that More was to appeal in his final speech at his trial, in 1535 (Roper 249–50).

The polemical writings of Thomas More display both the virtues and the vices of the genre. At their worst, they trade coarse insults or cheap debating points, as when he picks up an opponent's claim that monastic life is contrary to the Gospel and replies that, if so, the Gospel must stand for self-indulgence (*CW* 7:53). At their best they are witty and sharp. Their rhetorical influence would bear further investigation. More probably did more than anyone else to make 'Catholic' current in its modern sense, for 'catholyke chyrche', 'catholyque fayth, 'catholyke folke', and the substantive 'catholykes' crowd his pages in the 1530s. He may have coined the phrase 'good catholyke men' (*CW* 9:160), which was to become the watchword of Mary I's regime. In arguing about patristic testimony, More was no better placed than anyone else at that time to do justice to the rich variety of, for example, patristic teaching about the Eucharist. It is generally agreed that in his extensive discussions of two Tudor causes célèbres – the cases of the death of Richard Hunne and the recantation of Thomas Bilney – he was at best prejudiced.[16] The harsher judgement that he knowingly misrepresented, distorted or falsified the evidence in these cases is excessive.[17] It seems improbable that a man who showed so marked a revulsion from lying and perjury would act in such a way, whereas it is easy to see how a man's sympathies and prejudices might determine his choice of whom to believe in such hotly contested controversies.

In recent demonizations of More, particular weight has been placed on his insistent invocation of Luther's 'fylthy lechery' (CW 8:51), that is, his marriage to the former nun Katharina von Bora. It is indeed true that More returns again and again in his polemics, most insistently (over a hundred times) in *The Confutation of Tyndale's Answer*, to the idea that Luther taught by word and deed that 'a lewd friar may wed a nun'. The viciousness of Luther's public renunciation of his vowed virginity was doubled by his coupling with a nun, which for More made his act both bestial and incestuous. Twentieth-century scholars who had grown up amid the mythology of psychoanalysis found it irresistibly easy to uncover layers of hidden meaning in his coarse and relentless sarcasm on the subject of Luther's marriage. The man who had tested his own vocation to the religious life but had found celibacy beyond him, so the argument goes, poured out prurient invective against the man who had it all – Luther, sexually fulfilled yet a duly ordained minister of God's Word. A post-Freudian world could hardly ask for better material, and the psychohistorical interpretation of More was, somewhat uncharacteristically, pioneered by Geoffrey Elton and then, less surprisingly, taken up by Richard Marius in his influential biography.[18] It is not surprising that, in a cultural milieu demonstrably obsessed with sex, these fanciful speculations have become received wisdom.[19]

Judgements about other people's sexual psychology and pathology are cheap to issue, but whether twentieth-century notions of sexuality and sexual identity have anything to contribute to understanding an early sixteenth-century Englishman is, to say the least, questionable. What is clear is that More's allusions to Luther's sexual history are far from being the sort of psychological tic that some critics imply. Their theory rests on the dangerous assumption that a wordsmith as sensitive and masterful as More would at any point in a written work not be in overall control of what he was setting down. On this matter, at least, More is fully aware of what he is doing, for he knowingly likens himself at one point to 'a blynde harpar that harpeth all on one stringe'. The wedding of the friar and the nun is, in short, his 'rude refrain'.[20] It is no less a rhetorical device than Elton's decision to label More a 'sex maniac'.[21] For there is deliberate humour in the way in which More turns Luther's marriage into an alleged doctrinal principle that then becomes a rhetorical example in arguments of every kind against the dogmatics and hermeneutics of his opponents. The idea of friars in bed with nuns was as funny then as it is now, and More makes it a running joke. But he also seeks to take advantage of the taboo which attached then (but not now) to such sexual relations. Nevertheless, he is not obsessive: he can discuss Luther without discussing lechery, and lechery without Luther (or at least, he can rely on the reader to make the connection). If he was venting obsession or subconscious frustration, one would expect the subject to surface everywhere, whereas it is entirely absent from the letter to Frith and appears only a few times in the *Answer to a Poisoned Book* (*CW* 11:60, 106, 109, 128, 215). When he does harp on Luther's sexuality, he is not betraying any inner demons: he is implementing a considered strategy for discrediting Luther and his teachings, offering an explicit *tu quoque* to the charges of sexual vice that the Reformers levelled against Catholic clergy (*CW* 8:836). Thus an extended tirade against Luther's marriage forms a substantial coda to the first book of *The Confutation of Tyndale's Answer* (*CW* 8:140–2). The *Confutation* is monumental and, truth be told, somewhat tedious, and the recurrent asides on 'Luther and hys lemman' (8:262) do something to vary the monotony. But they also remind the reader that, from the perspective of traditional Catholicism, Luther cannot possibly be a moral leader and should properly be a figure of fun.

Modern critics often censure More for the intemperance and bitterness of his writings against heretics, and as a result the impression is given that his prose is an unbroken stream of vicious invective and vile scatology. The most widely cited proof text is his pithy epitaph on England's Protestant protomartyr, Thomas Hitton, 'the devil's stinking martyr' (*CW* 8:17, 'dyuyls stynkyng martyr' now well on its way to becoming More's best-known phrase). But equal weight is attached to the passage in the defence of Henry VIII in which More, under the pseudonym 'Rosseus', rounds on Luther and offers to 'throw back into your paternity's shitty mouth, truly the shit-pool of all shit, all the muck and shit which your damnable rottenness has vomited up'.[22] The spinsterish delicacy with which modern scholars admonish More's unbridled language rings somewhat incongruously in an age in which both popular and elite culture have, within living memory, abandoned so many verbal taboos, and in which unwelcome arguments and information are routinely dismissed as 'crap'. Perhaps the imaginative gap between More's attitude to heresy and ours might be bridged by the realization that he refers to heretics in the way that today passionate journalists or comedians refer to drug-dealers, child-molesters and suicide-bombers.

Modern censoriousness, however, has respected neither the text nor the context. The impression that More's polemics are brimming over with this sort of thing is entirely misleading. His *Responsio ad Lutherum* delves into the dungheap on perhaps a dozen occasions, two or three of them spectacularly revolting. But this is not typical of a text which amounts to about 350 pages in its critical edition.[23] Nor is it typical of his polemics in general, which otherwise rarely if ever descend to this level. Nor does More write in this vein under his own name. In this case, moreover, there is a specific reason given for the language deployed, which is entirely under authorial control. In offering to 'bespatter his English majesty with muck and shit' (*CW* 5:311), Luther had written something that, anywhere in Henry's jurisdiction, would on its own have earned him anything from physical mutilation to a slow and painful death. More's decision to respond in kind was precisely that – a decision – not some reflex of the 'real' Thomas More. He tells us so himself in acknowledging that you cannot touch pitch without being defiled and that he is ashamed of having to answer in kind. The necessity is defined as that of cleaning out 'the fellow's shit-filled mouth', but it is at least as much the necessity of showing that you cannot insult Henry VIII with impunity (*CW* 5:311–13).

Certainly More is not restrained by modern canons of academic politeness. But neither were his contemporaries. The Reformers had marked out the ground on which the contest was fought, with the definition of the pope as, personally, Antichrist in the centre circle. Their pamphlets offered a rich pageant of obloquy and obscenity featuring Catholic clergy, monks, nuns and theologians, along with their lay accomplices or dupes. Even today some of the cartoons printed in Germany in the sixteenth century have a genuine capacity to shock. The carnivalesque conceptual iconoclasm waged against Catholicism in print by the Protestant Reformers was a potent weapon in early modern culture, and the historian should be surprised, if anything, that their opponents did not do more to respond in kind. Impassioned invective often achieves more than reasoned discourse.

In reflecting on and justifying the burning of heretics, More makes no secret of the fact that he thinks those burned for Protestantism are likely to graduate to the fiercer fires of Hell (*CW* 8:590). He voices nothing but contempt for the readiness of heretics to take advantage of the English custom by which the full penalty of the law could be avoided, for a first offence, by formal abjuration. He reckoned perjury among the most heinous of crimes, and judged that its prevalence among heretics showed how defection from the true faith inexorably betrayed them into wider kinds of faithlessness and dishonesty: 'For when they fall to a false fayth in herte / theyr wordes can not be trew' (*CW* 9:127). In the early 1530s he was unconvinced by Christopher St German's claim that England's heresy laws were being inappropriately and excessively used by the clergy for their own ends, a claim he reckoned at best naive and at worst malicious. For More, the key argument in St German's *Salem and Bizance* was that, under the heresy laws, an innocent person might occasionally be condemned. In principle he regarded the argument as of little force, in that the risk of convicting someone innocent was common to the enforcement of all laws (*CW* 10:220–1). In practice, he took consolation in the fact that a first offence could be expiated by means of abjuration and penance, which, in the case of an innocent person wrongly convicted, offered the ultimate protection (*CW* 10:70). But the obstinate or relapsed, he felt, were 'well and worthely burned' (*CW* 9:113).

More's attitude to heretics is described in most recent literature as one of undiluted hatred, summed up in the epitaph he drafted for himself, in which he is taken to have declared his pride in having been 'hateful' to them. But, as More would have been the first to point out, translation is important: the *molestum* ('irksome') of his draft epitaph is not quite the same as the *odi* ('I hate') of his covering letter to Erasmus (*EE* 10:260–1; *SL* 180–1). The language of personal hatred does appear in his writings from time to time, most notably in the flaring anger of 'the devil's stinking martyr' (who, to More's evident annoyance, had disproved his thesis that heretics always availed themselves of escape by perjury if they could). But there is no justification for taking these scattered words as the 'real' More or 'almost the essence of the man'.[24] There is at least as much of the 'real' More in his personal efforts to win men back by argument, in his willingness to believe in Bilney's final recantation and consequent salvation, and in the heartfelt prayers for conversion and reconciliation which he offers:

> From whiche our lorde geue theym grace trewely to tourne in tyme, so that we and they to gether in one catholyque chyrche, knytte vnto god to gether in one catholyque fayth, fayth I saye, not fayth alone as they do, but acompanyed wyth good hope, and wyth her chyefe syster well workynge charytie, ... we maye be wyth them in theyr holy felyshyppe, incorporate in Chryste in hys eternall glorye Amen.
> (*CW* 11:223)

II

Notwithstanding such aspirations, six Englishmen were burned alive for heresy in the two and a half years of Thomas More's chancellorship, and More himself took a personal interest in three of those cases (Bainham, Bayfield and Tewkesbury), the three that arose in London.

However, that is not the whole story. More had been busy in proceedings against heretics for years before becoming lord chancellor. As chancellor of the duchy of Lancaster he led the raids on the Steelyard, the premises of the Hanseatic merchants, that turned up numbers of forbidden books over the Christmas season in 1525–6. He was present at the legatine court that proceeded against Thomas Bilney and Thomas Arthur in late 1527. His *Dialogue Concerning Heresies* shows that in 1528 he was also present at the interrogations of Dr Thomas Farman, the rector of All Saints Honey Lane, the man behind the circulation of prohibited books in London, Oxford and Cambridge in the mid-1520s (and it is hard to imagine that a man so fond of talking was present without taking part). More's eyewitness account of Farman's answers is the only record we have of this interrogation, and it shows that the suspect had thoroughly assimilated the Lutheran doctrine of justification by faith alone (*CW* 6:379–99). A passing reference in the *Apology* suggests that More was also involved in the uncovering of the Lollard cell in Essex that same year, which had probably come to light thanks to the investigations into the trade in forbidden books (*CW* 9:157).

More's duties as lord chancellor, far from distracting him from the fight against heresy, drew him into it still more intensely. Indeed, Peter Kaufman has recently put forward a strong case for concluding that his chief motive in accepting the office was 'to assyst the ordynaryes' in their judicial defence of the faith.[25] In his official capacity More presided over three Star Chamber cases relating to possession of forbidden books, most notably those in October 1530 against four Londoners. One of them, John Petyt, was an MP, and More had personally gone to arrest him.[26] He also turned out in person to pick up George Constantine, who subsequently escaped from detention in More's Chelsea home. Elsewhere More tells us that he had the Cambridge bookseller, Siger Nicolson, in his custody at Chelsea for a few days (*CW* 9:119).[27] He assisted at the interrogation of John Frith in the bishop of Winchester's palace in Southwark (*CW* 9:124–5). Thomas More, as lord chancellor, was in effect the first port of call for those arrested in London on suspicion of heresy, and he took the initial decisions about whether to release them, where to imprison them, or to which bishop to send them. He can be connected with police or judicial proceedings against around forty suspected or convicted heretics in the years 1527–33.

The *Confutation of Tyndale's Answer* shows that More kept Barnes under surveillance for almost every moment of his visit to England under royal safe-conduct in 1531. More is fond of letting slip in his writings how much he knows of the aliases and disguises under which heretics operated.[28] (He insinuates that the mere use of aliases is sinister and discreditable, although he had himself employed a pseudonym to write against Luther.) This kind of information does not come cheap or easy. It looks as though the network of informants that More built up during his time as undersheriff of London was something he employed throughout his public career. He was above all a Londoner, and he knew the city inside out. He knew what was going on, who was who, and where they were. We can see the importance of his London police role in a story that does not come to us from More himself, and does not concern heresy. In 1524 a servant of the imperial ambassador Louis de Praet was found leaving the city of London by night in suspicious circumstances. It was to More that the man was taken, and it was More who first read the compromising letter he was carrying, in which the ambassador unburdened himself of sundry unguarded observations on Cardinal Wolsey (*SP* 6:391).

When we add in the long hours spent, mostly by night, in his study at Chelsea writing against Tyndale, Barnes and Frith, we can safely conclude that heresy was the single most time-consuming issue Thomas More dealt with in his chancellorship, and probably in the whole of the last ten years of his life.

The degree of his commitment accounts for the particular sharpness with which he reacted when not only his personal involvement in heresy cases but also the nature and exercise of English heresy jurisdiction were called into question in the early 1530s. The personal accusations of the torture or maltreatment of suspects, mostly rumours but occasionally committed to writing or print, were rebutted by More with decisive indignation in his *Apology* (*CW* 9:116–28).[29] There is a delightful irony in the readiness with which those who, on the basis of unsupported allegations, convict More of maltreating prisoners then censure him for rushing to judgement against heretics and for his prejudice in the cases of Hunne and Bilney. The personal attacks made on More at the time need to be read in context. George Constantine's accusations of torture (which More flatly denied) sound suspiciously like excuses for his talkativeness under interrogation.[30] At a more general level, the persecution of heretics, which More implemented with such zeal, was without doubt the policy of the king. But criticism of royal policy was difficult to imagine as well as risky to express, and Tudor subjects therefore tended to blame their grievances on ministers and councillors. It was perfectly natural that criticism in this area should be directed at More, the leading agent of royal policy, and after his resignation and fall from favour it was equally natural for those

appealing for the redress of their grievances to seek to align the regime
with their cause by blaming More. Thomas More was as much a
whipping-boy for the grievances of heretics in the early 1530s as Cromwell was for conservatives in the middle of the decade.

Let us be clear. Thomas More's involvement in proceedings against
heresy was most unusual for a layman. The clergy did not normally
welcome lay intrusion into such matters. Indeed, an unusual degree of
interest in theology might very well embroil a layman in suspicion of
heresy! But More was a very unusual layman, undoubtedly the
cleverest and most learned Englishman of his generation, a man of
impeccable orthodoxy and European reputation, the perfect choice for
the shrewd bishops, led by his friend and diocesan, Cuthbert Tunstall,
to select as the lay face of the campaign against Protestantism.

III

While More's role as a lay theological polemicist was almost
unprecedented, his personal involvement in the physical repression
of heresy, though unusual in degree and intensity, was in kind entirely
legitimate and conventional. For it was first and foremost a function
of his public position. Since the time of Henry V, the oath sworn by
every man who took office under the crown had included an undertaking to assist the Church in the struggle against heresy.[31] More was
not the man to take an oath lightly, and in his *Apology* he reminds his
readers that the 'great officers of the realme' were 'solempnely sworen
to represse heretykes' (*CW* 9:162). He would doubtless have considered that, as the head of the judiciary, he was under a heavier
obligation than anyone else to fulfil that oath.

It is unquestionably true that Thomas More took a far closer interest in the repression of heresy than most of his contemporaries, and
that this was doubly remarkable in a layman: for heresy was very much
a clerical concern. It is easy, therefore, for hostile critics such as Jasper
Ridley, David Daniell and Brian Moynahan to dismiss More as an
unbalanced fanatic, a man whose obsession with doctrinal purity over-
whelmed his humanity and swept him into cruelty and irrational
hatred.[32] It is just as easy to mark the contrast between the tolerance
of More's Utopia and the intolerance of More's England. It is therefore
tempting to endorse John Guy's judgement about More's schizophrenia.

Yet the modern problem with More's pursuit of heresy is precisely
that – a modern problem. The suggestion that More is a victim of
'schizophrenia' precisely fails to take full account of the 'available

historical evidence'. Thomas More understood human societies much better than most people then or now. He understood Utopia as a place that, perfectly rationally, realized that it was not in possession of reliable religious truth. It did not persecute heresy because, quite literally, it had no reason to. It knew it had no orthodoxy, and therefore, perfectly rationally, it permitted reasonable discussion and doubt about religious possibilities, including, when it arrived, Christianity.[33]

More's own society, however, for all its faults, was confident in its possession of religious truth. For modern readers, that confidence is in itself one of that society's most egregious faults. But nobody in that society could think that such confidence was, in principle, inappropriate, however much, from time to time, different religious groups might consider that it was, in practice, misplaced. The tolerance of even the most tolerant of that era was only relative. John Foxe argued against executing dissidents, even Catholic priests.[34] But he had no problem with fines, exile, censorship, imprisonment or discrimination. There is a lot more to toleration than not killing people, although that is a good start.

The key to reconciling the More of Utopia and the More of Chelsea is to recognize, as Guy himself does in his most recent book on More, a magnificent dual biography of Thomas and his favourite daughter, Meg, that in discussing this most balanced and rational of men, the concept of schizophrenia is simply a category mistake.[35] You might think him wrong, but you cannot think him mad. Next, it is vital to realize that Chambers, notwithstanding the special pleading that Marius rightly exposed, was on to something when he emphasized the importance of notions of sedition and social breakdown in More's response to Protestantism. What Chambers realized, and what Marius does not exactly ignore but at times fails fully to appreciate, is how serious a threat More took Protestantism, in particular, to be.

This is not to advocate a simplistic revival of the Chambers thesis as an interpretation of Thomas More's attitudes towards heresy. Rather, it is to suggest that behind the special pleading of Chambers there remains an important perception. Ironically, Marius's refutation and the Chambers thesis itself share one and the same historiographical flaw. For both seek to bring More into the perspective of a Whiggish moralism: the one to defend, the other to condemn. Chambers wished to recruit More to the Whig pantheon, and so sought to transmute his persecution of heretics into the only kind of persecution condoned by pre-Second World War liberalism: persecution for the sake of social order and stability (a kind of persecution, one might add, no longer condoned by Western society). He applied to More the argument long used by Anglican and Whig apologists to exculpate the regime of Queen Elizabeth and William Cecil from the charge of persecuting Catholics, namely, that they were repressing not heresy but treason.

Marius rightly dismantled Chambers's arguments, but only in order to cast More down from the Whig pantheon to the Whig pande-monium. His historicism was adequate to the task of unpicking Chambers, but not to that of understanding More. Try as he might, he could never quite see things through More's eyes, which is why his vision of More, for all its mastery of detail, fails to carry conviction with those who retrace his investigative path rather than join him at his journey's end.

Thomas More acted as he did against heresy and heretics because he understood very clearly what was happening in England and in Europe. He scented change in the air. The 'new learning' was some-thing very different from the familiar, almost homely, tradition of Lollardy with which the English Church was still occasionally wrest-ling in the early sixteenth century. Lollardy was going nowhere, and the intensifying machinery of the Tudor monarchy was stamping it out in its few remaining strongholds – upland Kent, the Chilterns, London, Coventry, the Forest of Dean and the Norfolk Broads. There were no new Lollard treatises, and Lollard dissent was in general confined to the lower-middling reaches of small-town society.[36] It was an enemy, but it was not a threat. It is worth noting that More never discussed Lollardy as such. He felt no need to write against it. His writings do invoke the judicial measures against heresy intro-duced by Henry IV and Henry V, and allude on a few occasions to Lollards and to recent proceedings against them, but he shows little interest in their beliefs. There is no record of More's paying any special attention to heresy until Henry VIII took it upon himself to break a lance with Martin Luther, and summoned More to join him in the lists.[37]

Protestantism was different, and More knew it. It was recruiting among people like him, among people he knew, even among his relatives. His beloved daughter Meg was briefly in trouble in 1525 over the publication without a licence of her translation of a treatise on the Our Father.[38] Meg's husband, William Roper, dallied with Protestantism. A brother-in-law, John Rastell, at first a vigorous opponent of Protestantism, was converted to it by the polemics of John Frith. Thomas More himself was exactly the kind of man who might have become a Protestant. The cities of the Netherlands,

Germany and Switzerland were thronged with devout humanist lawyers or politicians who affiliated themselves with the exciting new learning of Luther, Melanchthon, Zwingli and Oecolampadius: men such as Lazarus Spengler of Nuremberg or Jakob Sturm of Strasbourg. In England, lawyers and royal servants such as Simon Fish, Christopher St German and Thomas Cromwell showed various degrees of engagement with it. Its appeal reached courtiers and clergymen, printers and booksellers, merchants and physicians, nobles and gentry. These were More's kind of people.

The early success of Protestantism brought about a subtle change in atmosphere that More, typically, picked up at once. He was far from obsessive: he did not see reds under the bed. He lacked that exaggerated fear of countless hidden foes that besets the imagination of the fanatic. On the contrary, in the *Apology* he poured cold water on the idle boast of Richard Bayfield that 'more then halfe of euery shyre' were Protestant sympathizers (*CW* 9:157). But, equally, he observed how, in just a few years, heresies that would have set people's hair on end a decade before had become the stuff of everyday conversation: 'it begynneth almost to growe in custume, that amonge good catholyke folke, yet be they suffred boldely to talke vnchekked' (*CW* 9:158). The taboo had been broken – and in any social revolution, exorcizing the taboo is half the battle. His response to all this was a variant of a modern axiom: for heresy to triumph, all that was needed was for the orthodox to do nothing (*CW* 11:3–4). Thomas More had, as ever, a pellucid realism that enabled him to see both the actualities and the potentialities of the situation.

Even more importantly, More saw doctrine, or religion, whether in Utopia or in Europe, as the foundation and touchstone of human society.[39] He realized that a new doctrine meant a new order. The facts of his public career suggest that he saw heresy as the greatest political issue facing his times and that he acted on that perception. The question is, was he right? The question is no sooner asked than answered, for the answer is found in precisely that term which we use to label the period of history in which he lived and died: 'the Reformation'. He would not have liked the label, but he would certainly have appreciated the reason we use it, namely because it signifies that the most important fact of his lifetime was the rise of an alternative account of the very essence of Christianity.

Finally, More saw that Protestantism could and might succeed. Hence the comment reported by Roper, in which More spoke airily of 'treading heretics under our feet like ants', is not at all the triumphalist rhetoric that it seems to critics who recite it out of context. His whole point is that the apparent security of Catholics might prove illusory, and that there might come a day when Catholics would be glad 'to let them have their churches quietly to themselves, so that they would be content to let us have ours' (Roper 216). That day was nearer than he dreamed. Did he realize already that Henry's divorce might pave the way for heresy? Quite possibly: but there was nothing he could do about that. His concentration on heresy as lord chancellor was not fanaticism; nor was it displacement activity; nor was it an attempt to influence the divorce controversy, from which he kept himself as far apart as he could. His policy was an attempt to confront the foremost political priority of his time. In short, the accumulation of evidence regarding the seriousness with which Thomas More addressed the issue of heresy shows precisely, notwithstanding the judgements of his modern critics, that he was not a fanatic but a statesman.

FURTHER READING

There are many valuable essays in the introductory materials to the editions of More's polemical writings in the Yale *Complete Works of St. Thomas More*. Besides those, the following works are of particular value. John Guy, *Thomas More*, not only offers a forensic account of More's dealings with heresy but also provides the best historiographical introduction to this and, indeed, most other aspects of More's career. Guy places More's concern with heresy in its political and biographical context in *The Public Career of Sir Thomas More*. The modern tradition of More as an unbalanced inquisitor derives chiefly from Richard Marius, *Thomas More*, and from the essays on More by Geoffrey Elton, most of them available in Elton, *Studies in Tudor and Stuart Politics and Government*, 4 vols. (Cambridge University Press, 1974–92). More's controversial writings are surveyed in Ranier Pineas, *Thomas More and Tudor Polemics* (Bloomington: Indiana University Press, 1968), and, again from a more revisionist perspective, in Alistair Fox, *Thomas More: History and Providence* (Oxford: Blackwell, 1982). His understanding of the Church is explored in Brian Gogan, *The Common Corps of Christendom: Ecclesiological Themes in the Writings of Sir Thomas More* (Leiden: Brill, 1982). A perceptive interpretation of the controversy between More and Tyndale is offered in James Simpson, *Burning to Read: English Fundamentalism and its Reformation Opponents* (Cambridge, Mass.: Belknap Press, 2007).

Notes

1. Brian Moynahan, *If God Spare My Life* (London: Little, Brown, 2002), 329–54, esp. 339–42; Rod Liddle, 'The English Bible has made us', *The Spectator*, 16/23 December 2006, 16–17; Hilary Mantel, *Wolf Hall* (London: Fourth Estate, 2009), 628–9.
2. John Guy, *Thomas More*, 122.
3. *The Statesman and the Fanatic: Thomas Wolsey and Thomas More* (London: Constable, 1982).
4. G. R. Elton, 'Thomas More, councillor', in his *Studies in Tudor and Stuart Politics and Government*, 1:134 (in 'Further reading'), for the date. Elton did not remark the coincidence.
5. For further detail, see below, 116 ff.
6. I should like to thank Pia Matthews for challenging the original title when I mentioned it to her. As Richard Marius is going to come in for his fair share of criticism in this essay, it is only fair to point out that he came up with this title first, in his 1962 Yale doctoral dissertation.
7. This, of course, is where Robert Bolt's classic play fails in historical terms. In having More justify his stand with the observation 'What matters is not that it's true, but that I believe it; or no, not that I *believe* it but that *I* believe it' (Bolt's emphases), the playwright affirms the exact opposite of More's account of conscience. See further below, 134 and 270–1.
8. Chambers, *Thomas More*, 274–82.
9. *Salvation at Stake: Christian Martyrdom in Early Modern Europe* (Cambridge, Mass.: Harvard University Press, 1999), chs. 3 and 4.
10. More to Erasmus, *c.* June 1532, *EE* 10:261; *SL* 181. The same triad appears at *CW* 9:120.
11. H. S. Herbrüggen, 'A letter of Dr Johann Eck to Thomas More', *Moreana* 2, no. 8 (1965), 51–8.
12. *Literarum, quibus inuictissimus princeps, Henricus octauus* (London, 1526; *STC* 13084).
13. *The Work of William Barlowe*, ed. Andrew M. McLean (Appleford: Sutton Courtenay Press, 1981). McLean does not accept the argument for More's role which is advanced by the series editor, G. E. Duffield, at 178–95. More's authorship was first proposed in the anonymous evangelical treatise *The Souper of the Lorde* (1533), which is reprinted in *CW* 11:303–40; see 332. In his reply to that work, *The Answer to a Poisoned Book*, More does not deny the claim, he simply ignores it: had it been entirely false, he would probably have been quick to accuse his opponent of another lie.
14. Marius, *Thomas More*, 276–8, 326, 432–3.
15. *CW* 5:117–43. See 141 for Fisher's reference to the general council, found in article 25 of the *Assertionis lutheranae confutatio*. See Fisher, *Opera omnia* (Würzburg: Fleischmann, 1597), cols. 543–4.
16. *CW* 6:317–30 (Hunne); *CW* 8:23–5 (Bilney).

17. See Marius, *Thomas More*, 123–41. Marius, characteristically, cites no evidence for his conclusion that, in More's view, the end of defending the Catholic Church would justify deliberate lying (141) and, equally characteristically, ignores More's frequent censures of lying and perjury. See also G. R. Elton, 'Persecution and toleration in the English Reformation', in W. J. Sheils, ed., *Persecution and Toleration* (Oxford: Blackwell, 1984), 163–87, at 171, where he states that More 'deliberately falsified the truth of Bylney's death', referring to J. F. Davis, 'The trials of Thomas Bylney and the English Reformation', *Historical Journal* 24 (1981), 775–90. Davis in turn (786 n. 27) cites two earlier articles, but neither he nor they pass such a severe judgement or give reason to do so.

18. Elton, 'The real Thomas More' (1980), in his *Studies in Tudor and Stuart Politics and Government*, 3:344–55, at 351–3; Marius, *Thomas More*, e.g. 14, 36–7 and 426. In this biography, the novelist indulges the technique, beloved of teachers of 'creative writing', of introducing complexity into character to make it more interesting. Marius is certainly as interested in More's sexuality as More was in Luther's. (The art of insinuation is easily learned.)

19. Guy offers an elegant deconstruction of the myth in *Thomas More*, 29–36.

20. *CW* 8:727. More uses the now archaic 'refrayte'.

21. 'Thomas More and Thomas Cromwell', in G. J. Schochet, ed., *Reformation, Humanism and Revolution* (Washington, D.C.: Folger Institute, 1990), 95–110, at 101.

22. *CW* 5:310–11. This passage includes the invitation to Luther, 'listen now, you pimp', translating the Latin 'audi nunc iam leno'. However, the charge of pimping is not one that I have noticed elsewhere in More's invective against Luther, and, unless similar comments are found, I would conjecturally emend 'leno' to 'lene' ('mildly'), which yields a more balanced rhetorical contrast with the previous clause, thus: 'sed si satis debacchatus es: audi nunc iam lene'.

23. Yet Marius, *Thomas More*, cites one of these few passages as 'one of the milder parts' (281) of a work characterized by 'monotonous scatology' (282).

24. Marius, *Thomas More*, xxiv, 289–91.

25. ' "To assyst the ordynaryes": why Thomas More agreed to become lord chancellor', *Moreana* 45, no. 174 (2008), 171–92.

26. Guy, *The Public Career of Sir Thomas More*, 173–4. See also Guy, *A Daughter's Love*, 192–3; and Susan Brigden, *London and the Reformation* (Oxford: Clarendon Press, 1989), 184–5.

27. The idea that More's detention of suspects in his home was illegal is a canard. As Guy has pointed out (*Thomas More*, 120–1), he was a JP for Middlesex, which gave him a range of summary powers.

28. For example, *CW* 8:19, 'Iohan Byrte otherwyse callynge hym selfe Adryane, otherwyse Iohan bokebynder'.

29. More admits and explains ordering beatings for two people, one a child in his household who had passed on heresy to another child, and the other an apparently deranged man who indecently assaulted women

at prayer (*CW* 9:117–18). Both punishments make sense in terms of sixteenth-century moral norms.

30. Marius, *Thomas More*, 402–4.
31. Guy, *Thomas More*, 120.
32. D. Daniell, *William Tyndale: A Biography* (New Haven and London: Yale University Press, 1994), ch. 10.
33. Even the Utopians punished what one might call practical atheism (the denial of the immortality of the soul or of the providential government of the universe), which they regarded as contrary to reason (*CU* 95).
34. Elton, 'Persecution and toleration', 174–7.
35. Guy, *A Daughter's Love*.
36. Richard Rex, *The Lollards* (Basingstoke: Macmillan, 2002), ch. 5. For a different view see Anne Hudson, *The Premature Reformation* (Oxford University Press, 1988), ch. 10.
37. Although More had perhaps had some contact with Richard Hunne (above, 95), and was doubtless aware of proceedings against Lollards before 1521, there is no evidence that he was engaged in such proceedings; and we only know about his awareness from comments made by him in the later context of the response to Protestantism.
38. Guy, *A Daughter's Love*, 157–8.
39. For a full account of how More's concerns in this area played out in the greatest of his polemical works, *A Dialogue Concerning Heresies*, see below, 209–12.

6 The last years

PETER MARSHALL

At around three o'clock on 16 May 1532, Thomas More met with the king in the garden of Cardinal Wolsey's former dwelling, York Place, near the palace of Westminster, and handed him a white leather pouch containing the Great Seal of England. More's resignation as lord chancellor marked an end and a beginning. A distinguished public career as a lawyer in royal service had come to a conclusion. Yet the final three years of Sir Thomas's life would be characterized by waves of intense activity and accumulations of dramatic incident – they would define the meaning of that life for posterity, supplying the lens through which More's character and motives must inescapably be read. Whether either of the old friends possessed any inkling of this that Thursday afternoon in Westminster is unknowable. Sir Thomas, declaring himself not equal to the responsibility, presented his stepping down from office as a withdrawal from the cares of the world, asking leave 'to bestow the residue of my life in mine age now to come, about the provision for my soul in the service of God, and to be your Grace's beadsman and pray for you'. Henry, for his part, graciously promised More 'that in any suit that I should after have unto your Highness, which either should concern mine honor … or that should pertain unto my profit, I should find your Highness good and gracious lord unto me' (*SL* 202). None of these undertakings were in the event to be honoured.

RETIREMENT AND OPPOSITION

More's decision to resign the chancellorship on 16 May was triggered by an event of the previous day: the decision of the convocation of the English Church, under intense royal pressure, to approve a Submission of the Clergy undertaking not to create any new canons or provincial constitutions without explicit royal consent. The legislative independence of the Church, for centuries an axiomatic principle of Catholic churchmen, had been surrendered, and Henry VIII's headship of the Church in England was in practice complete. More's departure was not an impulsive reaction to an unexpected development, but a final weary recognition that his hope of being able to steer the king into better counsels had failed, and perhaps he jumped before he was pushed. Writing a few days later to his master Charles V, the imperial ambassador, Eustace Chapuys, explained that 'the chancellor has resigned, seeing that affairs were going on badly, and likely to be worse, and that if he retained his office he would be obliged to act against his conscience or incur the king's displeasure, as he had already begun to do, for refusing to take his part against the clergy' (*LP* 5, no. 1046; and see above, 86–7).

More's life after 1532 is often portrayed in terms of a retreat from political engagement, a shift from action to contemplation. In particular, the pre-eminent Tudor political historian, G. R. Elton, saw the period of More's chancellorship as one of involvement in intense partisan politics, as the lord chancellor actively plotted with an organized grouping of fellow dissidents to derail the government's policies over the divorce and its campaign in parliament to put pressure on the pope and the clergy.[1] Much is made of a meeting More had only a few weeks before stepping down as chancellor with Sir George Throckmorton, a member of parliament for Warwickshire, who had apparently spoken in the house against Cromwell's bill for a parliamentary submission of the clergy. More sent word for Throckmorton to come and speak with him 'in a little chamber within the parliament chamber', where he told the outspoken MP that 'I am very glad to hear the good report that goeth of you, and that ye be so good a catholic man as ye be; and if ye do continue in the same way that ye began and be not afraid to say your conscience, ye shall deserve great reward of God and thanks of the king's grace at length'.[2] Throckmorton had already received advice and encouragement from several conservative clergymen, including Bishop John Fisher. But this hardly constitutes strong proof of More's role as an active leader of a faction. There is no evidence of his conducting private meetings with other members of parliament, and it is clear that he contacted Throckmorton – with this very guarded and coded encouragement – only after the latter had acquired a public reputation as an opponent of the government's anticlerical policies.

But if More was not a frenetic plotter before his resignation from office, neither was he a quiescent retiree afterwards. His sixteenth-century Catholic biographer Thomas Stapleton would have us believe that after handing back the Great Seal, 'More now lived at home in retirement, giving his time to prayer and study as he had always desired to do' (Stapleton 138). Yet as an account of More's priorities this will hardly do. In the first place, although deprived of coercive power, Sir Thomas continued his literary campaign against the English heretics, writing and seeing works into print at a prodigious rate. The first volume of More's massive *Confutation of Tyndale's Answer* was composed in the final months of his chancellorship, and the second volume was written and published in the course of 1533. Whether or not the *Confutation*, as Richard Marius claimed, 'rings with the clangor of More's own repressed sexuality',[3] it was certainly a work of robust and vigorous polemic, asserting the authority and identity of the institutional and visible Church against the alleged sectarianism of Tyndale and his associates. Its author was not a man who had given up the fight in order to concentrate on his private devotional life. Somewhat less strident in tone, but equally earnest in purpose, was the *Letter against Frith* (1533), a reply to a manuscript treatise on the nature of the sacrament by the brilliant young evangelical theologian John Frith, whom More urged to recant his 'sacramentarian' view of the non-real presence of Christ in the Eucharist. At the same time, More published his *Answer to a Poisoned Book*, a response to an anonymous printed attack on the Catholic theology of the Mass, *The Souper of the Lorde* (probably by George Joye).

In defending traditional Eucharist theology against these 'Zwinglians', More was on relatively safe ground. The *Letter against Frith* was prefixed with warm praise of the king, who 'lyke a moste faythfull catholyke prince' had forbidden the circulation in his realm of 'suche pestylente bokes as sowe suche poysened heresyes amonge his people' (CW 7:233). But More's two other polemical works of 1533, *The Apology* and *The Debellation of Salem and Bizance*, offered a more direct critique of policies and positions associated with the government itself, and with them More was treading a very fine line indeed. Although these books are larded with anti-Protestant arguments, their real target was not a heretic theologian, but an eminent common lawyer and legal theorist, Christopher St German. In *A Treatise Concerning the Division between the Spiritualty and the Temporalty* (1532) and *Salem and Bizance* (1533), works published by the king's printer and likely under the patronage of Thomas Cromwell, St German had criticized abuses of the church courts, especially in heresy cases, and argued more broadly for the subjugation of canon to common law, a programme effectively enacted in the clergy's Submission of 1532. These treatises were published anonymously, allowing More to affect ignorance of their author's identity (although he can hardly have been in doubt of it) and to imagine that they were the efforts of an ignorant country clergyman. In his rebuttals, More upheld the traditional divisions of power and responsibility between church and state. He was careful neither to defend the papal primacy nor directly to attack the Submission of the Clergy. But by claiming that church councils and provincial synods, inspired by the Holy Spirit, had the independent power to enact laws, More was implicitly rebuking both the Submission and the royal supremacy over the Church that Henry consolidated in 1533 with the Act in Restraint of Appeals, which declared the realm of England to be an 'empire', an entirely sovereign political entity. As far as he could be, More was cautious and circumspect. But St German's ideas seemed to him dangerously radical, demanding direct refutation. In undertaking that refutation, he had put his head above the parapet and issued a public rebuke to the king. The implicit bargain of May 1532 – that More would be left alone if he kept his mouth shut – was now in pieces, and Henry's anger against his former chancellor was beginning to swell.

In summer 1533, More missed a chance to assuage that anger, and most likely dangerously stoked it. The occasion was the coronation of Anne Boleyn as queen of England, following Henry's secret marriage to her in January, and Archbishop Cranmer's annulment in May of the marital bond to Catherine of Aragon. Like other dignitaries, More was expected to attend the new queen's coronation, on 1 June. According to Roper, three of the most conservative bishops – John Clerk of Bath and Wells, Stephen Gardiner of Winchester and More's old friend Cuthbert Tunstall of Durham – begged Sir Thomas to accompany them, and sent him £20 to buy a new gown for the occasion. More was happy to accede to one of their requests – he kept the money and bought a gown – but he also stayed at home. On next seeing the bishops, he regaled them with a story of a Roman emperor who had decreed that for a certain crime virgins would be exempt from the death sentence. Nonplussed when the first culprit happened to be a virgin, he was advised by a wily councillor, 'Let her first be deflowered and then after may she be devoured!' In the same way, the bishops risked loss of their spiritual virginity and worse in the matter of the marriage, as there were those 'that by procuring your lordships first at the coronation to be present, and next to preach for the setting forth of it, and finally to write books to all the world in defense thereof' were seeking to devour them. More, however, would keep his virginity.[4] If something like this was said, then it is likely that word of it got back to Henry VIII, and insult was added to injury in the king's mind.

At the beginning of 1534 More began to pay the price for his audacities of the preceding year. In January, the workshop of his printer-nephew, William Rastell, was raided at the instigation of Thomas Cromwell, to investigate reports that More had composed a reply to the *Articles devised by the whole consent of the king's most honourable council*, a recent piece of official propaganda in favour of the divorce containing vehement attacks on the authority and character of Pope Clement VII. The report was untrue, and More wrote to Cromwell to exculpate himself, protesting that he had published nothing since his *Answer to a Poisoned Book*, and promising that he would neither write against, nor urge anyone to write against, any book that should 'come abroad in the name of his Grace or his honorable Council' (*SL* 191).

If this was a warning shot, More became a target for real a few weeks later, when the government finally decided to remove one of the major political irritants of the preceding few years, the young visionary Elizabeth Barton, known as the Nun of Kent. Barton was a maidservant who had acquired a popular following, and a reputation as a prophetess and worker of miracles, after entering a convent in 1525. By the end of the decade, however, her prophecies had taken a sharp political turn, and she had the temerity to predict that Henry would not remain king if he put aside Queen Catherine. Her apparent sanctity won her influential patrons, among them Archbishop Warham of Canterbury and Bishop John Fisher. More, however, was much more cautious. He had met with the Nun at a monastery in London, but had refused to endorse her revelations. Nonetheless, when the authorities decided to deal with Barton in February 1534 by way of an attainder (a parliamentary act declaring her guilty of treason), the names of Fisher and More were added to the draft placed before parliament, as guilty of aiding and abetting her sedition. This was almost certainly at Henry's own instigation; Cromwell later let More understand that the king suspected 'all the Nun's business was wrought and devised by me' (*SL* 236). In the event, the guilt-by-association did not stick. Ever the procedural lawyer, More requested the right formally to present his case before the House of Lords. This Henry denied, but allowed him to appear before a committee of the Privy Council. Cromwell and the other members then persuaded a reluctant Henry to drop More's name from the attainder, probably because the evidence against him was so slight that it would endanger the passage of the bill. When the news came to More's family that the danger had passed, they were of course delighted. But Sir Thomas himself was more fatalistic, telling his beloved daughter Margaret, 'quod differtur non aufertur' (Roper 237; 'that which is put off is not taken away').

OATH AND INCARCERATION

On 5 March 1534, More wrote to Cromwell, thanking him for his 'charitable labor' in persuading the king to remove him from the attainder. He also took occasion to describe his position regarding the king's proceedings, and to explain some of the background to it. Nearly seven years earlier the king had first expounded to him his scruples about his marriage, and although More could not be persuaded over the rightness of the divorce, Henry had nonetheless graciously promised him on his entry into royal service that 'I should first look unto God and after God unto him'. The king exempted him from having to participate in the divorce proceedings, and More had neither then nor since written any word 'to the impairing of his Grace's part'. Now that Anne was formally anointed as queen, More would 'neither murmur at it nor dispute upon it', but would pray to God for the royal couple and their issue. As to the still larger political question, the primacy of the pope, More protested that he would 'nothing meddle in the matter', and had in fact said very little about it in his most recent controversial writings. Yet he made no secret of his view that to deny that primacy was a hazardous matter, since it had been recognized by the whole body of Christendom for more than a thousand years, and 'sith all Christendom is one corps [body], I cannot perceive how any member thereof may without the common assent of the body depart from the common head'. But there was no fault nor ill intention in him other 'than that I cannot in everything think the same way that some other men of more wisdom and deeper learning do' (SL 205–15). Thus More pitched the positions that he would maintain almost until the moment of his death: his views on the divorce and the royal supremacy were either known, or could be inferred, yet he intended in no way to criticize or work against royal policy. He was not a political threat, and therefore he could safely be left alone, as the king had promised he should be.

Perhaps this was from the outset a hopelessly unrealistic stance, and it was soon put sharply to the test. Fewer than three weeks after More's letter, in order to consolidate the legality and political security of the Boleyn marriage, parliament passed an Act of Succession, vesting the inheritance to the crown in Henry and Anne's heirs. One of the provisions of the act was that all the king's subjects should swear a formal oath recognizing this dynastic line. On 13 April 1534, the leading clergy of the capital were summoned before royal commissioners at Lambeth to take the oath, along with one layman, Thomas More. The commissioners were an assortment of old friends and new enemies: Archbishop Cranmer, Lord Chancellor Thomas Audley, the dukes of Norfolk and Suffolk, joined later by the abbot of Westminster and Thomas Cromwell. More asked to see the oath, and the text of the Act of Succession. After he had read them carefully, he told the commissioners that he did not wish to condemn the conscience of any man that swore the oath, and indeed that he was willing to swear to recognize the Boleyn succession. Nonetheless, as he reported to Margaret, 'the oath that there was offered me I could not swear, without the iubarding [jeopardizing] of my soul to perpetual damnation' (*SL* 217). There followed an elaborate dance of persuasions and arguments. The commissioners produced lists of the dignitaries who had sworn, and sent More off to a garden to think on the matter, and so that he could see the cheerful demeanour of the clergy, including some prominent conservatives, who had agreed to take the oath. More thought it a 'pageant', played for his benefit (*SL* 219). Yet still he would not swear, and, moreover, 'would not declare any special part of that oath that grudged [dissatisfied] my conscience', saying that he did not wish to offend the king further by doing so. He did offer to declare his reasons openly if he were to receive a royal licence under letters patent, affirming that his doing so would not put him in legal jeopardy. When this, inevitably, was refused, More avowed that 'it thinketh me, lo, that if I may not declare the causes without peril, then to leave them undeclared is no obstinacy' (*SL* 220).

This was More's famous 'silence', which he hoped would protect him from the violent revenge of the state. Writing shortly afterwards to Nicholas Wilson, one of the very few priests initially to refuse the oath, and in a letter he fully expected to be intercepted, More observed that 'as touching the oath, the causes for which I refused it, no man wotteth [knows] what they be, for they be secret in mine own conscience' (*SL* 232). But there was really no mystery about this. More would not swear because the preamble to the oath upheld the spiritual validity of the king's second marriage and implicitly rejected the authority of the pope. For him to swear such an oath against his belief to the contrary would have been perjury, not just a legal transgression but a cause of eternal damnation. Everyone understood that this was the position. Cranmer hoped to broker a fudge: More and Fisher should be allowed to swear to the succession without affirming the act's preamble, and the exact form of the oath they swore could be kept secret. But Henry was having none of it.[5]

Refusal to swear the oath was specified in the act as misprision of treason, the penalty for which was perpetual imprisonment, and confiscation of property. A formal legal conviction was required for this, yet, for the moment, More was neither put on trial nor convicted by attainder.[6] At first there may have been uncertainty over what to do with him, but after a delay of a few days he was sent on 17 April 1534 to the Tower of London.

PRISONER IN THE TOWER

The final fourteen months of Thomas More's life were spent in the Tower, at first in conditions of relative comfort, and later in more arduous ones. He was not deprived of human contact. He was able to communicate by letter with a number of correspondents, including an illustrious fellow prisoner of conscience, John Fisher. Moreover, he was able to receive visits, the most welcome of which were from his favourite child, Margaret Roper. As John Guy has persuasively argued, Margaret and Thomas collusively convinced the authorities that she was trying to argue him out of his 'obstinacy', in order to maintain their meetings.[7] The king and his ministers clearly hoped that even now More could be prevailed upon to change his mind; if not, then he could quietly rot while the world outside forgot about him.

For More, however, imprisonment was no occasion for inactivity. He continued, avidly, to write – not just letters to family and friends, but a series of meditative and theological pieces which have become known collectively as the 'Tower Works', and were grouped together in the last 320 pages of William Rastell's 1557 folio edition of More's English writings. These comprised a *Treatise on the Passion* (probably begun before he entered the Tower), a *Treatise on the Blessed Body*, *A Dialogue of Comfort against Tribulation*, a treatise *De Tristitia Christi* ('On the sadness of Christ'), and a variety of instructions, meditations and prayers.[8] These profound, contemplative works have helped to shape a tradition in More scholarship which holds that his months in the Tower were, paradoxically, the most peaceful and satisfying of his life, as well as, from a modern perspective, the most admirable. Imprisonment was, in a psychological if not theological sense, the salvation of More. Marius commented lyrically on 'the intense psychic freedom from care given him by his captivity', and on the calm resignation of a 'devout but divided man who had wrestled with the choice between priesthood and matrimony, the man of hair shirt and flagellation and with the lifelong thirst for the monastic life, now given the desire of his heart by a government that sought to punish him and ended by blessing him'.[9] Elton put it more succinctly: 'He had found peace; the demons were gone at last ... He had found the tonsure in the Tower.'[10] To an extent, such assessments echo the view of some of More's earliest biographers. Nicholas Harpsfield, for example, was keen to suggest that More embraced imprisonment and the prospect of martyrdom with serenity, never once asking God to deliver him from death, 'and thus by [his] gratious demeanour in tribulation, it well appered that all the troubles that ever chanced to him, by his patient suffering thereof, were to him no painfull punishmentes, but of patience profitable exercises' (Harpsfield 172).

Yet there is a danger with such approaches of sanitizing, or even trivializing, More's Tower experience, and of underestimating the intense spiritual and psychological struggle that it represented (see further below, 242–3). It is no coincidence that a major thematic focus of More's Tower writings is the agony of Christ in the Garden of Gethsemane, and Jesus's anguished prayer 'to let this cup pass from me', while surrendering himself to the will of his Father.[11] All scholars recognize that at no point was More actively seeking a martyr's death, although his evident desire not to become a martyr is sometimes discussed in surprisingly abstract and theological terms, focusing on a concern that too forceful a stand might be tantamount to suicide and thus constitute a mortal sin. Yet More simply did not want to die. Still more, perhaps, than the experience of death itself, he feared his own weakness, and the thought that desperation, or the prospect of torture, might impel him to give Henry what he wanted. As the character of Antony states in *A Dialogue of Comfort*, any Christian might wish that he had been put to death yesterday for the sake of Christ, 'but to feare while the payne ys coming, there is all our lett [obstacle]' (*CW* 12:319). There are further clues to these anxieties in More's prison letters. Writing to Margaret in 1534, he voiced the fear that a new law would be passed to deal with his case, and end the safety he had found in 'silence'. In contemplating this, he confessed that 'I found myself (I cry God mercy) very sensual [worldly] and my flesh much more shrinking from pain and from death than methought it the part of a faithful Christian man'. In a letter to a priest known to us only as 'Master Leder', More admitted his fear of giving way under torture: 'I trust both that they will use no violent forcible ways, and also that if they would, God would of his grace and the rather a great deal through good folks' prayers give me strength to stand' (*SL* 237, 243). Thus Sir Thomas found comfort in the Passion narrative of a human, suffering Christ, who may have chosen to undergo the mental anguish of Gethsemane precisely to give comfort and a supreme example of fortitude under pressure to Christians finding themselves in More's situation.

More's Tower writings are a rich source for the biographer, but they were not overtly autobiographical, and it would be a mistake to read them solely in this light. These works were self-consciously written for the utility of others, and the prayers More composed, even on the eve of his execution, were in a form that any Christian could recite. Garry Haupt has remarked that 'this predominantly public orientation of the Tower Works is richly symbolic of More's tenacious commitment to an objective, impersonal, universal order of Christendom' (*CW* 13:clxxx). Similarly, Eamon Duffy's examination of the annotations More made in the printed prayer book or primer he took with him to the Tower finds little 'autobiographical vehemence', or signs of a suppressed monastic vocation finally allowed to flower. Next to the opening of Psalm 84 ('my soul longeth and fainteth for the courts of the Lord') More wrote poignantly, 'The prayer of one shut up in prison, or lying sick in bed, yearning to go to Church.' In his physical and spiritual isolation, More's desire was for participation in a communal devotional culture.[12]

A further reason for not characterizing More's prison experience as a fundamentally 'monastic' one, or as a decisive turning away from the priorities of his earlier career, is the fact that, although he composed no further works like the *Confutation of Tyndale*, his polemics against heretics did not entirely cease. The *Treatise on the Passion* vigorously attacked heretical interpretations of the Mass, while *De Tristitia* castigated as Judases those who denied the real presence of Christ in the Eucharist, and compared the bishops who had failed in their duty to combat heresy to the sleeping disciples in the garden. The *Dialogue of Comfort*, although set in Hungary after the great Turkish victory there of 1526, is patently an allegory for the threat to Christianity posed by heretics, and of the sufferings to be expected in England by those standing up for the papacy and the unity of the Church. As Harpsfield patiently explained, More 'couloureth the matter under the name of an Hungarian, and of the persecution of the Turke' (Harpsfield 134; but cf. below, 218–20).

FINAL INTERROGATIONS

The persecutions of the Turk intensified for Thomas More in the final months of 1534. In November, parliament passed an Act of Supremacy, which removed any lingering doubts about the matter by insisting that Henry 'shall be taken, accepted, and reputed the only supreme head in earth of the Church of England'.[13] At the same time, a new Treasons Act was passed, which sought to do away with difficulties which had been experienced in securing the conviction of Elizabeth Barton and her associates. The law of treason was now extended to cover not just plotters, but those who denied the king's title by words alone, or who called him 'heretic, schismatic, tyrant, infidel or usurper of the crown'. In order to get the controversial legislation through parliament, it was specified that such words must be uttered 'maliciously', a straw at which Thomas More would tenaciously clutch.[14]

The treason law was not to come into effect until the following February, but a ratcheting up of the screws began in November, when More was belatedly attainted of misprision of treason under the terms of the Succession Act. The attainder noted that More had 'unkindly and ingrately served our sovereign lord by divers and sundry ways'. There is no such phrase in the parallel act which attainted Fisher, Wilson and several others for refusal of the oath, a circumstance which suggests that Henry himself may have been behind the decision to single More out and deal with him in a separate bill.[15] Certain privileges which More had been allowed – family visits, freedom to walk in the garden of the Tower – were now withdrawn. The confiscation of More's property also reduced his family to conditions of poverty. Although Lady Alice eventually secured a government pension, it is possible that some estrangement from her husband came about as a result of her inability to understand why he would force them all to suffer for a principle which few appeared to share.[16]

The increased pressure on More was probably a recognition that the strategy of hoping he would quietly fade out of public memory had failed, and that, worse, he was serving as an inspiring example of resistance to other dissidents. It was Cromwell's view, as More reported to Margaret Roper, that 'my demeanor in that matter was of a thing that of likelihood made now other men so stiff therein as they be' (*SL* 247). Cromwell had in mind here the three Carthusian priors, including the head of the London Charterhouse, John Houghton, who in early 1535 were still stubbornly refusing to recognize the king's title, and who, because of their reputation for sanctity and austerity of life, were both an embarrassment and a political threat to Henry. They were brought to trial on 28 April, and convicted of treason. Two days later, Cromwell interrogated More in the Tower, assisted by a team of legal officers. Reminding More that Henry was now ordained supreme head by an act of parliament, Cromwell demanded to know his opinion of the matter, and threatened him with the full rigours of the law. More's reply suggests the extent to which his imprisonment, and intimations of torture and death, had started to wear him down: 'I do nobody harm, I say none harm, I think none harm, but wish everybody good. And if this be not enough to keep a man alive, in good faith I long not to live' (SL 247–8).

On 4 May, the Carthusian priors, along with the Bridgettine monk Richard Reynolds, were taken to Tyburn for execution by hanging, drawing and quartering. More was able to watch their journey from his window in the Tower. With him was his daughter Margaret, whom Cromwell had allowed to visit on that day in the hope that her horror at the men's impending fate would work on her father's resolve. More observed, 'Lo, dost thou not see, Meg, that these blessed fathers be now going as cheerfully to their deaths as bridegrooms to their marriage?' He ascribed their serene demeanour to the penitential rigours of monastic life, and drew an unfavourable contrast with those, like himself, who had 'in the world, like worldly wretches ... consumed all their time in pleasure and ease'. For this reason God had decided to leave him a little longer, miserable in the world (Roper 242).

Cromwell and the commissioners were back on 3 June, and this time the pace was more urgent, the tone more aggressive and threatening. What had happened in the meantime was that Pope Paul III had decided to show his support for Fisher by creating him a cardinal, and had despatched the symbol of office to England. This turned out to be less a red hat to a bishop and more a red rag to a bull. Henry was furious, and ordered Cromwell to break the resistance of More and Fisher – now a scandal of European dimensions – forthwith. Cromwell began by telling More that 'the King's Highness was nothing content nor satisfied with mine answer, but thought that by my demeanor I had been occasion of much grudge and harm in the realm, and that I had an obstinate mind and an evil toward him' (SL 249–50). This was language redolent of the 'maliciousness' rendered a capital offence by the 1534 Treasons Act – it signalled that a final phase was beginning. More was now commanded on his allegiance to make plain answer if he thought the Act of Supremacy lawful or not. He remained at once plain-spoken and masterfully evasive. Comparing the act to a sword with two edges (*LP* 8, no. 974), More's statement that 'it were a very hard thing to compel me to say either precisely with it against my conscience to the loss of my soul, or precisely against it to the destruction of my body' was remarkably forthright, seeming to imply that he thought the act, literally, damnable. But he covered himself with a subjunctive construction: 'if it were so that my conscience gave me against the statutes ...' (*SL* 251). Once again, More's silence was hardly muteness. Marius suggests here that More simply 'could not break a lifelong habit of self-defense under attack, of argument, of simple gregariousness. He could not refrain from falling into the habitual practice of legal rebuttal that had engaged his fancy since childhood.'[17] Cromwell departed, saying 'he liked me this day much worse than he did the last time' (*SL* 253).

There was a momentous sequel. Under examination by the same commissioners later that day, John Fisher used the identical metaphor of the act as a 'two-edged sword', and immediately provoked suspicions of collusion. An investigation revealed that the two prisoners had indeed been in contact, and that letters had been exchanged, and burned. In retaliation, Cromwell ordered the confiscation of More's books and writing materials, and the solicitor general, Richard Rich, came to More's cell on 12 June to carry them away. The discussion that transpired between the two men on that occasion was to be the proximate cause of More's death, and there has been much debate about it since. Several accounts of the conversation exist, although the transcript with which Rich supplied Cromwell shortly afterwards seems likely to be closest to what actually took place. Rich appears to have taken it upon himself to play *agent provocateur*. More's sixteenth-century biographers all agree that Rich came to him in the Tower 'pretending friendly talk', although really 'with the intention of finding matter for accusation'.[18] It is possible that he had already played the same trick, successfully, with Bishop Fisher.[19]

Rich's gambit was to draw More out with a hypothetical 'putting of cases', of the sort that sixteenth-century lawyers enjoyed debating. What, he asked More, if parliament were to create him, Richard Rich, king of England? Would that be legitimate? Sir Thomas thought that it would be, as parliament had power to decide the succession, and he countered with an equally unlikely scenario: what if parliament declared that God was not God? Rich agreed that this was absurd, but then put a middle case: did parliament have the same authority to make the king head of the Church as it had to make Rich king? More's response, as reported by Rich to Cromwell, was that the cases were not alike. A subject, being a member of the parliament, could give consent to its making or unmaking a king, but in the other case he could not give his consent. More added that although the supreme headship might be accepted in England, countries overseas did not recognize it. This last point was a statement of the obvious, and the preceding assertion was not very much different from comments More had previously made in front of the commissioners. Rich himself seemed to think that no line had been crossed, and that this was another example of More's casuistical 'silence'. His closing retort was a warning that More might find 'your concealment to the question that hath been asked of you is as high offence as other that hath denied it'.[20] But on reading Rich's memorandum, Cromwell saw opportunity in it.

John Fisher had always been less circumspect than his fellow prisoner, and on 17 June, along with three Carthusians, he was tried for denying the Act of Supremacy. The monks were executed on 19 June, and Fisher followed them three days later. In an exercise of royal mercy, he was beheaded, rather than strangled, eviscerated and dismembered. Henry had now definitively decided that Fisher's fate was to be More's too. Cromwell was instructed to arrange a trial in Westminster Hall. The writs were issued on 26 June, and on 1 July 1535 More came out to face his accusers for the last time.

TRIAL AND EXECUTION

The outcome of Thomas More's tribunal was at no point seriously in doubt. Defendants in sixteenth-century treason trials were never, or hardly ever, acquitted. Nonetheless, its course and conduct were unexpected and dramatic: it was, perhaps quite literally, the trial of the century. For a man of advanced years, who had suffered the physical and psychological effects of fourteen months' incarceration, More's command of the proceedings, and his ability to influence and redirect them, was quite remarkable. But More was, first and last, a lawyer, and in his hour of greatest crisis he was also in his element.

The commission trying More comprised a group of professional judges and reliable courtiers, including Cromwell, Lord Chancellor Audley, the dukes of Norfolk and Suffolk, and Anne Boleyn's father, the earl of Wiltshire. Sir Christopher Hales, attorney general, led the prosecution. The jury contained members who bore personal grudges against More. As was usual in treason trials, the accused was given no copy of the indictment, no right to call witnesses and no legal counsel, although it is hard to imagine where More might have found a finer legal mind than his own to conduct his defence.

More listened intently as a long indictment in Latin was read out. There were four counts. The first was that in the Tower on 7 May 1535, before Cromwell and other commissioners, More had maliciously refused to give his opinion on the king's supremacy, saying that 'I wyll not meddyll with any such matters, for I am fully determyned to serve God, and to thynk uppon his passion and my passage out of this worlde.' The second was that on 12 May More had written a letter to Fisher reporting his own silence and maliciously encouraging the bishop in his treason. Third, he had maliciously conspired with Fisher, both men comparing the Act of Supremacy to a two-edged sword. The fourth count accused More, in conversation with Richard Rich on 12 June, of maliciously depriving the king of his title, and supplied an account of their verbal exchanges essentially identical to that Rich had written down for Cromwell.[21]

More now fought, brilliantly, for his life.[22] He began with a technical objection to the indictment: none of the charges constituted offences under the Treasons Act since the required 'malice' was not specifically demonstrated. When the judges rejected that argument, he asserted that the first three counts did not amount to constructive offences under the act because of the legal presumption expressed in the civil law maxim *qui tacet consentire videtur* ('he who is silent appears to consent'): in other words, his refusal to elaborate his reasons ought legally to be interpreted as assent to the king's supremacy rather than denial of it. Further, he pointed out that the letters to Fisher supposedly proving a conspiracy in the Tower no longer existed, and he swore on oath to their non-treasonable character. More admitted that the phrase about a two-edged sword had been used, but insisted that this was in reference to hypothetical legislation.

Remarkably, the judges upheld his argument, and three-quarters of the prosecution case fell apart. There remained the fourth count, to which More pleaded not guilty, and about which Richard Rich now stood to give evidence. There is uncertainty about what exactly he said in court. The fullest and most vivid near-contemporary report is in Roper's *Life* of his father-in-law. Roper was not in the court that day, and he wrote his account twenty years later, although drawing on the testimony of acquaintances who were present. In this version, Rich recounts the putting of cases in the Tower, although with a significant difference. After Rich had conceded that an act of parliament could not dethrone God, More had countered by denying the Act of Supremacy much more explicitly than he had ever done before: 'No more could the Parliament make the King supreme head of the Church' (Roper 244–5).

If Rich indeed said this (contradicting his own report of the conversation to Cromwell), then he committed perjury. In Roper's account, More immediately accused him of this offence, impugning Rich's character, and swearing that if what was said were true, 'then pray I that I never see God in the face'. Modern scholarship has been cautious – arguably too cautious – about the question of Rich's perjury. Elton inclined to the view that More did let his guard slip and say something genuinely incriminating on 12 June.[23] Guy admits the possibility of perjury, but notes that reports circulating in Europe within a few weeks of the trial do not mention it: 'we simply do not know'.[24] Marius argues that if Rich had told a blatant lie, More would hardly have gone on (in Roper's account) to propose that even if he had spoken as Rich alleged, 'it was spoken but in familiar secret talk, nothing affirming, and only in putting of cases'.[25] But More's persistent adherence to the legalistic defence that none of his words could be construed as 'malicious' is surely not surprising. Given his extraordinary care, over many months of intense pressure, in choosing non-incriminatory words and formulations, it does seem unlikely that he would have unbuttoned himself to the solicitor general, and false swearing is hardly inconsistent with everything else we know about the unsavoury course of Rich's self-serving career. On balance, Rich's perjury, although clearly serving a moral purpose for More's later hagiographers, seems more probable than possible.

It was enough to convict him. More's next submission – that even if he had withheld assent to the Act of Succession, he had already been punished for this by attainder, and no man could be punished for the same offence twice – was overruled. The jury returned swiftly with a guilty verdict, and Chancellor Audley proceeded to begin to pass sentence. But More threw the chancellor and the court into confusion by interrupting him with a final, ingenious, legal gambit. This was a 'motion in arrest of judgment', a plea that sentence should not be given because the act on which his conviction was based was invalid in law.[26] More's 'silence' was now irrevocably, volubly broken. The indictment was invalid (Roper tells us) because it was

> grounded upon an act of Parliament directly repugnant to the
> laws of God and His Holy Church, the supreme government of
> which, or of any part whereof, may no temporal prince presume

> by any law to take upon him, as rightfully belonging to the See
> of Rome, a spiritual pre-eminence by the mouth of Our Savior
> himself, personally present upon the earth, only to Saint Peter and
> his successors, bishops of the same See, by special prerogative
> granted ... [T]his realm, being but one member and small part of the
> Church, might not make a particular law disagreeable with the
> general law of Christ's universal Catholic Church, no more than
> the City of London, being but one poor member in respect of the
> whole realm, might make a law against an act of Parliament to
> bind the whole realm.
>
> (Roper 248)

He went on to accuse the act of being contrary to Magna Carta, and the
king of neglecting his coronation oath to defend the liberties of the
Church. The account in the 'Paris News Letter', a report of More's trial
and execution widely circulated immediately after the events, has less
on the dignity of the pope but adds the persuasive detail that More
alleged that the real reason they were seeking his blood was that he
would not consent to the Boleyn marriage (Harpsfield 264).

More's 'motion' was in all likelihood not so much a hopeful
attempt to overturn the indictment as a protected opportunity, finally,
to speak his mind. These were not quite his final words. When Audley
had recovered his composure, taken advice from the lord chief justice,
rejected the motion and finished passing sentence, More was given the
opportunity to plead for clemency from the court, and asked if he had
anything further to say in his defence:

> More have I not to say, my lords, but like as the blessed apostle Saint
> Paul, as we read in the Acts of the Apostles, was present and
> consented to the death of Saint Stephen, and kept their clothes that
> stoned him to death, and yet be they now both twain holy saints
> in heaven, and shall continue there friends forever, so I verily trust,
> and shall therefore right heartily pray, that though your lordships
> have now here in earth been judges to my condemnation, we may
> yet hereafter in heaven merrily all meet together.
>
> (Roper 250)

The sentiment was vintage More. Conforming himself to the pattern of
Christian martyrdom, as his meditations in the Tower had prepared
him to do, More extended the hand of charity to his enemies. But he left
them in no doubt where their future duty lay. As with St Paul, there
would be opportunities for them to repent and convert.

Thomas More was put to death at the Tower early in the morning of 6 July 1535 in front of a small crowd. Among his family, only his adopted daughter Margaret Clement was present: Margaret Roper probably could not bear to be. Like Fisher, More was granted the clemency of beheading. For a loquacious man, he said relatively little on the scaffold, probably because a deal had been struck whereby he agreed to keep things short in exchange for his family being allowed the body for burial.[27] The words of those about to be despatched carried a special charge for contemporaries. Conventionally, condemned criminals, especially traitors, freely confessed their guilt and warned the crowd to take advantage of their dire example. Once again, More rewrote the script. He urged those present to pray for him, and for the king, that it might please God to send him good counsel. According to Roper, he asked the bystanders 'to bear witness with him that he should now there suffer death in and for the faith of the Holy Catholic Church' – a formula that seems to have been used by the Carthusian priors and by Fisher.[28] The Paris News Letter, however, supplies the more famous tradition that More protested 'he died the king's good servant but God's first' (Harpsfield 266).[29] There may also have been a final Morean joke. To the lieutenant of the Tower, at the scaffold steps, More is reported to have quipped, 'I pray you, Master Lieutenant, see me safe up and, for my coming down, let me shift for myself' (Roper 254).

THE MEANING OF A MARTYRDOM

The business of claiming Thomas More began almost immediately. In a physical as well as an emotional sense, first off the mark was Margaret Roper. More's head was set on a pole on London Bridge as a warning to potential traitors. When it was taken down to make space for the heads of other malefactors, Margaret bribed the bridgemaster to let her take it away, having kept track of it by means of a missing tooth.[30] According to one sixteenth-century biographer, Margaret was summoned in front of the Privy Council 'and charged with keeping her father's head as a sacred relic' (Stapleton 193). She was able to persuade them, however, that she meant merely to bury it, although the head was not in fact buried (in the Roper family vault in Canterbury) till after Margaret's death, in 1544, she having preserved it with spices in the meantime.

The Council was right to worry about the propagation of a cult, for accounts hailing More as a martyr were soon circulating on the Continent. Within England, open recognition had to wait until the reign of

Mary, when, with the encouragement of Cardinal Pole, Harpsfield and Roper wrote their lives, casting Sir Thomas as a blessed martyr and saint in heaven. More's nephew William Rastell, who had himself begun a biography of his uncle, published his edition of More's English works in 1557; editions of his Latin works followed in 1563 and 1565. Collectively, these writings established a Catholic hagiographical tradition, which maintained that More, like Fisher, was a martyr for the papacy and the unity of the Church.

Yet the question of what exactly More died for has been a controversial one in modern times. The notion, implicit in R. W. Chambers's seminal biography of 1935 and explicit in Robert Bolt's famous play (and associated film), *A Man for All Seasons* – that More died to uphold the rights of individual conscience against the coercive authority of the totalitarian state – is fairly easy to dispose of. More spoke of his and others' consciences a good deal, but he did not have in mind the rights of individual subjective opinion in any modern relativist sense. Rather, 'conscience' was something individuals had a duty to frame in accordance with objective and accepted moral standards, principally the authoritative teaching of the universal Church.

The point at which the issue becomes clearest for us is perhaps an exchange with Cromwell during More's interrogation on 3 June 1535. Cromwell reminded More that, as chancellor, he and the bishops had compelled suspected heretics to answer on oath whether they believed the pope to be head of the Church. 'And why should not then the King, sith [since] it is a law made here that his Grace is Head of the Church, here compel men to answer precisely to the law here as they did then concerning the Pope.' More replied that there was a difference between the two cases. At that time, in England, as throughout Christendom, the pope's power 'was recognized for an undoubted thing which seemeth not like a thing agreed in this realm and the contrary taken for truth in other realms'. Cromwell's quick-witted, if cynical, response instinctively strikes a chord with the modern reader: 'they were as well burned for the denying of that as they be beheaded for denying of this, and therefore as good reason to compel them to make precise answer to the one as to the other.' But More stuck firmly by his insistence that a man's conscience could not be bound to affirm a 'law local' when there was 'a law of the whole corps of Christendom to the contrary in matter touching belief'. The difference, at root, was not one between burning and beheading, but 'between heading and hell' (*SL* 251–2).

The discussion here of the pope's power raises the question of how extensive More thought that power to be, and whether he can really, as Roper and Harpsfield were keen to suggest, be thought of as a martyr for the papacy. Some modern scholarship has been keen to depict More as a 'papal minimalist', or as a 'conciliarist' who doubted the divine origins of the papacy and considered a general council to be the supreme legislative authority in the Catholic Church.[31] There is certainly some support for this in More's utterances of the last years. In his letter to Cromwell of 5 March 1534, More confessed that 'I was myself sometime not of the mind that the primacy of that see should be begun by the institution of God'. But there was a characteristic twist: his mind had been changed on this question by reading 'those things that the King's Highness had written in his most famous book against the heresies of Martin Luther' (the *Assertio septem sacramentorum* of 1521). At that time, More claimed to have advised Henry to tone down his enthusiastic papalism, in case it embarrassed him in any future quarrel with a pope. There was an element of mischief about this recollection, but More was earnest enough in thinking denial of the divine institution of papal primacy to be a perilous thing, 'for that primacy is at the leastwise instituted by the corps of Christendom and for a great urgent cause in avoiding of schisms and corroborate by continual succession more than the space of a thousand year' (*SL* 212–13).

The letter suggests that the problem of whether More was prepared to give his life for the papacy, or for a united corporate Christendom, is something of a false dichotomy – he had come to see one as the guarantor of the other. It is certainly possible, as Guy suggests, that Roper's account of More's trial speech, with its strong emphasis on the commission to St Peter as first pope, is fanciful – a Marian Catholic version of what More ought to have said.[32] But it is equally plausible that the reality of schism, and the horrors that might flow from it, moved More towards a more positive assessment of the importance of the papacy, as it was to do (eventually) with churchmen on the other side of the argument in 1535, such as Stephen Gardiner and Cuthbert Tunstall. There is no doubt that, in a linguistic category first developed by Henry VIII's propagandists, Thomas More was a 'papist', and an 'obstinate' one at that.

In the end, however, such politico-theological analysis only takes us so far towards grasping how More understood the point of his own death. In the very last of his devotional writings, a prayer composed in the Tower after his condemnation on 1 July 1535, More prayed God for the grace 'in all my feare and agonye to have recourse to that great feare and wonderfull agonye, that thou my sweete saviour hadst at the mount of Olivete before thy most bitter passion' (*CW* 13:229). In the model of Christ as the righteous man unjustly convicted, the fearful human, shrinking but not turning from the prospect of death, and the loving saviour promising salvation to friend and foe, victim and persecutor, Thomas More found a pattern in pain, and a meaning in martyrdom.

FURTHER READING

More's last years are well covered in the standard modern biographies by Marius and Guy, and in Guy's dual biography of Thomas and Margaret More (below, 291). In addition, Peter Ackroyd's *Life of Thomas More* includes a memorably dramatized version of More's trial.

Good introductory discussions of the politics of Henry VIII's divorce and break with Rome are Richard Rex, *Henry VIII and the English Reformation*, 2nd edn (Basingstoke: Palgrave Macmillan, 2006), and the essays by Virginia Murphy and Diarmaid MacCulloch in Diarmaid MacCulloch, ed., *The Reign of Henry VIII: Politics, Policy and Piety* (Basingstoke: Macmillan, 1995). For more detailed discussion of these events in More's London milieu, see Susan Brigden, *London and the Reformation* (Oxford: Clarendon Press, 1989).

A comparison of More with the principal sparring partner of his last years, Thomas Cromwell, and highly favourable to the latter, is offered by G. R. Elton, 'Thomas More and Thomas Cromwell', in his *Studies in Tudor and Stuart Politics and Government*, 4 vols. (Cambridge University Press, 1974–92), 4:144–60. For a bracingly revisionist and anti-Eltonian account of More's opposition to Henry, see George Bernard, *The King's Reformation: Henry VIII and the Remaking of the English Church* (New Haven and London: Yale University Press, 2005), 125–51. Contrast and comparison with Henry's other problem case, John Fisher, can be followed up in Brendan Bradshaw and Eamon Duffy, eds., *Humanism, Reform and the Reformation: The Career of Bishop John Fisher* (Cambridge University Press, 1989).

On the Tower Works, in addition to the helpful interpretative essays in *CW* 12, 13, and 14, see Louis L. Martz, *Thomas More: The Search for the Inner Man* (New Haven and London: Yale University Press, 1990), and the final chapters of Alistair Fox, *Thomas More: History and Providence* (Oxford: Blackwell, 1982).

Anthony Kenny, *Thomas More* (Oxford University Press, 1983), 93–7, offers a very clear and persuasive short discussion of More's understanding of conscience. The myth-making potential of Bolt's

A Man for All Seasons, and a historiographical backlash, are assessed in Peter Marshall, 'Saints and cinemas: *A Man for All Seasons*', in Susan Doran and Thomas S. Freeman, eds., *Tudors and Stuarts on Film: Historical Perspectives* (Basingstoke: Palgrave Macmillan, 2008), 46–59.

Notes

1. 'Sir Thomas More and the opposition to Henry VIII', *EA* 79–91.
2. Throckmorton's later confession is printed as an appendix in Guy, *The Public Career of Sir Thomas More*, 207–12.
3. Marius, *Thomas More*, 426.
4. Roper 229–30. The story was adapted from a tale by Tacitus about a daughter of Sejanus, put to death with her family under Tiberius: Marius, *Thomas More*, 439.
5. Marius, *Thomas More*, 463–4.
6. Guy, *Thomas More*, 169.
7. *A Daughter's Love*, 234–42.
8. See the detailed accounts of the *Dialogue* and *De Tristitia* later in this volume. Rastell printed the unfinished *De Tristitia* in a translation by More's granddaughter Mary Basset.
9. Marius, *Thomas More*, 471, 465.
10. 'The real Thomas More?', in Elton, *Studies in Tudor and Stuart Politics and Government* (in 'Further reading'), 3:354–5.
11. Garry E. Haupt, 'Introduction', *CW* 13:clxxiv–clxxx.
12. Eamon Duffy, *Marking the Hours: English People and their Prayers 1240–1570* (New Haven and London: Yale University Press, 2006), 107–18.
13. Henry Gee and William John Hardy, eds., *Documents Illustrative of English Church History* (London: Macmillan, 1896), 244.
14. Ibid., 248.
15. G. R. Elton, *Policy and Police: The Enforcement of the Reformation in the Age of Thomas Cromwell* (Cambridge University Press, 1972), 402–3.
16. This is suggested by Roper 243–4.
17. Marius, *Thomas More*, 499.
18. Roper 244–5; Stapleton 160. Cf. Harpsfield 182–3; Ro. Ba., *The Life of Syr Thomas More*, 226–7.
19. *The Life of Fisher*, transcribed by Ronald Bayne from MS Harleian 6382, Early English Text Society, extra series 117 (London: Oxford University Press, 1921), 110, 115.
20. The most persuasive reconstruction of the meeting is that by John Guy, who has examined Rich's damaged memo under ultra-violet light in the National Archive, and I quote here from his transcription: *A Daughter's Love*, 257–8, 323.
21. The indictment is reproduced in Harpsfield 269–76.
22. I follow here the reconstruction of More's defence in Guy, *Thomas More*, 190–2.

23. *Policy and Police*, 415 (although Elton was not able to decipher all of Rich's memo to Cromwell).
24. Guy, *Thomas More*, 193–4.
25. Marius, *Thomas More*, 507; Roper 246.
26. All modern accounts of the procedure here depend on J. D. M. Derrett, 'The trial of Sir Thomas More', *EA* 55–78.
27. Guy, *Thomas More*, 210.
28. Roper 254; Peter Marshall, *Religious Identities in Henry VIII's England* (Aldershot: Ashgate, 2006), 177.
29. Guy doubts that More would have said something so bold (which might have provoked reprisals against his family), and speculates that he may in fact, 'with scarifying irony', have invoked Henry's injunction to him of years before that he should 'first look unto God and after God unto him': *Thomas More*, 211.
30. Guy, *A Daughter's Love*, 1–4.
31. Guy, *Thomas More*, 201; Francis Oakley, *The Conciliarist Tradition: Constitutionalism in the Catholic Church 1300–1870* (Oxford University Press, 2003), 135–6.
32. Guy, *Thomas More*, 203–4.

Part II

Five major works

7 Reading *Utopia*

DOMINIC BAKER-SMITH

The modern reader of *Utopia*, challenged by the provocations of More's traveller's tale, may find a degree of reassurance in the apparent failure of some among More's contemporaries to get the point. In 1518 the Alsatian humanist Beatus Rhenanus, who at that time was seeing the third edition of *Utopia* through Johann Froben's press in Basel, wrote to the imperial councillor Willibald Pirckheimer, reporting how he had praised the book to a group of respected men. One of these had responded with the observation that 'More deserved no more credit than a paid scribe, who simply writes down what other people say after the fashion of a pen-pusher ... Everything in the book, he said, came from the mouth of Hythloday; all More did was write it down' (*CU* 258–9). It is as well to be cautious here: maybe this dim individual, whose opinion was warmly supported by the others present, is just another literary invention. Certainly, his literal-mindedness seems to glance back at More's own prefatory letter to Peter Giles which had been part of the book since the first edition, printed at Louvain some two years earlier. There More plays on the same theme: 'I confess, my dear Peter, that having all these materials to hand left hardly anything at all for me to do.' His job was just to write down what he heard (*CU* 31). The author, in other words, is simply a passive conduit for the adventures described by the enigmatic figure of Raphael Hythlodaeus.

It can be no great surprise to learn that Beatus's group of wooden-minded literalists are theologians, representatives of that institutional scholasticism which forms a frequent target of Erasmus's satire. One revealing illustration of such a mentality, no doubt spiced up by Erasmus, occurs in a letter he wrote to More in 1520, describing his clash with the Louvain theologian Nicolaas Baechem. Exposed to a torrent of abuse by his opponent, Erasmus tries to put forward a proposition, ' "Imagine I ..." Here ... [Baechem] burst in at once with his large bargee voice: "I do not imagine, I will not imagine; I leave that to you.

You poets are all imagination, and all falsehood"' (*CWE* 8:92). The Latin verb employed here is *fingere*, to form, invent or feign, the root of our *fiction*. Baechem likes to know where he stands, and regards the introduction of imagination as seriously destabilizing. But then, that is just why Erasmus and More make use of it. The reader picking up *Utopia* and glancing through the introductory pages is immediately confronted by the issue of veracity.

For a start there is that map of the island, together with the Utopian alphabet and a poem in the language. Then More's apparently ingenuous letter to Giles stresses the passivity of his role; his major qualification is the accuracy of his memory, which is why he is so anxious to be precise over the length of the bridge in Amaurot. By contrast, Giles's letter to Jérôme de Busleyden extols the vividness of More's account, claiming that 'As often as I read it, I seem to see even more than when I heard the actual words of Hythloday' (*CU* 25). This teasing amalgam of historical circumstance and fictional elaboration is then taken further, when we venture on to the opening of the narrative itself. There, in Antwerp, we encounter 'historical' figures, notably those of More and Giles, respectively undersheriff of London and clerk to the Council of Antwerp, set against the background of a verifiable diplomatic mission. Yet their chance meeting after worship in the cathedral has an uncanny resemblance to the opening of Plato's *Republic*, and it also introduces us to the mysterious stranger, Raphael Hythlodaeus, who will be our guide to 'the new island of Utopia'.

There is, then, a sense of mischief lurking under the surface of the text, one that aims to stretch our reading capacity well beyond that of literal-minded men like Baechem, and this can be seen as part of More's debt to Lucian. Together with Erasmus, More had undertaken a study of the writings of the second-century Syrian ironist in 1505–6, while Erasmus was staying at More's house in Bucklersbury. The result was a collection of Latin translations from Lucian's Greek dialogues which was printed in Paris by Badius Ascensius late in 1506 (*CW* 3, Part 1). More is well known for his own sense of irony, a quality of mind that did not endear him to his opponents; it emerges clearly in the sharp turns of his Latin epigrams, and it gave him an instinctive sympathy with Lucian's exposures of human fatuity. In More's case, however, the laughter was invariably serious.[1] When Erasmus returned to Bucklersbury in 1509, the year of Henry VIII's accession, it was to complete and present to More his own Lucianic masterpiece, *The Praise of Folly*. Spoken by Folly (*Moria*), the book is dedicated to More, or, in his Latin form, *Morus*, a word that also designates a fool. That is a point that should be borne in mind when we meet More, or Morus, as one of the speakers in *Utopia*.

The Lucianic temper which marks the book can be detected in three features. In the first place, as we have already seen, there is an interpenetration between the actual world (that is, the setting for historical persons) and the imaginary world depicted in Raphael's travel story. In this interpenetration the prefatory materials, the *parerga*, play an essential part. In contrast to Beatus's group of literal-minded scholastics, More's ideal reader has to be nimble and alert, moving between a world of apparent objectivity and the startling fantasies of a traveller's tale. The effect is to give the fictional elements an extra ballast, to make the possibilities that they open up seem tantalizingly within reach.

A second Lucianic resource is the introduction of fanciful names, for the most part rooted in Greek, which make their own oblique comment on the main theme.[2] We have seen More's anxiety to establish the precise length of the bridge over the river Anyder at Amaurot, the chief city of Utopia (*CU* 35); Anyder, *Anydrus* in Latin, comes from the Greek *anydros*, 'waterless', while Amaurot derives from *amauros*, 'obscure' or 'unknown'. The negative connotations of a waterless river running through an invisible city fit aptly with the name of the island itself, Utopia, from *ou-topos* or 'no-place'. Indeed, More initially titled his book *Nusquama*, the Latin for 'nowhere', and its eventual emergence as the Greek-based *Utopia* may be an editorial liberty by Erasmus.[3] In any case, the negativity stands out and directs our attention to more serious themes.

In Lucian's *True History*, an example of the fantastic travel narrative which More certainly knew, the traveller arrives at the Isle of the Blest to find that of all the great ones of the past only Plato is missing: 'allegedly he was living in his imaginary city under the constitution and the laws that he drew up himself'.[4] In other words, along with his republic, he is lost in mental space. This is playful enough, but at the same time it points us to an important moment in Plato's *Republic* when Socrates discusses the philosopher's engagement with political affairs. Leaving the wider issues aside for the moment, it is worth noting Glaucon's description of the philosopher's city, 'whose home is in the ideal, for I think that it can be found nowhere on earth'.[5] Such a serio-comical approach is also evident in More's presentation of Raphael Hythlodaeus, the Portuguese traveller who has sailed to the New World with Amerigo Vespucci, encountered the remarkable island culture of the Utopians, and now resurfaces in Antwerp to tell his tale. Apart from his weather-beaten appearance and his long beard, Raphael wears his cloak with a casual informality (*neglectim*) which may be intended to suggest Lucian's stock image of a philosopher but certainly matches the bluntness (*neglecta simplicitas*) of his speech, which More is so anxious to reproduce (*CU* 31). It is his name, however, that merits special attention. Raphael is the name of an archangel, the messenger of God and a 'heavenly physician',[6] but it is followed by another teasing composite, Hythlodaeus, deriving from *hythlos*, 'nonsense', and either *daios*, 'destructive', or *daiein*, 'to distribute', offering the options of 'destructive of nonsense' or 'purveyor of non-sense'.[7] The one thing that is certain is the nonsense, and that glances back both to Plato's *Republic*, where the coarse and prag-matic Thrasymachus warns Socrates against talking about 'that which ought to be' or suchlike nonsense (336D), and also to Lucian's *True History*, where Socrates is in danger of being thrown off the Isle of the Blest precisely for talking nonsense. Simply by virtue of his name, then, Raphael might be said to hold complex credentials.

But there is a further insight which More and Erasmus must have come to appreciate in their encounter with Lucian, and that is his exposure of the distorting effects of social custom on our perception of the world. A basic factor here is the all-too-human tendency to confuse cultural signs with the qualities they signify, substituting outward gestures for actual qualities. Erasmus's *Praise of Folly* is in essence a catalogue of such confusions, the stunted vision of those dwellers in Plato's cave who take shadows for reality (*CWE* 27:119). It is this cultural disjunction between letter and spirit that drives the satire of More and Erasmus, and it is something they elaborated out of their reading of Lucian. But it is a disjunction sanctioned by custom, by established social practice, and thus custom is a frequent target for their anger.

A memorable example occurs in Erasmus's searing attack on the culture of war, that is to say on the institutions of chivalry, in his long essay 'Dulce bellum inexpertis', 'War is sweet for those who have not tried it' (*CWE* 35:399–440), first printed in 1515 in what has been called the 'Utopian' edition of his *Adages*. It was written in reaction to Henry VIII's invasion of France in 1513, but it touches on much wider themes of social alienation: at its core is a primitivist myth, deriving from Ovid, which identifies the fall of humanity from innocence with the consumption of animal flesh (*Metamorphoses* 15.75–142). Just as the Utopians despise hunting and butchery (although they still eat meat), so Erasmus finds the origins of military violence in the human war on animals, echoing in this Ovid's account of Pythagorean teaching. If it is acceptable to kill animals for food, then it is only a step to the clash of human rivals, and in time this is orchestrated into the elaborate killing fields of Renaissance Europe. Behind this process of degeneration is custom, whatever is made licit by society, 'so true it is that nothing is too villainous, or too cruel to gain approval if custom recommends it' (*CWE* 35:408). Custom, whether through the enactment of familiar rituals or through the uncritical adoption of established values, serves to spread infection through society. It is revealing here to jump ahead, to 1527, and the second book of Erasmus's *Hyperaspistes*, written as a response to Luther at the urgent prompting of More. Countering Luther's claim that sin is endemic to human nature, Erasmus detects its origins also in our social inheritance: 'For the most part it comes not from nature but from corrupt education, bad company, from a habit of sinning, and a will that is malicious' (*CWE* 77:575). This relatively optimistic reading of human nature means that while Erasmus admits a negative tendency, the malice of the will, he also sees the dangers coming from outside, from corrupt social perceptions. Original sin, the implication seems to be, is built into our social inheritance.

The hostility of both More and Erasmus to 'custom' is the basis for their criticism of contemporary society, and for them it carries the overtones of what would now be called structural sin, the distorting effect of unjust social structures on moral perception. It is for this reason that Erasmus's educational writings give such a strong emphasis to the implanting of positive values to resist the idols of society, just the policy adopted by Utopian educators: 'What is planted in the minds of children lives on in the minds of grown men and serves greatly to strengthen the commonwealth; its decline can always be traced to vices that arise from wrong attitudes' (*CU* 231). This may seem a far cry from Lucian, yet there is a common thread in the claim that society is founded on a conspiracy of shared delusions. *The Praise of Folly* is essentially an elaboration of this theme, and it has direct relevance to the argument of *Utopia*. As an illustration we can take the most Lucianic episode in the latter work, that of the Anemolian ambassadors.

This is inserted like a parable in the section that deals with the unusual attitude of the Utopians towards gold and silver, metals which have little practical use except for the fact that custom has endowed them with artificial value. The Utopians, thanks to their productivity in those things that sustain life, are able to trade their surplus to foreign nations, albeit on very generous terms, and receive in return not only genuine requirements like iron but also huge quantities of gold and silver. In the absence of any internal medium of exchange these are kept solely for use in time of war, when the Utopians use them to hire foreign mercenaries and to bribe enemy troops. Consequently, huge stocks of precious metal have to be stored against future use, but not as treasure, since this would only maintain its specious value, but rather in the form of chamber pots or the shackles of slaves and other insignia of public shame. This paradoxical linking of gold and excrement, a joke that had its classical antecedents, amuses most readers of *Utopia*, but it is important to see just how More places it.

Raphael introduces the section by raising the issue of belief: the Utopian practice would seem incredible if he had not seen it with his own eyes, because 'the more different a thing is from what the listeners are used to, the harder it is to believe' (*CU* 149). What 'the listeners are used to' is precisely *mos*, 'custom'. Customs define a society, so that – as Raphael implies – the odd way in which the Utopians handle gold is a consequence of their determination to rate it as a malleable but rather useless metal, instead of allotting it some inflated rarity value. This is the reason why, instead of storing it in a treasury, which would simply reinforce its artificial value, they use it for such sordid functions. This is part of their 'plan', *ratio*, 'which conforms with the rest of their institutions as sharply as it contrasts with our own'. That is why they can part with their gold without a twinge, while the rest of us feel its loss like disembowelling. In this they have at least one feature in common with other natives of the New World reported by Vespucci, who preferred feathers to gold or pearls.[8]

Authentic or 'natural' value is the issue, and Raphael introduces the picture of Utopian children, playing with gems and pearls, to illustrate the case. As they mature they discard such trifles (*CU* 151). The Anemolian episode rams home the point, but with particular irony. The Anemolians, from *anemos*, 'wind', are puffed up: when they hear of the Utopians' simplicity in manner and dress, they decide in typical Renaissance style to dazzle them with display, employing a large retinue in particoloured attire, while the ambassadors themselves are draped with gold chains. The objectivity of Raphael's account is borne out by a letter from 1514 (the year before More is writing) which describes the arrival of Henry VIII's sister, the Princess Mary, at Abbeville on her way to marry Louis XII:

On the road, in advance of her, were some fifty of her squires, dressed in silk of several sorts, with gold collars worth from 50 to 60 ducats each, some more, some less. Next came the Duke of Norfolk, the ambassadors, and other lords and barons, in pairs, according to grade, making a very fine show, all clad either in cloth of gold or silk of various qualities, in riding gear, and all wearing enormous gold collars [i.e. chains], some doubled and some trebled, round their necks, whilst some wore them prisoner fashion; so that never was such pomp witnessed; and the greater part of them had velvet bonnets, some of one colour and some of another.

(*CSPV* 2:208)

One can see here the basis for Erasmus's dry observation on courtiers, 'Their self-satisfaction rests on the weight of the chain their necks have to carry, as if they had to show off their physical strength as well as their riches' (*CWE* 27:137). Inevitably, the Anemolian ploy miscarries: the grander members of the embassy are assumed to be slaves or, worse still, fools, *moriones*, another term that leads back to the Latin cognate of More's own name. It is worth recalling that at the time he wrote this part of *Utopia* More was abroad as an ambassador and probably wore a gold chain when required.

This episode has its classical antecedents, notably in Lucian, whose *Nigrinus* describes a rich man, 'conspicuous for his vulgarity', who tries to make a splash in Athenian society and has to learn the same lesson as the ambassadors.[9] But this is the lesson of a moralist, making a point about individual conduct; what marks More's originality is his concern with the wider cultural perspective or 'belief'. As we have seen, Raphael's rather embarrassed introduction of the chamber pots implies that we, the readers, are to be included among those, whether Anemolian nobles or Hellenistic parvenus, who have a defective sense of value. We are, indeed, in the situation of Plato's cave dwellers, who cannot tell shadows from reality. Raphael's point is that customs are the guide to a 'cast of mind' or, as More's Latin puts it, *affectiones animorum*, a phrase which indicates, beyond mere intellectual assent, the whole disposition of the personality. Utopian attitudes are developed in part from their upbringing, since their social practices, such as using gold chamber pots, promote sound value judgements, but also in part from instruction and from good books (*CU* 155), among which we might feel inclined to put *Utopia* itself. Thinking back to those social causes of sin listed by Erasmus, one can see that Utopian education is precisely designed to counter them. In fact, it is entirely fitting that the discussion of false values, epitomized by the European lust for gold, should lead straight on to the account of Utopian education, grounded in mastery of the liberal arts, *bonae litterae*, which More so strongly urges in his 'Letter to Martin Dorp' (*CW* 15:15; see above, 31–2).

The 'Letter to Dorp' is dated from Bruges on 21 October 1515, the very time when More concluded his diplomatic duties in the Netherlands and returned to England. With him he carried the initial draft of the work, *Nusquama* as he called it, which had occupied his leisure hours since his visit to Antwerp in late July. *Utopia* has been described as a patchwork composition, and certainly More seems to have found out what he was doing as he went along. Recent scholarship, prompted by J. H. Hexter's classic study of *Utopia*'s 'biography', has attempted to recover the sequence.[10] This is not just a minor issue of literary history: in so far as it is possible to recover the most likely order in which More assembled the elements of his narrative, we can form a much clearer picture of his dominant preoccupations. The first clue, as Hexter pointed out, lies in Erasmus's biographical sketch of More, which he sent to Ulrich von Hutten in 1519 (*CWE* 7:24); there he claims that More wrote the second book when at leisure, and added the first book later 'in the heat of the moment'. This must mean that the first stage to be written dealt with the remarkable island and its institutions, and to it we can probably add the introductory pages set in Antwerp that lead us from the steps of Notre Dame into the privacy of the garden at More's lodgings. In brief, we have the setting of the scene, followed by Raphael's lengthy monologue about Utopian life.

At this point More returns to London and is swiftly sucked into a hectic routine, as Andrea Ammonio, the king's Latin secretary, reports: 'None bids my lord of York good morrow earlier than he' (*CWE* 3:239).[11] It is in this setting, 'in the heat of the moment', vividly described by More in his prefatory letter to Peter Giles, that he writes the remainder of the text, that is, the greater part of Book I and the closing section of Book II, that which follows after Raphael has concluded his account of the island. This has the effect of enclosing Raphael's monologue in the frame of a dialogue where he debates with More and Giles, those representatives of civic government, on issues of reform and political engagement. When, in September 1516, the completed work is sent off to Erasmus so that he can see it through the press, a third stage is initiated, that of the *parerga*, the prefatory letters and other materials collected by Erasmus, with their teasing questions about the objective existence of the island. It becomes possible to detect a pattern behind the evolution of the book.

To start off, in the enforced leisure of a lull in diplomatic negotiations, More is stirred to write an account of a fictional society. This society has struck readers in a variety of different ways, both negative and positive, but the one thing that can safely be said about it is that it is free from the dead hand of custom, at least as that is manifest in societies of the old or pre-Columbian world. More's return to London and his immersion in public affairs, however distracting it may have been, did provide a suitable backdrop for the dominant theme of Book I, dubbed by Hexter the Dialogue of Counsel.[12] Here, attention is switched from the depiction of a radically reordered social system to the actual possibilities for reform. How can a society driven by its own burden of custom and inherited perceptions be modified by new ideas? And, as a further refinement on this, what is the duty of the intellectual in the face of a corrupt or misdirected society? To put it briefly, More's book turns out to be less about the unveiling of some ideal model (which ironically is what 'utopian' has come to mean) than about the process by which such a model may, or may not, be put into practice. We could call it a parable of the political imagination.

It is not always noticed that the austerely anonymous society of Utopia does have its hero, the shadowy figure of Utopus, who is both its conqueror and the founder of its institutions. As it turns out, the two roles are inseparable. Utopus's opportunistic attack on the Abraxans (as they were originally called) took advantage of their religious squabbles to vanquish them and place them completely under his control. This creates that happy conjunction of power and intelligence necessary to overthrow inherited forms and make a fresh start, very much in the manner of Plato's philosopher-artist of the *Republic* or the consummate legislator of the *Laws*.[13] In the *Republic* a fresh start entailed banishing everyone over ten years of age. We do not hear much about the immediate steps taken by Utopus, but we do learn that his initiatives, which extend from town planning to religious affairs, have enabled the Utopians to evolve from relative barbarism to 'a high level of culture and humanity' (*CU* 111). The most striking of these initiatives had been to isolate the land mass of Abraxa from the mainland by excavating a channel fifteen miles wide, thus turning it into the island of Utopia, a territory inaccessible to the outside world, where its unique institutions can function in security, along with the moral dispositions that they encourage.

This link between institutions and attitudes is seminal for *Utopia*, as we have already seen. Thomas More was an astute observer of human behaviour and was fully alert to its dependence on surrounding circumstances. There had been that period at the Carthusian monastery in London, reportedly as a lodger (see above, 13–14), which brought him close to a highly organized way of life in which physical conditions were used to promote spiritual goals. Monastic observance is never far from the surface in his account of Utopian life. Further, as a lawyer active within the civic community of London, he would have been well aware of the tussle between civic idealism and the city's ever-expanding population.[14] It is hardly surprising that Raphael's account of Utopia is largely concerned with one representative city, Amaurot, since the island is a federation of identical city states, each comparable in scale to the Greek *polis* or to early Tudor London, although a Utopian city, with its population of 100,000 or more, was about twice the size of the latter.

In contrast to classical models of the ideal commonwealth, More makes his basic unit the individual household under its *paterfamilias*, which, according to Augustine, 'ought to be the beginning, or a little part of the city'.[15] Each urban household contains between ten and sixteen adults: since there are six thousand *familiae* in each city, this gives a median figure of 78,000 adults, although it is not clear if this includes those performing their two-year stint on the farms outside the city. These rural granges house forty adults, twenty of whom are replaced each year by a fresh intake from the city. It is really at this household level that the political system begins, in city and country-side alike, each household presided over by the senior couple, the *paterfamilias* and his wife. At the next level, the two hundred sypho-grants in each city and its surrounding farms, each one elected by thirty households, ensure a healthy continuity between domestic life and the higher levels of government. Elected on an annual basis themselves, they are responsible for the election of the governor and also, as far as one can make out, that of the twenty tranibors who constitute the senate and advise him. Moreover, whenever that body meets, usually every other day, two syphogrants are present as observers. All important issues are laid before the assembly of syphogrants, and they in their turn discuss the matter with their households before reporting back to the senate. Since it is a capital offence to initiate policies outside the senate, this democratic base provides a real check on the exercise of power; the essential distinction lies between the syphogrants, ordinary citizens, and the executive offices, which are filled by scholars.

Members of this privileged elite, only about three hundred in each city (*CU* 131 and n. 33), are first nominated by the priests, who oversee education, and then elected by the syphogrants. Their lives are devoted to study, but they also fill the major public offices and serve as ambassadors: they are, in other words, civic humanists. The key role of the syphogrants, therefore, is to maintain a dialogue between the executive and the citizens – by attending the senate, debating among themselves, and presiding in the urban halls. In some respects they can be compared to the members of the Common Council of London, drawn from the city's householders, much as tranibors match the aldermen, who advised the mayor.[16] Thus while it is clear that More drew on classical precedents for this 'mixed' mode of government, most notably on the Spartan model, and that he may well have had some conception of the Venetian constitution, with its provisions for curbing arbitrary power, it is also likely that a Londoner reading *Utopia* would have spotted familiar features among its institutions.[17]

More tells us relatively little about life on the rural granges, but it is clear that regular periods on the land ensure that all citizens are practised farmers, just as in the city they are enthusiastic gardeners. Close involvement with the cultivation of nature is seen as morally beneficial. It is a function of the syphogrants to ensure that all, in town or country, perform their allotted work, and this raises one unique aspect of Utopian life, the universal obligation to undertake manual labour. Only scholars and syphogrants are exempt, although the latter prefer to lead by example. This is in striking contrast to historical precedent and equally to theory: Aristotle had argued that citizens of his ideal constitution must avoid mechanical or agricultural labour, since it would interfere with the acquisition of virtue (*Politics* 7.8.2). The Utopians do both at once. This is possible because their labouring day, which amounts to a total of six hours, leaves ample time for study and self-improvement. There may be a monastic thought behind this elevation of labour to a place in the ideal life, but it has practical consequences in the ready supply of foodstuffs and other essentials which make leisure possible. It is this aspect of Utopian life that would have most astonished contemporaries. Out of a day of sixteen hours, six are given to work and the remainder that is not taken up by the communal meals and recreation is 'generally devoted to intellectual activity' (*CU* 127). Thus all Utopians, of both sexes, enjoy the opportunity for self-cultivation; indeed, those dawn lectures open to all (rising is at four o'clock) are arguably the most innovative feature of the Utopian system. Utopians also enjoy security in sickness and old age, a vivid contrast to the wretched existence of workers in Europe, described with barely suppressed rage by Raphael: 'After society has taken the labour of their best years, when they are worn out by age, sickness and utter destitution, then the thankless commonwealth, forgetting all their sleepless nights and services, throws them out to die a miserable death' (*CU* 243). Labour in Utopia, by contrast, has dignity and brings its rewards.

The best-known feature of Utopian life is its communism: when at the end of Book II More's fictional self, Morus, confides in us his objections to Utopian customs, it is their communal living and their moneyless economy that most disturb him. But what does this actually mean? In a monetary economy, where tokens based on conventional value replace inherent value, consumption and display are a predictable consequence of private ownership, and luxury trades pander to private gratification. So in Utopia there is no money, and there is no ownership: 'among friends all is common'. This ancient proverb is used by Erasmus to open the 1515 edition of the *Adages* (*CWE* 31:29–30), and there he attributes it to Pythagoras. We have already encountered this legendary figure in Erasmus's attack on war, and in both cases he is brought in to suggest some remote phase of cultural innocence, prior to the emergence of society as we know it.[18] The contrast is clarified, albeit unintentionally, in a passage from Cicero's *De officiis* ('On moral obligation'), cited by Erasmus, where he, too, deals with 'the Greek proverb': Cicero acknowledges 'the common right to all things that Nature has produced for the common use of man', but this is followed by the heavy qualification that 'everything assigned as private property by the statutes and by civil law shall be so held'.[19] For a moment we glimpse a primeval state of access to nature's resources, only for it to be blocked off by private property and the laws which protect it. Indeed, confronted by agrarian reform, Cicero claims that the original motive that drew men into civil association was 'the hope of safeguarding their possessions' (*De off.* 2.21.73).

In contrast to such Roman compromise, Erasmus offers the words of Plato, 'that a state would be happy and blessed in which these words "mine" and "not mine" were never to be heard'.[20] Plato makes this statement in the *Republic* (462C), but More could also encounter it in a very different source, the reminiscence of the Golden Age adopted by Peter Martyr d'Anghiera in his effort to describe the natives of Cuba: 'with them the earth, like the sun and water, is common, nor do "mine and yours", the seeds of all evils, fall among them'.[21] So More could look back to the primitivist myth of Pythagoras, or westward to those

new-found lands where Raphael had travelled, and find similar contrasts to the property-owning conventions of Europe. The thought that
established systems of law are the by-product of humanity's fall was
certainly in the air: Colet, in his *Exposition of Romans* (c. 1512–16),
distinguishes that unsophisticated nature which used common property from a 'law of a corrupter nature ... which brought in ideas of
meum and *tuum*'.[22] Budé, likewise, one of *Utopia*'s more perceptive
readers, sees the body of civil and canon law as undermined by Christ's
'Pythagorean rule' (*CU* 13). This is Erasmus's point as well: 'it is
extraordinary how Christians dislike this common ownership of
Plato's, how in fact they cast stones at it, although nothing was ever
said by a pagan philosopher which comes closer to the mind of Christ'
(*CWE* 31:30). What one can deduce from this is a clear sense that
community of goods is a defining note of Utopia not least because it
distinguishes it from the known world, from society as it has been
shaped by the inherited burden of custom and law.[23]

What the Utopians enjoy by natural right is the simple use
of commodities; what they do not claim is *dominium*, the power of
possession and disposal which is very much the product of civil
society as it has emerged in Europe.[24] As a result, there is a smooth
and equitable distribution of commodities throughout the community according to need. The natural discrepancies of shortage and
surplus are adjusted by the annual council in Amaurot, with the
result, as Raphael claims, that 'the whole island is like a single
family' (*CU* 147). In such an economy private ownership has no
place. What is more, without property there is no scope for self-
projection, for the intricacies of dress or manners that define individuality in Europe; in contrast to the gold-fettered slaves, the
anonymous citizens present a sober spectacle in their leather
working clothes and undyed woollen cloaks.

It says a lot about Utopian community life that those with permission to travel, whether within their own city's territory or further
afield, need take nothing with them: as their needs will be supplied
wherever they go, 'they are at home everywhere' (*CU* 145). Since
arrangements are identical throughout the island, the traveller can
pick up his trade at any point in order to earn his keep. The most
important means of cementing this social solidarity is the practice of
eating in common, a custom that had its Greek precedents but is used
in Utopia to the virtual exclusion of private catering. Each communal
hall serves a syphograncy, that is thirty families or anything up to 480
adults, and the syphogrant and his wife are seated centrally to keep

an eye on things. In such a society many eyes are kept on much. While infants are confined to the nursery and adolescents serve or stand silently by, at the tables young and old alternate, a means of bonding generations, and of restraining the young 'from improper freedom of words or gestures' (*CU* 143). Then, as in More's own house, the meal begins with a brief reading on some moral matter which can be reviewed in lively discussion between young and old. As Lewis Mumford remarks, these meals, combined with music and perfumes, restore 'the sharing and largesse that were common in simple communities before the introduction of a money economy'.[25] If here, as in so many areas of Utopian life, social control is emphasized, this is because the 'sharing and largesse', the whole concept of such Pythagorean community, depends on the curbing of private gratification.[26] Property and individuality go together.

It is in the context of such festive meals that Raphael sounds an initial note of caution, 'For they are somewhat inclined to think that no kind of pleasure is forbidden, provided harm does not come from it' (*CU* 143). This isolated comment may well mislead the reader, suggesting as it does a hedonistic way of life, but it soon becomes clear that the Utopian understanding of pleasure is a good deal more rigorous than we are led to anticipate. The point is that in the Utopian scheme pleasures are rated in an ascending order, rising from the easing of simple bodily needs to the intellectual contemplation of truth; no pleasure may be approved if it causes pain to oneself or others or if it blocks the enjoyment of a greater pleasure. By observing this hierarchical ordering of delights, 'the art of conducting one's life', as Augustine calls it, the Utopians are enabled to enjoy the full scope of human nature.[27] By contrast those false pleasures associated with courtly life, from sartorial display to the intricacies of hunting ritual, can only be rated as enjoyable on the basis of *vanissima conspiratio*, 'a grotesque conspiracy', where again it is social custom that perverts natural taste and projects an artificial 'nature'.[28] What strikes one here is that word *conspiratio*; the same term is used by Raphael at the very close of his account to describe the false commonwealth manipulated by the rich in their own interest. Compared to Utopia, then, society as we know it is a conspiracy to turn nature on its head.

That is why nature assumes such importance in More's treatment of the best state of a commonwealth: there human fulfilment is found in a life lived in accord with nature, and such a life will be a source of pleasure. It is essential to remember, too, that in Utopia, in contrast to the classical sources known to More, this life is accessible to all, a consequence of the favourable economic conditions that make leisure, *otium*, generally available. It can be no surprise that Utopians show little aptitude for the abstractions of scholasticism but rather, like good humanists, focus on moral philosophy and in particular on the nature of happiness (*CU* 157–9). This explains why they have such a positive response to the classical library that Raphael and his companions bring with them, and it is Greek literature in particular that captures their interest, making them a shining example to the reluctant Grecians of Europe (*CU* 181).[29] The Utopians have a natural affinity with the Greeks, and both are in agreement on the virtue of a life conducted in accord with nature – the whole Utopian enterprise identifies the reasonable with the natural.[30] From this arises their notion of pleasure as it ascends from delights of the senses, continues through the exploration of 'this beautiful mechanism of the world' (*CU* 183), to arrive finally at the recollection of a well-spent life and anticipation of joys in a life to come (*CU* 161). Behind this ascent we can detect the influence of those religious axioms which the Utopians accept as a necessary supplement to the reach of reason: the immortality of the soul, the instinctive appetite for happiness, and the prospect of post-mortem judgement. While their system betrays elements of Stoic and Epicurean thought, its controlling principle has much in common with the spiritual aspirations of Platonism as mediated by its great fifteenth-century advocate Marsilio Ficino.[31]

One Utopian virtue that is strongly emphasized by Raphael is openness to innovation; indeed, it is incorporated in the prayers offered by their priests (*CU* 239–41). We hear about the Utopians' adoption of Roman technology after an ancient shipwreck (*CU* 107), and their enthusiasm for Greek literature is the most obvious instance. It is this willingness to learn that has enabled them to rise from the barbarism of the Abraxans to their present level of culture, and a comparable pattern of evolution is discernible in their religious practice. Utopus's policy of toleration rests on faith in the eventual victory of truth; in Raphael's words, 'if one religion is really true and the rest are false, the truth will sooner or later emerge and prevail by its own natural strength' (*CU* 223). The liberal monotheism which results may sound rather like deism, but in context it is more accurately seen as a *prisca theologia* or 'ancient theology', a distillation of pre-Christian thought about the supreme being and the spiritual destiny of mankind which might easily be assimilated to Christian beliefs.[32] Indeed, once they hear about Christ and his teachings they respond with enthusiasm, especially because of his followers' communal way of life.

But there remain several perplexing aspects of Utopian life, not the least of them being the institution of slavery. It is important to remember that this is presented as an individual condition, rather than a hereditary one as was the case in the ancient world: it may be the result of choice, as in the case of those volunteers from abroad who find it better than life at home, but usually it is the penalty for some offence which violates rational order. Along with gold fetters and other signs of shame it provides a visible emblem of moral enslavement to irrational passion, and even prisoners of war fit into this category by virtue of their resistance to Utopian enlightenment. Since the workforce of citizens seems more than adequate to meet requirements, it is clear that slave labour is far from being the essential prop of the economy that it had been in the Greek polis. So one can only assume that More, as with the example of the Polylerites in Book I, is more concerned with presenting penal servitude as a viable mode of punishment which benefits society and holds open the chance of rehabilitation.[33]

Closely related is the issue of war, where Utopian practice may again seem unsettling. Put simply, the Utopians fight to win, and aim to do so with the minimum of casualties on both sides. Not only do they regard glory won in war with contempt, thus stripping away the chivalric veneer which disguises its brutality in Europe, but they use their reserves of gold to bribe the enemy and spread subversion, making a mockery of the entire heroic tradition and its thirst for glory. Gold also enables them to make use of mercenaries, especially the Zapoletans, whom they regard as supremely expendable. When necessary they can supplement these by auxiliaries drawn from their client states, but their own troops, held in reserve for times of crisis, form a civilian militia, including both sexes and ranged in family groups much as Socrates had proposed in the *Republic* (471D). Once engaged they again use unconventional but effective methods, prizing a victory won by cunning rather than brute force; they are fighting, after all, for the survival of their unique way of life in the face of a hostile and irrational world. It is important to remember, as well, the role played by the Utopian priests in restraining all unnecessary – that is to say irrational – violence on the battlefield (*CU* 233).

But the Utopians also fight for the extension of their way of life, adopting a policy of colonial expansion. Whenever the population rises above the stipulated quotas colonies are established on the mainland, at any point where the natives have left land unoccupied or unused. The Utopians improve the land and are prepared to assimilate the natives, provided that they are willing to conform to Utopian customs. But if they refuse they are driven out. So it is with their wars, which have a distinctly punitive character: while they protect their own lands, they also engage in hostilities to avenge ill-treatment of their client states, and 'in the name of compassion and humanity' (*CU* 203) fight to liberate oppressed peoples. One may suspect here some echo of Greek and barbarian relations as described by Plato in the *Republic* (469B–470B); like the Greeks, the Utopians represent a society based on reason and nature, and they distinguish themselves from other nations not on racial grounds but by rational conduct. This is why outsiders can be assimilated to their colonies and slaves liberated for moral perseverance; but there can be no true relationship between them and those other nations whose lives are directed by specious custom and corrupt institutions.

What, then, does Utopia represent in More's scheme of things? Here it is essential to remember that he was engaged in a work of fiction, not in a philosophical treatise: it is a mistake, in other words, to look for systematic coherence in all its features. But we noticed earlier how common ownership is integral to its identity. Among More's humanist contacts there is evidence of a nostalgia for social innocence, expressed in the Pythagorean ideal of mutual charity and community of goods. Pythagoras, significantly introduced by Ovid as one who 'through hatred of tyranny' chose exile, symbolizes this mythical phase in human development when, in Augustine's words, 'the first just men were established as shepherds of flocks, rather than as kings of men'.[34] Utopia has very few laws, we are told, and it relies more on domestic than on legal sanctions. This sets it in direct contrast to that law of nations, largely Roman in inspiration, which has evolved to protect ownership; in Budé's ironic formula, 'the stronger a man is the more goods he should have, and the more goods he has the more authority he should exercise over his fellow citizens' (*CU* 11).[35] So the channel dug by Utopus to separate Utopia from the mainland is indeed symbolic; somehow the island has avoided that institutional 'fall' which has shaped the world as we inherit it. If we think back to Erasmus's analysis in the *Hyperaspistes* of the causes of sin, one was 'malice of the will', and the presence of gaolers and executioners suggests that this is present also in Utopia; but those sources of moral infection which are built into the structures of European society would seem to be excluded. That is why Raphael can describe Utopian institutions as *prudentissima*, most prudent, but also *sanctissima*, most holy (*CU* 101).

At the end of October 1515, his diplomatic mission completed, More returned to London, taking in his baggage the account of Utopian institutions. Although his life on return appears to have been hectic, as he humorously indicates in his letter to Peter Giles (*CU* 33), the literary exercise which began as a diversion had now taken on sufficient weight for him to persist, encasing Raphael's description of 'the best state of a commonwealth' within a debate concerning issues that preoccupied him after his return. It was not until the following September that he could forward the manuscript to Erasmus who, together with Giles, prepared it for the printer, providing the marginal notes, prefatory material and – quite possibly – the title *Utopia*. The dominant issue of this secondary phase of composition is that of participation or, to put it another way, of contemplation versus action. Should one soil one's hands, and possibly one's character, in the service of the common good?

Giles's introductory comparison between Raphael and Ulysses or Plato establishes travel as an image for intellectual discovery, the quest for new horizons. So it is natural enough, after Raphael has told them something of the customs of new-found nations, that Giles should urge him to enter the service of a prince. But this well-meant suggestion prompts a fierce response: it would be slavery rather than service: 'As it is now, I live as I please, and I fancy that very few courtiers, however splendid, can say that' (*CU* 51). To 'live as you please' typifies for Cicero the life of retirement, the ideal of those who pursue calm of soul and withdraw from civic life, and it is this claim that draws the first intervention from More's own fictional persona, Morus.[36] His case is that it would be worthy of Raphael's 'noble and philosophical nature' to participate in public affairs. What we have, then, is a familiar confrontation between the ideal of contemplative retirement and the contrary belief, characteristic of civic humanism, that the noblest way of life is one devoted to virtuous public service. Raphael's resistance to the idea of 'active endeavour' is based on his conviction that the court society, the seat of actual power, is irreformable: counsellors are dedicated to self-interest and will resist all innovation. There is no point in sacrificing your independence when no benefit can ensue.

More's sense of the imagination is closely linked to the act of meditation, the inward stirring of subjective response: by 'beholding' a mural of the dance of death, for example, 'we shal fele ourselves stered [stirred] and altered, by the feling of that imaginacion in our hertes' (*The Last Things*, *CW* 1:139). No doubt he sees such use of the imagination as the feature of his account of the best state of a commonwealth which distinguishes it from Plato's.[37] While we pass the day in More's

Antwerp garden, Raphael wafts us away on two imaginary excursions to stir us: the main one, of course, is his account of the extraordinary island he has visited, but in Book I there is the brief but significant episode in Cardinal Morton's household, set in 1497, just a few years after More had served there as a page. This is the year of the Cornish insurrection, 'a lamentable slaughter', which may seem an odd event to recall, but it is one that provides a backdrop of social unrest and brutal suppression which is close to home. The central thread is the apparently ineffectual policy of hanging for theft, and it enables More to alert us to topics that will be thrust at us later, in Utopia. For a start there is the issue of human life and its worth: to take away a life for theft subordinates it to cash in a way that would appal Utopians (cf. *CU* 155). Then there is the inefficacy of a legal system which, like the common lawyer himself, is blind to social conditions. What are the factors that drive people to theft? Why do they persist in crime? As Raphael develops the scene he shifts our attention from individual crimes to the social conditions that make them all but inevitable, thus putting the wider community in the dock as well. Lurking in the background is the argument of medieval canonists that in times of necessity the poor were entitled to take what they needed to support life, without being guilty of theft.[38] It was an argument that, while it seems to have received little practical attention, remained as a subversive possibility. More would surely have known of it.

The issue is social utility, and in England many forces are at work against the common interest. One, certainly, is the number of unskilled vagrants, disbanded soldiers or discarded retainers who are parasitic on the economy; but dominating Raphael's account is the practice of enclosure, with its compound effects on local economies and employment. Indeed, the most memorable image of More's entire book is that of man-eating sheep (*CU* 63). Modern studies suggest that much of the damage to rural communities caused by conversion of land to pasture was done before 1485, but that it was the spread of printed books after 1500 that raised the sound level; indeed, in May 1517, six months after the publication of *Utopia*, a commission was established to report on enclosures.[39] But just how targeted More's criticism may be is secondary: for him the evils described by Raphael function primarily as images of social dysfunction, symptoms of that injustice so starkly conveyed by the oligopoly which manipulates wool prices (*CU* 65). These are the raw, local details of the conspiracy of the rich which Raphael will condemn at the close of Book II. However, it is when he turns to the question of equitable punishment, punishment designed 'to destroy vices and save men', that he introduces the first of his exotic models, the Polylerites, whose sophisticated penal system offers a telling contrast to the mass executions of England. As one might predict, it is not well received by the lawyer with whom Raphael is arguing, and the rest of the company follow his opponent's lead. In a sense, this is a pre-run for the reception of Utopia itself, and it is revealing that only the cardinal displays an open mind. More's portrait of his old patron is developed with care, displaying Morton's acuity of mind and authority of presence. The most striking of his qualities is pragmatism, a willingness to entertain new ideas and even to extend them, as in his proposal for vagrants; as Nelson observes, he is the only European in *Utopia* to accept 'Greek' advice.[40] An impressive figure as royal counsellor, within his own household – surrounded by flattering dependants – he can show both humour and social tact as he directs conversation. This image of an alert and perceptive man of affairs takes on particular importance in the remainder of Book I as we are confronted with an increasingly heated debate over the prospects of political action.

Again, it is Morus who puts the case for civic humanism, urging that it is the good man's duty to engage in public affairs: what began as a friendly suggestion from Giles has now been elevated to a moral obligation, placing in sharp relief the issues that dominate the final stages of More's composition. Raphael is identified as the spokesman for an uncompromising idealism, while Morus argues for more modest ambitions. While philosophers may not be kings, at least they can offer counsel (*CU* 81–3). So it is against the background of this discussion about counsel that Raphael elaborates the episodes that follow, depicting identifiable royal councils, the first French, the second – though unnamed – clearly English, as they debate external affairs and fiscal policy, both living up to Augustine's characterization of unjust kingdoms as robber bands.[41] In each case More contrasts a heavily ironic account of actual political practice with its ideal opposite, exemplified by the Achorians and Macarians, neighbours of the Utopians. It is this yawning discrepancy between custom and imagined possibility that prompts Raphael's claim that it is futile to relate the two – any appeal to moral idealism will fall on deaf ears.

Morus counters with the case for that distinctly humanistic concept, a sense of context. Against Raphael's 'school philosophy' he proposes one 'better suited to the role of a citizen' (*CU* 97), one, that is, which adapts itself to the situation like an actor to a script; it is by this 'indirect approach', rather than by outbursts of rectitude, that the counsellor must work, making what cannot be turned to good as little bad as possible. It seems a modest ambition, but nonetheless it brings us to the core of More's fictional exercise, when the very role of imagination in the life of politics is called into question, for, as Raphael speedily points out, such an 'indirect approach' implies tacit participation in the conspiracy which maintains society as we know it. He insists on speaking his mind without qualification.[42] It is at this point that private property emerges as the dividing issue between the customary world of Europe and the ideal worlds of Plato or Utopus. The intransigent Raphael, true to his mentor Plato, has no time for accommodation, which he equates with the leaden rule by which preachers adapt the Gospel, modifying Christ's teaching to match the way people actually live. Although he is not named, Aristotle is evoked here, since he uses the leaden rule as an image of the equity by which law is adapted to match individual cases (*Nicomachean Ethics* 5.10.7). So it is fitting, when Morus tentatively counters Raphael's case for common property (*CU* 105), that he should adopt an Aristotelian critique which stresses the way in which people really do behave rather than how they might behave.

Both books of *Utopia* follow similar patterns of closure. There is, of course, Raphael's bitter anger at the lot of the poor, which is repeated with searing force at the conclusion of his account of Utopia. But the dominant feature is the refusal of the two protagonists to agree. Raphael will not compromise; Morus has reservations. But we should note Raphael's tirade against money, 'that marvellous invention that is supposed to provide access to what we need to live' but which turns out to be 'the only barrier to our getting it' (*CU* 245). In fact, money, by its separation of value from worth, opens the gap that pride can exploit. The proud, characterized by Augustine as 'self-pleasers', use their property as a means to dominate others.[43] So to Raphael only the abolition of money along with the private ownership it sustains can result in a true commonwealth, one that is free from the social causes of sin and, moreover, one that may last forever.

Morus's feelings at the close are complex. On one hand he seems dismissive of Utopian practices, especially their moneyless society; yet his final words betray a certain fascination with the possibilities they raise. Again, there is an Aristotelian conservatism about his response to their system: it 'utterly subverts all the nobility, magnificence, splendour and majesty which (in the popular view) are the true ornaments and glory of any commonwealth'. The list is heavy with value-laden abstractions, and the deference to 'the popular view' is obviously ironic, yet the claim has its validity. The Aristotelian view had been canonized by Aquinas, and it emerges triumphantly in Medicean Florence in the writings of St Antoninus: 'God, indeed, has provided riches ... even artificial wealth like silver coin, cloth of gold, and the like, so that by means of devoted use of them we might merit eternal life.'[44] As Morus politely leads Raphael in to supper he offers a good illustration of the 'indirect approach' at work, and only we can actually share his thoughts. Have they softened? There is a positive ring about his wish to see Utopian features in society, yet there is a wistfulness about his fear that this will never happen. The final sentence hovers in the subjunctive – what happens next is up to the reader.

The majority of readers since 1516 have adopted a literal interpretation, in which Utopia is an ideal and Raphael is its prophet, something of a triumph for More's illusory art. For reasons that invite speculation, it is only in relatively modern times that the low-key stance of Morus has been taken seriously and his reservations given their due. But the most important thing has been the rediscovery of the work as a dialogue, where interplay between the characters is the important issue.[45] Like his model Plato, Raphael confines his politics to a city made of words; in contrast, Morus makes allowance for the shortcomings all too evident in society as we encounter it. If Raphael offers the excitements of a fresh start, Morus is reconciled to tinkering with the existing order. Perhaps his most revealing remark is the dry observation that 'it is impossible to make everything good unless all men are good, and I don't expect to see that for quite a few years yet' (*CU* 97). To Raphael the solution lies in liberation from ownership and all the subjective consequences that flow from it, but there is no Utopus in sight to impose this new order. It is Morus's Augustinian accommodation to a flawed world that offers some prospect of improvement: he may not expect to see Utopian habits adopted, but by the close he does at least wish that some might be.

In the course of his studies in the law More would have been trained in 'putting cases', that is, opening up the possibilities of conflicting views. So the question arises, do we need to arrive at a final position on the meaning of the book? Raphael offers the appeal of a radical stance, while the more conventional Morus makes some persuasive observations: whichever voice we favour, we cannot wholly disregard the alternative. Surely one indubitable quality of *Utopia* is that it unsettles familiar attitudes and prompts acts of political imagination, by which we 'fele ourselves stered and altered'. Its goal is a state of mind rather than a specified state of society. We can even catch a sense of this in the pattern of More's own life. In *The City of God* there is a sombre chapter which must have struck More when, as a young barrister, he lectured on the work (see above, 27, 28). Augustine asks whether, given the impenetrability of human motives, the wise man will sit as a judge: 'Clearly he will take his seat, for the claims of human society, which he thinks it wicked to abandon, constrain him and draw him to this duty.'[46] If More's legal career is anything to go by, such must have been his own conviction; and maybe, in the light of it, we ought to see Cardinal Morton, whom More would ultimately follow as lord chancellor, as the nearest thing to a hero in *Utopia*. Within eighteen months of the first publication of *Utopia* More had become a royal councillor, following in Morton's steps. Yet after the Submission of the Clergy in May 1532, when the political climate moved beyond the reach of accommodation, he resigned the chancellorship and endeavoured to withdraw from the public scene, in effect to 'live as I please' (*CU* 51). If we can believe William Roper, when Dame Alice accosted More in his prison cell for playing the fool and refusing the oath already taken by 'all the bishops and best learned of this realm', he responded, 'Is not this house ... as nigh heaven as my own?' Are these More's own words? Or is Roper merely recalling Raphael's favoured adage, 'Wherever you start from, the road to heaven is the same length'?[47] Whichever the case, the identification is clear enough.

FURTHER READING

The appearance of the Yale *Utopia* (*CW* 4) in 1965, edited by J. H. Hexter and Edward Surtz, prompted a renaissance in scholarly activity and, although its text has been superseded by *CU*, it remains an invaluable source of information, both in the Introduction (which includes Hexter's brilliant and challenging interpretation of the book) and in its extensive Commentary; there is an 'Index verborum' to *CW* 4 in *Moreana* 13, no. 52 (1976), 5–17, drawn up by Thomas I. White, and also a *Concordance*, edited by L. J. Bolchazy (Hildesheim and New York: G. Olms, 1978). Mention should be made of the generously annotated Latin–French edition by André Prévost (Paris: Mame, 1978). There is an English translation by David Wootton, '*Utopia*' *With Erasmus's 'The Sileni of Alcibiades'* (Indianapolis: Hackett, 1999), which includes a useful introduction.

Modern interpretation has tended to stress the inner tensions of *Utopia*, and a vivid instance is offered by Stephen Greenblatt in *Renaissance Self-Fashioning: From More to Shakespeare* (Chicago and

London: University of Chicago Press, 1980; repr. with a new Preface, 2005), 11–73. An entire section of *EA* is devoted to essays on *Utopia*, two of special importance: R. S. Sylvester, ' "Si Hythlodaeo credimus": vision and revision in Thomas More's *Utopia*' (290–301), and Elizabeth McCutcheon, 'Denying the contrary: More's use of litotes in the *Utopia*' (263–74). McCutcheon has also written the most penetrating study of More's verbal art, *My Dear Peter: The 'Ars Poetica' and Hermeneutics for More's 'Utopia'* (Angers: Moreanum, 1983). Dominic Baker-Smith, *More's 'Utopia'* (London and New York: HarperCollins, 1991; repr. University of Toronto Press, 2000), places the book in its intellectual context.

More wrote in dialogue with his classical predecessors, and an instructive guide to this relationship is George M. Logan, *The Meaning of More's 'Utopia'* (Princeton University Press, 1983). Thomas I. White has written on 'Aristotle and *Utopia*', *Renaissance Quarterly* 29 (1976), 635–75, and on 'Pride and the public good: Thomas More's use of Plato in *Utopia*', *Journal of the History of Philosophy* 20 (1982), 329–54, while the influence of Augustine is treated by Martin N. Raitiere, 'More's *Utopia* and *The City of God*', *Studies in the Renaissance* 20 (1973), 144–68. Also helpful is Ralph Keen and Daniel Kinney, eds., *Thomas More and the Classics* (*Moreana* 23, no. 86, 1985). More's highly original response to ancient, and in particular Roman, political ideas has been studied by Quentin Skinner in *The Foundations of Modern Political Thought*, 2 vols. (Cambridge University Press, 1978), as well as in his chapter 'Political philosophy' in Charles B. Schmitt *et al.*, eds., *The Cambridge History of Renaissance Philosophy* (Cambridge University Press, 1988), 389–452; of particular interest is his paper 'Sir Thomas More's *Utopia* and the language of Renaissance humanism', in Anthony Pagden, ed., *The Languages of Political Theory in Early-Modern Europe* (Cambridge University Press, 1987), 123–57; repr., with revisions, as 'Thomas More's *Utopia* and the virtue of true nobility', in Skinner's *Visions of Politics*, 3 vols. (Cambridge University Press, 2002), 2:213–44. Important modifications to Skinner's view are proposed by Eric Nelson, *The Greek Tradition in Republican Thought* (Cambridge University Press, 2004), and by Cathy Curtis, ' "The Best State of the Commonwealth": Thomas More and Quentin Skinner', in Annabel Brett *et al.*, eds., *Rethinking the Foundations of Modern Political Thought* (Cambridge University Press, 2006), 93–112. Finally, Andrew J. Majeske, *Equity in English Renaissance Literature: Thomas More and Edmund Spenser* (New York and London: Routledge, 2006), offers an illuminating reading from the perspective of More's legal interests.

Notes

1. One has to acknowledge here John Guy's brilliant perception that 'More was most witty when least amused': *The Public Career of Sir Thomas More*, 23.
2. James Romm, 'More's strategy of naming in the *Utopia*', *Sixteenth Century Journal* 22 (1991), 173–83.
3. The developments can be clearly followed in *CWE* 4:66, 79, 93, 98, 125, 131, 163–4: More initially refers to Nowhere in September 1516 (66); the first reference to Utopia is in a letter from Gerard Geldenhouwer to Erasmus (125); More uses it for the first time in early December (163–4).
4. Lucian, *Selected Dialogues*, trans. C. D. N. Costa (Oxford University Press, 2005), 223.
5. *Republic* 592A-B; Paul Shorey's translation from *Collected Dialogues of Plato*, ed. Edith Hamilton and Huntington Cairns (Princeton University Press, 1973), 819.
6. Pico della Mirandola, *On the Dignity of Man*, trans. C. G. Wallis (Indianapolis: Bobbs Merrill, 1965), 17.
7. The options are discussed in N. G. Wilson, 'The name Hythlodaeus', *Moreana* 29, no. 110 (1992), 33.
8. Amerigo Vespucci, *The Letters of Amerigo Vespucci*, trans. and ed. Clements R. Markham (London: Hakluyt Society, 1894, reissued by Cambridge University Press, 2010), 9; David Abulafia, *The Discovery of Mankind: Atlantic Encounters in the Age of Columbus* (New Haven and London: Yale University Press, 2008), 246. Utopian priests are vested in robes made of feathers (*CU* 239).
9. 'The wisdom of Nigrinus', in *Works*, trans. A. M. Harmon *et al.*, 8 vols. (LCL), 1:113–15.
10. *More's 'Utopia': The Biography of an Idea* (Princeton University Press, 1952; repr. with an Epilogue, New York: Harper Torchbooks, 1965), 15–27; also *CW* 4:xv–xxiii.
11. 'My lord of York' is Cardinal Wolsey, lord chancellor since December 1515.
12. *More's 'Utopia'*, 102.
13. *Republic* 473D (conjunction of power and intelligence), 501A (philosopher-artists); *Laws* 710D; cf. More's epigram 'What is the best form of government?', *CW* 3:228–31, lines 28–31.
14. On the interest in 'civic philosophies' among London officials see Sarah Rees Jones, 'Thomas More's *Utopia* and medieval London', in Rosemary Horrox and Sarah Rees Jones, eds., *Pragmatic Utopias: Ideals and Communities, 1200–1630* (Cambridge University Press, 2001), 123; only a quarter of Londoners were citizens, with the consequent privileges and obligations (ibid., 127).
15. *The City of God*, Book 19, ch. 16, trans. R. W. Dyson (Cambridge University Press, 1998), 944–5.
16. Jones, 'Thomas More's *Utopia*', 122; cf. *CU* 123; on the partnership of aldermen and common councilmen see Caroline M. Barron, *London*

in the Later Middle Ages: Government and People 1200–1500 (Oxford University Press, 2004), 136.

17. R. J. Schoeck, 'More, Plutarch, and King Agis: Spartan history and the meaning of *Utopia*', *EA* 366–75; for contemporary accounts of Venetian government see Jill Kraye, ed., *Cambridge Translations of Renaissance Philosophical Texts, 2: Political Philosophy* (Cambridge University Press, 1997), 117–45.

18. Erasmus also discusses Pythagoras at length in *Adages* 1.i.2, *CWE* 31:31–50.

19. *De officiis* 1.16.51, trans. Walter Miller (LCL).

20. *Adages* 1.i.1, *CWE* 31:30; cf. Budé's remarks in *CU* 9–13.

21. Cited in Abulafia, *Discovery of Mankind*, 181.

22. *Opuscula quaedam theologica*, ed. J. H. Lupton (London: G. Bell, 1876), 134–5.

23. On the theological view of property as a human convention see John T. Noonan, *The Scholastic Analysis of Usury* (Cambridge, Mass.: Harvard University Press, 1957), 28–9; as he notes, 'the official code of the Church appeared committed to the naturalness of communism'.

24. Thus 'the inhabitants consider themselves cultivators [*agricolae*] rather than landlords [*domini*]', *CU* 113; on *dominium* see Richard Tuck, *Natural Rights Theories* (Cambridge University Press, 1979), ch. 1.

25. *The City in History* (Harmondsworth: Penguin, 1966), 374.

26. On the lack of privacy see *CU* 119, 143, 145; even the dead observe the living (227).

27. The account of pleasure in *The City of God*, Book 19, ch. 3, seems relevant to Utopia; for classical sources see George M. Logan, *The Meaning of More's 'Utopia'* (in 'Further reading'), 168–78.

28. *CU* 166; my translation differs slightly.

29. More's championing of Greek studies is set in context by Simon Goldhill, *Who Needs Greek? Contests in the Cultural History of Hellenism* (Cambridge University Press, 2002), ch. 1; for an important account of 'the Greek view' see Eric Nelson, 'Greek nonsense in More's *Utopia*', in his *The Greek Tradition in Republican Thought* (in 'Further reading'), 19–48.

30. As Nelson argues (*Greek Tradition*, 10), Greek thinkers are concerned with 'freedom' as a life in accord with nature, rather than one of non-dependence as in the Roman tradition.

31. Dominic Baker-Smith, 'Uses of Plato by Erasmus and More', in Anna Baldwin and Sarah Hutton, eds., *Platonism and the English Imagination* (Cambridge University Press, 1994), 92–8; for the classical ingredients of Utopian thought see Logan, *Meaning*, esp. 144–81.

32. On the general concept see D. P. Walker, *The Ancient Theology* (London: Duckworth, 1972), 1–21.

33. On slavery as ameliorative see Plato, *Republic* 590C–D, and Augustine, *City of God*, Book 19, ch. 15, 942–4.

34. Ovid, *Metamorphoses* 15.61–3; *City of God*, Book 19, ch. 15, 942.

35. Augustine ironically summarizes the spirit of Rome, 'Let no one be brought to judgment unless he harms another's property' (*City of God*, Book 2, ch. 20, 75).

36. *De officiis* 1.20.69; for an earlier run of the debate, in the *Life of Pico*, see *CW* 1:84–8.

37. This is implied by the verses of Anemolius, the 'Utopian poet laureate', which are included among the *parerga* (*CU* 19); the actual author is not known.

38. 'According to natural law and even civil law, in a time of necessity "all things are common", as the saying goes. Whence he who is suffering from desperate hunger seems rather to be using his own rights than committing a theft.' Henry of Sugusio, *Lectura*, cited in Gilles Couvreur, *Les Pauvres ont-ils des droits?* (Rome: Analecta Gregoriana, 1961), 256 n. 8.

39. W. G. Hoskins, *The Age of Plunder: The England of Henry VIII* (London: Longman, 1976), 67–72; also Peter Gwyn, *The King's Cardinal: The Rise and Fall of Thomas Wolsey* (London: Barrie & Jenkins, 1990), 412–35.

40. *Greek Tradition*, 39.

41. *City of God*, Book 4, ch. 4, 147.

42. Cf. Erasmus's exasperated response to Luther's 'immoderate energy', Ep. 1202, *CWE* 8:203, lines 52–5.

43. *City of God*, Book 14, ch. 13, 609; cf. Budé to Lupset, *CU* 11.

44. *Summa*, cited in Peter Howard, 'Preaching magnificence in Renaissance Florence', *Renaissance Quarterly* 61 (2008), 338–9.

45. On the history of responses to *Utopia*, see below, 274–82.

46. *City of God*, Book 19, ch. 6, 927.

47. Roper 243; Raphael's adage (*CU* 45) derives from Cicero, *Tusculan Disputations* 1.43.104, where it is attributed to the dying Anaxagoras.

8 More on tyranny: *The History of King Richard the Third*

GEORGE M. LOGAN

Written around the time of *Utopia*, *The History of King Richard the Third* is More's other great political work, an account of the events of four tumultuous months in England from the death of King Edward IV, on 9 April 1483, through the several stages of the usurpation of the throne by his younger brother Richard. At the heart of both books is More's deep understanding of – and scathing contempt for – immoral, self-serving rulers and their enablers, his profound sympathy for their victims and his passionate desire to expose their machinations and depredations, in the (faint) hope of encouraging reforms that, in the final words of *Utopia*, he 'would wish rather than expect to see' (*CU* 249). Both books deploy in this effort all the resources of More's splendid literary gift, including narrative verve, dramatic immediacy, wit, irony, satire and, occasionally, pathos. Both are also supreme achievements of Renaissance humanism, imbued with their author's broad classical learning, participating in classical generic traditions and applying ancient paradigms in the attempt to elicit or confirm timeless lessons from observations of the present.

The *History* differs from *Utopia*, however, in two important respects. First, although More wrote a version of it in the simulated classical Latin of humanism (the language of *Utopia*), he also wrote an English version. Second, he did not complete *either* version. The Latin one breaks off immediately after a sour account of Richard's assumption of the kingship, on 26 June, and his formal coronation eleven days later.[1] The English version continues past the chronological endpoint of the Latin to narrate the supposed murder of Edward's two young sons (the rightful heirs to the throne); promises that we shall later hear Richard 'slain in the field, hacked and hewed', in just requital for his 'dispiteous cruelty' (*R3* 101–2); but then, a few pages later, stops abruptly in the middle of an episode narrating the defection (several weeks after Richard's coronation) of his principal ally, the duke of Buckingham.

Especially since the English version of the *History* is an utterly exhilarating work, and the most accomplished piece of English prose of the earlier sixteenth century, it is a pity that More did not finish the book.[2] The work's unfinished state did not, however, keep it from achieving enormous celebrity and influence. First published eight years after More's execution, in one of the popular sixteenth-century chronicle histories, and subsequently passed on to other such works, the English *History* quickly became the most admired segment of the chronicles. Its reputation was further enhanced by its publication, in a much better text, in the edition of More's collected English works (1557) by his nephew William Rastell. Rastell's text was adopted in subsequent chronicles, and it was in these that the most important student of the *History* – William Shakespeare – read it. Early in his career as a playwright, Shakespeare made More's treatment the principal source and historiographical model of his *Tragedy of King Richard III*, and the result was both a leap in the sophistication of his dramaturgy and a further blackening – and much wider dissemination – of the image of Richard for which the *History* was principally responsible. In turn, the two works provoked an impassioned and enduring reaction by supporters of Richard, inaugurating a running battle between defenders of the standard, More–Shakespeare view of him – as a Machiavellian monster hell-bent on attaining the throne at any cost in human life – and the apologists' view of him as a good and rightful king much maligned: a battle, still ongoing, that has made Richard the most controversial (and most studied) king in the long history of the English monarchy.[3]

THEME, SUBJECT AND INTENDED AUDIENCES

In the biographical sketch of More that Erasmus included in a letter of 1519 (by which time the two men had known each other for twenty years), he wrote that his friend 'has always had a special hatred for tyranny'.[4] Several decades later, Thomas Stapleton's biography of More (published 1588), which, although written well after his death, drew on anecdotes related by members of his circle, reported that More 'studied with avidity all the historical works he could find' (Stapleton 14). These two remarks, together with various indications of More's eagerness to establish himself in the community of European humanists (see above, 30–6 and 39), help to clarify why he chose to write a history, why he chose Richard III as its subject, and why he took the highly unusual step of writing versions of it in both English and Latin.

History was not only a personal passion of More's but one of the kinds of writing most strongly associated with humanism. As had been the case with the classical Greek and Roman historians whom they emulated, the humanists were interested almost exclusively in *political* history, which had the analysis and denunciation of tyranny as a recurrent subject – above all, in the Roman historians whom More most admired, Sallust and Tacitus. For More's own object lesson in tyranny, Richard was an obvious choice for several reasons: he was regarded as a tyrant by all More's compatriots (at least, all who ventured to offer a public opinion on the matter), and his usurpation of the throne was a scandal notorious not only in England but in Europe generally; More had access to excellent sources of information about him; and he had been defeated and killed by the father of More's king – the current representative of a Tudor line that, in view of the tenuousness of its own hereditary claim to the throne, had every reason for wishing Richard's reputation to be as black and (given this coloration) as widely disseminated as possible.

For More's purposes it made perfect sense for him to write the *History* in both English and Latin. First, versions in these different languages would appeal to different audiences and thus broaden the impact of the work (cf. above, 49–53). Clearly the English version was intended primarily for British readers, especially the less sophisticated ones who, although they would have studied Latin in school (since it was the working language of the grammar schools), were of course more at ease with English: the people of the middle and upper classes (those of the lower classes could not read at all) who made the English-language chronicle histories of the period enormously popular.[5] Additionally, the English version provided More, in an era when Latin was the normal medium of sophisticated prose, with the challenge and pleasure of writing literary prose in his native language.[6]

To be sure, the Latin version would have given him pleasure too. Like other humanists (and other well-educated people of his time in general), More was extremely comfortable in Latin; he also knew his principal models for the *History* – works of Sallust and Tacitus – in minute detail, and he must have found great satisfaction in emulating not only their subject matter but their language. The main purpose of writing a Latin version, though, was evidently to widen the audience of the work: this version was addressed primarily to readers on the European continent (where almost no one then read English). The fact that the Latin version was primarily addressed to a non-British audience is clear from the different handling, in the two versions, of English geography and institutions. In the English version, the settings of events are indicated simply by name: 'the palace of Westminster', 'Redcross Street without [outside] Cripplegate', 'Hornsey', and so on; and More assumes that he need not explain to his readers such matters as the heir-apparent's connection with Wales or the duties of the recorder of London. In the Latin version, though, most place names are either omitted entirely ('Redcross Street' disappears) or supplanted by information about the place's location relative to London: 'Hornsey' becomes an unnamed place 'four miles away' from London; 'Westminster' becomes 'the palace which is located next to the Benedictine abbey about a mile toward the setting sun from London'[7] – from which, incidentally, the *modern* reader learns that the precincts of Westminster had, in the sixteenth century, not yet been absorbed into the city. Similarly, English institutions and offices, identified only by name in the English version, are given more or less elaborate explanations in the Latin. In the most striking example, 'Parliament' in the English becomes, in the Latin (ironically, wishfully or both), 'Parliament, whose authority in England is supreme and absolute' (*CW* 15:321).[8]

DATING, AND THE PROCESS OF COMPOSITION

In part because neither version of the *History* was published during More's lifetime, it is impossible to date the composition of the work with any precision. The only pieces of external evidence on the matter are found in similar prefatory notes to the *History* in Rastell's edition of More's English works and in the first printing of the Latin version, included in the 1565 collected edition of his Latin works. In a headnote to the English version, Rastell says that his uncle wrote the book 'about the year of our Lord 1513', and the same assertion, probably also deriving from Rastell, occurs in the headnote to the Latin version.[9] The year 1513 falls in what is surely the right era of More's life for the *History*, for it was in the second decade of the sixteenth century that he wrote most of his humanist works (above, 30–6). But the date itself (which Rastell offers, after all, only as an approximation) seems too early for the *inception* of the book, since its first sentence refers to an event – the elevation of Thomas Howard II to the earldom of Surrey – that did not occur until February 1514. Moreover, the opening pages of the *History* appear to be modelled on a passage near the beginning of the opening books of Tacitus's *Annals*, which, lost for centuries, were first printed in 1515. To be sure, More could have begun the *History* in 1513 or even earlier, and later revised its opening. But there is little evidence of his having revised his English draft, and conclusive evidence that he did not do so in a thoroughgoing way: the 1557 edition of the *History* (printed, Rastell says, from a manuscript in More's own hand) includes a number of blank spaces, which were obviously left that way because at the time of drafting More was missing information – dates, place names, one personal name and the distance between two towns – that he meant to fill in later but never did; and there are also a few spots in the text that have obvious errors that he would surely have caught if he had read the passages over at any time after drafting them. The *History* thus seems just as likely, perhaps *more* likely, to have been begun after *Utopia* (written 1515–16) as before it. There is no way of knowing when More *stopped* working on it, although it seems probable that he had stopped by 1520, after which date he published no more humanist works and appears to have given over the great bulk of his writing time to anti-Lutheran polemics and devotional books.[10]

On those rare occasions when an author writes versions of a work in two different languages, the normal procedure is (of course) to write it first in one language and then translate it into the other – as was the case, for example, with several of Sir Francis Bacon's works, which were first published in English and later translated into Latin. Since in the case of More's *History* there is no reliable external evidence on the matter, reconstructing his procedure depends entirely on comparison of parallel passages in the two texts.[11] For one single passage, there is incontrovertible evidence that More wrote first in English and then translated into Latin. As Daniel Kinney shows, the most authoritative text of the Latin version of the *History* is a manuscript that he discovered – purely by good fortune, bound as it was with unrelated items – in a manuscript volume in the Bibliothèque nationale in Paris. This manuscript ('P') of the *History* is not in More's hand, but it is a careful copy evidently at a near remove from More's working manuscript and at a stage of revision more advanced than that represented in the only other complete manuscript of the Latin *History* that has survived or in the 1565 edition of More's Latin works (which offers the only sixteenth-century *printed* text of the Latin version). At one point in P, a blank appears in the latter part of a sentence (*CW* 15:340; cf. cxlvi). In the margin alongside this blank, we find the English word 'auauncement' (advancement) – which is also found in the English text at the corresponding point (*R3* 19). Unquestionably, in this passage More was translating from English into Latin but could not think of a satisfactory

Latin equivalent for 'auauncement', so left a gap to be filled in later, writing the English word in the margin as a reminder.

Unfortunately this is the only entirely certain indication of the direction of translation between the two versions. There are, however, many *likely* indications. In translating the *Life of Pico* from Latin into English, More had frequently used two words, joined by a coordinating conjunction, to translate a single Latin word – a common practice of translators in the period. The reverse practice – occasionally rendering English words by Latin doublets – would not be unexpected if More were translating from English into Latin; and in fact there are many instances where a single word in the English version of the *History* corresponds to a doublet in the Latin version: 'good' in the English corresponding to 'boni atque egregii', 'on a roar' to 'in armis ac tumultu', and so on. Of course More sometimes may have translated doublets into single words; but surely in most cases (though we can never know which particular ones) where two words correspond to one – and such cases are scattered throughout the text – we are justified in concluding that he was translating from English into Latin.

These examples, together with the blank awaiting a Latin equivalent of 'auauncement', would, in fact, appear to settle the question of the relative priority of the two versions – were it not that there are also many examples, likewise scattered throughout the text, of *English* doublets corresponding to single words in the *Latin* version (for examples see *CW* 2:lvii). These contrasting sets of instances strongly suggest that More worked on the two versions of the text in closely alternating, more or less simultaneous fashion – an almost unparalleled mode of composition.[12] Moreover, the *distribution* of the doublets – sprinkled as they are *throughout* both the English and Latin versions – suggests that he did not draft a number of pages in English, translate them into Latin, and then, for a similarly substantial section, draft in Latin and translate into English. As Richard Sylvester says, the shifts in the 'controlling' language are not on the order of section to section but on that of sentence to sentence (*CW* 2:lvii).

Then too, while More often translates quite closely, there are many passages where the English and Latin markedly diverge: phrases, entire sentences, and in a few places units of a paragraph or more in one version correspond to nothing at all in the other.[13] When translating others' prose (as in the *Life of Pico*) More generally stayed quite close to the original. Translating (in both directions) from *himself* – and having, moreover, different audiences in mind for the two versions – he clearly did not feel constrained to make source text and translation match. The very attractive result is, as another editor of the *History* – W. A. G. Doyle-Davidson – says, that each version 'has the air of being an original' (*EW* 1:48).

HISTORIOGRAPHY

When writing narrative histories, humanists usually employed only a single source: some previous narrative history (they did try to choose the most reliable one), which they rewrote in eloquent style and classical form. More, though, writing about relatively recent events that had occurred mainly in his hometown, and being a voracious reader of histories, could hardly not have had multiple sources. Indeed, he frequently refers to (oral) sources, although without identifying them: phrases such as 'this have I by credible information learned', 'as I have for certain been informed' and 'I have heard of [i.e. from] some (that said they saw it)' are scattered through his text. But only once in the history – and that only on a minor matter, and only in the Latin version – does he actually *identify* a source: his father, who, he says, had told him about an overheard conversation (*CW* 15:328–9). In 1483 John More had been a rising London lawyer, and, although he had not been an actor in the events of the usurpation, he presumably had more than *one* thing to tell his son about them.

As for the identity of More's other sources, we can only make plausible guesses.[14] It seems likely that the most important of his oral informants was John Cardinal Morton, Henry VII's lord chancellor, in whose household More served as a page for two years in early adolescence – about 1590–2, less than a decade after the usurpation (above, 9–10). At the time of Edward IV's death, Morton was bishop of Ely and an important royal counsellor, and he figured in several key episodes of the usurpation: among Richard's opponents, he was an unexcelled source for the events of 1483. One of More's duties as Morton's page was to wait table. It is hard to believe that the conversations at that table did not occasionally include something, perhaps a good deal, about Richard; and More was a precocious youth. For that very reason, too, Morton took a special interest in the boy, and seems to have been, to whatever extent, a mentor – as he was certainly an admired model – for him. Who knows what (if, indeed, any) conversations the two may have had before Morton's death in 1500?[15] As the distinguished Tudor historian A. F. Pollard showed in an article of 1933, More also knew a number of other individuals who had been involved in public affairs during Richard's reign.[16] These included Thomas Howard II, whose father and grandfather were allied with Richard. The grandfather – John Howard, whom Richard created duke of Norfolk two days after seizing the throne – was in fact, along with Buckingham, Richard's most important supporter (although More discreetly avoided naming either him or his son anywhere in the *History*).[17]

More's *written* sources surely included some of the many chronicle histories circulating in the period, and may also have included public records. But the only clear point of connection between the *History* and the latter comes in his version of the duke of Buckingham's speech at the Guildhall (*R3* 80–90; see below, 178), which in places strikingly resembles a petition, as found in the 1484 parliamentary Act for the Settlement of the Crown, urging Richard to accept the throne. (The original petition, undoubtedly engineered by Richard and his associates, was presented to him on 26 June 1483.)[18] As for the chronicles, these works routinely incorporated chunks from one another and, in consequence, are so closely interrelated that it is usually impossible to trace a particular fact or interpretation to a particular chronicle. There are, however, at least three passages where the *phrasing* of the English *History* is sufficiently close to that in corresponding passages of Robert Fabyan's *New Chronicles of England and of France* as to make it seem certain that More used this work – or another one that shared text with it.[19] More also had one true peer, who was also a close friend, among the historians living in London: Polydore Vergil (*c.* 1470–1555), an Italian humanist whose *Anglica historia* ('History of England'), commissioned by Henry VII about 1506–7, is a sophisticated work that became enormously influential as the origin of the 'Tudor myth' – an interpretation of fifteenth-century English history in which the Wars of the Roses were a protracted expiation of the sin of Henry Bolingbroke (Henry IV) in deposing Richard II, a process completed with the death of Richard III and the inauguration of the Tudor dynasty in the person of Henry VII. Polydore's treatment of Richard is somewhat more detached, and far less detailed, than More's, but it shares with his (and with almost all other accounts in the period) the conception of the usurper as deceitful, unscrupulous and tyrannical. Polydore completed a manuscript version of the *Historia* in 1513, but it is not clear whether More's book is directly indebted to it (although in any case the two friends may well have *discussed* Richard).[20]

In shaping the materials he obtained from a variety of sources into a coherent narrative, More applied the historiographical precepts and techniques revived by previous humanist historians from the ancient Greeks and Romans. The key fact about the classical tradition of historiography is that in it narrative history was normally regarded as a branch of rhetoric.[21] Rhetoric is the art of verbal persuasion; its aims, according to an influential Ciceronian dictum, are to teach, delight and move. When the genre is history, the teachings are moral and political, and we are moved to put them into practice primarily because they are embodied in vivid instances: as Thucydides – the father of classical political history – was reported to have said, 'history is philosophy teaching by examples'.[22]

The natural modern assumption is that these instructive examples would need to be *true*. And indeed Cicero – the pre-eminent Roman rhetorician and thus the single most potent authority for the humanists' literary theory and practice – asks (in two fine examples of the rhetorical question), 'who does not know history's first law to be that an author must not dare to tell anything but the truth? And its second that he must make bold to tell the whole truth?' (*De oratore* 2.15.62). In practice, however, the examples were often *not* entirely true, or not true at all. It was almost inevitable that this would be the case. First, the highest degree of eloquence – which history was thought to demand (*Orator* 11.37) – was not necessarily compatible with the exhaustive recital of 'the *whole* truth'. Second, if the purpose of history was to teach moral and political lessons, which for the most part meant deploying examples to illustrate familiar philosophical precepts, what difference did it make if the examples were strictly true, so long as they vividly conveyed the precepts? Indeed, it was often better, in this conception of history, *not* to use real examples (or, at least, to modify them), for, as Sir Philip Sidney notes in arguing the inferiority of history to poetry, history (that is, when it is veracious), 'being captived to the truth of a foolish world, is many times a terror from well-doing, and an encouragement to unbridled wickedness' – an observation he confirms by a recital of many historical examples of virtue punished and vice rewarded.[23]

That rhetorical historians had learned well both this lesson and the one about the ineloquence of historical detail is apparent in some kinds of materials they characteristically include, as well as in some they characteristically leave out. Eschewing whatever they deem pedestrian, and often not greatly interested (*pace* Cicero) in discovering the precise truth about historical events anyway, these historians normally decline to enter into detailed discussions of evidentiary questions, or to quote (or, for that matter, to consult) the unglamorous documents, private and public, that often constitute the most valuable historical evidence. On the other hand, their pages are full of

rhetorical set pieces – especially orations, character portraits and accounts of battles – that frequently have only tenuous connections
with known historical facts and are, indeed, often stereotyped in both
form and substance.

The elastic relation to fact in rhetorical historiography is especially
conspicuous in its orations. These are usually remarks supposed to
have been made by key actors in the events being narrated, speaking
at crucial junctures in them. But what these individuals actually said
on these occasions (if they spoke at all) was normally not known, or
known only in outline. Accordingly, it was standard practice for the
historian simply to *invent* the speeches. They were intended as – and
frequently were – dazzling displays of rhetorical prowess, and they
usually also served important thematic purposes, conveying the
writer's sense of the significance of the events being narrated and often
his understanding of their causes, which in this tradition of historiography were sought primarily in the character and ambitions of powerful
individuals. (None of these strictures should be taken to mean that
there was not, in the best rhetorical histories – as, in modern times, in
the best historical novels – profound exploration of historical events
and their causes and consequences, as well as beautiful writing: this is,
after all, a historiographical tradition that includes, to cite only three of
the most distinguished examples, Thucydides, Tacitus and Plutarch. In
hands of genius, rhetorical historiography drew lessons – often nuanced
and profound – *from* events rather than imposing text-book lessons *on*
them, and managed, through the stylization, and even the stereotyping,
that this way of writing history allowed, to display the constants in
human affairs.)

Since More did not complete his history – which would have
culminated in the battle of Bosworth Field (22 August 1485), where
Richard lost his crown and his life – he did not get to try his hand at
describing a battle. But he was an adept and enthusiastic practitioner of
the fictional oration and the other most common type of set piece, the
character sketch. Speeches – direct or reported, and including one
lengthy debate – constitute 40 per cent of the English version of the
History and more than half of the Latin one. Some of these speeches
(especially those that purport to record utterances made in the most
tightly guarded privacy) More probably fabricated from whole cloth.
Others convey the gist of what the speaker was known or thought
actually to have said on the occasion in question; but this core of more
or less accurate information was, in More's hands, only the starting
point for full-blown orations, fleshed out by his imagination and his

extraordinary mastery of (and evident delight in) rhetorical technique. Perhaps the most brilliant example is his account of the duke of Buckingham's speech at the Guildhall (the longest speech in the book), attempting to persuade the citizens of London to support Richard's bid for the throne (*R3* 80–90). Starting from such meagre materials as Fabyan's brief account of the occasion – in which it is admiringly reported (among other things) that Buckingham spoke in 'eloquent wise ...', without any impediment of spitting or other coun-tenance [comportment]' (quoted *R3* 128) – and evidently from the aforementioned petition 'presented' to Richard, More constructed an extraordinary scene centring on the speech of a master political moun-tebank promising instant cures for all social ills: a species of perform-ance with which we are only too familiar, but which is here far better done than we have ever heard it done, while at the same time marvel-lously satirizing itself and its genre. As for character sketches, the *History* includes word portraits of Richard; of Edward IV; of Lord Hastings; of his betrayer, William Catesby; and – the most famous portrait, along with that of Richard, and the longest – of Edward's favourite mistress, 'Jane' Shore.[24]

Rhetorical theory prescribes an elevated style for historical writing – a style that, as Cicero says, particularly 'indulges in a neatness and symmetry of sentences' (*Orator* 11.37; see also 20.66) – and one of More's great achievements in the English version of his work was to combine, especially in the set pieces, the elaborate symmetries and balancing of Latin 'high' style with a vigorous, fully idiomatic English. The most striking feature of this style (according precisely with Cicero's dictum) is its structures, often quite complex, of balanced parallel or antithetical elements – as, for example, in the final sentence of the character of Mistress Shore, on the indifference, to her present plight, of those whom she had formerly benefited: 'For men use [are accustomed], if they have an evil turn, to write it in marble; and whoso doth us a good turn, we write it in dust: which is not worst proved by her, for at this day she beggeth of many at this day living, that at this day had begged if she had not been' (*R3* 67).[25]

Rhetoric also calls for deft imitation of classical works, and More was an adept practitioner in this area, too. His imitations of Roman writers range from echoes of small phrases to large-scale appropria-tions that are of fundamental importance to his history. The small imitations – naturally more frequent and more recognizable in the Latin version of the work than in the English one – span Roman literature, but are concentrated especially on a few major authors: in descending order of frequency, Tacitus, Sallust, Seneca, Cicero, Vergil, Plautus, Terence, Ovid.[26] The large-scale imitations of classical works are confined to only three writers. In the reflections prompted by the charade, near the end of the history, where Richard pretends to decline the throne, More varies a passage – on human life as a stage play – of Lucian's dialogue *Menippus*. This is the only place in the history where More definitely imitates a *Greek* writer. He had rendered *Menippus* into Latin for the volume of translations from Lucian that he and Erasmus published in 1506 (above, 29–30); three years later, Erasmus incorporated a brilliant and profound variant of the stage-play passage into *The Praise of Folly* – from which More developed the idea that, when the play stars kings, it is dangerously unwise for a spectator to puncture the dramatic illusion.[27] With this notable exception, however, all the large-scale imitations in the history are confined to the works of two Roman writers on tyranny, Sallust and Tacitus.

From the first, it must have been clear to More that his principal models for a history of Richard III would be the classical histories of tyrants. Although Richard has always had his defenders, More and his contemporaries were – given the range of meanings the word 'tyrant' then carried – perfectly correct in applying the label to him. For the late medieval and early modern eras, the *Oxford English Dictionary* documents three senses of the word: usurper (irrespective of the nature of the usurper's subsequent reign); despot; absolute ruler (as a value-neutral term). It is very hard to argue that Richard did not qualify under at least the first heading. To be sure, he and his followers did attempt this argument (as later apologists also have), maintaining that Richard, rather than his brother Edward's sons, was the rightful heir. The grounds were that Edward's children did not belong to the line of succession, whether because Edward's marriage to their mother was invalid and his children therefore bastards, or because Edward himself was illegitimate.[28] But there is no real support for either claim; and Richard himself seriously undermined the argument for the illegitimacy of Edward's children by swearing (shortly after his brother's death), and causing many others to swear, allegiance to the young Edward V as the rightful heir.[29] Moreover, although Richard, once on the throne, did not rule despotically – he in fact made a great point of ruling by law, and through parliament, and manifested a special interest in law reform and the administration of justice[30] – he was still open to the charge of despotism, in consequence of the series of extrajudicial killings (several members of the queen's party, and his sometime ally Lord Hastings) that he certainly ordered on his way to the throne, and the two others (Edward V and his younger brother) that, having attained it, he likely ordered.[31]

The three senses of the word 'tyrant' in fifteenth- and sixteenth-century English were all inherited from classical culture. Greek τύραννος and its Latin successor, *tyrannus*, could mean simply 'king' – Vergil, for example, uses *tyrannus* of Aeneas (*Aeneid* 7.266) – but in early Greece it signified especially an absolute ruler who had achieved his position by usurpation. This application at first did not imply a value judgement on either the means of attaining power or the way in which the usurper subsequently exercised it. (Greek tyrants – a phenomenon especially of the seventh century BCE – typically gained power at the head of popular uprisings against a despised aristocracy, and often ruled beneficently.)[32] In the constitutional, republican milieu of fifth- and fourth-century BCE Athens, however, 'tyrant' is nearly always a pejorative term, in works of political philosophy, history and literature.

The Athenian view of tyrants was carried over into Republican Rome – with its hatred of monarchy – and even into the era of the Empire, in which republican sentiments remained strong, and where even the emperors liked to pretend that the Republic still existed. In particular, this view underpinned the great Roman histories of tyranny, the *Catiline* and *Jugurtha* of Sallust and the *Annals* of Tacitus – the works that were, inevitably, More's major models.

Sallust (86–35 BCE) and Tacitus (b. 56 or 57 CE; d. after 117) were important to More on all levels.[33] They are the authors whose turns of phrase he most frequently and tellingly adapts. Sallust was also the primary Roman writer in the particular genre of historical writing that the *History* exemplifies – the writer who provided, that is, the narrative paradigm that More employed to give his raw data a coherent design. Sallust's major works – *Catiline* and *Jugurtha* – are biographical monographs, both on monstrous villains: Catiline, whose failed Roman coup was also given lasting notoriety by Cicero's four orations on it; and Jugurtha, the nephew, adopted son and co-heir of the Numidian king Micipsa, whose blood sons he murdered in order to gain sole possession of the throne. The *History* is in general patterned more on the latter work than on the former, and the two passages where More's debts to Sallust are most substantial are both from *Jugurtha*: first, Edward IV's lengthy deathbed oration, which is, as Kinney says, 'an elaborate rearrangement and paraphrase' of Micipsa's (*CW* 15:cl n.1); and, second, a passage on Richard's insecurity and tortured conscience in the aftermath of the murder of Edward's sons.[34] The insecurity and unhappiness (extending to near-madness) of the tyrant was conventional in classical literature – as is indicated, for example, by the striking similarity between Sallust's passage on Jugurtha's state of mind and a parallel passage in *Catiline* (15).[35] The close connection between these passages and More's on Richard makes one wonder, of course, how solid a basis More had for what he here claims about Richard. This is, in fact, a standard question about imitative passages in rhetorical histories: to what extent does the imitation reflect the historian's recognition of genuine parallels between his subject and his predecessor's, and to what extent is the resemblance simply imposed for the sake of the imitation?

Tacitus was of even greater importance to the *History* than Sallust. I noted earlier that More's opening pages appear to be based on the opening of the *Annals*: Tacitus surveys the peaceful final years of Augustus's reign in order to set up a contrast with the terrible following reign of Tiberius; similarly, More opens by recounting the latter days of Edward IV's reign (the tranquillity of which he greatly exaggerates), which contrast starkly with Richard's times. The characterization of Richard himself – whose ruling traits, according to More, were dissimulation and a ready willingness to use cruelty to advance his ends – is strikingly similar to Tacitus's portrayal of Tiberius.[36] As Sylvester says, though, the specific parallels between the *History* and the *Annals* 'are ultimately of less significance than the common atmosphere that broods over both narratives' (*CW* 2:xcv). 'Sudden death and magnificent deception reign supreme' in both works (*CW* 2:xcvi); both powerfully convey the demoralizing and corrupting effect on the citizenry of such regimes. It is impossible to know to what extent the pervasive similarities between the works reflect More's having learned from Tacitus how to interpret Richard and his effects, and to what extent these parallels reflect, instead, his desire to call *attention* to similarities between tyranny and its effects in different times and places. In any case, the fundamental link between Tacitus and More is one of intellectual affinity: they saw the world in quite similar ways, a fact that is most clearly apparent in the striking resemblance between the narrative *voices* of their works – voices that are caustic, clinical, sceptical, superior and constantly focused on ironic contrasts between appearance and reality, expectation and outcome. At one point in the *Annals*, Tacitus steps back from his narrative to remark that 'the more I reflect on events recent or remote, the more am I haunted by the sense of a mockery in human affairs' (3.18).

This sense permeates More's work as thoroughly as it does Tacitus's, and gives it the same dark coloration – though More's *History* is constantly played over by his wit, which, unlike his irony, finds no parallel in the austere Roman.

All historical writing purports to teach, but More's account of Richard's rise evinces an especially rich, multifaceted didacticism. First, he had a good knowledge of the historical terrain he surveyed, and while the book, like other works in the tradition of rhetorical historiography, goes – especially in its manufactured speeches – much further in embellishment of the facts than modern historians normally do, it nonetheless presents an overview of the events of spring and summer 1483, and of the motives of the principal actors in them, that fundamentally does not differ much from the most authoritative accounts both early and modern.[37] More also offers many shrewd observations on the process of Richard's usurpation – lessons, of general applicability, on how a tyranny was established and how it might have been forestalled. The main points are made early in the book in two consecutive set pieces, both of great thematic importance – the character portrait of Richard and the deathbed oration of Edward IV.

The portrait of Richard (*R3* 9–12) lists – and much of the rest of the *History* illustrates – the personal qualities, good and bad, that enabled him to do what he did. He had 'wit [i.e. intelligence] and courage', as well as skill as a military leader; but he was also 'malicious, wrathful, envious'. Above all, there were his inveterate dissimulation and utter ruthlessness, which More brilliantly limns: 'He was close and secret, a deep dissimuler: lowly of countenance, arrogant of heart; outwardly companionable where he inwardly hated, not letting [refraining] to kiss whom he thought to kill; dispiteous and cruel ... Friend and foe was muchwhat indifferent: where his advantage grew, he spared no man's death whose life withstood his purpose.' Nor, examining the historical record for spring and summer 1483, can one easily dispute these claims.

But More saw that Richard's seizure of the throne also depended on certain qualities in the realm's *other* wielders of power – the aristocracy and the high clergy. This is the thematic point of Edward IV's deathbed oration (*R3* 15–17), which follows closely on the portrait of Richard. The speech is unhistorical: although there is an early report that Edward in his final illness tried to reconcile the feuding nobles of his court,[38] the speech More gives him is, as I noted earlier, a reworking of a similar thematic speech in Sallust. The point that More eloquently makes here is that factional divisions and selfish ambition among the powerful were necessary conditions for Richard's usurpation.[39] This speech is, in fact, the major thematic statement of the *History* – the major statement of More's explanation for what happened in England in the period of Richard's rise and reign. In the remainder of the unfinished book, More demonstrates how Richard's personal qualities, working (largely through his and Buckingham's powerfully deceptive rhetoric) on the ambition and factionalism of the other aristocrats, and on the initial gullibility of aristocrats and commoners alike, made possible his seizure of the throne.

As Richard rose, many fell; and More is very fond of drawing the standard moral lessons embodied in their falls, the commonplaces of the ineluctable turning of Fortune's wheel and 'the blindness of our mortal nature' (*R3* 61) that are illustrated especially by the murders of Richard's discarded henchman Lord Hastings and Edward's young sons, and the humbling of their mother, Queen Elizabeth Woodville (who, in the end, survived Richard and rose on the wheel again, when her eldest daughter became Henry VII's queen). But the most striking of all the book's moral lessons – and by far the least predictable – are those that More draws from the career of Mistress Shore, who, raised high by Edward's passion for her but cast down after his death, was, at the time More wrote, in 'beggarly condition, unfriended and worn out of acquaintance' (*R3* 66). What makes the passage remarkable is that More – who might have been expected to dismiss Shore as merely a fallen woman – was able to see beyond that stereotype and present a thoroughly individualized, and in many ways attractive, portrait of her as one who had great influence on Edward but never abused it, employing it instead 'to many men's comfort and relief': 'in many weighty suits [petitions] she stood many men in good stead, either for none or very small rewards, and those rather gay than rich: either for that she was content with the deed self well done, or for that she delighted to be sued unto and to show what she was able to do with the king, or for that wanton women and wealthy be not always covetous' (*R3* 66). The most vivid and nuanced portrayal of a woman in English literature between Chaucer and Shakespeare, More's few pages on Shore made her at once a byword and a legend, and gave rise to many later literary treatments.[40]

Ultimately, though, perhaps the most interesting – and certainly the most frequent – lessons of More's *History* are found not in its major thematic pronouncements or more formal moralizings but in the continual brief observations it offers on a wide variety of topics but especially on routine power politics, with its constant calculations of self-interest, constant manipulation and deception of others, and constant probing for, and exploitation of, others' weaknesses of vanity, naivety, wishfulness or cowardice. The man who tells us about these things is cynical and worldly-wise (like his mentor Morton, and like Tacitus) but also, in his observations on individuals, often – as towards Shore – exhibits a depth of moral insight and an attendant charity and tolerance that go far beyond the conventional. Thus Edward IV's lechery can, More thinks, be explained – and largely excused – on the grounds that 'health of body in great prosperity and fortune, without a special grace, hardly refraineth' (that is, finds it hard to refrain) from 'fleshly wantonness' (*R3* 5); and even of Richard, More is capable of entertaining the possibility that he did not (as was generally assumed) have a longstanding intention of usurping the throne but was put in mind of doing so only by his brother's unanticipated early death and the youth of his heirs: 'as opportunity and likelihood of speed [success] putteth a man in courage of that [encourages a man to do what] he never intended' (*R3* 13). There are scores of such pungent observations in the *History*, illuminating seemingly invariant aspects not of political life only but, often, of human life in general.

FURTHER READING

EW 1 (1931) prints a photographic facsimile of the first, 1557 edition of the English *History*, together with a modern-spelling transcription, extremely valuable introductory essays, and collations with the other early printings. The current full critical edition of the English version is Richard S. Sylvester's in *CW* 2 (1963), with superb, full introduction and commentary. For the Latin text, however, *CW* 2 has been superseded by *CW* 15 (1986), ed. Daniel Kinney. *R3* (2005) offers a modern-spelling version of the English text with full glossarial notes and a lean commentary, together with a substantial introduction and an appendix reprinting some sources and analogues of passages of the *History*.

The most authoritative contemporary accounts of Richard's usurpation are that by Dominic Mancini, ed. C. J. A. Armstrong as *The Usurpation of Richard the Third*, 2nd edn (Oxford: Clarendon Press, 1969), and the account included in the anonymous work known as the Second Continuation of the Crowland Chronicle, printed in *The Crowland Chronicle Continuations, 1459–1486*, ed. Nicholas Pronay and John Cox (London: Richard III and Yorkist History Trust, 1986). Alison Hanham, *Richard III and His Early Historians 1483–1535* (Oxford:

Clarendon Press, 1975), includes detailed accounts of a wide range of early written sources on Richard, with copious excerpts from many of them. Along with the *History*, the other important early-sixteenth-century account of Richard is found in the *Anglica historia* of More's friend Polydore Vergil. Part of this Latin work is available in a fine sixteenth-century translation by an unknown hand: *Three Books of Polydore Vergil's English History, Comprising the Reigns of Henry VI, Edward IV, and Richard III*, ed. Sir Henry Ellis (London: Camden Society, 1844). A superb brief introduction to the tradition of humanist historiography (to which Polydore's and More's accounts belong) is found in Felix Gilbert, *Machiavelli and Guicciardini: Politics and History in Sixteenth-Century Florence* (Princeton University Press, 1965), 203–26. For another overview, with copious references to the secondary literature, see Antonia Gransden, *Historical Writing in England*, vol. 2: *c. 1307 to the Early Sixteenth Century* (Ithaca, N.Y.: Cornell University Press, 1982), 425–30.

The most popular modern biography of Richard has been the colourful, highly sympathetic *Richard the Third* of Paul Murray Kendall (London: Allen & Unwin, 1955). A better balanced account (and the standard biography) is Charles Ross's *Richard III* (Berkeley: University of California Press, 1981). On the long-running controversy over the portrayal of Richard by More, other early historians and Shakespeare, see Kendall, 419–34; Ross, xlviii–liii; A. R. Myers, 'Richard III and historical tradition', *History* 53 (1968), 181–202; and, extending the overview to 1993, Keith Dockray, *Richard III: A Source Book* (Stroud: Sutton Publishing, 1997).

The modern critical tradition on the *History* began with the essays in *EW* 1 and A. F. Pollard's 'The making of Sir Thomas More's *Richard III*' (originally pub. 1933; repr. *EA*). Pollard's essay was influential in directing attention to the *History* as literature, and especially to its affinities with drama. *EA* also reprints (among other important articles on the *History*) Arthur Noel Kincaid's 'The dramatic structure of Sir Thomas More's *History of King Richard III*' (originally pub. 1972), which has been key to the development of a critical trend, predominant since the 1970s, that pushes the affinity between the *History* and drama so far that More's work has often been treated as if it really were a play, of one kind or another, rather than (as it clearly is) a member of a genre – rhetorical history – that has much in *common* with drama. Kinney, 'Kings' tragicomedies: generic misrule in More's *History of Richard III*', *Moreana* 22, no. 86 (1985), 128–50, is a notably wide-ranging and balanced member of this critical school.

Notes

1. It has sometimes been suggested (e.g. by the editor of the Latin version, Daniel Kinney, *CW* 15:clii and n. 2) that this passage – most of which, at least, did not appear in More's manuscript of the English version (see *R3* 95–6 and textual note, 123–4) – may have been intended as the *conclusion* of the Latin version, which would thus be a completed history of the usurpation rather than an incomplete one of Richard's rise, reign and fall. But even if this was More's intention (which is far from certain), it seems clear from various indications in the surviving sixteenth-century texts of the Latin version that he never completed revisions to it. See, e.g., below, 172–3.

2. *Why* he did not has been the subject of considerable speculation. For a summary, see *R3* xl–xliii.

3. For accounts of the reception of the *History*, see below, 271–4, and *R3* xliii–li (and, for further readings on the controversy over Richard, *R3* lviii, and 185 below).

4. *CWE* 7:18, which, however, translates *tyrannis* as 'absolute rule' (a defensible rendering: see below, 180). Especially from *Utopia* and one of his Latin epigrams – no. 198, entitled 'What is the best form of government' (*CW* 3, Part 2:228–31) – it is clear that More, like a good many other Renaissance humanists, harboured republican sentiments. Among the 280 or so epigrams (written in the period roughly 1500–20), tyranny is the subject most frequently treated.

5. On these readers see Annabel Patterson, *Reading Holinshed's 'Chronicles'* (Chicago and London: University of Chicago Press, 1994), esp. 15–16, 264–76.

6. More's previous English writings comprise, in addition to some poetry, the translated *Life of Pico* (above, 28), which includes, in its dedication and a few other additions, a small amount of original prose. Throughout the volume, More's prose style anticipates that of the more formal parts of the *History*. See W. A. G. Doyle-Davidson, 'The earlier English works of Sir Thomas More', *EA* 366–7, 371. In the 1520s and 1530s, of course, More wrote a great deal of English prose.

7. *CW* 15:317. All translations from the Latin *Historia* are Kinney's, from this edition.

8. In the Yale edition of the *History*, Richard S. Sylvester notes that this statement 'was not even true *de facto* in the early sixteenth century. *De jure* it has never been valid' (*CW* 2:164).

   For a discussion of the categories of differences between the English and Latin versions enumerated above, and a catalogue of instances, see *EW* 1:48.

9. The Latin Works appeared at Louvain, shortly after Rastell died in that city.

10. See further Sylvester's thorough and generally accepted analysis of the dating of the *History*, which concludes that More 'most probably' worked on it 'from about 1514 to 1518 and perhaps later' (*CW* 2:xx, also lxiii–lxv).

11. The most important discussion of the relations among the various sixteenth-century versions of the texts – both English and Latin – is Kinney's, in *CW* 15:cxxxiii–cliii (1986). Sylvester's discussion in *CW* 2: xvii–liv (1963), although full of interesting detail, must be corrected by comparison with Kinney. See also David Womersley, 'Sir Thomas More's *History of King Richard III*: a new theory of the texts', *Renaissance Studies* 7 (1993), 272–90.

12. The conclusion that the *History* was written in this fashion has been endorsed by all its major recent editors: *EW* 1:52; *CW* 2:lviii; *CW* 15:cl n. The only known parallel in a substantial work is Walter Savage Landor's epic poem *Gebir*. Landor says he wrote 'many parts' of that work first in Latin; he published versions of it in both English (1798) and Latin (1803). See Landor's *Complete Works*, ed. T. Earle Welby and Stephen Wheeler, 16 vols. (London: Chapman and Hall, 1927–35), 13:344.

13. The Commentary in *CW* 2 calls attention to many of the differences between the English and the 1565 Latin edition; *EW* 1:291–302 tabulates the 'most striking' differences, in a handy parallel-columns format. The tabulation includes about 110 places where the Latin is more expansive than the English and about 95 places where the opposite is true. (The counts are approximate because it is not always objectively clear whether a passage expands on its counterpart or is just a differently worded equivalent.)

14. For detailed surveys of the possible sources, see *CW* 2:lxv–lxxx and *R3* xxiii–xxxi.

15. Both of More's great political works include eulogies of Morton (*CU* 55; *R3* 105–6), and he is a major character in the *History* as well as in Book I of *Utopia*.

    From at least the late sixteenth century, there has been a durable suspicion, especially among Richard's defenders, that Morton *wrote* the Latin version of the *History*, and that More then merely translated it into English. This hypothesis – which has its only basis in a hearsay remark of Sir John Harington in his *The Metamorphosis of Ajax* (1596), and was from there taken up by Richard's apologists, who have understandably preferred Morton to More as their adversary – was demolished in a 1931 essay by R. W. Chambers (*EW* 1:24–41). There is some slight reason for thinking that Morton may have left a written account (though not the *History*) of Richard's usurpation: see *CW* 15: cxxxvi–cxxxvii n.

16. Pollard gives fourteen examples: see 'The making of Sir Thomas More's *Richard III*', *EA* 423–4.

17. That is, neither is named in the English version of the *History* as printed by Rastell from a holograph manuscript in 1557, or in the manuscripts or the printed text (1565) of the Latin version. At three points in the English version as initially printed in the chronicles, however, figures left nameless in Rastell's edition and the Latin text are identified as Howard *père* or *fils*. The provenance of these identifications – in themselves, quite plausible – is uncertain.

18. For excerpts from the act, see *R3* 129–31. Rosemary Horrox, *Richard III: A Study of Service* (Cambridge University Press, 1989), 118–19, argues plausibly that the 1584 version of the petition was very different from the original.

    Here and in a few subsequent places in the present essay, I have found it impossible to avoid echoes of corresponding passages in my introduction to *R3*.

19. Fabyan's book was complete through the reign of Richard by 1504, and More may have seen it either in manuscript or in the version printed in London in 1516 or 1517. For one of the close parallels between More and Fabyan, and an argument for More's debt to him, see *EW* 1:37 n.

20. For a careful treatment of the relation between the books, see *CW* 2: lxxv–lxxvii.

    There are two valuable early accounts of Richard that More almost certainly could *not* have read: an anonymous work known as the Second Continuation of the Crowland Chronicle, and a brief work, now called *The Usurpation of Richard the Third*, by Dominic Mancini, an Italian humanist residing in London at the time of the usurpation (for editions of both see 'Further reading'). The first of these works seems not to have been known to other historians before the end of the sixteenth century, and Mancini's account, written after he returned to the Continent, and preserved in a single manuscript (at Lille), was not published until 1936. They are now recognized as the most authoritative contemporary narrative sources on Richard's seizure of power. The striking closeness of agreement between them and More's *History* – on the basic facts of the usurpation and in the general view of Richard – constitutes the most important indication that More was well informed about the historical terrain he surveyed and that his unflattering view of its central figure was not mere Tudor propaganda but was harmonious with the interpretation of the best observers contemporary with the events.

21. E.g., Cicero, *Orator* 11.37, *De oratore* 2.12.50–4, 15.62–4. On the importance of rhetoric in humanism, see above, 47–8.

22. Ascribed to Thucydides by the Greek rhetorician and historian Dionysius of Halicarnassus (*Ars rhetorica* 11.2).

23. *A Defence of Poetry*, ed. Jan van Dorsten (Oxford University Press, 1966), 37–8.

24. More never gives Shore's first name, but in a 1599 play by Thomas Heywood she is called 'Jane', and the name has stuck. Her actual forename was Elizabeth.

25. The most useful discussions of the style of the *History* – that is, the discussions with the greatest number of instructively classified examples – are found in Doyle-Davidson, 'The earlier English works of Sir Thomas More', *EA* 371–2 and nn., and Elizabeth Story Donno, 'Thomas More and *Richard III*', *Renaissance Quarterly* 35 (1982), 428–9, 438–40. Both of these scholars claim (as others also have) that the *History* has two distinct styles: a Latinate high style for the set pieces, and an unpretentious, colloquial style for the narrative passages.

Although I formerly echoed this claim (*R3* xxxviii–xxxix n.), I now think it more accurate to speak of a stylistic *continuum* in the work, the stylistic differences between passages seeming to be differences of degree rather than kind.

26. My counts are based on the extensive documentation of echoes in the Commentary in *CW* 15.

27. For the three passages, see *R3* 94–5, 126–8.

28. Cf. *R3* 69–80, 85–6. The first of the two claims is explicit in the Act for the Settlement of the Crown, which also hints at the other one (which, since it impugned Richard's own mother, needed more delicate treatment). For the adoption of the argument for the bastardy of Edward's sons (and, more guardedly, of Edward himself) by Richard's most influential modern apologist and most popular biographer, see Paul Murray Kendall, *Richard the Third* (in 'Further reading'), 215–23 and nn. 16, 17.

29. On these matters see the current standard biography of Richard, Charles Ross, *Richard III* (in 'Further reading'), 70–1, 74, 88–93.

30. Ibid., 173–5, 184–90.

31. What actually happened to the little princes has been a subject of unending debate. But: they disappeared from view soon after Richard took the throne; the early accounts of Richard's usurpation agree that they were murdered; and, given the precedents (dynastic murders had been the rule in analogous circumstances), it would be surprising if they did *not* meet their deaths at the instigation – or, at the least, through the acquiescence or malign neglect – of the reigning monarch. See the balanced account in Ross, *Richard III*, 96–104.

32. A. Andrewes, *The Greek Tyrants* (New York: Harper Torchbooks, 1963 [1956]), provides an excellent overview.

33. By far the best treatment of More's relation to these writers is Sylvester's, in *CW* 2:lxxxvi–xcviii. See, above all, the masterly summarizing paragraphs, xcviii.

34. Deathbed orations: *Jugurtha* 9.4–11; *R3* 14–17 (and see below, 182–3); insecurity: *Jugurtha* 72; *R3* 102.

35. Uwe Baumann, 'Thomas More and the classical tyrant', *Moreana* 22, no. 86 (1985), 108–27, summarizes the conventions about tyrants, and More's use of them.

36. As also to the portrayal of Tiberius in another Roman work of the turn of the second century, Suetonius's *Lives of the Caesars*. But while there are a few passages of the *History* where echoes of Suetonius help to set Richard's England 'against the background of Tiberian Rome' (*CW* 2: xci–xcii), Suetonius's gossipy, scandalous work on the emperors from Julius Caesar to Domitian – essentially a collection of anecdotes – was not a formal model for More's *History*.

37. On More's general agreement with the best early accounts (those of the anonymous continuator of the Crowland Chronicle and of Dominic Mancini), see above, n. 20; his fundamental agreement with the best modern accounts becomes evident, for example, in reading Alison Hanham's outline of the 'basic facts' of the usurpation, 'as far as they can now be reconstructed', in *Richard III and His Early Historians*

1483–1535 (in 'Further reading'), 2–15, or Ross's *Richard III*, esp. 63–104, on the events of the usurpation and the fate of the little princes.

38. Mancini, *Usurpation*, 69.
39. Like More, Richard's best modern biographer attributes the success of the usurpation to 'the deep divisions ... among those who had held power at the court of Edward IV' and to 'Richard's own forceful character', including his willingness to use 'ruthless means' (Ross, *Richard III*, 93–4).
40. They are surveyed in Robert Birley, 'Jane Shore in literature', *Etoniana* no. 125 (4 June 1972), 391–7; no. 116 (2 Dec. 1972), 399–407.

9 'The comen knowen multytude of crysten men': *A Dialogue Concerning Heresies* and the defence of Christendom

EAMON DUFFY

A Dialogue Concerning Heresies, first published in June 1529, was the earliest of six interconnected vernacular treatises against the Reformation, culminating in 1533 in *The Answer to a Poisoned Book*. This controversial broadside, totalling an astonishing one million words, was the most sustained literary effort of More's life, and was produced in just five years, for three of which he held the highest secular office in the land as lord chancellor of England, and was busy as a zealous heresy-hunter.[1]

These books have had few admirers. Charles Lamb thought them informed by a wit and malice 'hyper-satanic', Richard Marius saw in them a dispiriting parade of 'ferocity and dreary dullness' and Alistair Fox 'a pattern of progressive deterioration' as 'dialogue gives way to debellation, self-control leads to loss of proportion and perspective, candour is replaced by dishonesty, and charity is displaced by violence'.[2] The sustained polemic in these works, against heretics in general and the Protestant preachers burned in the early 1530s in particular, has alienated even well-disposed commentators. In a sympathetic recent discussion of the *Dialogue*, James Simpson nevertheless deplored the 'heartless mockery' and 'frankly vicious self-confidence' on display in these works as a group.[3]

In this general chorus of condemnation or dismissal, the *Dialogue* has admittedly fared somewhat better than the rest. Couched, like Book I of *Utopia* and the very different *Dialogue of Comfort against Tribulation*, in More's favourite and most successful literary form, the *Dialogue Concerning Heresies* was written with evident zest, and published as the upward curve of More's career reached its zenith with his appointment as lord chancellor in succession to Cardinal Wolsey. C. S. Lewis put it in an altogether different class from the rest of the polemical works: written when 'the iron ... [had] not yet entered into

More's soul', it is a 'great Platonic dialogue: perhaps the best specimen of that form ever produced in English' (*EA* 392–3). While considering that its length (150,000 words) 'threatens to destroy' the dialogue form, Brian Cummings nevertheless sees in it 'a writer of genius writing at the extremity of his understanding of the meaning, significance and status of writing'.[4]

It needs to be insisted on that More intended the *Dialogue* as a real conversation between clashing accounts of Christianity. His fictional interlocutor, the Messenger, spokesman for the Reformation, is elaborately deferential to the 'More' character, and ultimately declares himself convinced. He has accordingly been dismissed as 'only a foil', 'a straw man' offering no real resistance to the fictional More's persuasions.[5] But the Messenger is a far more complex character than such a verdict suggests. He has 'a very mery wytte' and is 'of nature nothynge tonge tayed' (*CW* 6:25). More not only gives him space to develop a 'plausible impersonation of the best arguments of [his] opponents',[6] but wraps these polemical points in muscular, racy and often telling language, and he is given most of the best jokes in the book. He is indeed presented as a callow young intellectual, breezily and crassly dismissive of a learning he does not possess, and which, like the Cambridge heretic Thomas Bilney, he considers inimical to faith – 'Logycke he rekened but bablynge / Musyke to serve for syngers / Arythmetrycke mete for marchauntes / ... And as for Phylosophy / the most vanyte of all ... For man he sayd hathe noo lyght / but of holy scrypture' (*CW* 6:33).[7]

There was in fact plenty of warrant for these opinions in the writings of real Protestants, and More distilled much of the Messenger's talk from the writings of Tyndale and from the trial records of Bilney and his associates.[8] The Messenger is certainly a stereotype, 'a wanton' (*CW* 6:287), cockily enamoured of the latest intellectual fad, delighted to shock his elders. The poet John Skelton deployed much the same stereotype against the Messenger's real-life Cambridge counterparts in his 1528 'Replication' against 'certain young scholars abjured of late': 'these demi-divines, and stoical students, and friskajolly younkerkins ... basked and bathed in their wild burbling and boiling blood, fervently reboiled with the infatuate flames of their reckless youth and witless wantonness'.[9]

More, however, takes the Messenger and his opinions very much more seriously than Skelton took Thomas Bilney. The Messenger, although sometimes presented as thoughtless, is never witless. Indeed, More confessed himself 'halfe in a doubte' about the wisdom

and propriety of allowing his character to expound heresy 'so homly /
and in maner somtyme unreverently spoken agaynst goddes holy
halowes', and of giving him the 'tales and mery wordes whiche he
mengled with his matter' (*CW* 6:23). There is a real issue here. Given
More's ardent conviction of the intellectual and moral squalor of the
teachings of Luther and his followers, we will need to consider later
in this essay just why he opted to give the Devil so many of the
Dialogue's best tunes.

The *Dialogue*, then, is the 'record' of a fictional conversation, in
which the Messenger is urged to throw caution to the winds and speak
freely to a patient and sympathetic 'More' – 'Doubt on quod I bytwene
us twayne and spare not' (*CW* 6:109). James Simpson has recently
suggested, therefore, that 'trust surrounds and undergirds the text ...
at almost every point'.[10] In fact it would be truer to say that the entire
text is premised on suspicion rather than trust. More commits the
Dialogue to paper in case the Messenger's account of their conversation, by malice or mischance, should mislead or distort. The More
character indeed protests that he 'nothynge suspecte[s]' (6:21) the
Messenger, but over and over again the unfolding of the conversation
between them makes it clear that this is exactly what he *does* do. The
suspicion that the Messenger's account or recollection of their talk
might not be reliable is implicit in the elaborate fiction on which the
Dialogue is premised. An anonymous friend sends the impressionable
young Messenger, his own 'specyall secret frend' (6:24), to More, to
have his mind set at rest about the seductive claims of the new religion.
More spends several days in conversation with the Messenger, with a
three-week interruption, during which the young man visits his old
friends in Cambridge, returning to More's house full of outrage fuelled
by University gossip about the burning of Tyndale's New Testament
and the alleged clerical maltreatment of Thomas Bilney, abjured of
heresy in 1527. The young man is charged to recount the substance of
their conversations to the friend, but just in case he does not, and lest
garbled versions should be put about by heretics, More composes his
own verbatim report.

In this scenario, the Messenger is an ingénue, vulnerable to Protestant persuasions but in intention, at least, a docile Catholic seeking
correction, a mere mouthpiece for other men's views, anxious to learn
what the snags are. But More repeatedly subverts this innocent version
of things. The Messenger constantly reveals that he is no neutral
reporter: he is rabidly anticlerical, determined to believe the worst
of every priest, 'loke the holy horeson never so saintly' (*CW* 6:83).

His vehemence in expounding the Protestant case constantly betrays that he is in fact committed to many of the views he purports merely to report. As More tells the anonymous friend, the messenger 'set the matter so well and lustely forwarde / he put me somewhat in doubte whether he were (as yonge scolers be somtyme prone to newe fantasyes) fallen in to luthers secte' (6:34). Thus, despite occasional protestations of trust in his interlocutor's orthodoxy, all through Book I More slyly nudges the reader into doubting it. So at one point the fictional More offers to prove to the Messenger the reality of miracles at the shrines of the saints, 'whiche thynge ... ye seme to impugne'. Hastily the Messenger interjects, 'Nay syr ... / I pray you take me not so as thoughe that *I* dyd impugne it / but as I shewed you before / I rehersed you what I have herde *some other* say.' Undeflected, More begins his exposition: 'And fyrst, where ye say ...' Once more the Messenger nervously interrupts – 'Nay, quod he, where *they* say' – to which More sardonically replies, 'Well, quod I, so be it, where *they* say. For here ever my tonge tryppeth' (6:62–3).[11]

The *Dialogue* is, first and foremost, an *occasional* piece, addressed to very specific circumstances and to a large extent shaped by them. More's polemics were the result of a direct commission from his friend and collaborator in the struggle against heresy, Cuthbert Tunstall, bishop of London. In March 1528 Tunstall wrote to More, commissioning him to write some popular works in English which would help ordinary men and women (*'simplicibus et idiotis hominibus'*) to see through the 'cunning malice' of the heretics currently flooding the land with Lutheran propaganda. To help More, Tunstall sent him a bundle of confiscated books and tracts, including a marked copy of Tyndale's New Testament with the errors 'redy noted', and licensed him to read them (*Corr.* 386–8; *CW* 8:1139 n. 4).

This invitation was one move in an ongoing campaign against heresy being waged by every available means in the diocese of London, and in which More was already deeply involved.[12] Thomas Bilney and his Cambridge disciple Thomas Arthur had abjured their preaching against images and relics in December 1527, after lengthy examinations by a panel of bishops and theologians which had included Wolsey, Fisher and Tunstall. Within a fortnight of Tunstall's commission, More would be an eyewitness of Tunstall's lengthy interrogation of Dr Thomas Farman, Cambridge-trained rector of All Hallows Honey Lane in London, whose preaching was a magnet for evangelicals, and whose rectory was a centre of the contraband-book trade.[13] More would incorporate much detail from this campaign into the *Dialogue*, and the examinations of Bilney and Farman would provide major set pieces in the second half of the book (*CW* 6:255–80, 378–84). The *Dialogue* is, of course, a polemic against the Reformation as a whole, in which More touches on most of the issues in contention between Catholics and their opponents, from justification by faith and predestination to papal authority and the value of images and relics. But it is formally structured round issues arising from this London campaign.

Early in Book I, therefore, More declares that he will follow the Messenger's own agenda, beginning where he began, with the abjuration of Bilney, and consider whether the complaints that he had been 'borne wronge in hande' by his accusers and judges were justified. From there he will move on to the condemnation and burning of Tyndale's New Testament. Third, he will consider the nature and consequences of Luther's message. Finally he will consider the legitimacy of the use of force in defence of Catholic orthodoxy (*CW* 6:28–36). The Messenger is of course More's creation, and the agenda he sets is More's agenda. It is at first sight a puzzling one. Recent discussions of the *Dialogue* have focused on More's rejection there of the Reformation doctrine of *sola scriptura*. Accordingly, the work has been seen as essentially a defence of the spoken as against the written word, and an extended discussion of how the scriptures ought to be read. So for Brian Cummings More's book is 'a radical attack on the grapheme in favour of the phoneme', for James Simpson it is mainly about 'the licit function and limitations of sacred texts'.[14] These issues do loom large in the *Dialogue*, but they are not in fact its primary concern. A large proportion of the work is focused rather on the defence of the cult of the saints and, in general, of the practices and underlying assumptions of late medieval Catholicism. These were, of course, a major target of Protestant polemic, but they feature less prominently in the hierarchy of Protestant concerns than foundational doctrines of justification by faith or *sola scriptura*. Why, then, did More choose to lead his attack on the new religion with a defence of pilgrimage and images?

Certainly there was warrant for this focus in the Bilney affair. The articles alleged against him during his London examination included attacks on the intercession of the saints, the veneration of images and the practice of pilgrimage, and these issues were to dominate the East Anglian preaching tour which led to his execution as a relapsed heretic in 1531.[15] But it was neither obvious nor inevitable that More should fasten on these aspects of the affair, nor that he should devote almost half the *Dialogue* to them, deferring detailed discussion of Bilney's trial and the Messenger's other grievances for 250 pages.

The *Dialogue* starts with Bilney because Bilney's attack on images and pilgrimage allowed More to build the first half of his book round his own central conviction, the reality of Christ's guiding presence in the common life of the visible Church. Clearly, this choice of theme had implications for the debate about whether Christians look for guidance primarily to scripture or to unwritten tradition. For More, the Church cannot err in fundamentals, because of Christ's promise 'I am with you all the dayes tyll the ende of the worlde'. For his interlocutor that promise was fulfilled in the gift of the scriptures to the Church. Christ is present, the Messenger declares, 'bycause his holy scrypture shall never fayle / as longe as the worlde endureth'. More dismisses this as a confusion between mere text and the living word of God. Christ had promised that he and the Holy Ghost would abide with the Church, but 'wherto all this yf he ment no more but to leve the bokes behynde them and go theyr waye?' (*CW* 6:114–15). Texts may perish, and many scriptural texts have in fact perished. Those that survive may become corrupted in transmission by the ravages of time, or by some fault in the translator or the writer, 'or nowe a dayes in the prynter' (6:127). But the substance of God's word, his living truth embodied in the teaching and practice of the Christian community through the ages, can never perish, and is not dependent on the survival or stability of any text.

It is important to grasp that for More this was not in essence a debate about the primacy of the spoken as against the written word. Although he cites a *proposition* as an example of the Church's unwritten tradition – the belief that Mary had remained perpetually a virgin – he does not think of God's truth as consisting primarily of spoken propositions, any more than of written ones. By 'the lawe of Crystes faythe' he meant 'not onely the wordes wrytten in the bookes of hys evangelystes' but, much more, 'the substaunce of our fayth it selfe / whiche oure lorde sayd he wolde wryte in mennes hartes'. This he did by 'the secrete operacyon of god and his holy spyryte' in the work of grace – the regeneration of the baptized and the sanctification of believers – as well as by the fact that he revealed the heavenly mysteries 'fyrste without wrytynge ... by hys blessyd mouth / thorowe the eres of his appostles and dyscyples in to theyr holy hartes'. But More insists that in this transmission of the life and truth of God, the heart is just as important as the ear or mouth. Like the written word, even the *spoken* word was secondary. Indeed, God's truth was given to St Peter, 'the prynce of the appostles', without any words at all: 'as it semeth it was inwardly infused in to saynt Peter his harte / by the secrete inspyracyon of god / without eyther wrytynge or any outwarde worde'

(*CW* 6:143). The word of God was indeed first spread 'by the mouthes of his holy messengers', but it was the heart, not the ear or the eye, which received it. 'And so was it convenyent for the lawe of lyfe / rather to be wrytten in the lyvely myndes of men / than in the dede skynnes of bestes' (6:143–4).

All this did indeed have far-reaching consequences for the reading of scripture. More devotes a good deal of the later part of Book I to refuting the notion that the written scriptures and the faith of the Church can ever be truly at variance. The Bible can only be properly understood in the light of the Church's credo and its divinely inspired exegetical tradition, as embodied in the writings of 'the olde holy fathers'. The hermeneutic of suspicion, that systematic 'dyffydens and mystrust' which More thought characterized the exegesis of Lutherans like Tyndale, caused them to set Bible and Church over against each other: 'of all wreches worst shall he walke / that forsynge lyttell of the fayth of Crystes chyrche / cometh to the scrypture of god to loke and trye therin whyther the chyrche byleve a ryght or not' (*CW* 6:152–3).

But this opposition is not More's principal concern. For him the living truth of Catholicism was not primarily a matter of the *spoken* word any more than the written word, whether those words be Bible, creeds, conciliar decrees, or doctrinal statements, although naturally he acknowledged that Catholic tradition necessarily involved all these forms of expression. His principal concern in the *Dialogue* is rather to defend the presence of Christ in the life of the Church as embodied in its devotional and sacramental *practice*, the 'rytys & sacramentes and the artycles of our faythe' transmitted 'from hande to hande / from Cryst & his appostles unto our dayes' (*CW* 6:152), specifically in all the concrete forms of the cult of the saints. For that reason, the discussion of the right place and understanding of scripture comes as the conclusion of a far more extended discussion of the legitimacy of the symbolic forms in which devotion to the saints is expressed – pilgrimage, the veneration of relics and images, and the hope of miracles worked by their intercession. These forms of devotion were as ancient as Catholic Christianity itself: 'not thynges newly begon nowe a dayes', but attested in 'the godly bookes' of the 'olde holy doctour[s] of Crystes chyrche' (6:90). If, therefore, the devotion to the saints was indeed an appalling error, as Bilney maintained, 'dyspleasaunt to god / and by hym reputed as a mynyshment ... of the honoure dewe to hym selfe ... and taken as Idolatry', this would mean that the Church had for fourteen hundred years been out of the truth. Christ's promises to abide with his Church and keep in her 'the ryght fayth' would have failed (6:112).

The whole of Book I of the *Dialogue*, therefore, is an appeal not so much to a body of teaching, written or unwritten, as to the immemorial devotional practice of the Church, understood as a concrete manifestation of the life of God within her. For More, participation in that living tradition was the test of true understanding of the Gospel, and took precedence over all forms of argumentation. At the very outset of his exposition he declared that the best way for a simple layman like himself (!!) to discover the truth is 'in all thyngys / [to] lene and cleve to the comen faith / and byleve of crystys chyrche' (*CW* 6:37). All sorts of evidence might be mustered to prove the legitimacy of pilgrimage, not least the many miracles which God had worked through the saints: but for More 'the thynge that I holde stronger than any miracles ... is as I sayd afore the fayth of Crystes chyrche / by the common consent wherof these matters be decyded and well knowen' (6:62).

The main purpose of Book II of the *Dialogue* is the exploration of the meaning and implication of this 'common consent' for the nature of the Church itself. At the outset of the book, the Messenger concedes that perhaps Christ has indeed promised to remain personally present with the Church, and to ensure that she cannot err in faith. But since, as the reformers believe, scripture condemns the cult of the saints as idolatrous, might it not be that the true Church is not 'that people that ye take it for', but instead a hidden and persecuted remnant of true believers (like Tyndale or Bilney)? (*CW* 6:189–90).

Characteristically, More's reply to this is to insist that the true Church cannot be hidden, and is known precisely in the visibility of its common life. Even in times of persecution, the early Church had come together 'to the prechynge and prayer', and had expressed its identity in a shared public life of grace, in 'fastyngys / vygylys kepte / the sondayes halowed / the masse sayd / holy servyce songe / and theyr peple howselyd [administered Communion]'. What was true then must be true now: 'suche thyngys must there be therin / yf it be any chyrche or congregacyon of Cryste' (*CW* 6:190). This common cult was the expression of a common faith and a shared life of grace. The early Church 'were all of one mynde and of one harte', for the indwelling of the Holy Spirit 'maketh all of one mynde in the house of god'. The Messenger counters this by pointing to the visibility of an alternative church rejecting superstition, to be seen among Luther's followers in Saxony, and the Hussites in Bohemia. More, however, seizes on this as corroboration of his point, because these heretics manifestly have no unity of heart or mind. 'For in Saxony fyrst and amonge all the Lutheranes there be as many heddes as many wyttes. And all as wyse as wylde geese ... the maysters them selfe chaunge theyr myndes and theyr oppynyons every day.' And Bohemia was the same, 'One fayth in the towne / another in the felde. One in prage / another in the next towne' (6:191–2). There is therefore no hidden remnant with special access to an allegedly pure gospel truth: Christ's church is 'knowen and not hyd ... And he wolde have his fayth dyvulged and spredde abrode openly / not alway whyspered in hukermoker' (6:202). The Church must always be 'the comen knowen multytude of crysten men good and bad togyther' (6:205).

It is notable that in the *Dialogue* this appeal to the common life of the Church as the ultimate criterion of Christian authenticity never becomes merely or mainly an appeal to hierarchy or to the teaching authority of the clergy. Although More insisted that Peter was Christ's Vicar and head of the Church, 'and alway synce the successours of hym contynually' (*CW* 6:206), More never once appeals to the teaching of a pope or council to clinch his argument. Although the authority of 'the olde holy fathers' is repeatedly invoked in defence of current practice, it is always as a witness to the shared faith of the Church as a body. 'I do not talke of one doctour or twayne / but of the consent and comen agreement of the olde holy fathers', expressing the 'comen consent of the chyrche' (6:169). Even when More's argument might seem to be leading him inexorably towards an appeal to clerical authority, he steers instead towards this insistence on the shared belief of the whole Church. So at one point he asks the Messenger to suppose that some fundamental truth such as the divinity of Christ were to be called in doubt which the balance of biblical texts seemed unable to resolve. If God were then to reveal that there was a wise man who understood the true interpretation of such texts, would we not be bound to seek him out and accept his judgement, rather than remain in doubt? The Messenger agrees that we would have to believe such an infallible guide, at which point More invokes neither the pope nor the bishops, but asks 'What yf it were a certayne knowen company of men and women togyder?' (6:161). Here the inclusion of women in the 'knowen company' makes explicit the non-clerical nature of this appeal to the 'comen corps of crystendome' as the ultimate authority.

That same non-clerical emphasis surfaces also in the course of More's defence of pilgrimage. The Messenger characteristically suggests that pilgrimage thrives mainly because the clergy 'norysshe this superstycyon ... to the parell of the peoples soules / for ... lucre and temporall advauntage'. But More insists that this devotion had been 'planted by goddes owne hand in the hertes of the whole chyrche', *not* among the clergy only, 'but the hole congregacyon of all crysten people'. As a result, 'yf the spyrytualyte were of the mynde to leve it / yet wolde not the temporalyte suffre it' (*CW* 6:53–5). For More, the most fundamental mark of the Church was this holy unanimity, as much a lay as a clerical possession. Correspondingly, the mark of heresy was the pride and love of singularity which set heretics, 'in spekynge and prechyng of suche commune thynges / as all crysten men knowe', to 'shewe them selfe ... merveylous' and set out 'para-doxis and straunge oppynyons / agaynst the commen fayth of Crystes hole chyrche' (6:123).

So far, I have alluded only in passing to More's use of humour as a controversial weapon. Humour, however, and particularly that of the 'mery tales' which punctuate the text, is integral to More's purpose in the *Dialogue*.[16] The insistence on the devotional and doctrinal unan-imity of 'the comen corps of crystendome' which undergirds these books might have become an argument for inertia and the total irre-formability of Christian belief and practice. If what the Church did and taught was the expression of the mind of Christ, must it not be con-sidered perfect? For the humanist author of *Utopia* and the dedicatee of *Encomium Moriae*, Erasmus's great satire on the absurdities of contem-porary Christendom, such an argument would indeed have represented a retreat to reaction. And some influential interpreters of the *Dialogue* have read it in just this way, as when Richard Marius characterized the work as a 'rigid affirmation of unshakable certainty'.[17]

The *Dialogue*, however, is far from rigid, and More's defence of traditional religion, however benign, is by no means uncritical. Convinced of the essential wholesomeness of Catholic religious prac-tice, he can simultaneously poke fun at its excesses while making the case for the value of the core institutions. More's handling of criticisms of traditional religion in the *Dialogue* is therefore self-consciously pragmatic and moderating, puncturing rhetorical posturing, challeng-ing sweeping generalizations. He is insistent that to portray the laity as the helpless dupes of the clergy is to traduce them: 'the flocke of cryst is not so folysshe as those heretyques bere them in hande'. If even a dog can tell 'a very cony from a cony carved and paynted', then 'crysten peple that have reason in theyr heddys / and therto the lyght of fayth in theyr soulys' are in no danger of thinking that images of the Virgin 'were our lady her selfe' (*CW* 6:56).

In this defence of religion as it is actually practised, the 'mery tales' allow More to highlight religious foibles and abuses while maintaining that abuse does not outlaw right use. He gives most of these scandalous stories against orthodox piety to the Messenger. Most of the fun in the Messenger's stories has a sour edge to it, in line with More's belief in the self-righteous censoriousness of the reformers. But the humour is nevertheless genuine, not least in the most notorious (and funniest) story in the book, the Messenger's ribald account of the shrine of St Walery in Picardy. There, he claims, pilgrims resorted for the healing of genital diseases and impotence, and the votive offerings hung round the shrine were 'none other thynge but mennes gere and womens gere made in waxe' (*CW* 6:228).

Richard Marius rightly pointed to the similarity between these 'mery tales' and the humour in Erasmus's *Colloquies*, the satirical Latin dialogues in which, into the mid 1520s, Erasmus lampooned aspects of popular Catholic practice which he judged to be remote from Gospel teaching.[18] 'The Shipwreck', published in 1523, and 'A Pilgrimage for Religion's sake', of 1526, ridicule many of the very practices complained of by the Messenger, and in much the same terms. So the panic-stricken travellers in '*Naufragium*' make extravagant vows to curry favour with the saints, chant hymns to the Virgin to still the waves, or deploy 'certain private little prayers, like charms, to ward off danger'; the somewhat supercilious narrator, who of course knows better, by contrast resorts 'straight to the Father himself, reciting the Paternoster' (*CWE* 39:356).

More was undoubtedly prepared to tolerate a good deal that Erasmus deplored as 'superstition'. The Messenger relates a hair-raising catalogue of abuses – 'ryot / revelynge / and rybawdry' in pilgrimages, the confusion of simple souls between the images of the Virgin and the Virgin herself, the wives of London praying to St Wilgefortis to uncumber them of their husbands, the universal resort to particular saints for special purposes (St Scythe to find keys, St Roke against plague, St Loye to heal horses) – not to mention more exotic abuses like the procession of the image of St Martin, where people emptied their pisspots on the statue if the weather had been bad (*CW* 6:226–9). More agrees that dousing St Martin with urine may be stretching the legitimate bounds of piety, and concedes that the Sorbonne should perhaps investigate the goings-on at St Walery's shrine. But he dismisses most of the Messenger's complaints as hypercriticism: 'somewhat is it in dede that ye say / and yet not all thynge to be blamyd that ye seme to blame' (6:232). '[A] fewe dotynge dames make not the people' (6:237). Even simple women well understand the difference between a favourite statue and the spiritual reality it represents. More saw 'nothing moche amysse' (6:234) in the practices the Messenger condemned. It is 'no wytche-crafte' to pray for relief from the toothache to St Appolonia, 'consyderyng that she had her tethe pulled out for Crystys sake', or to invoke St Loye, a smith, 'for the helpe of a poore mannes horse'. These were natural Christian intuitions in time of need, an extension of faith in God's providence in all our necessities fully in the spirit of the petition of the Lord's Prayer, 'Give us this day our daily bread' (6:232–3).

More treads a delicate line here, guying the scandalous side of popular religious practice jokingly in his own fictional persona or more abrasively through that of the Messenger, conceding the existence of deceptions and abuse, but defending the essential soundness of the institutions themselves and the religious instincts of the laity who used them. Accordingly, a great deal has been made of the contrast between More's intentions in the *Dialogue* and those of the Erasmus of the *Colloquies*. Marius declared that 'Erasmus ends by attacking popular piety and More by defending it', and suggested that although Erasmus was not mentioned explicitly by name, 'Much in the *Dialogue* sounds like a refutation of views expressed in the *Familiar Colloquies*'.[19] The implication here is that in the *Dialogue* More repudiated his earlier concern for the reform of Christendom, abandoned his erstwhile Erasmianism, and exerted himself instead to defend precisely those aspects of religion which Erasmus most deplored. It was a claim made in More's own time. Tyndale, in his reply to the *Dialogue*, claimed that he, not More, was following in the footsteps of Erasmus, and speculated that More had held back from attacking his 'derelynge' Erasmus only because the great humanist had written *The Praise of Folly* in More's house. But from that same book, 'if [it] were in englishe / then shulde every man se / how that ... [More] then was ferre other wise minded than he nowe writeth'.[20]

It is true that Erasmus's *Colloquies* and More's merry tales poke fun at the same targets, but for rather different ends. To left-leaning correspondents, Erasmus could confess that the cult of the saints had indeed 'run to idolatry'. He admitted that 'practices good in themselves should [not] be condemned because they are abused', but he thought the Church had itself to blame for the Protestant rebellion. Catholics, he insisted, 'instead of repenting of their sins, pile superstition on superstition'.[21] He told the Dominican Johann Fabri that the best way to refute Luther was to reform the abuses which had provoked Luther's protest.[22] That was why, when the rest of Europe was polarizing religiously in the 1520s, Erasmus went on doggedly producing his satirical dialogues, to orthodox outrage, determined not to be deflected from the course which he had marked out for himself before Luther had ever been heard of. More, by contrast, thought that Protestant denunciations of abuses were a mask for outright rejection of essential Catholic practices and the theology behind them. This no reform would ever quieten, since what they looked for was not to purify but 'to mynysshe and quenche mennes devocyons' (CW 6:47). Both men were aware that despite all they had in common, therefore, their religious instincts did not exactly coincide. Erasmus regretted More's polemical writings, although he defended his activities against heresy as lord chancellor, and he understood the respect for traditionalist piety which motivated More, for, as he told Fabri, More 'detests the seditious doctrines with which the world is now convulsed ... He is profoundly religious, and if he inclines either way, it is towards superstition'.[23]

For his part, More never criticized, much less repudiated, Erasmus or his writings, but, unlike the less grounded Erasmus, he did think that changing circumstances made a profound difference as to how those writings were likely to be perceived. In 1531 he denied Tyndale's claims to kinship with Erasmus, who 'detesteth and abhorreth the errours and heresyes that Tyndale playnely techeth'. Erasmus's satire was licit because it was without 'malycyouse entent' towards the saints, their relics and images. The Praise of Folly 'doeth but in dede but ieste uppon the abuses of suche thynges', like a jester in a play, 'and yet not so far neyther by a greate deale, as the messenger doth in my dyalog'. But 'erronyouse bokes ... settynge forth Luthers pestylent heresyes' by Tyndale and others had so poisoned public discourse about religion 'that men can not almost now speke of such thynges in so mych as a play, but that such evyll herers wax a grete dele the worse'. In this fraught context, More lamented, where men could take harm from the 'very scrypture of god', it might even be necessary 'to burne ... wyth myne owne handes' not only 'my derlynges bokes but myne owne also ... rather than folke sholde (though thorow theyr own faute) take any harme of them' (CW 8:176–9).

More made that gloomy assessment when, riding on the back of the king's divorce, anticlericalism and heresy were gaining ground in England, 'turning all hony in to posyn' (CW 8:179). It was a prescient judgement: the humanist movement would indeed by hijacked by the proponents of far more drastic reform, and Erasmus himself would be annexed posthumously as a Protestant avant la lettre. Even as early as 1528 Tunstall was turning up heresy suspects in his diocese who attributed their fall from orthodoxy to reading Erasmus. Thus Thomas Topley, an Augustinian friar of Stoke by Clare, began his recantation, 'All Christen men beware of consentyng to Erasmus fables [i.e. the *Colloquies*], for by consentyng to them, they have caused me to shrinke in my fayth.'[24] Given his closeness to Tunstall, and their shared love of Erasmus, More must certainly have known about Topley's examination and recantation, throughout which Erasmus features very negatively. That makes all the more striking, therefore, his unequivocal public defence of Erasmus's innocence and orthodoxy in 1531, as well as his lavish deployment of Erasmus's satirical technique in the merry tales of the *Dialogue* in 1529. These are emphatically not the actions or attitudes of a man in denial about his humanist past.

In Books III and IV of the *Dialogue* More changes gear, and mounts a detailed defence of the role of the clergy in combating heresy. This he develops into a general consideration of the solvent effects of heretics and heresies on Church and society, ending with a rationale and defence of the use of the death penalty in suppressing error. En route, the discussion takes in the legitimacy of the vernacular Bible in general, and Tyndale's version in particular. After the relatively leisurely pace and comic interludes of Books I and II, this second half of the dialogue is more closely focused on specific events, and its later pages are fiercer and more urgent in their analysis of what More sees as the destructiveness of Lutheran teaching, and the measures needed to fight it.

Modern readers of the *Dialogue* have recoiled from these chapters especially. Richard Marius, convinced that the *Dialogue* in general represented an abandonment of More's earlier humanism, was baffled by More's apparent advocacy of a vernacular Bible in Book III, which he thought 'at odds with his general and oft-expressed thoughts on the Bible'. Marius speculated that More included this material to curry favour with Henry VIII.[25] James Simpson focuses, instead, on More's apologia for the burning of heretics. In these chapters, Simpson argues, More contradicted the humane views of *Utopia* (*CU* 221–3) about the futility of the use of force in religion. The 'weak' argumentation More deploys in favour of persecution stems, Simpson believes, from his unwitting surrender to the 'exclusivist, distrustful and utterly self-convinced' understanding of Christian truth maintained by his evangelical opponents.[26] At the risk of appearing perverse, however, I want to maintain that in these final two books it is More's remarkable consistency in defence of Christian humanism which is most striking. The allegations of discrepancies between the author of *Utopia* and the author of these parts of the *Dialogue* arise from a failure to grasp the force of More's urgent analysis of the special dangers threatening Catholic Christendom in the 1520s.

As Book III opens, the Messenger has returned to Chelsea after a visit to Cambridge, where all the talk has been of the abjuration of Thomas Bilney for heresy, and where 'some of them semed to take very sore to hart / the hard handelyng of the man' by his clerical judges (*CW* 6:247). As More knew, Bilney had a reputation for personal holiness and theological zeal: anger against the clerical establishment was being fuelled by rumours that he had been framed, by implacable heresy-hunters, for heresies he never held. More, who had been present at Bilney's examination, knew better. He had heard the testimony of twenty witnesses about Bilney's preaching, he had seen incriminating letters in Bilney's own hand which had not been brought in evidence against him, and he knew that he had previously been summoned before Wolsey himself on suspicion of heresy, but that the cardinal, 'for hys tender favour borne to the unyversyte', had chosen not to proceed against him. Bishop Tunstall had delayed sentence against Bilney even when his heterodoxy had become clear, and he was eventually offered a form of abjuration so laxly ambiguous that More's professional instincts as a lawyer were outraged (6:268–71).

More's account of these proceedings was not in fact unfair to Bilney. The most thorough modern examination of his trial concluded that Bilney throughout displayed 'a degree of contrivance and calculation difficult to reconcile with his pose as an injured innocent', and that this 'shrewd young man' was 'more a schemer than a saint'.[27] But whatever the facts, in addition to exonerating Bilney's judges, More was concerned to present the man himself – whom he never names, since he had abjured and was at liberty – as a paradigmatic case of lapse into heresy. More's Bilney is the victim of religious neurosis, pride and *amour-propre*, whose reluctance to confess his errors, simply and sincerely, boded ill for the future. (In the light of Bilney's relapse two years later, More here showed himself remarkably percipient.) More's portrayal of Bilney's religious trajectory has considerable psychological plausibility, and was crucial for the overall scheme of the last two books of the *Dialogue*, through which some of its key themes would be elaborated. Afflicted with neurotic scruples which drove him to obsessive religious observance, Bilney, according to More, had eventually recoiled into antinomianism: 'wyth the werynesse of that superstycyous fere and servile drede / he felle as farre to the contrary'. So, under the pretext of Christian love and liberty, he 'waxed so dronke

of the new must of lewd lyghtnes of mynd and vayn gladnesse of harte /
whyche he toke for spyrytuall consolacyon that what so ever hym selfe
lysted to take for good / that thought he forthwith approved by God'.
Thus deluded, he 'framed hym selfe a fayth / framed hym selfe a
conscyence / framed hym selfe a devocion' (*CW* 6:257–8).

Bilney provides More with an *exemplum* of a talented man's
progress into heresy, in reaction from a diseased and disproportionate
piety: there is, More tells the Messenger with characteristic humanist
emphasis, 'a meane [that] may serve' between fanaticism and
carelessness. But the arch-heretic of the *Dialogue* is William Tyndale.
Outrage at the solemn burning of Tyndale's New Testament was
another complaint the Messenger had encountered in Cambridge,
and in chapter 8 of Book III More turns to justify this apparently
obscurantist act. Such a defence was certainly a test of his own
fidelity to the humanist project. A decade earlier, in the *Letter
to Dorp* and related writngs, he had thrown his weight behind
Erasmus's controversial new Greek and Latin edition of the New
Testament. Some of the most controversial renderings in Tyndale's
English version had their origins in Erasmus's rejection of the
vocabulary of St Jerome's Vulgate and the substitution of words free
of the theological freight of the medieval schools. More himself
defended one such substitution (*sermo* for *logos* in the prologue of
St John's Gospel), in the *Letter to Dorp*.[28] In defending the banning
and destruction of Tyndale's translation, therefore, More's own integrity and consistency were on the line.

More tackles this delicate task by confining his discussion to just
three words. The marked copy of the New Testament supplied by
Tunstall had noted 'wronge and falsly translated above a thousande
textys by tale [tally]', More tells the Messenger, but he will demon-
strate Tyndale's malicious error by focusing on the terms *priest*,
church and *charity*. Tyndale systematically substitutes for these terms
the words 'senyor', 'congregacyon' and 'love'. More's objections to
Tyndale's renderings are both linguistic and theological. By rejecting
the traditional terms, Tyndale deliberately drives a wedge between the
text and the Church's understanding of the text, developed over fourteen hundred years of divinely guided reflection, prayer and preaching.
In the three examples he has chosen, More insists, a tendentious
Lutheran agenda masquerades as scholarly objectivity. Luther and
Tyndale deny the sacramental priesthood and so translate the Greek
presbyteros to exclude the notion of priesthood altogether. Yet,
according to More, Tyndale's preferred translation, 'senior', has no claim

to greater fidelity to the Greek. In implying *age* it is over-literal – the presbyter Timothy was a young man – and its semantic resonances in English were both inadequate and misleading: 'in our englysshe tonge this worde senyor sygnyfyeth no thynge at all / but is a frenche worde used in englysshe more than half in mockage / whan one wyll call another my lorde in scorne' (*CW* 6:285–6).

In the same way, More argues, the tendentious use of 'congregation' instead of 'church' is rooted in Tyndale's repudiation of the visible Church in favour of 'an unknowen congregacyon of some folke here two and there thre no man wote where' (*CW* 6:289). Tyndale deliberately empties the New Testament concept of the Church of its resonance as a *holy* assembly, for the term 'congregation' makes no distinction between 'a company of crysten men or a company of turkes' (6:286). And the systematic choice of the word 'love' in place of 'charity' is intended to insinuate Luther's doctrine of justification by faith alone. More accepts that there is a linguistic warrant for that particular translation. Although he thinks that 'charity' better conveys the nature of that 'holy virtuous affeccyon', yet 'If he called charyte sometyme by the bare name of love / I wolde not stycke therat'. Tyndale's real agenda, however, is revealed in the fact that he 'studyously flee[s]' the traditional term, and so 'laboureth of purpose to mynysshe the reverent mynde that men bere to charyte' (6:288). His repudiation of Tyndale's work, therefore, is not a rejection of the possibility or desirability of translation, but of the tendentious nature of the translation which Tyndale has actually produced.

And so More's justification of the suppression of Tyndale's translation is balanced by robust and forceful argument for the legitimacy and desirability of English Bible translation.[29] There were those among the clergy, he conceded, who thought it best to withhold the Bible because if it were to be in every man's hand 'there wold grete parell aryse / and that sedycyous people sholde do more harme therwith / than good and honest folke sholde take fruyte therby' (*CW* 6:332). But that argument, he declared, weighed nothing with him. Although 'sedycyous' readers might twist meaning to their own purposes, that could not justify denying well-intentioned Christians the nourishment of the scriptures. The Messenger's eager assertion that lay people can easily understand the Bible is slapped down by More, who insists on lay inability to grasp the 'high secrete mysteryes of god / and harde textes of hys holy scrypture': scripture often exceeds 'the capacyte and perceyvyng of man'. And so disputing God's mysteries in 'pot parlyamente[s]' (6:343), when 'the wyne were in and the wytte out', can breed only 'folyshe wordys and blasphemye': interpretation is a task for trained theologians and approved preachers. But that was no reason for withholding an English Bible. English was a language well fitted to translation, the sacred writers had written in the vernacular in the first place, and 'I wolde not for my mynde withhold the profyte that one good devout unlerned ley man myght take by the redyng / not for the harme that an hundred heretykes wolde falle in by theyr owne wylfull abusyon' (6:335–40).

More somewhat took the shine off this heartfelt apologia for lay Bible reading by suggesting that a reverent and devotional use of scripture might be ensured if individual books of the Bible were to be printed in separate fascicles and doled out by the bishop 'to suche as he perceyveth honeste sad [serious] and virtuous' (*CW* 6:341). It is hard to believe that More seriously imagined that such a paternalistc scheme was remotely workable in an age of print. But his support for an orthodox Bible translation was in any case rapidly overtaken by events. In May 1530 Henry VIII, anxious to offset his increasingly anticlerical behaviour by proving his credentials as Defender of the Faith, summoned leading bishops and theologians from both universities to discuss measures against heresy. The assembly condemned a long list of evil opinions from Tyndale's writings, and advised the king that, given the spread of 'pestilente bookes and ... evill opynyons', the publication of an English New Testament at this stage would bring 'confusion and destruction' rather than the edification of souls.[30]

More was the only layman at the Whitehall consultation: he must certainly have had a hand in its detailed condemnation of Tyndale's writings; he probably drafted and he vigorously enforced the proclamation issued in June 1530 banning those writings. In 1531 he would include a brief defence of the ban on an official translation of the New Testament in his *Confutation of Tyndale's Answer* (*CW* 8:178–9). Yet More retained his long and vehement argument for the legitimacy of lay Bible reading, whatever the dangers, in the 1530 reissue of the *Dialogue*, although it directly contradicted the official rationale for the Whitehall ban. This cannot have been an oversight, for this second edition was significantly revised. It therefore seems likely that the prohibition of an official English New Testament originated with the clerical members of the consultation. If More did eventually retreat from his Erasmian commitment to the benefits of lay Bible reading, that retreat was the reluctant product of the increasingly fraught circumstances of his last two years as chancellor, when anticlericalism was given its head by Cromwell, and heresy established a foothold even at court. There is no such retreat in the *Dialogue*.[31]

The fourth and last Book of the *Dialogue* is in many ways its craggiest. In it, More argues two positions. Luther's teaching, however speciously attractive, is the worst of heresies, lethal to Christian society, because his exaltation of faith alone as the key to salvation makes virtue irrelevant and thereby dissolves all order and moral cohesion. From this it follows that Christian rulers have a duty to protect their people from this demonic teaching, and in doing so the use of force, including the death penalty, is legitimate and necessary.[32] More was unusual among Luther's Roman Catholic opponents in the 1520s in emphasizing the Wittenberger's teaching on justification. But like other Catholic writers, including King Henry, he interpreted Luther's teaching on justification as leading directly to antinomianism, 'plunging [men] headlong into that licentious way of life which you strive to introduce under the pretext of evangelic liberty'.[33] For More this had a special horror, for he recognized that Luther's teaching of justification was underpinned by his teaching on predestination, and was an outright repudiation of human free will. This was the issue on which Erasmus and Luther had decisively quarrelled just three years earlier, and it went to the heart of More's own Christian humanism. For him salvation was the crowning and purification by grace of man's natural inclination towards virtue. The Utopians, even before conversion, believed that in the afterlife vice is punished and virtue rewarded. This was the *only* religious opinion they would not permit to be disputed, and 'Anyone who denies this proposition they consider nor even one of the human race', since such a man put humanity on a level with the beasts, placed himself beyond the reach of morality, and could have no respect for anything but force (*CU* 225).[34] More shared all the Utopians' horror at what he took to be Luther's repudiation of the foundations of human morality and, specifically, Christian virtue. That, and not some personal sexual obsession, was the significance for More of Luther's marriage. A friar in bed with a nun was bad enough, the stuff of a thousand medieval satires. But a friar in bed with a nun claiming that this was a Christian marriage, that solemn religious vows had no power to bind and that holy chastity was an offence against the Gospel, he regarded as the ultimate repudiation of the ancient Christian moral order (*CW* 6:434). He regarded the religious iconoclasm and violent acts of desecration which accompanied the early Reformation, and the secular upheavals of the Peasants' War, as the inevitable outcomes of Luther's antinomian Gospel, a conviction strengthened by the atrocities perpetrated during the sack of Rome in 1527 by the mutinous army of the emperor Charles V, which consisted partly of German Lutheran mercenaries. And for More the doctrine of predestination was an attempt by the reformers to absolve themselves of any moral responsibility for their evil actions: 'He that thus beleveth / what careth he what he dothe?' (6:403).

It is these convictions which underlie More's passionate insistence that the Reformation had to be halted at all costs before it took hold in England. Otherwise, the fate of Germany would befall England. That urgent warning informs one of the most eloquent passages in the *Dialogue*, the extraordinary single sentence passionately evoking Luther's doctrine as the ruin of Christian coherence as More and Erasmus conceived it. In Germany,

> theyr secte hath all redy fordone the faythe / pulled downe the chyrches / polluted the temples / put out and spoyled all good relygyous folke / joined freres and nonnes togyther in lechery ... caste downe Crystes crosse / throwne out the blessyd sacrament / refused all good lawes / abhorred all good governaunce / rebelled agaynste all rulers ... and finally that most abhomynable is of all / of all theyr owne ungracyous dedes lay the faute in god / taking away the lybertye of mannes wyll / ascrybyng all our dedes to desteny ... whereby they take away all dylygence and good endevour to vertue / all withstanding and stryvyng against vyce / all care of hevyn / all fere of hell / ... all desyre of devocyon / ... all the lawes of the worlde / all reason among men / set all wretchedness a broche / no man at liberty / and yet every man do what he wyll / calling yt not his wyll but his desteny / layng theyr syn to goddes ordenaunce / and theyr punysshment to goddes crueltye / and finally turnyng the nature of man in to worse than a beste / and the goodness of god in to worse than the devyll.
>
> (*CW* 6:427–8)

That vision of the chaos and destruction which Luther's Gospel brings lies at the root of the apologia for the use of force against heresy and its propagators with which the *Dialogue* concludes. James Simpson, deploring what he took to be the feebleness of More's arguments here, claimed that More had weakened an already weak case by dragging in just-war theory.[35] But this is to miss the specificity of More's argument. Heresy, More believed, was always a force for destruction and rebellion. It was this inherent violence which had moved St Augustine to call for the forcible repression of heretics. In England a millennium later, Oldcastle's rebellion had demonstrated that heresy ran true to type (6:409). But the real rhetorical weight of More's argument turns on a comparison between the duty of Christian rulers to resist militant Islam in the form of the Turkish threat to eastern Europe, and their matching duty to punish and repel internal heresy (6:411–18). More was here invoking a very real danger, which preoccupied him and his humanist friends. In 1529, Islam was knocking at the doors of Europe. Suleiman the Magnificent had captured both Belgrade and Rhodes, 'the outworks of Christendom', and in 1526 his armies occupied Budapest. A stream of humanist publications lamented the divisions of Christians, and Erasmus himself called for unity against the common enemy.[36] Suleiman's attempts to buy the neutrality of the Protestant Schmalkaldic League, and Luther's teaching that the Turk was the scourge of God and therefore not to be resisted, seemed to More proof of a demonic conspiracy against 'the comen corps of crystendome'. More would deepen and spiritualize this comparison in the greatest of his Tower Works, the *Dialogue of Comfort* (see *CW* 12:xxii–xxxv). In the *Dialogue Concerning Heresies*, however, the comparison, although no less deeply felt, is strictly practical. Christendom was in deadly peril from without *and* from within. The same imperative which required the princes to defend Christian civilization from Turkish conquest mandated and demanded the forcible elimination of heresy.

More's argument here has about it something of the manifesto. In the London campaign against heresy, no evangelical had so far been burned, and More at this stage did not believe that any heretic possessed the courage or conviction to persist to the point of death. 'I never yet founde or herde of any one in all my lyfe', he tells the Messenger, 'but he wolde forswere your fayth to save his lyfe' (*CW* 6:201). For their part, Tunstall and his colleagues had bent over backwards to avoid sending anyone to the flames, if only because, as the Messenger declares early on in the *Dialogue*, 'of the asshes of one heretyque spryngeth up many' (6:31). More makes much of that reluctance in defending the clergy against charges of cruelty. But he clearly foresaw the possibility that Protestant resistance might force Church and state to resort to the ultimate sanction, and at the conclusion of the *Dialogue* he mounts a vehement defence of such a step. Notoriously, as chancellor he would translate theory into grim fact. No modern reader of the *Dialogue* is likely to find that defence compelling. In its own time and place, however, it carried great weight, and most of his contemporaries would have felt the force of More's urgent advocacy.

The *Dialogue* is More's most effective polemical work. Its conversational sprawl masks a carefully controlled argument setting the teaching of Luther, Tyndale and their English followers against the holy unanimity of 'the comen corps of crystendome'. More defends the religious value of traditional religious practice while laughing at its absurdities, and comes forward as the champion of the religion of ordinary Christian men and women. But he also advocates the renewal of lay piety by devout encounter with an English Bible. He deploys an unrivalled mastery of the detail of the Henrician campaign against heresy to defend the bishops and clergy, while resisting a clericalist ecclesiology. He offers a powerful if one-sided analysis of the evils of Lutheran teaching, informed by a humanist vision which he had laboured alongside Erasmus to defend, and which he never repudiated. And at the end of his book he justified the death penalty for unrepent-ant heretics, summoning up a sombre and terrifying vision of the devastating consequences for Christian souls and the fabric of Chris-tian belief and practice, if Protestantism were to gain a hold in England. What he would have considered the worst elements of that dire vision – the destruction of the monastic life, the rejection of the cult of the saints, the dismantling of the sacramental system – would all be real-ized within a generation, testimony to the prescience of the polemical masterpiece in which he had predicted just such an outcome.

FURTHER READING

The introductory essays in the editions of More's polemical writings in *CW* 6, 8 and 9 all contain material relevant to the *Dialogue*. More's concern with heresy is placed in its political context by John Guy, *The Public Career of Sir Thomas More*. Most recent accounts of the *Dia-logue* are distorted by a largely baseless psychological reading of More. A key influence here has been Richard Marius, *Thomas More* (1984), which nevertheless remains worth reading, as do the essays on More in G. R. Elton, *Studies in Tudor and Stuart Politics and Government*, 4 vols. (Cambridge University Press, 1974–92). More's controversial writings are surveyed in Ranier Pineas, *Thomas More and Tudor Polemics* (Bloomington: Indiana University Press, 1968). Alistair Fox, *Thomas More: History and Providence* (Oxford: Blackwell, 1982), has been influential, but offers a perversely Freudian misreading of the controversies: there is a salutary review by Brian Vickers in the *Journal of Medieval History* 56 (1984), 311–16. A crucial reappraisal of the controversial writings was provided by Brendan Bradshaw, 'The contro-versial Thomas More', *Journal of Ecclesiastical History* 36 (1985), 535–69. Also useful is Eiléan Ni Chuílleanáin, 'The debate between Thomas More and William Tyndale, 1528–33: ideas on literature and religion', *Journal of Ecclesiastical History* 39 (1988), 382–411. More's understanding of the Church is explored in Brian Gogan, *The Common Corps of Christendom: Ecclesiological Themes in the Writings of Sir Thomas More* (Leiden: Brill, 1982). James Simpson's *Burning to Read: English Fundamentalism and Its Reformation Opponents* (Cambridge, Mass.: Belknap Press, 2007) is stimulating if sometimes wrong-headed: a more sober reading by another distinguished literary historian is Brian Cummings, 'Reformed literature and literature reformed', in David Wallace, ed., *The Cambridge History of Medieval English Literature* (Cambridge University Press, 1999), 821–51, at 834–8. Margaret Aston's 'More's defence of images', in her *England's Iconoclasts*, Vol. 1: *Laws Against Images* (Oxford: Clarendon Press, 1988), 173–94, offers a valuable study of some of the changes More made in the second edition of the *Dialogue*.

Notes

1. There is an extensive survey of More's polemical writings by Louis A. Schuster, in CW 8:1137–1268.
2. Lamb, quoted *CW* 8:1208; Marius, *Thomas More*, 338; Fox, *History and Providence* (in 'Further reading'), 111. The outstanding exception to this negative consensus is Brendan Bradshaw's seminal defence of the controversial writings, to which I am much indebted: 'The controversial Thomas More' (in 'Further reading'), 535–69. See also the robust defence of the effectiveness of More's arguments in the later polemical treatises, especially the *Debellation of Salem and Bizance* and the *Apology*, in Henry Ansgar Kelly, 'Thomas More on inquisitorial due process', *English Historical Review* 123 (2008), 847–94.
3. *Burning to Read* (in 'Further reading'), 265.
4. 'Reformed literature and literature reformed', in David Wallace, ed., *The Cambridge History of Medieval English Literature* (Cambridge University Press, 1999), 834–5.
5. Marius, *Thomas More*, 346; David Daniell, *William Tyndale: A Biography* (New Haven and London: Yale University Press, 1994), 263–4. See also Roger Deakins, in 'The Tudor prose dialogue: genre and anti-genre', *Studies in English Literature* 20 (1980), 5–23, at 14.
6. Cummings, 'Reformed literature', 834.
7. One of the articles alleged against Bilney in 1527 was that he had denied 'moral Philosophy and natural, to preuaile any thing for the better vnderstanding of the scriptures, & for the exposition and defence of the truth': John Foxe, *Actes and Monuments* (London, 1583), 1000. Cf. H. C. Porter, *Reformation and Reaction in Tudor Cambridge* (Cambridge University Press, 1958), 61.

   In texts of this period, the virgule (/) is regularly used where we would use a comma or, sometimes, another punctuation mark.

8. For parallels in Tyndale's *Obedience of a Christian Man* to the Messenger's views on philosophy, see Thomas Russell, ed., *The Works of the English Reformers: William Tyndale and John Frith*, 3 vols. (London, 1831), 1:190–4.

9. *The Complete Poems of John Skelton*, ed. Philip Henderson, 3rd edn (London: Dent, 1959), 415.

10. *Burning to Read*, 240.

11. I have added punctuation and emphasis to clarify More's irony. Cf. *CW* 6:84.

12. Indispensable context for More's dealings with heresy is provided in Guy, *The Public Career of Sir Thomas More*, 97–174.

13. For the campaign against heresy in London in 1528, see Susan Brigden, *London and the Reformation* (Oxford: Clarendon Press, 1989), 110–18. The commonly accepted form of Farman's name, 'Robert Forman', is incorrect, as entries relating to him in Queens' College archives and his own signature in his copy of Erasmus's edition of Jerome in St John's College Library make clear. My thanks to Dr Richard Rex for this correction.

14. 'Reformed literature', 835; *Burning to Read*, 243.

15. Foxe, *Actes and Monuments*, 999–1000, 1010–11.

16. Cf. below, 221–2.

17. *Thomas More*, 345.

18. Ibid., 339–42.

19. Ibid., 342, 339.

20. Anne M. O'Donnell and Jared Wicks, eds., *An Answere vnto Sir Thomas Mores Dialoge*, Vol. 3 of *The Independent Works of William Tyndale* (Washington, D.C.: Catholic University of America Press, 2000), 14.

21. Erasmus to Johann Botzheim, 13 August 1529, in *Erasmus*, ed. Richard DeMolen (London: Edward Arnold, 1973), 170–1.

22. James Anthony Froude, *Life and Letters of Erasmus*, new edn (London: Longman, Green, 1895), 342–3.

23. Ibid., 413.

24. Foxe, *Actes and Monuments*, 1046–7; James McConica, *English Humanists and Reformation Politics* (Oxford: Clarendon Press, 1965), 106–49, esp. 145–7.

25. *Thomas More*, 348–9.

26. *Burning to Read*, 261–71.

27. Greg Walker, 'Saint or schemer? The 1527 heresy trial of Thomas Bilney reconsidered', *Journal of Ecclesiastical History* 40 (1989), 219–38.

28. For More's writings in defence of Erasmus, see *CW* 15:lxxii–xcii and above, 30–6.

29. It is prefaced by a lengthy rebuttal (*CW* 6:317–30) of the Messenger's accusation that the English clergy have always been the enemies of an English Bible, in which More argues that the fifteenth-century legislation forbidding unauthorized translations had been intended to outlaw only heretical versions. He claims that it had always been possible for a bishop to allow 'suche as he knew for good and catholyke folke' to read

the Bible, and many had done so. There was special pleading here, and More was undoubtedly making a small amount of evidence go a long way, but his basic claim is in fact borne out by recent study of the circulation and censorship of the so-called 'Wyclifite' Bible: Mary Dove, *The First English Bible* (Cambridge University Press, 2007), 37–67.

30. David Wilkins, *Concilia Magnae Brittaniae et Hiberniae*, 4 vols. (London, 1737), 3:727–37.

31. And in fact, despite the official ban and the opinion of 'well lerned ... & very vertuouse folk' against an English Bible, in 1533 More declared himself 'of the same opynyon still' about the desirability of translating the New Testament, 'yf the men were amended and the tyme mete therfore' (*CW* 9:13).

32. For a related account of how these concerns played out in More's polemical writings in general and in his involvement in the detection and prosecution of English heretics, see Richard Rex's essay earlier in this volume.

33. David V. N. Bagchi, *Luther's Earliest Opponents: Catholic Controversialists, 1518–1525* (Minneapolis: Fortress, 1991), 159, 128 (quotation from Henry VIII's *Assertio septem sacramentorum*).

34. On this subject, see Brendan Bradshaw, 'More on Utopia', *Historical Journal* 24 (1981), 1–27, esp. 9–14.

35. *Burning to Read*, 263.

36. See below, 217.

A Dialogue of Comfort against Tribulation

ANDREW W. TAYLOR

CIRCUMSTANCES

In consequence of refusing the Oath of Succession on 13 April 1534, Thomas More was incarcerated in the Tower of London for the final fourteen months of his life (above, 121–3). Yet imprisonment did not prevent him from writing, with a fluency approaching that of his anti-Lutheran polemics of the immediately preceding years. He composed, in addition to a series of letters and other brief writings, the main 'Tower Works': *A Treatise on the Passion* (begun before his imprisonment but perhaps completed during it), *A Dialogue of Comfort against Tribulation* and, finally, the unfinished *De Tristitia Christi*.[1] In differing ways, these last compositions reveal More's transmuting of personal experience into enduring monuments of faith.

The *Dialogue of Comfort* was More's third major work in dialogue form, after *Utopia* (1516) and *A Dialogue Concerning Heresies* (1529). In those previous works he represents himself as a speaker in the dialogue. By contrast, the *Dialogue of Comfort*, divided into three 'books', presents two voices in a fictional dramatic setting distanced in both place and time from the author. A disconsolate young Hungarian, Vincent, has turned to his sick uncle, Antony, for counsel in the face of imminent Turkish persecution of Christians, following the calamitous Hungarian defeat at Mohács on 28 August 1526 by the forces of the Ottoman Empire under its sultan, Suleiman the Magnificent.[2] Vincent complains, 'me thynketh the gretest comfort that a man can haue, ys when he may see that he shall sone be gone' (*CW* 12:3). It is against such despair and the temptations of fear that the *Dialogue* is ostensibly addressed, and in so doing artfully interweaves fact with fiction, and the present with the recent past.

Prior to his resignation from royal service in 1532, More's diplomatic and informal secretarial duties had apprised him of papal dispatches to Henry VIII, some of which relayed information from the nuncio at Buda, Baron de Burgio, whose trepidation arose more from the disloyal 'Turks' (turncoat Christians) of Hungary than from the real ones.[3] Moreover, Europe's internecine preoccupations, even in the face of impending Ottoman incursions, attracted sustained criticism and pleas for unity, several from humanists well known to More. In 1526, for example, the Spanish humanist Juan Luis Vives responded to Mohács with his *De Europae dissidiis et re publica* ('On the dissensions and state of Europe'), in which the blind Theban seer of Greek tragedy, Tiresias, bewails the European monarchs' bellicose thirst for power: Europe will be overrun just as the enfeebled Roman Empire had yielded to godless hordes.[4] In 1529, Vives added his *De concordia et discordia in humano genere* ('On concord and discord in humankind'), including a tract on the wretchedness of Christians under the Turk, in which he retold martyrs' histories; Erasmus contributed his *De bello Turcis* ('On the war with the Turks') the following year.

Despite this counsel, in 1527, the year after Mohács, with Vienna exposed to the Turks, the troops of the Holy Roman Emperor, Charles V, sacked Rome, effectively capturing Pope Clement VII. In the struggle for power, the French king, Francis I, whose hereditary titles included the recently acquired 'Most Christian King', but whom Cardinal Wolsey called 'the real Turk', had encouraged the Turkish invasion of Hungary as part of his country's grand strategy (*CSPSp* 2:444). In *A Dialogue Concerning Heresies*, More condemned such 'ambycyon' and 'dedly dyscencyon', and also denounced the cruelty of the Lutheran *Landsknechte* mercenaries who had shared in the spoils of Rome (*CW* 6:413–14, 371–2).[5]

Thus the threat of the infidel Turk to Christendom offered a rich source of analogy for the censuring of faithlessness or heresy among Christians at a time of growing religious and political turmoil. Situated grimly between Mohács in 1526 and the second invasion of Hungary in 1529, the *Dialogue of Comfort* is also set against the outcome of the civil war into which Hungary was plunged following the demise of the Hungarian king, Louis II, at Mohács. For in 1529, János Zápolyai (John Zapolya), voivode of Transylvania, who opposed Louis' son, Ferdinand of Austria, turned Turk with ten thousand troops, swearing allegiance to Suleiman on the very same battlefield, prior to the Turkish siege of Vienna that began in late September.[6] Early in the *Dialogue of Comfort*, we hear Vincent's anxiety over apostasy and betrayal: 'for there ys no born Turke so cruell to christen folke, as is the false christen that falleth fro [from] the fayth' (*CW* 12:7).

ANALOGY OVER ALLEGORY

More's early biographer Nicholas Harpsfield asserted that More's object in the *Dialogue* was to stir and prepare the minds of English Catholics facing imminent persecution: 'Albeit full wittily and wisely, that the bookes might the more safely goe abrode, he doth not expressly meddle with those matters, and couloureth the matter vnder the name of an Hungarian, and of the persecution of the Turke in Hungarie, and of a booke translated out of the Hungarians tonge into the latin, and then into the englishe tonge' (Harpsfield 134). Although it is tempting to refer the beleaguered situation of the *Dialogue* to More directly – to read the Turks as Protestant heretics and the Grand Turk as Henry VIII – More's literary handling of the consolatory dialogue develops complex overlapping patterns of enduringly rich and elusive analogy, instead of merely an historical and autobiographical allegory.[7] More's fictive 'colouring' involves the reader in both dialogical and digressive interests which resist such direct and reductive mappings. The distorted echoes of More's life and circumstances resounding throughout the work inform a general spiritual counsel, developed through the universal application of scripture and theological argument.[8] Nor, despite sharing something of his creator's ironic wit and demeanour, can Antony, the major speaker and source of counsel, be identified simply with the author. The interplay of the voices, however unequal, offers in part a consolatory and exemplary catechism in the face of tremendous fear, so that the bolstering trust and faith in the saving grace of Christ emerges through colloquy.[9]

The *Dialogue* is lightly but carefully punctuated with reminders of the dramatic setting. At the start, Antony recalls his youth in Greece before the Turkish threat, then the fall of Belgrade in 1521, and of Rhodes the following year. Later, in Book II, chapter 12, he reminisces about his youthful soldiering south of Belgrade, while the preface to Book III returns to Hungary's vulnerability to the Turkish advance and the commitment of the invaders to 'minysh the fayth of Christ, & dilate the fayth of Mahumet' (*CW* 12:190). However, other historical details – the Turks' dispersal of smaller nations as slaves, the exacting of tribute from larger ones, the trouble over succession, and the threat to Europe of Hungary's fall – provide for the discussion not of Turkish actions but Christian ones. The threat makes Christians 'more glad to fynd fawtes at euery state of christendome, prestes, princes / rites / ceremonies / sacramentes laues [laws] and custumes spirituall temporall & all' (12:192).[10] In the context of the Reformation, 'turning Turk' becomes a similitude for any turning away from true faith, or conversion to the Lutheran 'sect'.

Turkish persecution is finally revealed as but the latest instrument of the continual assaults on faith by the great Tempter, a matter More is keen to distinguish from any apocalyptic misinterpretation. His Antony is more historically optimistic: 'this vngraciouse sect of Machomete, shall haue a foule fall, & christendome spryng and sprede, floure and increace agayne' (*CW* 12:194). However, the threat of the Turk's merciless cruelty engenders fear, through which the Christian is tempted to fall from faith in attempting to avoid pain. Tribulation emerges as temptation towards false and potentially damning solace in worldly values, whatever their apparent virtue: 'none can be his [i.e. Christ's] disciple but yf he love hym so far above all his kynne, & above his own lyfe to, that for the love of hym rather than to forsake hym / he shall forsake them all' (12:174).

The intertwining of apostasy and heresy with Hungary and England is paralleled in the Latin annotations More made, in the Tower, in the psalter of his Latin prayer book. Writing *tribulatio* twenty-seven times and *contra turcas* six times alongside verses of the Psalms on which he depended most particularly in prayerful meditation, More plotted the imaginative landscape explored more fully in the *Dialogue*. Thus, against Vulgate Psalm 68:7–21 (Psalm 69 in the Hebrew numbering), he wrote, 'to be said in [time of] tribulation by the faithful among the Hungarians when the Turks grow strong and many Hungarians fall away into the false faith of the Turks'.[11] Engagement with Vincent and Antony is larger than that of the stricter correspondences of allegory, with their human dimensions being inseparable from the work's consolatory potential, a matter both inscribed within the fiction between Antony and Vincent and relating the author to his readers, including those who in tribulation have complied with persecution and now fear for their own salvation.

The Tower Works have been seen as a return to non-dogmatic literary priorities following the exhausting and futile campaign of controversial writings against heresy and the incursion of temporal power over the spirituality.[12] Yet More's want of polemical or apologetic outspokenness here may reflect not merely a restored faith in providence but his understanding of the proper relationship between private citizen and instituted authority. Against the Psalmist's profession of deafness and muteness in the face of calumny and betrayal (Psalm 37:12–20), More, in his prayer book, noted that

> a meek man ought to behave in this way during tribulation; he should neither speak proudly himself nor retort to what is spoken wickedly, but should bless those who speak evil of him and suffer willingly, either for justice's sake if he has deserved it or for God's sake if he has deserved nothing.[13]

As Dermot Fenlon has observed, More considered active resistance to Henry's authority illegitimate, that which 'only the Church could do – openly to admonish the ways of a tyrant, which in practice meant one who commanded men to imperil their salvation'.[14] Yet we may find in More's strictly regulated resistance a loyalty to the king greater than obedience, in which, as Fenlon concludes, his death might prompt the king's repentant conversion from tyranny.[15] The *Dialogue* then becomes less a Boethian consolation of philosophy, more an *ars moriendi*, a treatise on dying well, but adapted to the possibility of martyrdom under tyranny and with a consolatory rather than oppositional, polemical or apologetic emphasis.

More's weaving together of argument, the tolerant interpretation of scriptural witness, rich anecdotal digression, and meditation on Christ's suffering for the faithful displays a literary and rhetorical mastery which serves to foster trust and faith in Christ as the only 'treacle [antidote] agaynst the poyson of all desperat dreade, that myght rise of occasion of sore trybulacion' (*CW* 12:9). The absolute nature of the challenge is immediately evident in Antony's unmitigated response to Vincent's desire to hold on to life: the 'holsom dew ... of goddes grace' should moisten and vivify the longing 'to be with hym in heven' (12:4).

MERRY TALES AND MEMORIALS

As the *Dialogue* progresses, interest shifts from faith to hope to charity. Whereas the twenty discrete and intellectually stimulating chapters of Book I, the shortest, lay out the benefits of tribulation in faith but remain relatively abstract and divorced from quotidian experience, Book II, which with Book III spans a day about a month after the time when Book I takes place, bristles with anecdotes. Marking the shift, Book II opens with Vincent's compassionate concern at having exhausted his old and sick uncle, 'in talkyng so long together without interpawsyng betwene' on unavoidably distressing matters; Antony quips that 'a fond [foolish] old man is often so full of wordes as a woman', confessing that it was 'great comfort, & nothyng displesaunt at all' (*CW* 12:78–9). Moreover, Vincent, we learn, has already conveyed Antony's comforting words to others – in fictive terms, publication of the *Dialogue* seems afoot.[16]

We are also reminded not to fixate anxiously on the clearly imagined possibility of persecution, but to review 'the comfort that may grow theron' – comfort from, as well as against, tribulation. In this serious and urgent literary game, More refashioned at a time of crisis (and justification) both deeply personal and less private episodes into anecdotes and tales articulating and countering the doubts and fears impeding, yet finally facilitating, the ultimate understanding of a faithful Christian life.[17] More wittily sustains this literary reflexivity in having Antony desire that he and Vincent had 'had more often enterchaungid wordes / & partid the talke betwene vs, with ofter enterparlyng vppon your part / in such maner as lernid men vse betwene the persons / whom they devise disputyng in their faynid diologes' (*CW* 12:79). Antony then elaborates on this topic with a story of a brother visiting his sister at a nunnery. At the locutory, she delivers 'a sermon of the wretchednes of this world, & the frayelte of the flesh, & the subtill sleight of the wikked fend' – thematically not unrelated to the *Dialogue* – before criticizing her brother's lack of 'some frutfull exortacion', learned as he is. He retorts that he has lacked the opportunity, 'for your tong haue neuer ceasid, but said inough for vs bothe' (12:80). Agreeing that *they* will share the talking, Vincent returns Antony's anecdote with another on loquacity, this time involving 'a kynswoman of your own / but which will I not tell you, gesse there and [i.e. if] you can' (12:81). She learns from her husband's friend that the reason for his absence from her dinner table is his friend's allowing him to hold forth at his. Whereupon she replies 'that am I content he shall haue all the wordes with good will as he hath euer had / but I speke them all my selfe, & give them all to hym / & for ought that I care for them so shall he haue them styll / but otherwise to say that he shall haue them all / you shall kepe hym still rather than he get the halfe'. The vivid mimicry of this kins-woman's garrulousness encourages recognition in it of More's relation-ship with Dame Alice, just as Antony's recollection of the learned young woman who advised him about the tertian fever from which he had suffered is both imaginatively located within the *Dialogue* and playfully celebrates Margaret Giggs and her husband John Clement, the former servant-scholar and tutor to both Margaret and More's daughters, who worked on the Aldine *editio princeps* of Galen

(*CW* 12:88–90). Despite their appealing to common knowledge of human types, these memorials also suggest More negotiating his gradual detachment from the world in approaching Christ.

Although Antony is far from sanctioning 'wanton idell talys', he admits that, for many, 'some honest worldly myrth' relieves the 'hevy burdeyne' of heavenly discourse: 'Our affeccion toward hevenly ioyes waxith wonderfull cold / yf drede of hell were as far gone / very few wold fere god' (*CW* 12:83). Accounts of hellfire captivate an audience, but heavenly joys are less compelling. The early Christian theologian John Cassian, as Antony recalls, tells of a preacher's celestially sweet-sounding sermon on heavenly matters inducing sleep in his listeners, who earn his rebuke when they are roused by his promise of a merry tale. But although Antony laments such human frailty, he cannot deny that most lack the spiritual perfection that would make 'all worldly recreacion be but a grief to thinke on' (12:84).

The liveliness of Book II, then, reflects More's understanding of a necessary accommodation of frail human capability. Its discursive sops of 'recreacion' both entertain and prepare appetites for graver fare within the text's larger economy of comfort. But Book II is also analytical, with Antony, at chapter 3, recapping Book I's tripartite division of tribulation: that taken willingly, that willingly suffered, and 'such as he can not put from hym[:] ... siknes, imprisonment, losse of good, losse of frendes, or such bodely harm as a man hath all redy caught & can in no wise avoyd' (*CW* 12:86–7). Antony reminds those with wit and faith that 'by freting & by fumyng' against apparent vicissitudes of fortune they increase their pain and also, with their 'froward behaviour', displease God, a theme echoed in a later passage on making a virtue of necessity (12:254). Antony's brief rehearsal of the first kind of tribulation at II.4 points towards penance and charitable works, neither of which, he argues, requires comfort: the grace which prompts such actions will supply the comfort too; the promise that 'the pleasure of his sowle shall passe the payne of his body' (12:88) also anticipates the counsel for combating a violent death for faith. This circuit, from the discussion of penance, through the anecdote of Antony's fever, to Jerome's maxim *Et doleas & de dolore gaudeas* – the simultaneous joy and sorrow of comfortable suffering – back to the original matter of penance, illustrates the discursive enrichment typical of this part of the *Dialogue*.

Antony, emphasizing the need for habitual preparation for the ultimate test, warns against the example of the thief saved 'at his last end' at the Crucifixion: 'Now he that in hope to be callid toward night,

will slepe out the mornyng, & drinke out the day, ys full likely to pass
at night vnspoken to / & than [then] shall he with shrewid [vexatious]
rest go souperlesse to bedd' (*CW* 12:92). Sinners should thus recognize
that the 'mynd may be the let [hindrance] that grace of frutfull repent-
yng shall neuer after be offred hym / but that he shall eyther gracelesse
go lynger on careles, or with a care fruteles fall into despayre'. But
instead of turning directly either to the inability to repent (II.7) or to
suicide (II.15), here the consideration of penance ramifies further.

More invests Vincent with a vivid eyewitness account of a Saxon –
that is, Lutheran – preacher, to portray the laity's vulnerability to loud
and shrill indoctrination by heretics: 'he cried euer owt vppon them to
kepe well the lawes of christ / let go their pevysh penaunce & purpose
them to amend, and seke nothing to saluacion but the deth of christ /
for he is our iustice, & he is our saviour, & our hole satisfaccion for all
our dedly synnes / he did full penaunce for vs all vppon his paynfull
crosse' (*CW* 12:94). This verbal bombardment made Vincent's 'heare
stand vp vppon myne hed'. If the *Dialogue* is to expound Christ as the
sole source of comfort, here it deals with how the availability and
sufficiency of Christ's saving work may be misconstrued. Antony's
animus momentarily recalls More's polemical *Dialogue Concerning
Heresies*: he marvels at the attack on fasting and other bodily penance
as unscriptural. But Antony then simply asserts the consensus of the
'old holy doctours' and of scripture (12:96), similarly eschewing polemical language in his teaching that fasting and penance prepare the sinner
for God's grace and strengthen the spiritual affections through which
Christ is apprehended. In place of the Saxon's hair-raising rhetoric and
the disputation of theological language of penitence, repentance, attri-
tion and contrition, Antony cites the French reformist theologian Jean
Gerson, a writer whose presence is also felt in the *De Tristitia Christi*
(see below, 243–5): 'sith the body & the sowle together make the hole
man / the lesse affliccion that he felith in his sowle, the more payne in
recompence let hym put vppon his body, & pourge the spirite by the
affliccion of the flesh' (*CW* 12:98).[18] Arguing through probability and
personal commitment, Antony bets his life that such bodily penance
will finally yield the 'sowle in an holsome hevynes & hevenly gladness
to / specially yf (which must be ioynid [joined] with euery good thyng)
he ioyne faythfull prayour therwith', so countering gently the evangelical doctrine of salvation by faith alone.

Fiction, fable and anecdote blur into the deep plot or teleology of
the *Dialogue*. The resulting obliqueness offers the reader both distance
and distraction from More's particular circumstances. This 'art of

improvisation', instead of suggesting an unrevised work, is better seen as strategic.[19] The intervening discussions confront or anticipate objections, to clear the path towards the consolatory goal while suggesting that little from life in faith can be excluded from consideration. This unpredictable and ostensibly untidy growth of Book II arises from the application of the more abstract and theoretical spadework of Book I. But where meanderings, loss of momentum or distracting intricacy might have resulted, a new focus emerges midway through Book II, which determines the shape and structure of the rest of the *Dialogue*.

PSALM 90

In chapter 10 of Book II, Antony reasserts that God can be trusted to provide the faithful with 'strength agaynst the devilles might, & wisdome agaynst the devilles traynes [traps]' (*CW* 12:102). God thus prevents 'sore brosyng [bruising]' from those occasional but inevitable lapses in faith. Antony moves from Vulgate Psalms 117(118):14 and 36(37):24 to the comforting promise against all temptation in Psalm 90(91):1: '*Qui habitat in adiutorio altissimi, in protectione dei celi comorabitur*: who so dwellith in the help of the hiest god, he shall abide in the proteccion or defence of the god of hevyn' (*CW* 12:102–3). Henceforth, Antony will labour to convince Vincent of the full significance of this verse. Yet even in the work's penultimate chapter, he still admits that heaven's joys are almost inaudible and ineffable because 'our carnall hartes hath so feble & so faynte a felyng / & our dull worldly wittes so litle hable to conceyve so mych as a shadow of the right Imagynacion' (12:308). But by that point, as a hopeful response, the word *vincenti* (to him who triumphs) rings out repeatedly from such scriptural promises as '*vincenti dabo edere de ligno vite* / To hym that ouercometh, I shall give hym to eate of the tree of lyfe [Revelation 2:7]' (12:309). The fearful nephew who seeks comfort from Antony has to apprehend this 'triumph' embedded in his name.[20]

Through Psalm 90:5–6, More asserts the fundamental recognition of fear as temptation: '*Scuto circumdabit te veritas eius* / *non timebis a timore nocturno* / *a sagitta volante in die, a negocio perambulante in tenebris, ab incursu & demonio meridiano*: The trouth of god shall compasse the about with a pavice [body-length shield], thow shalt not be aferd of the nightes feare, nor the arrow fleyng in the day, nor the bysynes walkyng about in the darknesses / nor the incursion or invacion of the devill in the mydde day' (*CW* 12:105). Verses 5 and 6 are drawn from a context of solitary penitential combat against temptation, while verses 11 and 12 are misused by the devil in tempting Christ to cast himself down unharmed from the pinnacle of the Temple (Matthew 4:6). Thus Psalm 90 became the main psalm text for Mass on the first Sunday of Lent, and also the main night prayer of compline, the day's final Divine Office, which fortifies the tired and vulnerable spirit in the darkness of night.[21] From his time at the London Charterhouse (above, 13–15), More knew the Carthusian practice of saying compline alone.

Antony asserts that temptation is 'incident' to persecution: 'For both by temptacion the devill persecuteth vs, & by persecucion the devill also temptith vs / and as persecucion is tribulacion to euery man, so is temptacion tribulacion to euery good man' (*CW* 12:100). The first three tribulations – 'nightes feare', 'the arrow fleyng in the day', and 'bysynes walking about in the darkness' – are the 'devilles traynes' or traps, which are discussed in the remainder of Book II; the fourth, 'playne open fight' of 'mydde day', consumes Book III: 'his fierce malicious persecucion agaynst the faythfull christens for hatrid of christes trew catholike fayth' (12:200).

Despite these sober verses, the *Dialogue* loses none of the wit it shares with More's Tower letters. Some of these play ironically with serious matters which overlap with the *Dialogue*, sustaining that complex relationship between fact and fiction. The lengthy, sophisticated letter in the name of his daughter Margaret Roper (and probably composed jointly with her) replies to one by Alice Alington, More's step-daughter by his second wife's previous marriage (*Corr.* 511–32; cf. above, 58). Lady Alice's letter records the condemnation of More by the lord chancellor, Thomas Audley, as 'so obstinate in his owne conceite' over the Oath of Succession (*Corr.* 512). The second of the two fables Audley employed to illustrate his point concerns the confession of a lion, an ass and a wolf (*Corr.* 520). More readily owns to the ass, 'signifieng (as it semeth by that similitude) that of ouersight and folye, my scrupulous conscience taketh for a great perilous thing towarde my soule, if I shoulde swere this othe, which thinge as his Lordship thinketh, wer in dede but a trifle'. It is to this 'trifle' that More has Antony turn in treating the temptation 'Of the dowghter of pusillanimitie a scripelous [scrupulous] conscience', the title of Book II, chapter 14.

The veil of fiction becomes thinner here, as Audley is sounded as 'mother mawd / I trow [believe] you haue hard of her', More rewriting the fable to better effect, as 'there is al most no tale so folysh, but that yet in one mater or other, to some purpose it may hap to serue' (*CW* 12:114). The lion now omitted, a scrupulous ass and a wolf make Lenten confession to Father Reynart, the fox. The ass receives moderation as penance for his venial gluttony, while the wolf, for his ravenous excesses, is forbidden to eat above the value of sixpence during the year. We feel More's mordant satire of evangelical doctrine, hypocrisy and spiritual degradation in his having the fox confide that he believes fasting to be a human invention rather than a divine commandment, that he secretly eats flesh throughout Lent, and that in his judgement the wolf is so stuck in his rapine that 'were it folye to forbid it you / & to say the trouth agaynst good conscience to' (12:117). However, their performance of penance drives home the point of the fable. The ass's scrupulosity leads to his starving himself before being counselled better by Reynart. The wolf, initially pricked more by conscience than hunger, factitiously avoids dining on two unappetizing horses, one dead, one lame almost to death, to prey on a cow and her calf: 'I neuer saw ded horse sold in the market ... but in my conscience I set hym farre aboue vj^d [sixpence]', while the other is a soft ambler and is factitiously deemed even more valuable. But 'the cow is in my consciens worth but iiijd, my consciens can not serue me for sinne of my soule to prayse her calfe aboue ijd / & so passe they not vjd betwene them both' (12:119). Thus the mediocrity of Audley's use of fable matches that of his conscience, which serves 'on euery side for his own comoditie [advantage]'. Moreover, behind the mitigation of the ass's scrupulosity lies More's interrogation of his own conscience in relation to both apostasy and presumption.

The subsequent discussion of spiritual pride and temptations to self-destruction is extended through anecdotes of darker humour, which serve to define temptation deriving from fear, for which tribulation, comfort can be sought. In one, an ultra-ascetic monk, reputed for sanctity and visions, is seduced by the devil to commit suicide for God (*CW* 12:131).[22] The issue of martyrdom and the sin of presumption must have preoccupied More in the Tower, even before he was sure of his sentence. Was his refusal of the Oath merely provocation? As More stated in a later letter, to Margaret, one ought not to presume: it is left to God to draw the martyr to victory, and from God comes the necessary grace and strength to be a witness to his faith (*Corr.* 559, 3 June 1535). The Carthusians' strictly cloistered life, a prison self-imposed within the world's prison to bring them nearer God, is celebrated in the *Dialogue* as exceptional (*CW* 12:276); More witnessed from the Tower their bride-like walk to execution. Cato's 'honourable' death, exposed as a false triumph of pagan pride over worldly shame, counterpoints that 'sleight' of the devil, despair, against which the faithful should humbly trust in God's saving grace through penance and prayer. Antony advises seeking out 'a conyng pylote' (12:120) to assist the spiritual navigation between the Scylla and Charybdis of fearful doubts and irascible stubbornness against God (12:111–12). While Antony in some ways stands in for this guide, More encourages the reader to consider the relationship of the *Dialogue* to such consolatory conversation.

The last sections of Book II handle the world more directly. The arrow flying in the day – that is, prosperity – is the devil's distraction: 'how proud we be, buzzyng above bysily like as a bumble bee fleeth about in somer, neuer ware that she shall die in wynter' (*CW* 12:158). The proud fall to hell, not to earth. Antony identifies 'the dedly desier of ambiciouse glorye' (12:160) as a tribulation, anatomizing the way in which power and riches corrupt, exposing their ephemeral nature and grievous final cost, and, again, the need for habitual confession to 'some vertuouse goostly father' of frailty, negligence and readiness to fall (12:164). The seclusion of 'some secret solitary place' is also advocated – More had built one on his estate, and found another in the Tower – in which to imagine confession of sin directly before God, assisted by meditation on 'some pitifull image of christes bitter passion'.

The long closing chapter of Book II handles *negocium perambulans in tenebris*: 'bumblyng bysynes' is the endless pursuit of insatiable physical pleasures through which the devil draws the blind to hell, the centre of this 'besy mase'. Antony counsels that those who, in the 'day light of grace', perceive their painful folly and fear the loss of God are being overfearful. Moreover, it is not that worldly goods are ungodly, but rather 'the will & the desire / and affeccion to haue & the longyng for it' (*CW* 12:171). In having Antony counter Vincent's objection that any economic advantage implies 'an inordinate affeccion', More again addresses all those incapable of observing the most ascetic Christian life (12:172–3). The *Dialogue* is shaped to the needs not of exceptional spiritual athletes, but to ordinary human beings who unavoidably find themselves in exceptional circumstances. Thus, although Antony acknowledges that 'wilfull pouertie' may well sharpen the 'hungrye desire & longyng for celestiall thinges' (12:174), he interprets Christ's challenge that all goods be forsaken and family and friends be hated (Luke 14:33, 26) as the willingness finally to abandon them rather than displease God. In his poised handling of the question whether riches always endanger the soul, Antony prefers pragmatic wealth creation to something more Utopian: he criticizes radical redistribution as generally impoverishing, because it destroys the entrepreneurial potential of those from whom everyone should benefit (*CW* 12:180). But the rich man, he emphasizes, should, 'havyng it fall habundantly vnto hym, taketh to his own parte no greate pleasure therof / but as though he had it not, kepeth him selfe in like abstynence & penaunce prively, as he wold do in case he had it not' (12:184). Here, and in passages which follow, concerning the use of wealth in maintaining good Christian households, on behaving consistently in public and private to avoid charges of hypocrisy, and on the occupying of high office, we again feel the connection with More's own experience and behaviour.

AFFECTIONS SPIRITUAL

After Book II's more leisurely and discursive exposition of how to live faithfully in the world, Book III confronts 'the incursion or invacion of the devil in the mydde day'. Vincent has news of imminent invasion. Preparation against the possibility of persecution becomes essential and particular, raising affection for God above that which 'we bere to our own filthy flesh':

> while the thing shall not apere so terrible vnto them / reason
> shall bettre entre, & thorow [through] grace workyng with their
> diligens / engendre & set sure, not a sodayne sleyght affeccion of
> sufferaunce for godes sake / but by a long contynuaunce, a strong
> depe rotid [rooted] habit.

(*CW* 12:205)

The *Dialogue* turns to guide and discipline more keenly those habits of thought and action towards saving souls rather than skins. Anecdotes, merry tales and digressions on the unreliability and insecurity of the gifts of fortune (goods, lands, reputation, honour and authority) define their virtuous use against their inflaming of desire. The 'tribulacion of the Turke', in threatening the loss of worldly goods, presents a crisis between outward and godly things, and a 'towch stone' to tell 'the faynid fro the trew myndid' (12:226). There can be no compromise in their surrender: trying to hang on to goods for future virtuous employment is a loophole Antony immediately closes.

Role-playing, so pleasing to More, is now added, to intensify engagement.[23] Antony asks Vincent to 'conjecture' the part of a wealthy lord who must choose between faith and riches (III.14). In this fiction within the fiction, Vincent is able to inhabit the arguments for accommodation with the Turks, so as 'not [to] be compellid vtterly to forsake christ / nor all the whole christen fayth, but onely some ... partes'. The performance of this interlude licenses Antony's vehemently uncompromising retorts: 'what feleship [fellowship] is there betwene light & darknes, betwene christ & Beliall ... no man may serve two lordes at ones' (CW 12:229–30). The absurdity of temporizing is thus ruthlessly exposed. Against the certainty of God's promise, that of a 'great prince' depends on his personal conception of honour, which might (as in the case of Henry) be subject to revision. Even a constant Sultan's promise dies with him. True treasure is the security to be hoarded in heaven rather than on earth (Matthew 6:19–21), and this provides the basis of Antony's comprehensive response (III.15–20); to invest elsewhere is folly.

Meditative preparation now comes to the fore: how to grub up 'the thornes & the breres & the brambles of our worldly substaunce' (CW 12:241) and sow and root hope in the heart. Antony urges the cultivation of a spiritual discourse to free the heart from the world:

> we shall (that ones [once] done) fynd our hartes so conuersaunt in hevyn, with the glad consideracion of our folowyng the graciouse counsayle of christ, that the comfort of his holy spirite inspirid vs therfor / shall mitigate, minish, asswage, & in maner quench, the greate furious fervour of the payne that we shall happen to haue by his lovyng suffraunce / for our ferther merite in our tribulacion /

Moreover, Christ's example, both in poverty and in 'his gret grievous agony' on the Cross, provides a powerfully affecting image through which to apprehend this 'graciouse counsayle'. As the *Dialogue* turns unflinchingly to the possibility of violent death in the realization of this divine economy, Vincent's trembling heart understandably betrays his need for greater assurance. Although Antony states that not all are called to be martyrs, the focus remains on fear and pain; he has already deplored the prevalent faintheartedness: 'the greater, the more bittre that the passion were / the more redy was of old tyme the feruour of fayth to suffre yt' (12:204). Fear arises not only from the 'devill with all his faythles tourmentours' but also from 'our own fraylty'. But God, Antony adds reassuringly, 'will not suffer vs to be temptid above our power' (12:247–8). Just as Antony refers the efficacy of his counsel to the necessary inward work of the 'sprite [spirit] of god', so the *Dialogue* only shows the way to comfort rather than guaranteeing it. Nevertheless, the work exercises reason and the affections through a literary art which blends dialectic and colloquy, and it is through this combined appeal that More sought to dispose the receptive reader to co-operate with grace.

In purging illusory dependencies on the world, tribulation plays an essential part in realizing a glimpse of the ultimate, inviolable sanctuary of heaven; the Turk, whether defeated or persecuting, is God's gift. Through confronting the challenge of 'tharldome / imprisonment / paynfull & shamfull deth' (*CW* 12:250) in Book III, chapter 18, Antony continues to loosen Vincent's grasp on the world: we are pilgrims and wayfaring men, without country; exile is a 'wrong Imaginacion', for the world is no home. Vincent needs to rethink his notion of liberty from the divine perspective of the Fall. The world is a prison and God the gaoler; divine and human laws constrain us, while 'he that commyttith synne, ys the thrall or bondman of synne' and the devil (12:253). Without grace, 'we fynd in our naturall fredome our bond seruice'. Even if we should be forced to act against our will, we should make a virtue of necessity, as Seneca counselled (12:254). Antony meets Vincent's objection with a finer distinction between the unruly resistance to servitude and the consolatory service to God, where Christ's example of 'grete humble meknes' as a 'bond man or slaue' offers salvation to the believer. In such faith, he concludes, it is only reasonable to endure temporary worldly bondage for everlasting liberty, rather than the reverse. Similar logic applies to confinement itself: what true freedom is compromised by physical constraint? Antony manages to balance rigour with humanity in his dogged pursuit, acknowledging the unavoidable fear of pain, yet evoking that fear to expose the terrifying fantasies of anticipation as temptations to forsake faith.

Antony attempts to expose the essence of imprisonment through the methodical marginalizing of its 'accidentes'. Vincent's interruptions and objections perform important rhetorical work within the fiction in clarifying and sharpening the intellectual analysis of sundry tribulations, discovering more convincingly the comfort available in each. Antony leads Vincent through the argument with commendable precision; absolute freedom is quickly exposed as unobtainable: is someone less imprisoned for being in a larger cell? How widely need a person range to be said to be free? The Great Turk and the beggar both face constraints of one sort or another. However, Vincent's creditable resistance to Antony's subordination of every lack of freedom to the condition of imprisonment adds dramatic vitality: 'euer me thinketh that these thinges wherwith you rather convince & conclude me than enduce a credence & perswade me / that euery man is in prison all redye / be but sophisticall fantasies / & that / except those that are comenly callid prisoners / other men are not in any prison at all' (*CW* 12:262). Antony then enquires whether a man is at liberty if physically unconstrained between attainder and his execution, another *frisson* of contact with the author's own circumstance. Vincent concedes that the shadow of execution would make him 'a very playne prisoner styll' (12:265), with brief but brutal incarceration being preferable. But another, more haunting suggestion is that the guilty fear of God's punishment experienced by the faithful who fail to follow their conscience leads to the prison of despair.

To address Vincent's resistant distinction between 'generall imprisoning' and dreadful 'speciall prisonmentes' of vulgar understanding (*CW* 12:270), Antony advances the argument of inverted values, of seeing the truth in the opposite of common sense; the worldly pursuit of glory, unlike the Carthusians' cloister, builds a prison in the prison of the world. Distracted, we forget our true relation to God and errantly abhor the state of those in 'speciall prisonmentes'. Likewise, we fail to see migraine, quinsy, palsy, gout, cramp and other restricting diseases as God's 'invisible instrumentes' (12:274). Antony seemingly acknowledges Vincent's point about physical confinement, then tells of a charitable woman, not unlike the uncomprehending Dame Alice, who aroused a prisoner's inward laughter by lamenting his being locked in, when she locked herself into her house every night; Dame Alice also viewed More's principle as stubbornness (cf. above, 126). Antony insists that comfort comes from debunking the fantasy of apparent liberty: nothing compares to the self-fashioned prison of fallen human nature unsupported by faith: 'But now yf we haue not lost our fayth al redye, before we come to forsake it for feare: we know very wel by our fayth, that by the forsakyng of our fayth, we fall into the state to be cast into the prison of hell / & that can we not tell how sone' (12:279).

Finally, Antony turns from countering the fear of imprisonment to 'the last & vttermost poynt of the drede' (*CW* 12:280). Euphemistically reducing 'the terrour of shamfull & paynfull deth' to a 'sore pynch', he asserts that faith and understanding need to be deeply rooted to withstand the ultimate challenge (12:281). Reason can, in part, he argues, mitigate the terror of death, but its working depends on the grace of God's inspiration, which disposes man to spiritual rather than sensual affections; godly counsel and prayer assist this but cannot entirely purge sensual dispositions. Antony yet again assists reason, here dividing the fear of shameful death (III.23) from that of a painful one (III.24). Whether a death is shameful depends on whether it is perceived faithfully or fearfully: Christ's triumph on the Cross seemed a foolish and humiliating defeat to unbelievers. Antony's strategy tends to the ecphrastic: Vincent should imagine an affirming, glorious company of heaven witnessing his faithful march to martyrdom, against the 'shamfull gestyng & raylyng of those mad folysh wretchis' of the world (12:289). The proper pride of the Apostles in 'that shame & velenouse [atrocious] payne put vnto them' is also invoked – they had not disdained this part of Christ's example (12:291). Antony sets his vivid description of Christ's suffering against the previous mirages of glory. Through such arguments and inspiring images Vincent is persuaded that, although perfect spiritual vision is unachievable, so that shame cannot be entirely avoided, its brevity on earth is as nothing compared with everlasting glory in heaven.

Antony, with characteristic scrupulousness, admits that pain, unlike shame, is not culturally determined. Yet if reason cannot obliterate pain itself, it should prefer an ephemeral and lesser pain to eternal agony. Faith and grace are required, 'first to engendre in vs such an effeccion / and after by long & depe meditacion therof, so to contynew that affeccion, that it shall tourne into an habituall fast & depe rotid [rooted] purpose, of pacient suffryng the paynefull deth of this body here in earth, for the gaynyng of euerlastyng welthy lyfe in hevyn, & avoydyng of euerlastyng paynefull deth in hell' (*CW* 12:294). Vincent, however, countering with a fable of an old hart unable to find sufficient courage from his friend to face a hunter's pursuing bitch, is far from convinced that God's presence, where two or three are gathered in his name, will triumph over fear. Antony reiterates that although reason can only be followed through grace, God's help is ever available, even to those who have cast it aside (12:294–6), perhaps another tacit message to those whose religious convictions had been compromised by Henry's incursions.

Antony applies further euphemistic discourse to shift Vincent's perspective. But mention of death, 'though bytter & sharp / yet short for all that, & in a maner a momentary payne', still causes Vincent to flinch, and he clutches at the report of a Nicodemite – one who outwardly complies, but believes that true faith can be hidden. Antony's sustained denunciation of this position as 'fantasticall feare / false fayth / false flattrying hope' (*CW* 12:297) signals the importance to More of striving to be a true witness to faith. The premeditated forsaking of faith in the hope of future forgiveness is, Antony argues, a presumptuous sin against the Holy Ghost quite unlike Peter's fearful denials of Christ, for which he sorely repented and later found a martyr's death in Rome. True faith cannot conceal itself. Antony turns the screw: repentance for such denial would be nearly impossible, a slender 'perhaps' to contrast with the certainty of salvation in a faithful, if violent, death. Nor does *nature* necessarily spare us excruciating and protracted deaths. Antony fights fear with fear through Christ's words: *'ita dico vobis hunc timete* ... So I say to you be aferd of hym' (Luke 12:5). God's eternal punishment of hell is 'an hundred thowsand tymes more intollerable', a 'deth in which folke shall euermore be dyyng' (*CW* 12:303–4). The terrifying metaphysics of Revelation 9:6 – *'vocabunt mortem et mors fugiet ab eis* / They shall call & cry for deth, and deth shall flye from them' – reinforces Antony's trenchant (and alliterative) enlarging of his exasperation: 'In how wrechid foly fall than [then] those faythlesse or feble faythed folke.'

Although Vincent claims to be convinced, Antony's work ends not in fear of God but in the love of Christ and, again, the difficulty of apprehending the affective power of heaven. Hell's pains may be imagined as extrapolated worldly agonies – more intense, and interminable – but spiritual pleasures are at odds with fleshly sensations. The penultimate chapter addresses this challenge of cultivating 'desire expectacion & hevenly hope' of something beyond 'experimentall tast' (*CW* 12:306). Yet, although the 'carnall myndid man', trapped in the literal meaning of Christ's similes in scripture, cannot benefit from the promise of heaven, even the most virtuous can only imagine such joys as the blind perceive colours. Nevertheless, even as Antony asserts that scriptural celebrations of heaven barely penetrate our 'carnall hartes ... & our dull worldly wittes' (12:308), his dramatic speech rises to a rapturous, paraphrastic commentary which conveys paradoxically, and at times in an almost hymn-like way, the ineffability of the incomprehensible joys for which we should long. From this emerges the refrain of 'hym that overcometh' (Revelation 2:7) – again that play on Vincent's name – which signifies 'his holy martires that suffer for his sake', and who receive 'a speciall kynd of Ioy' (*CW* 12:309). To the ravishing and inspiring effects of the most mystical of biblical authors, Antony adds Paul's sundry 'perelles' and 'passions', which the Apostle considered 'but light & as short as a moment in respect of the wayghty glory that yt after this world wynneth vs' (12:311). And, at last, Antony's urgent voice, increasingly subsumed by scripture in Latin and English, turns to the climactic example of the Passion.

The final chapter begins with an unsparing description of the agony of Christ's physical persecution, to help 'conceyve in our myndes a right Imagynacion & remembraunce' (*CW* 12:312). Sustaining his antithetical approach, Antony contrasts 'our kay cold [cold as a key] hartes' towards God's 'fervent love & Inestimable kyndnes' with the 'hote affeccion many of thes fleshly lovers haue borne & dayly do, to those vppon whome they dote' (12:313). Analogous preoccupation with worldly honour and glory is again invoked, but here momentarily referred to the false martyrdoms of heretics.[24] However, instead of a sustained epitome of the sundry arguments of earlier chapters, Antony concludes with the Last Things: the Passion, heaven and hell, and how the mind's rapture renders it impervious to both the fear and the pain of persecution. The clamorous and vivid image of hell is raised as if to be exorcized. Even as the invocation of the beckoning heavenly company is presented to counter the image of everlasting torment, Antony iterates the 'marvelouse paynfull deth' some face to escape it. Hope of heaven, with which the *Dialogue* has sought to combat despair, transfigures the Turk's persecution into 'inestimable good' (12:316). We are reminded that the strength of previous martyrs was God's gift for faith, whatever their mortal attributes; confidence in human abilities should therefore be forsaken. Martyrdom is thus not the triumph of human virtue, but available to all those who, through devotional preparedness, fasting, prayer and alms-giving, and with God's freely given help, stand firm in their faith and struggle to overcome temptation. The *Dialogue* dispels seductive worldly illusions by revealing the paradoxical truth: to endure pain and death through grace is the way to eternal freedom and joy; to disbelieve or abandon God's truth, his pavice, for one's own tissue is to become defenceless against eternal servitude and agony.

In conclusion, Antony expounds what is seen through faithful sight: 'the Turke is but a shadow', no allegory, but the deceiving instrument of the midday devil 'that maketh ... his ministers to make vs fall for feare / For till we fall, he can neuer hurt vs ... Therfor whan he roreth out vppon vs by the threttes of mortall men / let vs tell hym that with our inward yie, we see hym well ynough, & intend to stand & fight with hym evyn hand to hand' (*CW* 12:317–8). And if the Turk is the shadow, the real, invisible enemy is combated with the three paramount Christian virtues: 'let vs fence vs with fayth, & comfort vs with hope, & smyte the devill in the face with the firebrond of charitie'. The complex workings of the intricately structured *Dialogue* are thus ultimately directed towards rectifying our perception of persecution. To educate the inner or spiritual eye, Antony has supplied both images on which to fasten and argument to clarify thought. His last gesture is to amplify the workings of love and pity, ostensibly for the Turk, but again speaking to the author's opponents, as he deplores what persecutors bring on themselves. Paul's conclusion provides Antony's summary text (Romans 8:18): 'the passiones of this tyme, be not worthy to the glory that ys to come, which shalbe shewid in vs' (*CW* 12:319). Antony's rhetoric has soared aloft, leaving the world's pain and anguish far below as merely a 'trowble' set before everlasting joy. The labour spent in deeply rooting this perception has profoundly wearied him, and he suddenly ends the 'tale'.

Vincent breaks his long silence, undertaking not only to record Antony's counsel but to translate it 'in the Almayne tong to'. This final deflection from Hungary, not to England but to the persecution by heretics in Germany, should be set against the title page, which announced that the dialogue has been rendered from Hungarian into English via Latin then French. If Vincent's promise associates Hungary with Germany, and thus the Turk with Lutheran heretics, as More had done in his controversial works, translation itself becomes a trope for the spread of persecution across Europe, expanding how the *Dialogue* negotiates between the particular and the universal. But it remains a work as personal as it is elusive. Dialogue allowed More to intertwine argument and scriptural testimony, the drama of objection and reply, and the interplay of witty anecdote and pointed fable, to produce a powerfully fortifying rhetoric (*confortare*: to strengthen) in which the Hungarian setting served not merely as an enabling fiction but as a way of understanding his life as a Christian: he drew on personal experience and the political circumstances so as to withdraw to a position conditioned by revelatory spiritual affections. The fiction allowed memory, learning and earthly attachments to be set in proper perspective to one another, whereby More sought to subordinate his affections to the divine, and in so doing created perhaps his most masterful English writing. Antony's weariness so reflects More's seemingly exhaustive spiritual, intellectual and literary labour (and the exertions he challenges the reader to take up) that Harpsfield's appraisal, then speaking of all three Tower Works, may command our assent: 'he doth so wonderfully, so effectually, and so strongly prepare, defence and arme the Reader, that a man cannot desire or wish any thing of more efficacie or importance thereto to be added' (Harpsfield 133).

FURTHER READING

The definitive edition of *A Dialogue of Comfort* is *CW* 12, which includes important introductory essays both by Louis L. Martz, on the text and the place of the *Dialogue* among the Tower Works, and by Frank Manley, on the argument and the audience of the work. Manley also edited a modern-spelling version (see below, 290).The *Dialogue* is compared with the Catholic consolatory works of John Fisher, Robert Southwell and Benedict Canfield in Paul Strauss, *In Hope of Heaven: English Recusant Prison Writings of the Sixteenth Century* (New York: Peter Lang, 1995). Anne Dillon, *The Construction of Martyrdom in the English Catholic Community, 1535–1603* (Aldershot: Ashgate, 2002), begins with a consideration of More. Germain Marc'hadour, *The Bible in the Works of St. Thomas More*, 5 vols. (Nieuwkoop: B. de Graaf, 1969–72), shows the depth and range of More's knowledge and literary use of the Bible. More's correspondence from the Tower has been gathered as *The Last Letters of Thomas More*, ed. Alvaro de Silva (Grand Rapids, Mich.: Eerdmans, 2000). Anne M. O'Donnell relates the *Dialogue* to classical and patristic traditions in 'Cicero, Gregory the Great, and Thomas More: three dialogues of comfort', in Clare M. Murphy *et al.*, eds., *Miscellanea Moreana: Essays for Germain Marc'hadour* (Binghamton, N.Y.: Medieval & Renaissance Texts & Studies, 1989), 169–97. David Marsh, *The Quattrocento Dialogue* (Cambridge, Mass.: Harvard University Press, 1980), gives an overview of the form, which can be continued in Virginia Cox, *The Renaissance Dialogue* (Cambridge University Press, 1992). The humanist handling of laughter and wit in theological and other contexts is richly explored in Michael Screech, *Laughter at the Foot of the Cross* (Harmondsworth: Penguin, 1997), with folly handled more specifically in Nancy Yee, 'Thomas More's *Moriae Encomium*: the perfect fool in *A Dialogue of Comfort against Tribulation*', *Moreana* 27, no. 101–2 (1990), 65–74, available online, with other *Moreana* essays of interest on the *Dialogue*, at the Center for Thomas More Studies.

Notes

1. The chronology of the Tower Works, especially the degree of completion of the *Treatise on the Passion* before More's imprisonment, is discussed by Louis L. Martz in his introductory essay to the Yale edition of the *Dialogue* (*CW* 12:lvii–lviii) and by Garry E. Haupt in his introduction to the *Treatise* (*CW* 13:xxxvii–xliii).

2. For a historical overview see Halil Inalcik, *The Ottoman Empire: The Classical Age 1300–1600*, trans. Norman Itzkowitz and Colin Imber (London: Weidenfeld and Nicolson, 1973).

3. See item 2056 (copy of letters of the nuncio in Hungary to the pope) in *LP* 4, Part 1:925.

4. On Vives's anthology as part of his peace writings, see E. V. George, 'Juan Luis Vives' *De Europae dissidiis et bello Turcico*: its place in the 1526 ensemble', in J. F. Alcina *et al.*, eds., *Acta Conventus Neo-Latini Bariensis* (Tempe, Ariz.: Medieval and Renaissance Texts and Studies, 1998), 259–66.

5. See C. A. Patrides, ' "The Bloody and Cruell Turke": the background of a Renaissance commonplace', *Studies in the Renaissance* 10 (1963), 126–35.

6. Paul Lendvai, *The Hungarians: A Thousand Years of Victory in Defeat*, trans. Ann Major (Princeton University Press, 2004), 90–1.

7. See R. J. Schoeck, 'Thomas More's "Dialogue of Comfort" and the problem of the real Grand Turk', *English Miscellany* 20 (1969), 23–37.

8. See Romuald I. Lakowski, 'Thomas More, Protestants, and Turks: persecution and martyrdom in *A Dialogue of Comfort*', *Ben Jonson Journal* 7 (2000), 199–223.

9. This idea is explored in Howard Norland, 'Comfort through dialogue: More's response to tribulation', *Moreana* 24, no. 93 (1987), 53–66.

10. In texts of this period, the virgule (/) is regularly used where we would use a comma or, sometimes, another punctuation mark. Both virgules and commas are found in the most authoritative manuscript of the *Dialogue* (although in the original form of this manuscript commas may not have been used at all: see *CW* 12:xxxvi).

11. *Thomas More's Prayer Book: A Facsimile Reproduction of the Annotated Pages*, ed. Louis L. Martz and Richard S. Sylvester (New Haven: Yale University Press, 1969), xxxv, 114 (facsimile)/197 (transcription and translation). The translations are by the editors. In the present essay, Psalms are numbered following the tradition of the Gallican Psalter (after the Greek Septuagint) included in the Vulgate text of the Bible, rather than after the Hebrew Psalms of the Masoretic text favoured in the Protestant tradition of the English Psalter and Bible. The Hebrew numbering is given in parentheses.

12. Against Alistair Fox's development of this thesis in *Thomas More: History and Providence* (Oxford: Blackwell, 1982), see Brendan Bradshaw's essay 'The controversial Sir Thomas More', *Journal of Ecclesiastical History* 36 (1985), 535–69.

13. *Thomas More's Prayer Book*, 75/194.

14. 'Thomas More and tyranny', *Journal of Ecclesiastical History* 32 (1981), 453–76, at 471.

15. Ibid., 476.

16. Although More evidently wrote the *Dialogue* for publication, the work could only be read in manuscript copies during the eighteen years between his death and its eventual printed publication in 1553.

17. On humour in *A Dialogue Concerning Heresies*, see above, 200–4.

18. More is referring particularly to *The Imitation of Christ*, which at the time was attributed to Gerson, but is now thought to have been written by the fifteenth-century German mystic Thomas à Kempis (see *CW* 12:374 n.).

19. 'More's art of improvisation' is Louis Martz's phrase. For it, and on More's literary use of digression, see Martz, 'Thomas More: the Tower Works', in Richard S. Sylvester, ed., *St. Thomas More: Action and Contemplation* (New Haven: Yale University Press, 1972), 59–83; 63 ff. Much of this essay was subsequently incorporated in *CW* 12:lvii–lxxxvi.

20. For a fuller exploration of More's punning on Vincent's name, see Germain Marc'hadour, *Thomas More et la Bible* (Paris: J. Vrin, 1969), 334.

21. Joaquin Kuhn, 'The function of Psalm 90 in Thomas More's *A Dialogue of Comfort*', *Moreana* 7, no. 22 (1969), 61–7.

22. See Paul D. Green, 'Suicide, martyrdom, and Thomas More', *Studies in the Renaissance* 19 (1972), 135–55; and cf. below, 254–6.

23. For a wide-ranging account of More's sustained interest in role-playing and performance – clearly related to his interest in dialogue – see Howard B. Norland, 'The role of drama in More's literary career', *Sixteenth Century Journal* 13 (1982), 59–75, at 74–5.

24. See Anne Dillon, *The Construction of Martyrdom in the English Catholic Community, 1535–1603* (in 'Further reading'), 18–27.

11 The lessons of Gethsemane: *De Tristitia Christi*

KATHERINE GARDINER RODGERS

DATE, CIRCUMSTANCES AND HABITS OF COMPOSITION

De Tristitia Christi, an unfinished commentary on the agony of Christ in the Garden of Gethsemane, is the last of Thomas More's major works, composed while he was imprisoned in the Tower of London on a charge of misprision of treason. According to the preface to the work which William Rastell supplied for its first translation – by More's granddaughter, Mary Basset, in the 1557 edition of the English works – More began *De Tristitia* 'beyng then prisoner, and coulde not atchieue and finishe the same' because he was 'bereaued and put from hys bookes, pen, inke and paper' (*1557* sig. QQ₇v; *CW* 14:1077–8). On the basis of this information, we can place the composition of the work sometime between April 1534, when More was taken prisoner, and June 1535, when his books and writing materials were confiscated by the royal authorities (see above, 128). Such circumstances as these are enough to stimulate interest in the work's composition and content, but we are also fortunate that More's manuscript has survived, having been found in 1963 at the Royal College of Corpus Christi in Valencia, Spain, and analysed in detail by Clarence H. Miller in the Yale editon of *De Tristitia* (*CW* 14:695–724). The only surviving holograph of a major work by More, the Valencia manuscript affords a rare glimpse into his methods and process of composition, if not in general, at least under the straitened circumstances of his imprisonment.

The Valencia autograph (reproduced in the Yale edition as a facing-page facsimile with Miller's transcription and translation of the Latin text) leaves an impression both of the urgency of More's circumstances and of the privations of his Tower cell. As Miller shows, More composed quickly, revising as he went, crossing out what he wished to change and making interlinear additions with carets (*CW* 14:745–54). The manuscript reveals an almost mercurial process of composition; many of More's corrections were necessary to amend false starts where what was in his mind to put on the page simply 'outran his pen' (14:745). In addition to a lack of time, he seems to have been constrained by a lack of materials, particularly as he neared the end of the work. Although the manuscript includes blank leaves at the beginning and end of the first four gatherings, and three pages which he cancelled entirely, More seems elsewhere to have tried to spare paper: he tended to write up to the edge of most pages and (towards the end of the manuscript) on both sides of each leaf (14:701). At one point he made a lengthy addition to the text in the right margin, separating the new material from the old with a neat line (14:178). Overall, the appearance of the manuscript suggests a writer consciously making maximum use of limited materials.

The limitations of More's resources should, however, not be overstated. Some of his letters from the Tower were evidently written 'with a coal', but the notion that More was deprived of every amenity during the entire fourteen months of his imprisonment is contradicted by the Valencia manuscript itself, which is written in ink and has definitively laid to rest the rather romantic legend that the longer Tower works were composed without a pen.[1] Still, perhaps partly owing to the relative scarcity of his resources, More took great care in preparing the manuscript, and (as Miller shows) the speed with which he composed the work by no means compromised the legibility of the copy (*CW* 14:747). Indeed, because some pages include long and involved sentences without any cancellations at all, Miller speculates that at times More may have composed on separate leaves of paper and later copied into the manuscript what he had drafted (14:751). In general, he seems to have written quickly but purposefully, providing a clear and legible holograph (14:747). Although the work accommodates great complexity of expression and literary style, More thus seems utterly confident about the *points* he wishes to make (if not always about the particular words he wishes to use in making them), and it is tempting to speculate that he had the work's possible printing in mind even as he composed. Miller cautions that the manuscript alone does not permit us to draw conclusions on this matter with any degree of certainty, but the very presence of the work's careful, deliberate revisions suggests a high degree of audience awareness and (along with the clarity of More's hand in writing) makes at least plausible the idea that *De Tristitia* was written with a public readership in mind (14:747).

'DE TRISTITIA' AND THE OTHER TOWER WORKS

Despite limited access to writing materials in the Tower, More made good use of his imprisonment by writing some of his most remarkable and substantial works. *De Tristitia* is part of a group that includes *A Dialogue of Comfort against Tribulation*, more than a dozen artfully composed letters, and a series of *Instructions and Prayers* that appear at the end of the Valencia manuscript. By tradition, other writings from the period after More's resignation of the chancellorship have also become known as 'Tower Works'. As early as 1557, the *Treatise on the Passion* and the *Treatise on the Blessed Body* were included in this group; indeed, More's sixteenth-century readers believed that *De Tristitia* continued in Latin what More had begun in English in the likewise unfinished *Treatise on the Passion*. Thus in the 1557 edition of More's works, Mary Basset's translation of *De Tristitia* follows directly after these words at the end of the *Treatise*: 'Syr Thomas More wrote no more in englishe of thys treatise of the passion of Chryst. But he (still prisoner in the tower of London) wrote more thereof in latine (after the same order as he wrote thereof in englyshe:) the translacion whereof here foloweth' (sig. QQ₇; qtd *CW* 14:740). More's earliest biographers cemented the impression that the works are related, by asserting that More began to prepare himself for martyrdom as soon as he resigned the chancellorship, dedicating himself to study and meditation on the Passion (Roper 227–8; Stapleton 158–9).

The Yale editors of both works have convincingly discredited the suggestion (probably introduced into the 1557 edition by Rastell) that *De Tristitia* is a continuation of the *Treatise on the Passion*; for one thing, setting aside the difference in language, the *Treatise* is largely concerned with the theological necessity of Christ's death, while *De Tristitia* recounts and reflects on his agony in the Garden of Gethsemane (*CW* 13:xxxviii–xli; *CW* 14:740–1). There is no obvious coherence between the place where the *Treatise* ends and *De Tristitia* begins; as Miller observes, the two works should be regarded as separate compositions on similar subjects. In fact, it is probable that the *Treatise on the Passion* was begun before More's imprisonment, and although he may have continued to work on it in prison, it is thus only partly a 'Tower Work' (see *CW* 13:xl–xli). In his introduction to the Yale edition of *A Dialogue of Comfort*, Louis Martz has offered the plausible suggestion that the short English *Treatise on the Blessed Body* (which deals with the proper manner of receiving the

Eucharist), not *De Tristitia*, may be the missing conclusion of the *Treatise on the Passion* (*CW* 12:lxxix–lxxxv).

Modern scholarship has thus reached a consensus that the sequence of More's last works in the 1557 edition is misleading, and some have speculated that the arrangement of the works there may have been part of an effort in the More circle to correct the Henrician version of More's image as a traitor, disseminated in the aftermath of his trial and execution.[2] The legend of the coal, the portrayal of More settling his affairs as soon as he resigned the chancellorship, and the grouping together by Rastell of *De Tristitia* with the treatises on the Passion and blessed body of Christ could indeed seem designed to suggest that More was a Christlike victim of Henry's tyranny. As Martz and others have pointed out, the explanation of the work's unfinished state that Rastell prefixed to Mary Basset's translation very clearly suggests a parallel between Christ's death and More's execution: 'ere he could goe thorow [through] therwith, (eauen when he came to thexposicion of these wordes, *Et incecerunt* [sic] *manus in Iesum*) [he] was bereaued and put from hys bookes, pen, inke and paper, and kepte more strayghtly than before, and soone after also was putte to death hymselfe'.[3] The general impression suggested by the grouping in *1557* is that the Tower Works are devotional and private, full of veiled references to More's personal predicament.

The argument that the last works are evidence of a spirituality that became increasingly inward and withdrawn from the world has persisted among some of the very scholars who have questioned the *1557* grouping. Martz, for example, characterized *De Tristitia* as a 'Latin meditation on the Agony' which is marked by 'numerous occasions, long and short, in which the speaker hears the voice of his Redeemer answering his meditation' (*CW* 12:lxxxiv, lxxxvi). Tracing a movement in More's work from a 'dark night of the soul' in the last polemics to 'calm regained' in the Tower Works, Alistair Fox reads *De Tristitia* almost as if it were a commentary on More's agony rather than one on Christ's: 'More, in effect, did not need to finish *De Tristitia*', Fox writes, 'for its ending was left implicit, and soon to be literally supplied' by More's own execution.[4] Even John Guy (whose biography of More argues persuasively that he continued to be engaged in public debate well after resigning from public office) has suggested that the 'otherworldliness' of the *Dialogue of Comfort* and *De Tristitia* assisted More's sixteenth-century biographers in their attempt to show that after resigning the chancellorship, in 1532, More renounced public life and devoted himself wholly to prayer and meditation as he prepared his soul to meet God.[5]

Undoubtedly, the major works More composed before and after entering the Tower contain passages influenced by the meditative tradition of 'inward speaking'. It docs not undermine More's sainthood, however, to assert that these last works, including *De Tristitia*, are fully alive to the world and primarily address an audience beyond the self. Among them, the *Treatise on the Passion*, the *Dialogue of Comfort* and *De Tristitia* offer a summation of More's characteristic habits of mind – his dialogic imagination, his fondness for digression, his mordant 'merry tales' and ironic wit, and his employment of certain exegetical methods. The last of these is especially relevant to an understanding of the sources and strategies of scriptural interpretation in *De Tristitia*.

THE TEXT OF SCRIPTURE: GERSON'S 'MONOTESSARON'

The works More composed after resigning the chancellorship differ in language and form, but a thread common to all of them – both those begun before his imprisonment and those begun during it – is dependence on Jean Gerson as a source of scriptural narrative and moral theology. Gerson (1363–1429) served as chancellor of the University of Paris, and his views on reforming the Church from within through conciliar action in many ways anticipate More's own.[6] Gerson's works ranged from the doctrinal to the devotional, and the fact that the widely influential devotional manual *Imitatio Christi* was erroneously attributed to him throughout the sixteenth century is a measure of his lasting influence.[7] It is clear that More had access to at least some of Gerson's works in the Tower, for he explicitly acknowledges his debt to them at several points in the Tower Works, notably at the end of *De Tristitia*, where he is discussing 'exactly when'[8] the Roman guards laid hands on Jesus – whether the capture occurred immediately after Judas had identified Jesus with a kiss or only after events made it clear that Jesus was capable of resisting arrest but chose instead to allow himself to be captured (*CW* 14:619–25).

In this instance, More rejects what he claims to be Gerson's view that Christ was seized as soon as Judas kissed him. The rejection, however, is framed less as criticism than as an appreciation and acknowledgement of Gerson's *Monotessaron* as a source for the Passion narrative presented in *De Tristitia*: 'And this is the opinion adopted not only by many celebrated doctors of the Church but also approved by that remarkable man John Gerson, who follows it in presenting the sequence of events in his work entitled *Monotessaron* (the work I have generally followed in enumerating the events of the passion in this discussion)' (*CW* 14:623). In the *Treatise on the Passion*, More similarly praises 'the worke of that worshipful father maister Iohn Gerson, whych worke he entitled *Monotessaron*', and announces that 'I wil not in any worde wyllinglye, mangle or mutilate that honourable mans worke' (*CW* 13:50).

The *Monotessaron* (1420), to which the subtitle *Unum ex quattuor* ('One from four') was frequently attached, harmonizes the four Gospels, presenting the life of Christ in a single narrative of 150 chapters divided into three parts: 'De origine Christi et ingressu ejus' ('On the lineage and birth of Christ'), 'De praedicatione Joannis et de progressu praedicationis Christi' ('On the preaching of John and the spread of Christ's preaching'), and 'De egressu passionis et resurrectione Christi' ('On the passion and resurrection of Christ'). Chapter 143 essentially serves as the scriptural basis of *De Tristitia*; indeed, More seems in the *Treatise on the Passion* to ascribe to Gerson an authority nearly as great as that of scripture itself, pausing to give 'A warning to the Reader' that he plans to 'rehearse the wordes of theuangelistes in this process of the passion, in latyne, word by word after my copy' (*CW* 13:50) – that is, Gerson's text.

In *De Tristitia*, this commitment to following Gerson 'word by word' does not preclude the attribution of passages to the different evangelists, and the original biblical context of the Gospel narratives is duly acknowledged. At the same time, the somewhat combative tone of the warning in the *Treatise on the Passion* is reminiscent of debates in the polemical works over the nature of scriptural authority, and serves as a reminder that for More the text of the Bible might legitimately be derived from any number of sources and could not be adequately understood without recourse to the *sensus fidelium* – the received interpretation of oral tradition and custom, of the Church Fathers and Doctors, and of doctrine as established by councils of 'the whole corps of Christendom'.[9] For one thing, as More was keenly aware through his familiarity with Erasmus's Greek New Testament, the text of scripture is not an unchanging artefact but is, rather, subject to ongoing philological investigation. For another, in his view the text of scripture is 'teeming with various mysterious meanings' (*CW* 14:21) and its interpretation requires the help of time-tested authorities. More may have used an edition of the Bible similar (and perhaps identical) to one published by Froben in 1498 and 1502, in which the Vulgate was printed along with the *Glossa ordinaria*, the *Glossa interlinearis* and the commentary of Nicholas de Lyra, so that no passage is ever encountered without extensive commentary.[10]

As More's use and treatment of Gerson's *Monotessaron* as a scriptural text thus indicate, the reading and interpretation of scripture in *De Tristitia* are based on deliberate consideration of 'credible witnesses and the likelihood of evidence' for particular readings.[11] Even the apparently straightforward task of collating and harmonizing the Gospels had forced Gerson, More's own authority, into interpretive decisions. Thus in deciding the question of 'exactly when' Christ was taken prisoner, More, lawyerlike, first considers one possibility, affirmed by 'some commentators' including Gerson, then examines another held by other 'celebrated authorities', and finally determines that 'probable inferences' compel him to favour the second view because it better demonstrates what More takes to be the essential point of the passage – the voluntary nature of Christ's submission to his captors' power. In fact, Gerson's sequence is closer to the one More favours than he here suggests, and no debate on the issue of the precise moment of Christ's capture turns up in patristic or medieval commentary.[12] But this is beside the point, for our purposes. The point here is that More actively seeks to determine the meaning of scripture by finding precedents for a reasonable interpretation within the community of faithful readers.

BIBLICAL EXEGESIS IN 'DE TRISTITIA'

In his influential study of Renaissance self-fashioning, Stephen Greenblatt remarks on 'a very odd quality of the Tower Works, namely, their mysterious passage from intensely personal meditation to what appears to be dry, tedious elaborations of scholastic theology'.[13] This characterization does not fairly or fully describe the tone, style or exegetical methods of *De Tristitia*. The work includes passages of great intensity, to be sure, but these are rarely 'intensely *personal*'. And while More's methods occasionally recall those of scholastic exegesis, his primary approach to biblical interpretation is better understood with reference to the tradition of *patristic* homiletics advocated and described by St Gregory in the *Praefatio in Iob*: 'he that treats of sacred writ should follow the way of a river ... if, in discussing any subject, he chance to find at hand any occasion of seasonable edification, he should, as it were, force the streams of discourse towards the adjacent valley, and when he has poured forth enough upon its level of instruction, fall back into the channel of discourse which he had prepared for himself'.[14] Gregory's approval of digression (expressed in the metaphor of the river of discourse), his emphasis on instruction and his attention to the needs of his audience are aptly applied to the kind of biblical exposition More practises in *De Tristitia*.

More exhibits his willingness to digress throughout *De Tristitia*. Thus as he begins to comment on 'the story of that time when the apostles were sleeping as the son of man was being betrayed', More allows himself to be drawn into an explanation of the term 'son of man', from there proceeds into the consideration 'that Christ is also betrayed into the hands of sinners when His most holy body in the sacrament is consecrated and handled by unchaste, profligate, and sacrilegious priests', and then offers the warning that we, too, must 'stay awake, get up, and pray continually' (*CW* 14:339–61). Acknowledging the circuitous route his discussion has taken, he concludes, 'But so much for my digression into these mysteries; let us now return to the historical events'.

As this passage suggests, More's digressions are sometimes related to another important feature of his exegetical methods: his application of the traditional four 'senses' of scripture identified by the Church Fathers. The determination to 'return to the historical events' from a 'digression into these mysteries' specifically invokes the idea that scripture has both literal (historical) and non-literal (spiritual) meanings. The spiritual senses of scripture, which More here groups together as 'mysteries', had different nuances in medieval theology: they might be allegorical (related to Christ and the Church), tropological (related to morality), or anagogical (related to the Last Things).[15] As Garry Haupt shows in his introduction to the Yale edition of the 'treatyce hystorycall' on the Passion (*CW* 13:lxii–lxv), More often privileges literal, historical readings, but he is by no means averse to offering spiritual ones as well, for (as he maintains early in *De Tristitia*) scripture offers 'a store of sacred mysteries' (*CW* 14:15) ripe for interpretation.

Moral and allegorical readings, for example, inform such passages in *De Tristitia* as the involved consideration of the Apostles' cowardly flight from Gethsemane and the identity of the young man described in the Gospel of Mark, who shed his linen cloth and fled naked when the Roman guards seized Christ. Here More's discussion of the strictly historical matter of the young man's identity is easily transposed into an exposition of the 'figurative meaning' (*CW* 14:599) of these events: 'it will be of no small use for us to gather wholesome spiritual counsels from the flight of the disciples before they were captured and from the escape of this young man after he was captured' (14:589). In fact, More devotes more space to moral and allegorical interpretations of the episode than he does to the question of the young man's identity: eighty-five lines as compared to sixty-five.

It is true that this kind of interpretation occasionally leads More to adopt what we might call 'quasi-scholastic' methods and style. For example, commenting on the significance of Peter's impulsive attempt to sever Malchus's ear in defending Jesus against the Roman guards, More explains that 'Christ chose not to reprove Peter sharply' (*CW* 14:489) and pursues this line of interpretation by offering a rather structured and formal three-part examination of the choice: 'He first rebuked him by giving a reason, then He declared Peter's act to be sinful, and finally He announced that even if He wished to avoid death He would not need Peter's protection ...' This approach is certainly reminiscent of the scholastic method of *divisiones*, the technique of dividing the text under discussion into parts and subparts. But More's treatment of the different aspects of Christ's response appears fluid and casual next to a full-blown scholastic commentary.

A comprehensive overview of scholastic exegesis is beyond the scope of this discussion, but the nature of high-medieval interpretation can perhaps be glimpsed in this passage of St Bonaventure's thirteenth-century commentary on the Gospel of Luke, where the Franciscan '*doctor seraphicus*' offers a preamble to his own commentary on Christ's betrayal as recounted in Luke 22:

> Now since Christ during his arrest was betrayed by a disciple and denied by Peter, this part has two components. The first treats *the manner of his arrest* while the second treats *Peter's denial* ... So in expressing *the manner of Christ's seizure and arrest*, the Evangelist introduces four items, that is, *the wiles of the betrayer, the zeal of the disciples, the power of the Savior,* and *the deceit of the Jews.*[16]

More's presentation of the same event is, by contrast, supple, wide-ranging and dynamic, less arid and analytical than Bonaventure's. He considers the significance of Judas's kiss as a signal to the Roman guards, compares Judas with Joab (another biblical traitor, in 2 Kings), addresses both Judas and Christ directly, and comments on the words 'If you seek me, let these go their way' by paraphrasing them in a dramatic, first-person amplification:

> If my blood is what the chief priests, the scribes, Pharisees, and the elders of the people are longing to drain away with such an eager

thirst, behold, when you were seeking me I came to meet you; when you did not know me, I betrayed myself to you; when you were prostrate, I stood nearby; now that you are arising, I stand ready to be taken captive.

(*CW* 14:436–7)

The effect of such an elaboration of the scriptural text is far from 'scholastic' – if by that term we mean a text so analytical that the drama and emotional intensity of scripture are obscured. In More's hands, Christ is portrayed as a fully realized human being, speaking in his own voice and responding emotionally to his betrayers.

If this passage undercuts the claim that *De Tristitia* is scholastic in its methods, it might also stand as a rebuttal of the idea that the work mixes scholasticism with specifically *personal* intensity. Certainly many of the examples More chooses to illustrate his points inevitably resonate with the circumstances under which he wrote *De Tristitia*, and it would be perverse to argue that some of the work's most important themes (martyrdom in particular, but also the use of prayer to allay fear, despair and spiritual laxity) have no bearing on More's personal predicament. In one notable passage, for example, he compares the intentional way in which Christ conducted his supplications at Gethsemane with the ill-considered, half-hearted prayers of ordinary Christians: 'Imagine, if you will, that you have committed a crime of high treason against some mortal prince or other who has your life in his hands but who is so merciful that he is prepared to temper his wrath because of your repentance' (*CW* 14:129). While the metaphor suggests More's own circumstances, its personal implications are nevertheless clearly limited – unless we are prepared to claim that More here implies repentance for a crime he officially and vehemently denied having committed. Indeed, throughout *De Tristitia*, the person on whom More focuses is Christ, and however tempting it is to do so, we would need to make unwarranted assumptions to see the dramatic and emotional passages of *De Tristitia* as merely autobiographical.

This is not to deny the *meditative* character of several key passages in *De Tristitia*; the influence of the meditative tradition has long been recognized as an important feature of More's prose in the Tower Works.[17] It can, for example, be observed in the same passage where we are admonished to conduct ourselves in prayer as if we were addressing someone who holds our life in his hands: More's instruction to the reader ('Imagine, if you will') specifically invokes the meditative practice of visualizing a scene for prayer and contemplation, and as this section of *De Tristitia* begins, More likewise urges, 'Reader, let us pause for a little at this point and contemplate with a devout mind our commander lying on the ground in humble supplication' (*CW* 14:114–15). This language draws on the terminology of such meditative classics known to More as the *Scala perfectionis* by the fourteenth-century mystic Walter Hilton, where meditation, contemplation and prayer are commended as essential to the reading of scripture (*CW* 13:lxxxiii–cxiii). Indeed, humanist exegesis of scripture (and More's is no exception) welcomed such affective interpretive practices and affirmed that 'interpretation, meditation, and prayer are one and the same'.[18]

But the meditative strains of *De Tristitia* are subsumed in its homiletic and didactic features even when the work is most personal. When More exhorts the reader to 'imagine' or to 'contemplate', the exhortation is also an invitation to engage in a *shared* experience. This awareness of an audience to whom he addresses himself suggests that in this last work More was less inwardly focused than we are sometimes led to believe. In some ways, the circumstances under which he composed *De Tristitia* may have led us as readers to search the work too diligently for what it reveals about the inward motions of his soul, causing us to see purely individualistic or private significance where he rather attempts, like a preacher addressing a congregation, to engage public and communal ones. Thus, in a passage full of obvious personal resonance, he considers the example offered by 'a thousand' martyrs who have (like Christ) faced death despite their fears (*CW* 14:73). Significantly, though, the treatment of martyrdom seems here to deflect (rather than enforce) personal references, when More addresses the reader much as a homilist might address his listeners: 'For do you imagine that, since most holy martyrs shed their blood for the faith, they had no fear at all of death and torments? On this point I will not pause to draw up a list; to me Paul may stand for a thousand others.' The subject of martyrdom is a major theme of *De Tristitia*, but the manner and tone in which More explores it are not introspective and personal. And while the choice of subject and the intensity of More's engagement with it surely reflect the circumstances under which he wrote the work, in general *De Tristitia* looks not inward but outward – to Christ and to Christian believers.

At times, More seems to imagine himself addressing an audience consisting of an overly analytical (perhaps even scholastic) theologian, rather than a naive congregation, as if he were engaged in a debate on the question of Christ's humanity. Thus, anticipating the objections of 'some meticulous fussy dissector of the divine plan' to Christ's apparently futile and certainly unnecessary efforts to rouse the Apostles from sleep, More answers the question of an imagined interlocutor – 'Could He not at one and the same time speak the command and ensure its execution?' (*CW* 14:197) – with an impatient dismissal: 'Doubtless He could have, my good man, since He was God.' The argument which follows (Christ could have, but did not, enforce his command to stay awake because he desired the Apostles' voluntary co-operation) effectively moves the interpretation to the level of allegory, in which both More and his audience are involved as a general condition of being fallen human beings: 'such is God's kindness that even when we are negligent and slumbering on the pillow of our sins, He disturbs us from time to time' (14:203).

More's occasionally pithy and even vulgar language also reveals his awareness of an audience and draws attention to an overlooked side of *De Tristitia*, which as we have seen has sometimes been regarded as 'otherworldly'. When, for example, More compares the prayer habits of Christ with those of sixteenth-century Christians, his tone and diction are those of the homilist chastising his congregation. Thus, by comparison with Christ, 'we' merely pretend to pray in church, cushioning ourselves in our pews 'like a propped up house that is threatening to tumble down' (*CW* 14:127), and revealing our lack of attention to the words of the Mass: 'We scratch our heads, clean our fingernails with a pocketknife, pick our noses with our fingers, meanwhile making the wrong responses.'

But if the Christ of *De Tristitia* exceeds ordinary Christians in the fervency and focus of his prayer life, he also exceeds them in his very human fear of death; he is no disembodied spirit impervious to human emotion. In the best-known passage of the work, More imagines Christ speaking directly to those among his followers who may be experiencing fear at the prospect of dying:

> O faint of heart, take courage and do not despair. You are afraid, you are sad, you are stricken with weariness and dread of the torment with which you have been cruelly threatened. Trust me. I conquered the world, and yet I suffered immeasurably more from fear, I was sadder, more afflicted with weariness, more horrified at the prospect of such cruel suffering drawing eagerly nearer and nearer.
>
> (*CW* 14:101)

As in many other passages, Christ is here made to seem a living, suffering, speaking person, one who admits to his own fear and fatigue even as he comforts others similarly afflicted. The portrayal suggests that an advantage of both the meditative and homiletic tendencies of More's exegetical methods is the ease with which they shade into dramatic colloquy. Through such vivid realizations as this, More's commentary comes very close to being less exegetical than literary.

THEMATIC STRANDS AND LITERARY STYLE

The chapter of the *Monotessaron* which More tells us he has 'generally followed in enumerating the events of the passion' in *De Tristitia* is entitled simply 'De oratione Jesu et sua captione' ('The prayer and capture of Jesus'), a heading which summarizes the main narrative events of the Agony in the Garden. That More's commentary expands on these events to address themes of psychological depth and theological complexity is suggested by the work's full title, over which he took some care: *De tristitia tedio pauore et oratione Christi ante captionem eius* ('The sadness, the weariness, the fear and the prayer of Christ before he was taken prisoner').[19] Despite the manuscript's digressions, it is artfully constructed and was perhaps nearing the final stages of its composition when More was forced to cease working on it (see *CW* 14:752–3). Two subjects, prayer and martyrdom, are of primary concern throughout, and More's subtle returns to the emotions and behaviour attributed to Christ in the title function as a structural leitmotif, framing and unifying the whole. This loosely but carefully structured framework allows More to explore such questions as how the humanity of Christ is revealed by the Gethsemane story, whether fear is compatible with martyrdom, and in what way spiritual attentiveness is essential to effective prayer and Christian life in general, particularly for bishops and others who are responsible for guarding the Church against heresy. At least two of these concerns (the acceptability of fear on the part of the martyr and the spiritual attentiveness necessary for embattled Christians) were of obvious personal importance to More as he composed *De Tristitia*. But these and other themes of the work are treated as matters of public moment and with such literary sophistication that we ought to suspect that More envisioned the work being read by a public audience beyond the More family circle and intended it for more than private, devotional uses.

The importance to More of portraying Christ's humanity is apparent early in *De Tristitia*, when he comments on the verse '*Tristis est anima mea usque ad mortem*' (Matthew 26:39, Mark 14:34, John 12:27). As Miller notes, the passage in the *Monotessaron* which treats this verse suggests three points for discussion – the selection of Peter, John and James to keep watch with Christ in prayer, Christ's 'sadness unto death', and his command to the selected three Apostles to 'stay here' while he himself withdraws to pray alone – but after cancelling a first draft which drew him into an extended discussion of the first and third points, More deliberately chose to emphasize the second (CW 14:797, note to 45/2–47/1). In the final version, the scriptural adjective (*tristis*) is expanded and amplified as a list of nouns, so that Christ is portrayed as experiencing a decidedly human 'sharp and bitter attack of sadness, grief, fear, and weariness' ('*tristitiam / mesticiam / pauorem ac tedium / tam acriter e uestigio ac tam acerbe in se sensit irruere*'). Christ's sadness, More argues, is no more surprising than his hunger, thirst or fatigue (the perfectly normal vulnerabilities of all human beings), and his agony, like these other characteristics, thus demonstrates commonality with his merely human followers.

It is possible that More's emphasis on the humanity of Christ in *De Tristitia* owes something to Erasmus's debate with John Colet on the nature of Christ's Agony at Gethsemane, published in 1503 as *Disputatiuncula de taedio, pavore, tristicia Iesu, instante crucis hora* ('A short debate concerning the distress, alarm, and sorrow of Jesus, as the Crucifixion drew nigh'), a title suggestive of More's; and (as we have seen) a number of passages in *De Tristitia* have the character of a polemical disputation.[20] Erasmus advocates the view that the supplication 'Let this cup pass from me' (Matthew 26:42) should be interpreted to mean that 'Christ's dread arose from the simple fact that his mind felt in advance, as it were, the pain of such an affront to nature' (*CWE* 70:48). The point for Erasmus is that Christ truly 'feared his own death'; like More, he asserts that Christ 'had reason to fear death not only as other mortals do, but even more keenly than anyone else' (70:25).

Whether he relied on Erasmus's work or not, emphasis on Christ's willingness to share the weaknesses of mortal flesh allows More to develop a contrast between the sadness and weariness of Christ and other, less salutary forms of fatigue which can lead to sin. The Apostles also suffered from sadness (*tristicia*) in Gethsemane, but their grief caused them to fall asleep, rather than to obey Christ's command to watch and pray. While the Apostles' sorrow is understandable and even commendable, their sleep is not: 'Certainly the apostles' feeling of sadness because of the danger to their master was praiseworthy, but for them to be so overcome by sadness as to yield completely to sleep, that was certainly wrong' (*CW* 14:263). The contrast between Christ's sadness, which leads (properly, in More's view) to prayer, and the

Apostles', which leads (dangerously) to sleep, occasions a digressive and tropological interpretation of the negligence of sixteenth-century bishops, whose metaphorical nodding off has allowed heresy to infiltrate the Church (14:259–75).

Indeed, as Brenda Hosington has demonstrated in her comprehensive and perceptive discussion of the imagery of sleeping and waking in *De Tristitia*, More consistently associates falling asleep with spiritual laxity and inattention.[21] When More castigates those whose minds wander during prayer by commenting on the fervent prayers of Christ (*CW* 14:113–59), he specifically compares their 'absurd fantasies' (14:121) to dreams which enter the mind during sleep. The dangers of sleep, during which the devil has access to the unguarded mind, is a well-known trope, and More returns to it seven times in the course of *De Tristitia*. Even the Apostles' flight from the garden in response to Christ's capture by the Roman guards (an otherwise energetic action) is pictured as the result of their inattentive, drowsy state of mind: drowsy and insensible ('*nutantes et incogitantes*'), their earlier failure to stay awake and pray weakens their will and renders them unable 'to bear all with patience' (14:563).

The drowsy sadness of the Apostles must thus be distinguished from the wakeful sadness of their master. More insists and even dwells on the theological justification for sadness from the very beginning of the work, offering an extended allegorical application of the hidden meanings of the place names 'Cedron' (Sadness) and 'Gethsemane' (Most fertile valley): 'we must (I say) cross over the valley and stream of Cedron, a valley of tears and a stream of sadness whose waves can wash away the blackness and filth of our sins' (*CW* 14:19). In thus validating a certain kind of sadness as an acceptable mental state for the Christian, More appears to depart from the teaching of such standard authorities on the subject of sin as John Cassian. For Cassian, writing in *De caenohioruni institutis libri XII*, a handbook of monastic conduct, *tristitia* is a prelude to the deadly sin of despair (*acedia*).[22] Arising from a sense of anger or frustration over undeserved afflictions or wrongs against the self, sadness, for Cassian, signalled a moral disorder of the soul which, if left untreated, could have grave consequences for the monk who suffered from it.[23] But as the pattern of sleep imagery in *De Tristitia* makes clear, spiritual inattention (pictured figuratively as sleep), rather than sadness, is the real enemy for More.

Such thematic contrasts as that between spiritual sleep and wakefulness are an important feature of the work throughout. The contrast between the sadness of the Apostles and the sadness of Christ, for example, is itself embedded in a contrast between the wakefulness of Christ in prayer and the wakefulness of Judas in betrayal (*CW* 14:259–93). Elsewhere, Christ's humanity is contrasted with his divinity, the body is contrasted with the soul, the literal sense of scripture is contrasted with the spiritual sense, and reluctant martyrs are contrasted with eager ones. Clarence Miller's brilliant discussion of the Latin style of *De Tristitia* has demonstrated how frequently these thematic contrasts are enforced stylistically by parallel constructions (14:754–76). A typical example of such parallelism shows the contrast between eager and fearful martyrs. Here, the contrast is rendered through a *sic … ut* construction and a pair of clauses beginning with *alius*: 'And so God proportions the temperaments of His martyrs according to His own providence in such a way that one rushes forth eagerly to his death, another creeps out hesitantly and fearfully, but for all that bears his death bravely' ('*Sic pro sua prouidentia martyrum suorum affectus temperat / ut alius alacer ad mortem prouolet / alius cunctanter et timide prorepat*') (14:249).

Stylistic parallelism in the service of paired contrasts bespeaks a sense of balance and restraint, and this impulse can also be observed on the thematic level. As the passage quoted above suggests, not only does More validate sadness in the face of spiritual torment; he also recognizes fear as an acceptable response to martyrdom. Although More is reported by his biographer and son-in-law William Roper to have told his family that 'if he might perceive his wife and children would encourage him to die in a good cause, it should so comfort him that, for very joy thereof, it would make him merrily run to death' (Roper 228), martyrdom was not a vocation for sixteenth-century Catholics, and the discussion of martyrdom in *De Tristitia* carefully (and significantly, for readers inclined to understand the work as a key to More's own martyrdom) balances willingness to die for Christ with reluctance to die at all.[24]

In fact, the official position of the Catholic Church with regard to martyrdom was (and remained throughout the sixteenth century) marked by complexity. The New Testament word μάρτυς (which More adopts as a Latin cognate) designates 'a witness' in the legal sense of 'one who testifies to a fact on the basis of personal observation'.[25] Thus, for example, the word is applied in Acts 2:32 to the Apostles as first-hand observers of the resurrection: οὗ πάντες ἡμεῖς ἐσμεν μάρτυρες ('to which we are all witnesses'). However, even within the lifetime of the Apostles, this usage was gradually replaced by the more familiar meaning of a person who, without the benefit of personal observation, nonetheless dies attesting to faith in the fact of the Resurrection and its efficacy for believers.[26] By the second century CE, in reaction to over-zealousness on the part of some Christians (including those in positions of ecclesiastical power, such as Ignatius, bishop of Antioch), Rome began to weigh claims of martyrdom against evidence that individual martyrs might have attempted too actively and for the wrong reasons to make the ultimate sacrifice.[27] Riding a fine line between honouring self-sacrifice and discouraging acts which could threaten civic stability, the medieval Church sought to emphasize the heroic qualities of its martyrs and in so doing to distance them from ordinary believers.[28] Thus (as Karen A. Winstead has recently shown), the message of the *Legenda aurea* (*The Golden Legend*, the collection of hagiographies that became a primary source of knowledge about the saints and martyrs for the lay medieval reader) was that 'Fearlessness is the mark of sanctity'.[29]

For all that post-Reformation martyrologies consciously tried to separate themselves from the *Legenda aurea*, the ideal of Protestant martyrdom in the latter half of the sixteenth century followed a similar pattern of highly individualized, heroic acts.[30] Foxe's *Acts and Monuments*, published at the beginning of Elizabeth's reign, abounds with examples, but his hagiographical portraits of superhuman heroes of the faith may be adequately represented by the following account of the martyrdom of James Bainham, burnt during More's chancellorship: 'as he was at the stake, in the midst of the flaming fire, which fire had half consumed his arms and legs, he spake these words: "O ye papists! behold, ye look for miracles, and here now ye may see a miracle; for in this fire I feel no more pain, than if I were in a bed of down."'[31] The implied argument of such popular works as the *Legenda aurea* and *Acts and Monuments* is that martyrs possess heroic courage and bravery and thus are fearless in the face of death. More makes precisely the opposite argument in *De Tristitia*. Fearlessness, he asserts, is fine as far as it goes, but it does not go very far, since few flesh-and-blood people, saintly or otherwise, are unafraid to die. In keeping with the homiletic and didactic methods which inform *De Tristitia* throughout, More challenges the idea that martyrs should face death without fear by anticipating the objections of his audience to his description of the 'bitter attack of sadness, grief, fear, and weariness' (*CW* 14:43) that Christ experienced while praying and awaiting capture by the Roman guards.

These hypothetical objections are that it is not possible that Christ was afraid of captors over whom he had divine power; that we know that Christian martyrs have 'rushed to their deaths eagerly and joyfully', and Christ is 'the very prototype and leader of martyrs, the standard-bearer'; and that Christ sets the precedent for Christian behaviour and could not therefore encourage 'slackness' by approving the fear and hesitation of reluctant martyrs (*CW* 14:53–7). More's answers to these objections are carefully balanced and precisely worked out. Here as elsewhere in *De Tristitia*, a style featuring parallel constructions is one way in which he achieves balance and precision in making complex theological points. Thus, for example, commenting on Christ's reluctance to drink the cup of martyrdom, More carefully argues that 'He said all these things not as God, but insofar as He was man', and drives the point home with sentences that are symmetrical in both thought and construction: 'We ourselves provide a parallel: because we are composed of body and soul, we sometimes apply to our whole selves things which actually are true only of the soul and on the other hand we sometimes speak of ourselves when strict accuracy would require us to speak of our bodies alone. For we say that the martyrs go straight to heaven when they die, whereas actually only their souls are taken up to heaven' (14:181–3).

To such a finely observed synecdoche as this, More adds other elements which convey a sense of balance. Miller's analysis of revisions to the Valencia manuscript shows that More at times exercises 'a lawyerlike caution'; this is certainly evident in such passages as those where he enumerates circumstances and exceptions under which he believes 'it is not very safe' to undertake martyrdom (*CW* 14:241). Still another device which reveals the cautionary note in More's treatment of martyrdom (and other major themes of the work) is his occasional use of ironic understatement. Anticipating that his imagined interlocutor will cite the scriptural proverb (quoted by Paul in 2 Corinthians 9:7) that 'God loves a cheerful giver' and therefore prizes a joyful martyr more highly than a reluctant one, More counters that God also loves such paradigmatic sufferers of tribulation as Tobias and Job, although 'neither of them, so far as I know, was exactly jumping with joy or clapping his hands out of happiness'.

From even this brief list of illustrations, it is clear that More's attitude towards martyrdom in *De Tristitia* is balanced and restrained. But martyrdom in *De Tristitia* is also paradoxical. If More insists that authentic martyrdom may properly be accompanied by fear, he also consistently pictures the martyr as a soldier whose death acts as a blazon for others. In a pattern that is repeated throughout the work, martyrdom is associated with images of warfare and testimony: Christ is 'the standard-bearer' ('*antesignanum*') of martyrdom, its authoritative exemplar ('*authorem christum*'). At the same time, Christ's trepidation in Gethsemane authorizes a humanizing timidity on the battlefield of martyrdom, and his agony paradoxically provides 'a fighting technique and a battle code for the faint-hearted soldier who needs to be swept along, as it were, into martyrdom' (*CW* 14:109). If More's martyr is a soldier of the faith, he is a decidedly unheroic one.

Indeed, although he praises heroic martyrs for their courage, it is clear that More endorses the paradox of reluctant martyrdom. Pressing the paradox home, he suggests that the courage of the eager martyr offers but one paradigm for authentic martyrdom, and may be the result of a kind of anaesthetizing divine inspiration, an ecstatic joy ('*gaudio*'), that masks the natural fear of physical pain, just as 'we often see it happen that some men do not feel wounds inflicted in battle until their awareness, which had been displaced by strong feeling, returns to them and they notice the injury' (*CW* 14:244–5). According to More, such displacement is 'an unearned felicity, ... not the measure of future reward in heaven' (14:245). Returning to the leitmotif of the title, More suggests (again paradoxically and ironically) that a reluctant martyr may thus in fact be more courageous than an eager one, 'unless someone perhaps imagines he ought to be thought less brave for having fought down not only his other enemies but also his own weariness, sadness, and fear – most strong feelings and mighty enemies indeed' (14:249).

The paradoxical image of the brave but reluctant soldier – one whose enemies include his own fears and whose most courageous act may be his mastery of them – is related to a stylistic tendency in *De Tristitia* that works against balance, a tendency to multiply meanings beyond the demands of precision, to shift viewpoints and to disrupt parallel structures. Miller has commented that despite its many balanced constructions, More's style in *De Tristitia* is 'restless, nervous, and muscular', and this, too, is observable when the question of martyrdom is at issue (*CW* 14:770). More thus concedes that both eager and fearful martyrs should be admired, but he amplifies and exaggerates the concession with a burst of additional verbs by which we may respond to martyrs: 'we should admire both kinds of most holy martyrs, we should venerate both kinds, praise God for both, we should imitate both when the situation demands it, each according to his own capacity and according to the grace God gives to each' ('*ut sanctissimorum martyrum utrumque genus admiremur / utrumque deueneremur / in utroque laudemus deum / utrumque quum res postulat pro suo quisque captu prout gratiam dederit deus imitemur*') (14:251). Although the verbs follow the same pattern, they add different and, in this case, not entirely logical shades of meaning: the idea that 'we should imitate both when the situation demands it' disrupts the pattern and begs the question (how a single martyr faced with imminent death might both rush forward and hang back is exactly the problem), causing More to finish the sentence with the qualifying *'pro ... prout'* clause.

It is possible that More's style – at once balanced and cautious, paradoxical and profuse – may reflect complicated and somewhat conflicting motives for writing the work. For reasons both political and doctrinal he may have wished to quell suspicion that he had courted his own martyrdom. Letters More wrote from the Tower (*SL* nos. 200, 210, 213, 214, 216) repeatedly refer to the charge made against him by his interrogators that in refusing to explain the 'reasons of conscience' which prevented him from taking the Oath of Succession, he was 'obstinate', a posture that could have been interpreted as a deliberate and passive provocation, one which could only achieve the outcome it actually did – execution. (In *De Tristitia*, the imaginary interlocutor's anticipated objections to More's validation of reluctant martyrdom are, after all, largely concerned with the apparent passivity of Christ in Gethsemane.) The nuanced argument against overzealous martyrdom could certainly answer this objection, as well as establish More's orthodoxy on this issue.

Then, too, More may have been conscious of the danger of unduly inciting 'copycat' martyrs, imitators who might find themselves better equipped to face persecution and death after reading the work than they had been before. Miller has suggested that the choice of Latin as the language in which to write *De Tristitia* freed More to dwell at length on the negligence of bishops who had 'fallen asleep' to the dangers of heresy, a subject he would have been unlikely to have wanted to make more accessible to readers at this point in time by discussing it in English (*CW* 14:711–12). By the same reasoning, it is possible that the choice of Latin also enabled the work's complicated and subtle treatment of martyrdom without running the risk of encouraging less sophisticated readers to follow suit without cause. In Latin, More might easily express theological subtleties to an audience of educated people in England and on the Continent, an audience he perhaps wished to persuade that in refusing to swear the Oath of Succession he had not sought the scaffold through wilful pride, but had rather imitated Christ, 'who teaches by his own example that his soldier should take humility as his starting point' (14:113).

These are possible explanations for the complex style of *De Tristitia*, for its nuanced attitude towards difficult subjects and the choice of Latin in which to convey them. Yet if these possibilities allow us to glimpse More's own motivation as a martyr, they ought not to encourage us to read *De Tristitia* too exclusively as a semi-autobiographical account of More's own spiritual predicament. More's sixteenth-century editors and biographers, along with many later observers, have sometimes made it seem that the primary achievement of *De Tristitia* is its transcendence of public concerns, its personal and devotional nature. Yet both its exegetical and its literary methods suggest that the work's public concerns are just as significant as what it implies for More's private and personal dilemma. Homiletic impulses, didacticism, awareness of and interaction with its audience, such highly rhetorical literary devices as irony and paradox, complexity of argument and style: all these characteristics of *De Tristitia* bespeak a work entirely consistent with the rest of More's lifelong dedication not merely to the inner workings of the self but to 'the whole corps of Christendom'.

FURTHER READING

The definitive edition of *De Tristitia* is *CW* 14 (1976), ed. Clarence H. Miller and including the Latin text with modern English translation, an invaluable facsimile of the Valencia manuscript in More's hand, Miller's superb Introduction and Commentary, and the translation by Mary Basset which first appeared in the 1557 edition of More's English works. A useful recent edition intended for non-specialist readers is *The Sadness of Christ and Final Prayers and Benedictions* (Princeton, N.J.: Scepter, 1993), which reprints Miller's translation along with a brief introduction to More's career by Gerard B. Wegemer. Miller's 'The heart of the final struggle: More's commentary on the Agony in the Garden', in Michael J. Moore, ed., *Quincentennial Essays on St. Thomas More* (Boone, N.C.: Albion, 1978), 108–23, condenses some of the discussion of the Valencia manuscript and More's exegetical methods found in the Introduction to *CW* 14.

The publication in the Yale edition of *De Tristitia* and More's other late writings has generated renewed interest in them as devotional and literary works. In addition to his Introduction to *CW* 13 – an indispensible guide to the Tower Works in general and *De Tristitia* in particular – Garry E. Haupt wrote an important assessment of 'The personal and impersonal in the late works of Sir Thomas More', *Interpretations: Studies in Language and Literature* 6 (1974), 14–23. Louis L. Martz's discussion of the last works in *Thomas More: The Search for the Inner*

Man (New Haven and London: Yale University Press, 1990) concludes with a chapter on *De Tristitia* as a deeply personal expression of More's humanism and fear of martyrdom. Seymour Baker House's 'A martyr's theology of assent: reading Thomas More's *De Tristitia Christi*', *Renaissance and Reformation* 29 (2005), 49–63, focuses on *De Tristitia* as a devotional work offering More and his readers a rationale for accepting martyrdom. In 'Endgame: the genesis of *The Sadness of Christ*', *Moreana* 45, no. 174 (2008), 33–54, House argues that it is possible to date More's composition of *De Tristitia* in late spring 1535, when he realized that his martyrdom was unavoidable. In the same issue of *Moreana*, Miller addressed the variety of More's methods as a biblical commentator, in 'More's biblical exegesis in *De Tristitia Christi*' (17–32).

For general background on the history of martyrdom in the Christian tradition, see W. H. C. Frend's classic work, *Martyrdom and Persecution in the Early Church* (Oxford: Blackwell, 1965). Helen C. White's still unsurpassed *Tudor Books of Saints and Martyrs* (Madison: University of Wisconsin Press, 1963) (which includes substantial discussion of *De Tristitia* in a chapter on 'The Catholic martyrs under Henry') is complemented by the excellent comparative, cross-confessional survey in Brad S. Gregory's *Salvation at Stake: Christian Martyrdom in Early Modern Europe* (Cambridge, Mass.: Harvard University Press, 1999).

Notes

1. For the letters written 'with a coal' (that is, a pencil of charcoal) see *SL* 234–5, 254, 256. For the unlikelihood that the longer works were composed without pen and ink, see *CW* 12:xlvi.
2. See e.g., John Guy, *Thomas More*, 180–1.
3. See lviii of Martz's introduction to *CW* 12, and Alistair Fox, *Thomas More: History and Providence* (London: Blackwell, 1982), 253. Basset translates the Latin phrase (quoted from the Vulgate, with a misspelling of *iniecerunt*) as 'they laid hands on Jesus'.
4. *History and Providence*, 253.
5. *Thomas More*, 181.
6. See John J. Ryan, *The Apostolic Conciliarism of Jean Gerson* (Atlanta: Scholars Press, 1998). On More's conciliar views, see Richard Marius, 'More the conciliarist', *Moreana* 17, no. 64 (1980), 91–9.
7. The modern edition of his writings (with a brief biographical introduction) is Jean Gerson, *Oeuvres complètes*, ed. Mgr Palemon Glorieux, 10 vols. (Paris: Desclée, 1960–73). The *Monotessaron* appears in 9:245–373.
8. *CW* 14:619. Throughout, I quote *De Tristitia* in Miller's translation (although sometimes adding More's Latin).

9. More uses this phrase in *The Debellation of Salem and Bizance* (*CW* 10:9, 229) and in the later letters (*SL* 252); see also above, 81, 199–200. His convictions about the authority of the laws of Christendom are discussed by James Hitchcock, 'Thomas More and the *sensus fidelium*', *Theological Studies* 36 (1975), 145–54, and Brian Gogan, *The Common Corps of Christendom: Ecclesiological Themes in the Writings of Sir Thomas More* (Leiden: Brill, 1982).

10. See Germain Marc'hadour, *The Bible in the Works of St. Thomas More*, 5 vols. (Nieuwkoop: B. de Graaf, 1969–72), 4:20–32; Richard Marius, 'Thomas More and the early Church Fathers', *Traditio* 24 (1968), 379–407; and Gogan, *Common Corps of Christendom*, 69–70.

11. James Simpson, *Burning to Read: English Fundamentalism and Its Reformation Opponents* (Cambridge, Mass.: Belknap Press, 2007), 251.

12. See Miller's Commentary, notes to *CW* 14:619/8–621/3 and 621/5–623/5.

13. *Renaissance Self-Fashioning: From More to Shakespeare* (Chicago and London: University of Chicago Press, 2005 [1980]), 72.

14. Quoted and translated by Beryl Smalley, *The Study of the Bible in the Middle Ages* (Notre Dame, Ind.: University of Notre Dame Press, 1978 [1952]), 33.

15. Ibid., 28, and Henri de Lubac, *The Four Senses of Scripture*, trans. Mark Sebanc, 4 vols. (Grand Rapids, Mich.: Eerdmans, 1998), 1:15–74.

16. *Commentary on the Gospel of Luke*, trans. and ed. Robert J. Karris, in *The Works of St. Bonaventure*, ed. Philotheus Boehner and M. Frances Laughlin (Saint Bonaventure, N.Y.: Franciscan Institute, 1955–; 2001–4), 8, Part 3:2090.

17. Haupt, *CW* 13:lxxxiii–cxiii; Martz, *CW* 12:lxxvii–lxxxvi.

18. Michel Jeanneret, 'Renaissance exegesis', *The Cambridge History of Literary Criticism*, 9 vols. (Cambridge University Press, 1989–), 3:33–44.

19. On the carefully weighed composition of the title, see Miller, *CW* 14:738–40.

20. Giovanni Saltinello, 'Thomas More's *Expositio Passionis*', *EA* 455–61. The *Disputatiuncula* is translated in *CWE* 70:9–67.

21. '*Quid dormitis?*': More's use of sleep as a motif in *De Tristitia*', *Moreana* 26, no. 100 (1989), 55–68.

22. See *Institutes*, trans. Boniface Ramsey, Ancient Christian Writers: The Works of the Fathers in Translation, no. 58 (New York: Newman, 2000), 211 (9:1).

23. Cassian's views are discussed in detail by Kenneth C. Russell, 'John Cassian on sadness', *Cistercian Studies Quarterly* 38 (2003), 7–18.

24. I owe this point to Guy, *Thomas More*, 168. On More's attitude to martyrdom, see also above, 226 ff.

25. Allison A. Trites, *The New Testament Concept of Witness* (Cambridge University Press, 1977), 78–80.

26. See W. H. C. Frend, *Martyrdom and Persecution in the Early Church* (Oxford: Blackwell, 1965), 88.

27. Henry Chadwick, *The Early Church* (New York: Dorset, 1967), 28–31; Frend, *Martyrdom*, 216–20.

28. Sherry L. Reames, *The 'Legenda aurea': A Reexamination of Its Paradoxical History* (Madison: University of Wisconsin Press, 1985), 199–202.

29. 'Fear in late-medieval English martyr legends', in Johann Leemans, ed., *More Than a Memory: The Discourse of Martyrdom and the Construction of Christian Identity in the History of Christianity* (Louvain: Peeters, 2005), 204.

30. Helen C. White, *Tudor Books of Saints and Martyrs* (in 'Further reading'); John R. Knott, *Discourses of Martyrdom in English Literature, 1563–1694* (Cambridge University Press, 1993).

31. *The Acts and Monuments of John Foxe*, ed. George Townsend, 8 vols. (New York: AMS, 1965 [1843–49]), 4:705.

Part III

Reception

12 Afterlives

'Utopia' is a 'medieval fantasy game ... where the lowliest of peasants can become the world's greatest heroes ... Every decision, every challenge will be yours and yours alone.

From a Google search of 'Utopia'

Sometimes a neologism's afterlife is even busier than that of its inventor. A recent Google search of 'Thomas More' brought 2,500,000 hits, but a search of 'utopia' yielded exactly 18,000,000. All those zeros! How fitting for More's Nowhere, even though its name is now nearly everywhere, even reimagined – witness my epigraph – as a computer game combining feudalism with American get-up-and-go.

What of the man who coined 'utopia'? More's early biographer William Roper reports that after his arraignment More told his judges (as he told others) that he and they would 'in heaven merrily all meet together' (Roper 250). This essay, however, will focus on More's earthly afterlife and that of his two major works *The History of King Richard the Third* and *Utopia*. In his own day his Latin epigrams were widely enjoyed, his savage polemics roundly condemned but just as savagely answered by William Tyndale and other Reformers, and his eloquent Tower Works (particularly the *Dialogue of Comfort against Tribulation*) published and, if we may judge from a few allusions, read with appreciation. But More's later fame was shaped largely by ambivalent memories of the man, by the usurping duke of York whom he helped make an archetype of pathologically cunning tyranny, and by the famous island that gave us the word 'utopia', the genre of utopian fantasy, and eventually, in an expansion of More's pun on u/eutopia, the word 'dystopia'. It is on these three afterlives – of the person and his two most influential books – that I will focus.

More went to his death a convicted traitor, and yet his posthumous reputation even in Protestant England (under Mary Tudor there was no danger in praising him) remained high, whatever the accusations of the Reformers with whom he had tangled in his polemical works. To look through the allusions to him before 1640, so usefully collected or cited in Jackson Boswell's *Sir Thomas More in the English Renaissance* (and hence not stressed in this essay), is to find compliments to his wit, his learning, his filial piety, his integrity and his imagination, as well as the exploitation of Utopia as a convenient nowhere to put ideas or people and a dangerous impracticality, if also as a source of anecdote.[1] True, one also finds denunciations, many printed before the start of Elizabeth's reign, of what Protestants thought Catholic errors and malicious anti-Reformist propaganda.

Even modern scholars who find Thomas More a darker figure – burner of heretics, front man for the Tudors – than the better known brave soul of more popular fame usually agree that More had a lively wit, however deployed. How that wit has been imagined, though, has shifted over the centuries, and now sophisticated readers of *Utopia*, for example, need to keep repeating, to those for whom the island is primarily a dream of perfection, that both books of the work vibrate with irony and that Utopia itself is in part a carnivalized non-England, a world without lawyers by a lawyer, one in which slaves, not European statesmen, wear gold chains (or are those statesmen slaves to the kings who own them?). For earlier generations, though, More had seemed to many less witty than 'merry', given to foxy subtlety, maybe, but also to jests and practical jokes.

Contemporary evidence for this 'merry' More includes notice of the sort of anecdotes and snappy comebacks that writers on rhetoric had long recommended to lawyers and orators; even the practical jokes credited to More had a place in a statesman's life, or so suggests a section on jests in Castiglione's *Courtier*. The early modern More was broadly humorous, sharply observant and given to puns and ingenious analogies that unfold in the imagination. His writings are indeed remarkable for the 'merry tales', especially in the polemics and, as pills to purge melancholy, in the *Dialogue of Comfort*.[2] More's early translations of Lucian may have contributed to his image, although allusions to them are few, but the mini-anecdotes among his epigrams are jests of the sort some humanists, with classical precedent, were collecting.[3] A few jokes in Ottmar Luscinius's *Joci ac Sales Mire Festivi* (Augsburg, 1524/5), for example, turn More's verses to prose. Because it is so easy to confuse an author with his persona, moreover, and because even so learned a poet as John Skelton, who played the fool in verse, became the protagonist of a jest-book, one can speculate that had More not been a statesman with a tragic end, he might well have figured in such a work. A hint of what might have been shows in the margins of a book in which Gabriel Harvey scribbled jokes credited to More.[4]

This 'merry', if also wise, More figures comfortably in early biographies. Two seventeenth-century volumes each devote a separate section to his 'wit and wisdom', both indebted to the pages on More's 'quick wit' in the Catholic Thomas Stapleton's *Vita Mori*.[5] Made longer, published separately, these collections might look something like jest-books, if perhaps more akin to the early humanist ones than to the later world of Robert Armin's *Nest of Ninnies* (1608) or the anonymous *Pasquils Jests with the Merriments of Mother Bunch* (1629; true, the clowning seventeenth-century 'Water-Poet' John Taylor wrote some verses in Utopian).

One collection appears in John Hoddesdon's *History of Sr. Thomas More ... Collected Out of Severall Authors* (1652), printed early in republican England by a man of mildly Puritan sympathies. Hoddesdon much admires More, although offering no comment on *Utopia* (after all, he was living in what some might call a utopian experiment), and he claims implausibly that Henry VIII had meant to kill only More's body, not his reputation. He enlivens his text with familiar anecdotes and sayings taken from earlier biographers, including such examples of More's scaffold humour as saying, 'I pray you Mr. Lieutenant see me safe up, and for my coming down let me shift for myself' (129; from Roper 254). Hoddesdon ends with 'A view of Sir Thomas More's wit and wisdome' and a selection of apophthegms taken from Stapleton. The wit is not always entirely kind: one story concerns a friend who, following More's advice, converted a book to verse and was then told, 'Yea marry, now it is somewhat; for now it is Rime, before it was neither Rime nor Reason' (139).

Hoddesdon claims that More's 'merry jests and witty sayings, were they together, were sufficient to fill a volume', evidence that the never-realized Thomas More Jestbook was imaginable, but he concludes with what his margin calls 'An Apologie for Sir Tho. M. pleasantnesse of wit', necessitated by 'an English Chronologer that terms him a scoffing man' because 'his writings and doings were full of witty jests, calling him a wise foolish man; or a foolish wise man' (an old pun on *moro*soph). So 'I think it very fit to set down in this place, the reason (out of his own writings) why he hath used so many pleasant passages in his books'. There follows a page or so (147–8), mostly credited to More himself, yet taken – without acknowledgement – from *The Life and Death of Sir Thomas Moore* by More's great-grandson Cresacre More (Douai, ?1631).⁶ Just as doctors put something sweet in medicine to make it taste better, Hoddesdon quotes More as saying, so fables and jests encourage readers to 'hearken to serious and grave documents'. Jests are like 'sawce whereby we are recreated, that we may eat with more appetite'. Not quite. The passage that he quotes from More's 'great volume' (his 1557 *Workes*) but in fact found, citation and all, in Cresacre More, had actually said that 'reste [not 'jest'] and recreation shoulde be but as a sawce. And sawce ... should serve for a faint and weake stomake, to get it the more appetite to the meate.'⁷ Does the error spring from Cresacre More's own wishful thinking? More did believe that jokes serve us well and on occasion stopped to defend their use in theological discourse. What seems interesting here is less the defence than Hoddesdon's need for one.

Another collection heavily indebted to Stapleton is in Thomas Bayly's *Witty Apophthegmes Delivered at Several Times ... by King James, King Charles, the Marquess of Worcester, Francis Lord Bacon, and Sir Thomas Moore* (1658). Bayly's preface calls these 'the timely fruit of those once Famous Monarchs, and Peeres of this Realm, whose yet living Fame for Majestick Wisdom and high Discretion, is able still to gain them life and Glory, maugre all the dirt, and filth, which this ungratefull Age hath flung both upon their Persons and works' (sig. A3). It is not clear what filth he has found on More. More was killed by a king, but Bayly wants to show that other kings were wise and good. Perhaps he thought it was time to seek the favour of Charles I's son.

Bayly includes the story, not entirely to modern squeamish taste, that when visited in the Tower More jokingly examined his own urine, a common method of diagnosing illness, and gave the prognosis that he would die. This More has a talent for puns: a man who owes him money does not repay it, on the grounds that More might die, saying 'in Latin, the better to please Sir *Thomas*, *Memento morieris* [remember you will die]: to which Sir *Tho.* presently answer'd, *What say you Sir? methinks you put your self in mind of your duty herein, saying*, Memento Mori aeris, *Remember* Moor's money [i.e. the 'aeris' or coins of More]' (163). There are further puns on More's name, his sage sayings and the witticisms as he ascends the scaffold. To say – whether the real More did or not – that the headsman should spare the beard that had grown since its owner's conviction might later seem distastefully frivolous, and one eighteenth-century writer notes it with dismay.⁸ To early modern readers, though, this famous jest might signal a golden balance of humours.

Tastes in execution behaviour change. Even in *Sir Thomas More*, a play by Anthony Munday to which Shakespeare contributed several pages, More makes some of the usual jokes but then goes to his death saying, 'Here More forsakes all mirth, good reason why: / The fool of flesh must with her frail life die' (5.4).[9] In James Hurdis's neoclassical tragedy *Sir Thomas More* (1792) there is no terminal mirth at all: we hear only that More showed 'cheerful constancy' at his trial and was 'patient' and 'heroic' on the scaffold. No joking. Even the assurance that he and others will meet again in heaven drops the word 'merry' (120). As for the final moments of Robert Bolt's 1960 *A Man for all Seasons*, the martyr's rest is not jokes but silence.

More's cleverness had not always pleased readers. (The index to George Buck's biography of Richard III, on which see below, sneers that More 'dyed scoffing'.) Answers to and comments on his polemics included counter-sarcasms and puns on his name even by later readers such as John Day, who otherwise admired him: 'Can the blacke More change his skin? Or the Leopard his spots? Sr Thomas hath only his Teeth white, all is els as blacke as coale' (1614; Boswell #169). Nor did More the heresy-hunter vanish. Thomas Mortimer's *British Plutarch* (1762) laments that this great man 'carried his aversion against heterodoxy to such a height, as even did great dishonour to his humanity', citing More's polemics and his whipping of a heretic (71; cf. above, 107). The 1795 edition drops this story but adds a concluding paragraph on More's 'most celebrated work' *Utopia*, *Richard III* and 'many other pieces' that are 'now little known, being chiefly in defence of the Roman catholic religion' (86). Mortimer mentions More's 'great fund of wit and humour' (1795; 61), and the description of his execution gives the old stories, but Mortimer shows less interest in the teller of jests; there is no section on 'wit and wisdom'.

In the next century commentary on More became entangled with the question of Catholic emancipation, and the polemical and persecutory More once more drew unhappy notice.[10] The Anglican bishop Mandell Creighton, for instance, objected that More was no good example of expansive tolerance; his *Persecution and Tolerance* (1895) even accuses him of 'justifying what was convenient for the moment' (qtd Wyland 55). Some modern biographers have shared this stress on the heretic hunter: Jasper Ridley, with (in the American edition) a book jacket that features a scowling revision of Holbein's portrait, reads More as a cruel persecutor, and even the more moderate Richard Marius insists that those who admire More should not let the incense-surrounded saint obscure the angry combatant.[11]

Neither goes as far as the critic James Wood, who offers the confident statement in 'Sir Thomas More: a man for one season' that 'no man can ever be a saint in God's eyes, and no man should be one in ours, and certainly not Thomas More'.[12] After all, the man hunted heretics, was 'astonishingly disingenuous' and died for a 'sanctioned truth' that excludes freedom. Nor is Wood alone. When in 2009 Hilary Mantel, a subtle novelist, set a mellow Thomas Cromwell against a punitively idealistic More, the reviewer for the *Times Literary Supplement* explained that in the latter's 'utopian eyes' it 'is a "blessed" act to torture a heretic or trick one into a confession'.[13] The 'real' Utopia, of course, has a religious freedom that, to be sure, More did not wish in any Christian country, whatever his later melancholy remark (as reported in Roper 216) that the English might yet see the day when Catholics and heretics would have to live and let live. The reviewer's wording does show how the word 'utopian' has multiplied its meanings into near meaninglessness. Much of modern commentary on More has been hagiographic (after all, More was canonized in 1935), but the reviewer has company, not least among those who forget that saints are canonized for heroic virtue and posthumous miracles, not for perfection.

More's more positive current image is due in substantial part to the impact of Bolt's *A Man for All Seasons*, a play that spoke to a fear of collectivist socialism on the one hand and memories of fascism (and in America of McCarthyism) on the other – and perhaps also to distaste for the conformism of the 1950s.[14] In this regard the play has many cousins, from the film *The Man in the Gray Flannel Suit* to Arthur Miller's play *The Crucible* to Anthony Burgess's dystopic *A Clockwork Orange*. Many who applauded in 1960, then, thought that we needed to stiffen the spines of our inner Mores. Bolt's is not the 'real' More, but he remains the More many admire: witty and ironic (if not 'merry') and protective of an inviolate self. When he tells Norfolk that 'what matters to me is not whether it is true or not but that I believe it to be true, or rather not that I *believe* it, but that *I* believe it', the historical More might be chilled by what he would call pride, self-love (see also above, 113 n. 7, 134). Roper's More tells Cromwell that the vast majority of the dead disagree with that statesman on the matter of the king's supremacy over the English Church; nor is More himself bound 'to conform my conscience to the council of one realm against the general council of Christendom' (Roper 249–50). A crucial point, for More died not just for conscience in the sense of an inner individual self, although he had one, but for a *con*science that was in his view *con*nected to an outer world. That outer world is itself a body, comprising the pope in council and the 'common corps of Christendom'. *That* More is less useful than Bolt's to those who fear incorporation into groupthink – the sort of conformity that some dislike in ... Utopia.

Twentieth-century science fiction, too, could adopt this modern More; nor is this surprising, for much of the eu/dystopian impulse has moved into the future or out into space. In R. A. Lafferty's 1968 *Past Master*, Henry's good servant, not yet under arrest but expecting it, is transported to an earth colony of the future that in its utopian perfection (or what its semi-robotic rulers think is perfection) makes many flee to outlying areas of stink, rot, work, pain – and freedom. Lafferty's More, the novel's protagonist, is wittily ironic, aware of his future martyrdom, shaky in his faith and easily angered. Although Lafferty thinks *Utopia* a satirical nightmare vision of where More feared his culture was headed, on the golden eu/dystopian planet Astrobe, More at first likes this 'golden mediocrity' – Lafferty's witty play on the geometer's golden mean – but then opposes it and, his religious faith recovered, is beheaded. As for the rest of us, this novel seems to hint that in a conformist America it might be better to turn on and drop out. The counsel of despair? No, for at the very end of the novel, Lafferty imagines his ambiguous world now waiting and hoping.

More's biography of Richard III found a vigorous afterlife largely by way of Tudor chronicles as reworked by Shakespeare.[15] But is this brilliant portrait of ruthless tyranny on the part of a clever if spiritually diseased hypocrite true? Doubts have been felt since early modern times, although at first prudence recommended silence.

The two most relentless denunciations of More's biography before the twentieth century may be a life of Richard by Sir George Buck, written under Elizabeth but published posthumously in 1646, and, generations later, *Historic Doubts on the Life and Reign of King Richard III* by the antiquarian and man of letters Horace Walpole.[16] For neither author is More honest. Buck treats him with nothing but contempt and anger, claiming that his reputation for erudition was unearned, citing two of More's sixteenth-century detractors, the French humanist Germain de Brie (Brixius) and the Protestant polemicist John Bale, to show that More was a 'man of slender reading'. A note – marginal as though to sideline such trivia – explains further that More 'wrote many Poems and Epigrams, sundry pretty Comedies, and

Enterludes' (and indeed 1638 saw an edition of the *Epigrammata* printed in London). More applied his 'poeticall straine' to King Richard, says Buck, and from malice. Had he not been beheaded, moreover, he would have 'hazarded the best Queene that ever was, the sacred and eternally honoured *Elizabeth*', to whom he had been an adversary even before she was born (75–9). Buck also takes a swipe at *Utopia*, echoing Reformers who sneered at More the 'poet' for imagining such other nowhere places as Purgatory.[17] It would indeed be good, he says, if statesmen were perfect in body, gesture and act – but this 'must be so defined by the laws of Utopia'. Not that More himself has any utopian virtues, for had Richard been the victor at Bosworth his denigrators 'would have sung Peans to his glory' (78).

In his *Historic Doubts* (Dublin edition, 1768), Walpole is happy to praise the famous statesman as a writer, and says of More's biography that 'It is in truth a composition, and a very beautiful one', written when More was 'in the vigour of his fancy, and fresh from the study of the Greek and Roman historians, whose manner he has imitated in divers imaginary orations' (21). Yet its well-written speeches are 'no more to be received as genuine, than the facts they are adduced to countenance'. Walpole does not think More's inaccuracies mere courtiership. The man, he says,

> who scorned to save his life by bending to the will of the son, was not
> likely to canvass the favour of the father, by prostituting his pen
> to the humour of the court. I take the truth to be, that Sir Thomas
> wrote his reign of Edward the Fifth as he wrote his Utopia: to amuse
> his leisure and exercise his fancy. He took up a paltry canvas and
> embroidered it with a flowing design as his imagination suggested
> the colours. (23)

And so Walpole pronounces the work 'invention and romance' (24). But his later strictures are less charitable, and he makes witty fun of what he thinks over-dramatized, over-Senecan. Quoting one vivid passage he gets down to serious history: 'Let us strip this paragraph of its historic buskins' and say in plain English '*the queen's party took up arms*' (38–9). As the text proceeds, the impatience with More increases and Walpole grieves that both More and Bacon (in his history of Henry VII) distort history. 'And here let me lament', he says, 'that two of the greatest men in our annals have prostituted their admirable pens, the one to blacken a great prince, the other to varnish a pitiful tyrant' (77–8). Not even More's sympathetic portrait of Mistress Shore escapes censure, for the writer's historical distortions, says Walpole, make even his condemnation of Richard's mistreatment of her itself morally suspect (144).

More than many scholarly biographers might like, the modern image of Richard III has been shaped by a detective-story writer, Elizabeth Mackintosh, writing under the pseudonym Josephine Tey. In *The Daughter of Time* (1951), a bedridden detective entertains himself by deducing the true identity of the king who killed young Edward V and his brother. (There is some irony to the title, for it comes from the proverb 'Truth is the daughter of Time', a hopeful sentiment that Mary Tudor, Henry VII's granddaughter, adopted as her motto.) Thanks to More's pro-Tudor propaganda, the novel concludes, we have long mistaken the innocent for the guilty – the true murderer was Henry VII. The historical More, though, was not the first to promulgate what some have called the 'Tudor myth': others had already read England as first the victim of a destructive usurper bearing a boar as his crest and then liberated into the sunlight and fertility of the Tudor years.[18] Whether More (or Shakespeare) fully accepted this myth in its simple form is subject to doubt, for More's *History* is not without irony. Whatever the doubts of Richard's modern defenders, though, More's extraordinarily compelling text, freed both from the author's subtly insinuated doubts about how anyone can know the truth of the past and from his equally subtle scepticism towards Richard's enemies, has proven resilient, if only because Shakespeare's own Richard III lives. Tyranny, ambition and political manoeuvring are going to be with us for some time, and so the play and its protagonist can be modernized, allegorized, often associated with Richard Nixon's dark suspiciousness in the 1970s, and in a 1995 film version set in a fantasized fascist England by the director Richard Loncraine. More's Richard is too culturally useful to lose.

The *History* had one more effect. More's portrait of 'Jane' (Elizabeth) Shore, whatever the distortions on which Walpole leaped, is among early modern England's most riveting comments on women who exploit their sexuality – or who have it abused – and then grow old. More is sympathetic, not condemnatory; even the soft prose rhythms of this particular passage (R3 63–7) seem to rebuke those who now harshly neglect her.[19] Not surprisingly, the poet Thomas Churchyard contributed a poem by her shade to the 1563 edition of *The Mirror for Magistrates*, a poem that in turn helped to inspire a fashion for laments in the voice of a woman, often a 'fallen' one. One impetus for this fashion was Ovid's *Heroides*, but another was More by way of Churchyard, and his interest not in condemning the morally

274 Anne Lake Prescott

lapsed but in imagining the pathos of beauty and power fallen victim to error, time and male indifference.

Because so many readers have found More's *Utopia*, canonized as a major text long before the author himself was canonized as a saint, so apt to engage the imagination in so many ways (stirring desire, fear, dismay, amusement or curiosity; inspiring imitation; or providing a useful nowhere in which to put airy nothings or whatever else seems impossible or ridiculous), and because the text has shifted significance as the times themselves have shifted, both Utopia and 'utopia' now mean too much for coherent definition. To browse in the huge field of modern 'utopian studies', in print or on the Web, where such studies proliferate beyond the power of any essay to catalogue, or even to note how the word 'utopian' is used in casual modern discourse, is to find, over and over, the equation of 'utopian' with 'ideal', 'perfect' or 'too good to be true' and hence 'idle'. Even Renaissance scholars can assume that Utopia itself was meant to be 'ideal' or 'perfect'. (One may wonder if More's early plan to call his island 'Nusquama' would have proved as useful, for 'nusquamian' seems less easy on the tongue.) Utopias have websites, electronic journals, special issues or collections, and courses. On the other hand, the utopian genre, even in its punning sense of 'eutopian', has in more recent times generated its dark other, the 'dystopia', impelled in particular by historical developments that rendered what was once amusingly 'nowhere', or at least a merely parodic 'somewhere', all too likely to be made real, at huge human cost. Eutopias look like dystopias, moreover, to those with different political or social assumptions. It is now a commonplace that the last century saw a turn away from u/eutopian speculation and dream, although some who write on this shift too readily ignore the dreams of the civil rights or women's movements, perhaps because if hopes are even partially realized then they are, by definition and even in retrospect, no longer 'utopian'. For the seventeenth-century Mary Astell to imagine higher education for women used to be utopian. No longer. Now it is just prescient – like, for that matter, Sébastien Mercier's utopian prophecy that in seven hundred years vehicles will have started to drive on the right (but not his protagonist's report that in 2500 women will have learned to stay home where they belong).[20] To say that we live without speculative hope is to forget how much some hopes are no longer speculation and how much of what we accept (speed limits, expiration dates, in America the obligatory 'Have a nice day') might look coercive if described by some alien visitor. The word 'utopia' has paradoxes within its paradoxes.

What, though, not of Utopia or utopias but of *Utopia*? The after-life of More's most famous text has seen explosive expansion. There is no way in a brief study of tracing *Utopia*'s history (although I cite some studies in the notes and 'Further reading'), not least because the advent of Early English Books Online and Eighteenth Century Collections Online (ECCO) has made available even the most obscure allusions and imitations. At the latest count, for example, ECCO provides 2,266 hits for 'Utopia', although many are duplicates or book catalogues. What follows, then, are close to random observa-tions – with, I hope, point.

One concerns the frequent expansion of Utopia, if sometimes only implicitly, from an important *part* of More's larger ambiguous dialogue to the *whole* of the text, as though the island Hythloday describes in Book II had somehow colonized Book I and its discussions and debates: the part has become the whole. In editions over the centuries, the evolution of the title itself illustrates this tendency. From the mere object of a preposition in the first Latin titles, More's island would eventually become a solitary italicized name: *Utopia*. With this shift, moreover, hints on how to read the book vanish.[21] Titles of the early Latin editions vary somewhat but offer similar guides to how to read the text. This is a *Libellus vere aureus nec minus salutaris quam festivus de optimo reip[ublicae] statu, deque nova Insula Utopia*, says the 1516 Louvain edition: 'A truly golden little book as healthful/salutary as it is festive concerning the best state of a commonwealth and concerning the new Island Utopia'. The prettiest title page, that of the Basel edition of March 1518, says much the same, although the Paris edition of 1517, perhaps more fashion-conscious, tells the reader that he (almost certainly a 'he', for Utopia had its birth in the largely homosocial world of Latin humanism) has here an *opusculum illud vere aureum Thomae Mori non minus utile quam elegans de optimo reipublicae statu, deque nova Insula Utopia*: 'a truly golden little work by Thomas More no less useful than elegant on the best state of a commonwealth and on the new Island Utopia'.[22] From 'festive' to 'elegant' in Paris.

The first English edition, Ralph Robinson's 1551 translation, echoes the Latin: 'A fruteful and pleasaunt worke of the beste state of a publique weale, and of the newe yle called Utopia: written in Latine by Syr thomas More knyght ...' True, this is no longer a 'golden little book', although the translator is identified as a goldsmith (he would, Robinson may have reflected, have found work in Utopia making chamber pots and manacles). The time was ripe, under Edward VI's reforming advisers, to think hard about the 'publique weale'. In 1556, with Mary Tudor on the throne, came Robinson's second edition: 'A frutefull, pleasaunt, & wittie worke, of the beste state of a publique weale, and of the newe yle, called Utopia: written in Latine, by the right worthie and famous Syr Thomas More knyght ...' The stress is heavier on More's distinction and wit. Under Elizabeth, a 1597 edition calls itself 'A Most pleasant, fruitfull, and wittie worke of the best state of a publique weale and of the new Yle called *Utopia*. Written in Latine, by the right worthie and famous Syr Thomas Moore Knyght.' Italics for *Utopia* hint at the future, for in a 1624 edition the title page reads 'Sir Thomas Moore's **UTOPIA**: Containing An Excellent, Learned, Wittie, and Pleasant Discourse of the best state of a Publike Weale, as it is found in the Government of the new Ile called *Utopia*'. The wit remains, as does the 'best' state – but the suggestive ambiguity of 'concerning the best state of a commonwealth *and* concerning the new island of Utopia' has been eliminated, as the best state is now *identified* with Utopia; 'salutary', too, has gone, while the island is promoted, along with the author, to the top of the page. In 1639, on the eve of the Civil War, the author is demoted to the bottom of the page but Utopia stars: 'The COMMON-WEALTH of *UTOPIA*: Containing a Learned and pleasant Discourse of the best *state of a Publicke Weale, as it* is found in the government of the new Ile called *Utopia*'. 'Salutary' has become 'learned', and the festive is now 'pleasant' (carnival yields to wit), but most important is the continued identification of Utopia with the 'best'.

After the Commonwealth, we are in modern times: an Oxford Latin edition of 1663 is merely *Thomae Mori Utopia* and the new translation by Bishop Gilbert Burnet says almost as tersely: '**UTOPIA:** Written in Latin by Sir *THOMAS MORE*, CHANCELLOR OF ENGLAND: Translated into English' (1664). Burnet's introduction explains that because English has now divested itself of pedantry (humanist pickiness?), a 'trifling way of dark and unintelligible wit' (a slap at the Metaphysicals) and an 'extravagant Canting' (so much for Puritan radicals), it is now time to retranslate a book 'writ by one of the greatest Men that this Island has produced', a book filled with 'fine and well-digested notions'. For Burnet, though, Utopia is no simple ideal. More himself, he says, could not have desired the 'taking away of all *Property*, and the levelling of the World', words that during the Restoration would recall with a shudder the Commonwealth's Levellers and Diggers. He concludes by suggesting that More often 'only intended to set many Notions in his Reader's way; and that he might not seem too much in earnest, he went so far out of all Roads to do it the less suspected'. After all, he could not seriously have advocated the hiring of assassins or assisted suicide (no, one might reply, but the logic of Utopia may require these). In any case, Burnet will leave his author's 'Thoughts and Notions to the Reader's censure'. Burnet's take on *Utopia* is thoughtful (even if he implausibly considers the Utopian custom of premarital nude viewing to be possible evidence that More had 'had a misfortune of his own choice' of a wife). Still, More's interrogatory fantasy in Book II triumphs over Book I's provocative dialogue, and nowadays the work is always called 'Utopia', not something like 'Considerations on Democracy' or 'How Might We Rearrange a Republic?'[23]

Burnet was not alone in reading *Utopia* as meant to inspire reflection. Milton, at least, says that More and Bacon taught us 'better and exacter things', not perfect dreams, and in France the Robespierrist Etienne Cabet would say that the plan for a better society in his *Icaria* (1840) came to him after reading *Utopia* had plunged him into thought.[24] Perhaps most notably, in his *Complaints of the Poor People of England* (1793) George Dyer, recently returned from 'Utopia, a country that allows the freest inquiry', asks a central question: 'How far a nation, REALLY FREE, may improve in political knowledge; how far it may extend its capacity for promoting PUBLIC HAPPINESS, without encroaching on private' (97). Can there even *be* a 'best state' to satisfy those who long for both liberty and social harmony?[25] Still, the evolution of English titles is a story of fading ambiguity, of dialogue becoming dream, the whole becoming the part, and what George Logan has called a 'thought experiment' becoming, often, a fantasy of desire.[26]

So it did not take long for Utopia to stop being 'best' or contributing to a discussion of the 'best' and become, usually, a dream of perfection, which is for most people its current definition even when associated specifically with More. As the 2009 Wikipedia entry put it, with at least a 'seemingly' somewhat to modify the definition, 'Utopia is a name for an ideal community or society, taken from the title of a book written in 1516 by Sir Thomas More describing a fictional island in the Atlantic Ocean, possessing a seemingly perfect socio-politico-legal system'. In fact More is less specific about his island's whereabouts, but more important is the shift by which Utopia floats from political discussion or satire to fantasy, and often from Nowhere into that ocean in which we find (or do not find) the land of Cockaigne and its cousins. Since some might call this a foolish reading it seems appropriate that as early as 1549 Thomas Chaloner, in his translation of Erasmus's *Praise of Folly*, has his protagonist send the Stoics' impossible 'wiseman' to dwell in 'Platos citee, or in the lande of Fairie, or Utopia' (sig. E4v).

'Utopian', in this text, has not only come to mean 'perfect' or, in another subtle distortion of More's description, characterizing a place fit only for people better than ourselves; it has also become a space for whatever might seem good but is unreal. Because it is both nowhere and semi-satirical, Utopia could even be the location of a play, such as Edward Howard's failed Restoration comedy, *The Six Days Adventure, or The New Utopia* (1671), or Gilbert and Sullivan's *Utopia Limited* (1893; the 'limited' is a witty touch) – in which a newly perfected but boring society is gratefully returned to the *status quo ante* by the reintroduction of political parties.

Chaloner was thus to have company in sending the unreal or the unwanted for storage in Utopia or utopia. Earlier examples may be found in Boswell's collection, but others proliferate in later times, perhaps precisely because 'utopian hopes' were themselves both increasing and, sometimes, becoming actual plans. Must radical hopes be in fact 'utopian'? Many said so, but not all. John Saltmarsh, writing in 1643 against a conservative sermon by Thomas Fuller, urges us to stop describing schemes for serious reform as fit only for 'Plato's *Common-wealth*, and Moores *Utopia*'. Let us, rather, 'think it as possible to be the best, as easie to be the worst' and no longer dismiss as fit for Utopia what we might with effort make real (*Examinations, or, A Discovery of Some Dangerous Positions*, sig. B3). Not surprisingly, and as it had in response to the English civil wars, the word 'utopian' invaded arguments over the French Revolution – the 1790s saw a flood of Tory texts condemning Jacobin hopes as 'utopian', yet some thoughtful defences of radical reform also cite More. Thus the author of *The Trial of Thomas Muir ... before the High Court of Justicary, at Edinburgh* (1793; 82) finds it irrational to censor Tom Paine and allow More: 'did not Sir Thomas More, enjoying the confidence of the King, and placed at the head of the law, publish his Utopia, the plan of his republic, of which an equal division of property, an Agrarian Law, an universal community, formed the basis?' More conventional is the assurance by Henry Yorke, in *These Are the Times that Try Men's Souls! A Letter to John Frost. A Prisoner in Newgate* (1793; 58), that reformers wish only equality of rights, for 'an equalization of property is unknown to the thoughtful men of this age, and is to be found only in the visionary republic of Plato, and the Utopia of Thomas More'.

Such examples could be multiplied many times. Not that all are political: *Moore's Fables for the Female Sex* (Edinburgh, 1793) versifies a witty girl's mockery of a would-be seducer: she will 'demand, without a cavil, / What new Utopia do you travel? – / Upon my word, these high-flown fancies / Shew depth of learning – in romances' (28). It is a pleasure, if disconcerting, to imagine a lover finding romantic compliments in Utopia. And one finds parodies throughout the century: an entertaining report on the 'Empire of Nothing' in *The Looker-On* for 15 May 1795 describes a world of projectors, imitators of Shakespeare, academic punsters, rebus-makers and philosophers who are 'going on embassies from his Inane Majesty to Plato's republic, Utopia, Lilliput, and Laputa' (274; or see the equally funny *Tale of a Tub Reversed*, 1705, in which a queen has conquered Utopia – obverse of modern postcolonialist accusations against Hythloday).

Nor is there room here to describe the many utopias that owe something to More, if only in their dissent, but an extended consideration of his text's afterlife, even in Anglophone countries alone, would include such early modern works as Bacon's *New Atlantis* (1627), Gabriel Plattes's *Macaria* (1641), James Harrington's *Oceana* (1656, although this 'utopia', like that of Plattes, reads more like a plan than a fictional speculation), or Margaret Cavendish's *Blazing World* (1666). Some utopias are translations, including the surprisingly sex-obsessed *History of the Sevarites* by Denis V. d'Allais (1675), set like so many no-places in the Antipodes; for another one see Sir Thomas St Serfe's Menippean *Bourlasque News From the Antipodes* with its 'Utopia Nova' (1661). The next century offered some more utopias, including some parodies, but the great age for them is the nineteenth century, not least William Morris's socialist *News from Nowhere* (1888; like *Utopia*, this medievalist fantasy of communal work and artistic fabric has carnival touches, such as the conversion of the parliament building into a place to store manure – has, the implied question delicately asks, much changed?). Samuel Butler's *Erewhon* (1872) is a reminder that one way to Nowhere is nominal reversal; compare Thomas Lupton's 1580 *Siuqila* ('aliquis', subtitled *Too Good to be True*), and its 1581 sequel *Mauqsun* ('nusquam'). Edward Bellamy's *Looking Backward* (Boston, 1888) reverses not the name but the temporal pattern of utopias: the protagonist has had not a dream of the future but a nightmare about his past (our present). Women? More's *Utopia* has more equality than England in 1516, and Astell wished for more, but for feminists who want to fly higher there are the winged equivalents in Inez Gillmore's 1914 *Angel Island*, who marry male visitors and with some difficulty teach them to allow their sons, too, to fly. Charlotte Perkins Gilman's *Herland* (New York, 1915; in Gilman's magazine, *The Forerunner*) does not even bother with taming men: in her imaginary world our species survives without them.

In the wider history of European thought, the good place, *eutopia*, moves from a past Eden or Golden Age, or from distant Isles of the Blessed or of the Hesperides, to the future, or even to outer space or to our own world after a benign alien invasion, as in Arthur Clarke's 1953 *Childhood's End*. This means, perhaps inevitably, that Utopia and utopia become yet more ambiguous and, for some, repellent. That is why nowadays students often need to be reminded that at first *Utopia* was both 'salutary' *and* 'festive', that it was a dialogue, not a tract, and that Utopia is 'best' only in the opinion of a speaker who may be talking nonsense to an author whose name looks much like 'fool'.

And thus for many readers (often the comfortably off and socially privileged), More's *Utopia* is dystopic. One complaint any professor hears is that the place is boring, which may be in part an artifact of the utopia game: *Utopia* is not a novel and we see few individual Utopians (rightly so, for rounded characters bring tension and mess), and so some of our impression of smothering conformity is a result of narrative distance. We never hear the Utopian military discussing which enemy to assassinate or the excuses of a man condemned to hard labour for adultery. Perhaps no 'utopia' can survive a full-scale novelistic treatment, although H. G. Wells tried in his *A Modern Utopia* (1905); his dystopias remain better energized. Another issue for those who live in a world more tamed than was More's England is Utopia's rationalized political space, although its clarity might please those living near large animals and with few roads. More himself might be puzzled by Richard Wilbur's lovely 'In Trackless Woods'[27] and its concluding praise of natural forms 'Not subject to our stiff geometries' – the geometries that help make Utopia seem, perhaps unjustly, totalitarian.

Among the first dystopias, cheerfully unburdened by serious thought on the 'best' society, is Joseph Hall's *Mundus Alter et Idem* (*c.* 1605), a text with various Antipodean lands ruled by women, thieves, gluttons and fools, the joke being that so is England. It was only after the full implication of utopian hopes and utopian possibilities had struck the late nineteenth and early twentieth centuries that frightening dystopias began to appear. If the French Revolution had accelerated English conservatives' use of 'utopian' (often more hopefully than prophetically dismissive) to mean 'unreal', the later doubts expressed by leftist writers such as H. G. Wells in his *Time Machine* (1895) could be less dystopic than monitory. But the USSR's arrival gave more serious pause. Sights that inspired Lincoln Steffens to say, famously, 'I have seen the future and it works' inspired Yevgeny Zamiatin to write *We* (c. 1920; pub. 1924); the very title of this futuristic dystopia signals a fear of just the Platonic stress on social harmony that characterizes Hythloday's thinking. Others could dread the trajectory of modern capitalism and technology towards what in 1932 Aldous Huxley ironically called a *Brave New World*. Even the more benign worlds of corporate culture or sexual timidity as imagined for some eloquent or funny late-twentieth-century cinema and television made the conformism of most utopias seem unbearable. As many have said, furthermore, one person's utopia is another one's dystopia. B. F. Skinner's *Walden Two* (1948), a behaviourist dream, seems to many sheer nightmare, violating every human right except that to pursue happiness – if to be manipulated into happiness is to be happy. No wonder, all things considered, that one essay on such matters is titled 'More to Orwell: an easy leap from *Utopia* to *Nineteen Eighty-Four*'.[28] Nor did a fashion for irony make serious literary speculations about something better, best, or perfect easy to take seriously.

This shift from utopia to dystopia (or their collapse into each other) has been often noticed and, indeed, Ursula K. Le Guin plays with this ambivalence in her 1985 *Always Coming Home*, in which a voice within the text itself forces the author to confess that her creation is in part a utopia. But is utopia dead? The coroner is undecided. A recent book by Russell Jacoby, who objects to the association of utopia with totalitarianism and who thinks that More himself, frightened of the Reformation, became an anti-utopian, laments that we have stopped dreaming of something better. And yet the statement that 'Buoyant idealism has long disappeared' (ix), although published several years before shouts of 'Yes we can' shook the American campaign trail, ignores much in the past half century, from flower power to the 'I have a dream' speech that helped to generate what is now a national holiday in the United States (nor does Martin Luther King figure in the index).[29] Does utopia live? The Manuels' classic history of utopian thought (see 'Further reading') concludes with the suggestion, based on dream research, that since REM (rapid eye movement) sleep is essential to health, banishing its fantasies would risk getting waking hallucinations instead. And since some utopian dreaming has come true and hence, perhaps, dull (would Plattes's plan in *Macaria* for a secretary of agriculture (sig. A3v) now race any pulses?), those who dislike fantasy may hope that good utopias die soon and go not to heaven but to reality. In that (non)utopian future we may also hope that More's Utopia and *Utopia* will be read even more often as offering neither solemn ideal nor idle play, let alone a dream of perfection, but as both *festivus* and, at least in some ways, *salutaris*. After all, the Internet itself has brought dangers but also Utopian hopes, such as the reconciliation of blogging or tweeting individual selves with an increased sense of community. Cyberspace, like outer space, has room for experimental thinking and play – utopia lives here, at least, and often with a Utopian indifference to private property and social status; nor is it averse to modifying existing political habits. Eu, U, or Dys, our *cyber-topoi* are now complex and ambiguous playgrounds for the imagination – but then so is More's own anamorphically mapped, provocative and dialogic thought experiment.

FURTHER READING

On More's afterlives see essays listed on the *Moreana* website and in the forthcoming *Yearbook of Thomas More Scholarship* (Arizona Center for Medieval and Renaissance Studies), sponsored by the International Association for Thomas More Scholarship. Jackson Boswell, *Sir Thomas More in the English Renaissance: An Annotated Catalogue* with an Introduction by Anne Lake Prescott (Binghamton, N.Y.: Medieval and Renaissance Texts and Studies, 1994), is a major source, although it usually cites previously reprinted allusions without quoting them. Albert Geritz has published several bibliographical guides: 'Recent studies in More (1977–1990)', *ELR* 22 (1992), 112–40; *Thomas More: An Annotated Bibliography of Criticism, 1935–1997* (Westport, Conn.: Greenwood Press, 1998); and 'Recent studies in More (1990–2003)', *ELR* 35 (2005), 123–55. See also Michael D. Wentworth, *The Essential Sir Thomas More: An Annotated Bibliography of Major Modern Sources* (New York: G. K. Hall, 1995). The prologue and final chapter of John Guy, *A Daughter's Love: Thomas & and Margaret More*, describe the first stage of More's earthly afterlife.

On *Richard III*, *R3* xliii–li gives a brief pungent survey of the printing history, the incorporation into the chronicle histories that Shakespeare used, early praise such as that by Queen Elizabeth's tutor Roger Ascham, early disagreements and recent scholarship.

Two useful online bibliographies are, for *Utopia* itself, Romuald Ian Lakowski's 'A bibliography of Thomas More's *Utopia*', *Early Modern Literary Studies* 1 (1995), and Clare Jackson and R. W. Serjeantson, *Utopian Writing, 1516–1798* (2009). For scholarship on Enlightenment utopias, see Nicole Pohl, 'The quest for Utopia in the eighteenth century', in Blackwell Publishing's online *Literature Compass* 5 (2008), and, for more chronological sweep, Lyman T. Sargent, *British and American Utopian Literature, 1516–1985: An Annotated, Chronological Bibliography* (New York: Garland, 1988).

J. C. Davis's Introduction to *Utopia and the Ideal Society: A Study of English Utopian Writing 1516–1700* (Cambridge University Press, 1981) comments on the hard task of defining 'utopia', as does that to George Slusser *et al.*, eds., *Transformations of Utopia: Changing Views of the Perfect Society* (New York: AMS, 1999), an imaginative collection including such 'utopias' as, for example, Club Med. Frank and Fritzie Manuel's magisterial *Utopian Thought in the Western World* (Cambridge, Mass.: Belknap Press, 1979) notes the later efforts to haul More's *Utopia* into ideologies from Marxism to deconstruction. A humanist impulse that had been playful and ironic as well as serious in Erasmus, Rabelais and More, they say, becomes solemn and absolutist. (Perhaps this complaint results in part from a focus on utopian *thought* rather than on literary or parodic utopias and popular culture.) Nicole Pohl, *Women, Space and Utopia, 1600–1800* (Burlington, Vt.: Ashgate, 2006), notes the 'shift from *eu/utopias* to *eu/uchronias* in the mid-seventeenth century' (3), and Alessa Johns, 'Engendering utopias: examples from eighteenth-century England', in Slusser *et al.*, 17–30, comments on gender difference and on utopias that owe more to Mary Astell's 1694 *Serious Proposal to the Ladies* than to More.

On utopias and dystopias of the nineteenth and twentieth centuries, with a glance at More, see Krishan Kumar, *Utopia and Anti-Utopia in Modern Times* (Oxford: Blackwell, 1987), as well as the online Society for Utopian Studies and its journal. The Ralahine Centre for Utopian Studies, based at the University of Limerick, produces *Ralahine Utopian Studies*. Literature on science fiction and u/dystopia is growing rapidly. See, for example, William H. Hardesty III, 'The programmed utopia of R. A. Lafferty's *Past Master*', in Richard D. Erlich and Thomas P. Dunn, eds., *Clockwork Worlds: Mechanized Environments in SF* (Westport, Conn.: Greenwood, 1983), 105–13, and Raffaella Baccolini and Tom Moylan, eds., *Dark Horizons: Science Fiction and the Dystopian Imagination* (London and New York: Routledge, 2003). Utopia and its discontents may be found even in books for young adults: for a subtle exploration of how well-intentioned utopias can be *nice*, very *nice*, but also suffocating and literally colourless, see Lois Lowry's prize-winning *The Giver* (New York: Delacorte, 1993).

Finally, as an example of negative views of modern utopian thinking (and sometimes of More himself), see Edward Rothstein, Herbert
Muschamp and Martin E. Marty, *Visions of Utopia* (Oxford University
Press, for the New York Public Library, 2003) – and, as an example of
how varieties of utopian and ideal thinking can inspire a range of
compelling visual images, the illustrated collection of essays, a com-
panion to a joint exhibit at the Bibliothèque nationale and the New
York Public Library, Roland Schaer, Gregory Claeys and Lyman T.
Sargent, eds., *Utopia: The Search for the Ideal Society in the Western
World* (New York: Oxford University Press, 2000).

Notes

1. Not everyone had agreed on More's learning, or at least on his prowess as
   a Latinist, and doubts continued. In *Corruptae latinitatis index* (1755),
   William Massey, scorner of post-classical Latin, often cites *Utopia*,
   saying of *'ribaldus'*, for example, that 'I wonder so elegant a writer as
   Sir *Thomas More* should disgrace his Stile with this paltry word' (61).

   Unless otherwise indicated, the place of publication of pre-twentieth-
   century books is London.
2. The jests in the polemics circulated. In *Veritas Redux. Evangelical
   Truths Restored* (1707), John Edwards writes of a young man 'in
   Sir Thomas More's time' who says he was predestined to steal and the
   judge who replies that he was predestined to hang him (218). The story, a
   'reversible' paradox *by* More, is in his *Dialogue Concerning Heresies*
   (*CW* 6:404). For more on merry tales, see above, 200–4, 221–2, 225–6.
3. Anne Lake Prescott, 'The ambivalent heart: Thomas More's merry
   tales', *Criticism* 45 (2003), 417–33.
4. S. A. Tannenbaum, 'Some unpublished Harvey marginalia', *Modern
   Language Review* 25 (1930), 327–31.
5. Douai 1588; Stapleton, 121–31.
6. Pp. 384–9. Cresacre More himself identifies More's critic as the 'bauld
   English Chronicler [John] *Hall*' (384). For a modern facsimile see
   *The Life and Death of Sir Thomas Moore, Lord High Chancellour of
   England* (Menston: Scolar Press, 1971).
7. Cresacre More is misquoting More's *Answer to . . . the Poysoned Booke*
   (*1557*, 1048).
8. *The Miscellaneous Remains of Cardinal Perron [et al.]* (1717/8), 2:248;
   at such moments, says the author, we 'should despise all the things of
   the World', not make jokes.
9. In Gerard Wegemer and Stephen Smith, eds., *A Thomas More Source-
   book* (Washington, D.C.: Catholic University of America Press, 2004),
   156. Ambiguity attends More in *The True Chronicle Historie of the
   Whole Life and Death of Thomas Lord Cromwell* by 'W.S.' (1613). He
   can jest: to pledge a 'health' may hurt one's 'health', for 'though the
   drops be small, / Yet have they force, to force men to the wall' (sig. D2v;

i.e. they can defeat a man but also make him find a wall against which to urinate). And when Cromwell modestly denies that he deserves his new power, More says, 'O content thee man, who would not choose it? / Yet thou art wise in seeming to refuse it' (D4v) – still genial, but more cynical than 'merry'.

10. Memories of More, says Russell Wyland, in 'Thomas More's reputation in nineteenth-century England', *Moreana* 33, no. 127–8 (1996), 37–56, show how this interest led, after controversy, to a reaction that first focused on More as a tolerant reformer but then edged into a more complex view and thence to modern scholarship.

11. Ridley, *The Statesman and the Fanatic: Thomas Wolsey and Thomas More* (London: Constable, 1982); Marius, *Thomas More*. Even sympathetic biographies such as Peter Ackroyd's *Life of Thomas More* now acknowledge the moral complexity of More's personality and career.

12. Collected in *The Broken Estate: Essays on Literature and Belief* (New York: Random House, 1999), 3–15. Wood calls *Utopia* a 'beautiful lament' with an 'air of mournful surmise', which may sentimentalize it.

13. *Wolf Hall* (London: Fourth Estate, 2009); *Times Literary Supplement* 15 May 2009.

14. Much has been written on this play. For some it erases More's persecutory hatred of heresy, whereas for others it minimizes his religion while exalting his conscience; see Peter Marshall, 'Saints and cinemas: *A Man for All Seasons*', in Susan Doran and Thomas S. Freeman, eds., *Tudors and Stuarts on Film: Historical Perspectives* (Basingstoke: Palgrave Macmillan, 2009), 46–59.

15. For a compact overview, see *R3* xliii–xlviii.

16. George M. Logan, *R3*, who notes that Walpole provoked replies (l), observes that Shakespeare takes More's own irony and gives it to his protagonist, adding a touch of the Medieval Vice and the Renaissance Machiavel (xlvii–xlviii). Sir William Cornwallis wrote a defence of Richard III in his *Essayes of Certaine Paradoxes* (1616), together with praises of syphilis, nothing and debt; he does not engage More.

17. On accusations that More was a 'poet' in theology see Peter C. Herman, *Squitter-wits and Muse-haters: Spenser, Sidney, Milton and Renaissance Antipoetic Sentiment* (Detroit: Wayne State University Press, 1996), 37–43. In his *Answer unto Sir Thomas More's Dialogue* 3.16, Tyndale asks in a typical scoff, 'What maye not Master More saye by auctorite of his poetrie?' (Boswell #645).

18. See above, 175. On Richard's role as the wintry boar of Greek myth – as read by Renaissance mythographers – that More includes but does not stress as much as does Shakespeare, see Anne L. Prescott, 'The equinoctial boar: Venus and Adonis in Spenser's garden, Shakespeare's epyllion, and *Richard III*'s England', in J. B. Lethbridge, ed., *Shakespeare and Spenser: Attractive Opposites* (Manchester University Press, 2008), 168–86.

19. Parts of the passage are quoted above, 178, 183.

20. *Memoirs of the Year Two Thousand Five Hundred*, trans. W. Hooper (1772), 27.

21. *Thomas More's 'Utopia' in Early Modern Europe: Paratexts and Contexts*, ed. Terence Cave (Manchester University Press, 2008), gives the paratexts, but this invaluable collection does not comment on what the evolution of English titles indicates about shifting views of Utopia's place in More's book.

22. *L'Utopie de Thomas More*, ed. André Prévost (Paris: Mame, 1978), gives the title pages (219, 227, 235). See also Richard Sylvester, ' "Si Hythlo-daeo credimus": vision and revision in Thomas More's *Utopia*', *EA* 290–301, and Steven Hutchinson, 'Mapping utopias', *Modern Philology* 85 (1987), 170–85. For Richard Marius, '*Utopia* as a mirror for a life and times', *Early Modern Literary Studies* (July 1995; online), 'festivus' is the 'key word'.

23. The admiring anonymous life of More that prefaces the 1795 edition of Burnet's translation, though, cites More's 'Eutopia', the only one of his works that survives 'in the esteem of the world', as 'de optimo rei-publicae statu dequa [*sic*] nova insula Utopia Etc.' – adding, of the polemics, that 'His answer to Luther has only gained him the credit, of having the best knack of any man in Europe of giving men bad names in good Latin' (xlvii). Early French editions take a different course, but the trajectory is the same and the shift faster, to judge from works available on the Gallica website. A poem by the translator in 1550 says that we should now refer to Utopian, not Elysian, Fields, and calls Utopian customs 'sainctes'. The first illustration, either because Elysium is pagan or because the translator has been thinking of Plato and Cicero, shows the speakers dressed like Romans. A 1730 translation by Gueudeville calls the book (I translate) '*Idea of a Happy Republic or* THE UTOPIA *of Thomas More*'. Note the 'or'.

24. John Milton, *Apology ... against Smectymnuus* (1642), sig. B1v; Etienne Cabet, *Travels in Icaria*, trans. Leslie Roberts and introduced by Robert Sutton (Syracuse University Press, 2003), x.

25. One subtle comment on this matter appears in *A Collection of Fables* (London, 1705), a verse translation with no named author that provides prose commentary, including a conservative note on the tension between individual rights and community that cites 'that wise and wonderful Man *Thomas More*', if only to disagree with what the author believes to be his espousal of communism (275–6).

26. *The Meaning of More's 'Utopia'* (Princeton University Press, 1983), 139 n., citing Ursula K. Le Guin; the phrase, originally from German, is most often applied to philosophy and science but seems wonderfully apt for both More's and Le Guin's experiments in postulation and extrapolation.

27. *The New Yorker*, 31 March 2003, 92.

28. Janice L. Hewitt, in Courtney Wemyss and Alexej Ugrinsky, eds., *George Orwell* (Westport, Conn.: Greenwood, 1987), 127–33.

29. Russell Jacoby, *Picture Imperfect: Utopian Thought for an Anti-utopian Age* (New York: Columbia University Press, 2005). Cf. Robert Appel-baum, *Literature and Utopian Politics in Seventeenth-Century England* (Cambridge University Press, 2002): 'We live in an age of the

End of Utopia', for in the last twenty-five years we have 'shed even the last vestiges of an ideal "ought"' (3–4). Again, this probably erases too much, although 'ideal' begs the question – the more practical the aims of those who demand gay marriage, a tighter European Union, a green revolution, or universal health care even in America, then the less 'utopian'. By turning 'utopian' from 'best' or even 'better' to 'ideal' or 'dream' we have – *pace* Martin Luther King – made it *by definition* impossible.

Foundational resources for More studies[*]

THE YALE EDITION

Volumes of *The Yale Edition of the Complete Works of St. Thomas More* (New Haven and London: Yale University Press, 1963–97). Original-spelling editions with full introductions, textual apparatus and commentaries; Latin works printed with facing modern English translations. Apart from published open letters, the edition does not include More's correspondence. For modern-spelling editions in Yale's supplementary Selected Works series, see below, under 'Correspondence' and 'Some other notable editions of works by More'.

1. *English Poems, Life of Pico, The Last Things.* Ed. Anthony S. G. Edwards, Clarence H. Miller and Katherine Gardiner Rodgers. 1997.
2. *The History of King Richard III.* Ed. Richard S. Sylvester. 1963. English and Latin versions (see also entry for vol. 15).
3. In two parts, separately paginated:
   Part 1: *Translations of Lucian.* Ed. Craig R. Thompson. 1974.
   Part 2: *Latin Poems.* Ed. Clarence H. Miller, Leicester Bradner, Charles A. Lynch and Revilo P. Oliver. 1984.
4. *Utopia.* Ed. Edward Surtz, S. J., and J. H. Hexter. 1965.
5. *Responsio ad Lutherum.* Ed. John Headley. 1969.
6. In two parts, continuously paginated: *A Dialogue Concerning Heresies.* Ed. Thomas M. C. Lawler, Germain Marc'hadour and Richard C. Marius. 1981.
7. *Letter to Bugenhagen, Supplication of Souls, Letter against Frith.* Ed. Frank Manley, Clarence H. Miller and Richard C. Marius. 1990.
8. In three parts, continuously paginated: *The Confutation of Tyndale's Answer.* Ed. Louis A. Schuster, Richard C. Marius and James P. Lusardi. 1973.
9. *The Apology.* Ed. J. B. Trapp. 1979.
10. *The Debellation of Salem and Bizance.* Ed. John Guy, Clarence H. Miller and Ralph Keen. 1988.
11. *The Answer to a Poisoned Book.* Ed. Clarence H. Miller and Stephen M. Foley. 1985.

---

[*] For works on particular topics treated in the essays in this volume, see the 'Further reading' appendices to the individual essays.

12. *A Dialogue of Comfort against Tribulation*. Ed. Louis L. Martz and Frank Manley. 1976.

13. *Treatise on the Passion, Treatise on the Blessed Body, Instructions and Prayers*. Ed. Garry E. Haupt. 1976.

14. In two parts, continuously paginated: *De Tristitia Christi*. Ed. Clarence H. Miller. 1976.

15. *Letters to Dorp, Oxford, Lee and a Monk; Historia Richardi Tertii*. Ed. Daniel Kinney. 1986. Supersedes vol. 2 for the Latin version of the *History*.

CORRESPONDENCE

The Correspondence of Sir Thomas More (Corr.). Ed. Elizabeth Frances Rogers. Princeton University Press, 1947. The Latin letters are printed without translations.

St. Thomas More: Selected Letters (SL). Ed. Elizabeth Frances Rogers. *The Yale Edition of the Works of St. Thomas More: Modernized Series*. New Haven and London: Yale University Press, 1961. The Latin letters are in translation.

Sir Thomas More: Neue Briefe. Ed. Hubertus Schulte Herbrüggen. Münster: Aschendorff, 1966.

'Thomas More's letters to Frans van Cranevelt including seven recently discovered autographs: Latin text, English translation, and facsimiles of the originals'. Ed. Clarence H. Miller. *Moreana* 31, no. 117 (1994), 3–66.

The Last Letters of Thomas More. Ed. Alvaro de Silva. Grand Rapids, Mich.: Eerdmans, 2000. Modernized versions of *Corr.* nos. 194–5, 197–218, with extensive commentary.

SOME OTHER NOTABLE EDITIONS OF WORKS BY MORE

The workes of Sir Thomas More Knyght, sometyme Lorde Chauncellor of England, wrytten by him in the Englysh tonge (1557). Introduction by K. J. Wilson. 2 vols. London: Scolar Press, 1978. A facsimile reprint.

The English Works of Sir Thomas More (EW). Ed. W. E. Campbell *et al.* 2 vols. London: Eyre & Spottiswoode, 1931. Discontinued after two volumes; these include facsimile reprints, modern-spelling transcriptions and full and valuable editorial apparatus (Vol. 1: Early Poems, *Life of Pico, History of King Richard the Third, The Last Things*; Vol. 2: *A Dialogue Concerning Heresies*).

The Utopia of Sir Thomas More. Ed. J. H. Lupton. Oxford: Clarendon Press, 1895. Latin text and the earliest English translation, by Ralph Robynson, 1551; valuable commentary.

L'Utopie de Thomas More. Ed. André Prévost. Paris: Mame, 1978. Facsimile of November 1518 text, modern French translation and voluminous commentary.

Utopia: Latin Text and English Translation (CU). Ed. George M. Logan, Robert M. Adams and Clarence H. Miller. Cambridge University Press, 1995. Latin text with normalized spelling and modern punctuation and paragraphing; modern translation; relatively lean editorial apparatus.

The History of King Richard III and Selections from the English and Latin Poems. Ed. Richard S. Sylvester. *The Yale Edition of the Works of St. Thomas More: Modernized Series*. New Haven and London: Yale University Press, 1976.

The History of King Richard the Third: A Reading Edition (*R3*). Ed. George M. Logan. Bloomington and Indianapolis: Indiana University Press, 2005. Modern-spelling edition of the English version with relatively lean apparatus.

A Dialogue of Comfort against Tribulation. Ed. Frank Manley. *The Yale Edition of the Works of St. Thomas More: Modernized Series.* New Haven and London: Yale University Press, 1977.

The Tower Works: Devotional Writings. [*A Treatise upon the Passion, A Treatise to Receive the Blessed Body of Our Lord, The Sadness of Christ*, and *Instructions and Prayers.*] Ed. Garry E. Haupt. *The Yale Edition of the Works of St. Thomas More: Modernized Series.* New Haven and London: Yale University Press, 1980.

Thomas More's Prayer Book: A Facsimile Reproduction of the Annotated Pages. Ed. Louis L. Martz and Richard S. Sylvester. New Haven: Yale University Press, 1969. With transcription and translation.

EARLY BIOGRAPHIES

William Roper. *The Life of Sir Thomas More* (Roper). In *Two Early Tudor Lives.* Ed. Richard S. Sylvester and Davis P. Harding. New Haven and London: Yale University Press, 1962. Written *c.* 1557.

> *The Lyfe of Sir Thomas Moore, knighte.* Ed. Elsie Vaughan Hitchcock. EETS Original Series no. 197. London: Oxford University Press, 1935. Original-spelling edition of Roper's *Life.*

Nicholas Harpsfield. *The life and death of Sir Thomas Moore, knight, sometimes Lorde high Chancellor of England* (Harpsfield). Ed. Elsie Vaughan Hitchcock. EETS Original Series no. 186. London: Oxford University Press, 1932. Completed 1558 or 1559.

Thomas Stapleton. *The Life and Illustrious Martyrdom of Sir Thomas More* (Stapleton). Trans. Philip E. Hallett, ed. E. E. Reynolds. London: Burns & Oates, 1966. Originally published 1588 (in Latin).

Ro. Ba. *The Lyfe of Sir Thomas More, Sometymes Lord Chancellour of England.* Ed. Elsie Vaughan Hitchcock and P. E. Hallett, with additional notes and appendices by A. W. Reed. EETS Original Series no. 222. London: Oxford University Press, 1950. Written *c.* 1599.

Cresacre More. *The Life of Sir Thomas More* (CMore). Ed. Joseph Hunter. London, 1828. Written *c.* 1616–20, by More's great-grandson. Largely derivative from earlier biographies, but well executed.

SOME NOTABLE MODERN BIOGRAPHICAL STUDIES [*]

Ackroyd, Peter. *The Life of Thomas More.* London: Chatto & Windus, 1998.

Chambers, R. W. *Thomas More.* London: Jonathan Cape, 1935.

---

[*] All of these studies are referenced, sometimes with brief critiques, in essays in this volume. See the index entries for the studies' authors.

Elton, G. R. 'The real Thomas More'. In his *Studies in Tudor and Stuart Politics and Government*. 4 vols. Cambridge University Press, 1974–92. 3:344–55. Originally published 1980.

'Thomas More, councillor'. *Studies in Tudor and Stuart Politics and Government*. 1:129–54. A lecture given in 1970, originally published 1972.

Greenblatt, Stephen. 'At the table of the great: More's self-fashioning and self-cancellation'. Chapter 1 of *Renaissance Self-Fashioning: From More to Shakespeare*. Chicago and London: University of Chicago Press, 1980; repr. with a new Preface, 2005, 11–73.

Guy, John A. *A Daughter's Love: Thomas & Margaret More*. London: Fourth Estate, 2008.

The Public Career of Sir Thomas More. New Haven and London: Yale University Press, 1980.

Thomas More. Reputations. London: Arnold, 2000.

Marius, Richard. *Thomas More: A Biography*. New York: Knopf, 1984.

Martz, Louis L. *Thomas More: The Search for the Inner Man*. New Haven and London: Yale University Press, 1990.

Reynolds, E. E. *The Field Is Won: The Life and Death of Saint Thomas More*. London: Burns & Oates, 1968; repub. 1978 with title and subtitle reversed.

BIBLIOGRAPHIES AND CLEARING HOUSES

For a list of printed and online bibliographies and literature reviews of More editions and More studies, see above, 282–3. The great clearing houses for More scholarship are the Société des Amici Thomae Mori (currently based in Péronne, Somme, France), with its journal *Moreana* and *Newsletter/Gazette*, and the Center for Thomas More Studies at the University of Dallas. See the websites for both. The Center's website includes an extensive online library of writings by and about More, and about his works.

Index*

* Front matter, back matter, and the 'Further reading' appendices to the essays are not
  indexed.

THE CAMBRIDGE COMPANION TO REFORMATION THEOLOGY
edited by David Bagchi and David Steinmetz (2004)
ISBN 0 521 77224 9 hardback   ISBN 0 521 77662 7 paperback

THE CAMBRIDGE COMPANION TO AMERICAN JUDAISM
edited by Dana Evan Kaplan (2005)
ISBN 0 521 82204 1 hardback   ISBN 0 521 52951 4 paperback

THE CAMBRIDGE COMPANION TO KARL RAHNER
edited by Declan Marmion and Mary E. Hines (2005)
ISBN 0 521 83288 8 hardback   ISBN 0 521 54045 3 paperback

THE CAMBRIDGE COMPANION TO FRIEDRICH SCHLEIERMACHER
edited by Jacqueline Mariña (2005)
ISBN 0 521 81448 0 hardback   ISBN 0 521 89137 × paperback

THE CAMBRIDGE COMPANION TO THE GOSPELS
edited by Stephen C. Barton (2006)
ISBN 0 521 80766 2 hardback   ISBN 0 521 00261 3 paperback

THE CAMBRIDGE COMPANION TO THE QUR'AN
edited by Jane Dammen McAuliffe (2006)
ISBN 0 521 83160 1 hardback   ISBN 0 521 53934 × paperback

THE CAMBRIDGE COMPANION TO JONATHAN EDWARDS
edited by Stephen J. Stein (2007)
ISBN 0 521 85290 0 hardback   ISBN 0 521 61805 3 paperback

THE CAMBRIDGE COMPANION TO EVANGELICAL THEOLOGY
edited by Timothy Larsen and Daniel J. Trier (2007)
ISBN 0 521 84698 6 hardback   ISBN 0 521 60974 7 paperback

THE CAMBRIDGE COMPANION TO MODERN JEWISH PHILOSOPHY
edited by Michael L. Morgan and Peter Eli Gordon (2007)
ISBN 0 521 81312 3 hardback   ISBN 0 521 01255 4 paperback

THE CAMBRIDGE COMPANION TO THE TALMUD AND RABBINIC LITERATURE
edited by Charlotte E. Fonrobert and Martin S. Jaffee (2007)
ISBN 0 521 84390 1 hardback   ISBN 0 521 60508 3 paperback

THE CAMBRIDGE COMPANION TO LIBERATION THEOLOGY, SECOND EDITION
edited by Christopher Rowland (2007)
ISBN 9780521868839 hardback   ISBN 9780521688932 paperback

THE CAMBRIDGE COMPANION TO THE JESUITS
edited by Thomas Worcester (2008)
ISBN 9780521857314 hardback   ISBN 9780521673969 paperback

THE CAMBRIDGE COMPANION TO CLASSICAL ISLAMIC THEOLOGY
edited by Tim Winter (2008)
ISBN 9780521780582 hardback   ISBN 9780521785495 paperback

THE CAMBRIDGE COMPANION TO PURITANISM
edited by John Coffey and Paul Lim (2008)
ISBN 9780521860888 hardback   ISBN 9780521678001 paperback

THE CAMBRIDGE COMPANION TO ORTHODOX CHRISTIAN THEOLOGY
edited by Mary Cunningham and Elizabeth Theokritoff (2008)
ISBN 9780521864848 hardback   ISBN 9780521683388 paperback

THE CAMBRIDGE COMPANION TO PAUL TILLICH
edited by Russell Re Manning (2009)
ISBN 9780521859899 hardback   ISBN 9780521677356 paperback

THE CAMBRIDGE COMPANION TO JOHN HENRY NEWMAN
edited by Ian Ker and Terrence Merrigan (2009)
ISBN 9780521871860 hardback   ISBN 9780521692724 paperback

THE CAMBRIDGE COMPANION TO JOHN WESLEY
edited by Randy L. Maddox and Jason E. Vickers (2010)
ISBN 9780521886536 hardback   ISBN 9780521714037 paperback

THE CAMBRIDGE COMPANION TO CHRISTIAN PHILOSOPHICAL THEOLOGY
edited by Charles Taliaferro and Chad Meister (2010)
ISBN 9780521514330 hardback   ISBN 9780521730372 paperback

THE CAMBRIDGE COMPANION TO MUHAMMAD
edited by Jonathan E. Brockopp (2010)
ISBN 9780521886079 hardback   ISBN 9780521713726 paperback

THE CAMBRIDGE COMPANION TO SCIENCE AND RELIGION
edited by Peter Harrison (2010)
ISBN 9780521885386 hardback   ISBN 9780521712514 paperback

THE CAMBRIDGE COMPANION TO C. S. LEWIS
edited by Robert MacSwain and Michael Ward (2010)
ISBN 9780521884136 hardback   ISBN 9780521711142 paperback

Forthcoming

THE CAMBRIDGE COMPANION TO THE TRINITY
edited by Peter C. Phan

THE CAMBRIDGE COMPANION TO THE VIRGIN MARY
edited by Sarah Boss

THE CAMBRIDGE COMPANION TO BLACK THEOLOGY
edited by Dwight Hopkins and Edward Antonio